Personality Traits of Money
1st Printing -
Copyright © 1989 - Dr. Nova Dean Pack
Revised Copyright 2024 - Dr. Nova Dean Pack

Photos used by attribution;

All rights reserved. No part of this publication may be reproduced, distributed, or transmitted in any form or by any means, including photocopying, recording, or other electronic or mechanical methods, without the prior written permission of the publisher, except in the case of brief quotations embodied in critical reviews and certain other noncommercial uses permitted by copyright law.

For permission requests, write to the publisher, addressed "Attention: Permissions" by electronic mail to: packnovapack@aol.com

Scriptures taken from the New King James Version. Copyright © 1982 by Thomas Nelson, Inc. Used by permission. All rights reserved.

Scriptures taken from the King James Version, originally published in 1611. Public domain.

Personality Traits of Money

DR. NOVA DEAN PACK

Content

Dedication — Page 8

Introduction — Page 9

Christian Money Beatitudes Test — Page 33

1- The Natural And Spiritual Origin Of Money — Page 44

Content

2 - Today's Mystical Or Spiritual Significance Of Money — Page 63

3 - Using Money For The "Safety Personality Trait Of Money" — Page 82

4 - Using Money For The "Control Seeking Personality Trait Of Money" — Page 104

5 - Using Money For The "Freedom Seeker Personality Trait Of Money" — Page 132

Content

6 - Using Money For The "Romantic Attraction Personality Trait Of Money" Page 172

7 - Using Money For The "Personal Magnetism Personality Trait Of Money Page 187

8 - Money For The "Other Kinds Of Personality Traits Of Money" Page 199

9- Three Great Genius Inventors Who Were Denied The Wealth From Their Inventions Page 204

Content

10 - Why Some Stay Wealthy While Others Stay Poor Page 236

Conclusion Page 262

Dedication

I would like to dedicate this book to my supportive wife, Linda Mundinger Pack. Her knowledge and skill as a certified Counsellor in addictions and additional mental health issues were invaluable research for my further understanding the complexities of people with behavior issues regarding the personality traits of money disorders.

Linda graduated from Whitworth University, a Christian University in Spokane, Washington with a Bachelor's Degree in History and Education.

She received her Master's Degree of Education and Counseling from Eastern Washington University in Cheney, Washington. She received a Certificate of Addiction Studies from Seattle University. She has 35 years of training in mental health issues and behavioral problems with adolescence. She has 22 years' experience as a counselor and as an Intervention Specialist in the Seattle and Lake Washington School Districts.

Washington Governor Gary Locke awarded Linda for her work in mediation and violence prevention at the school. Linda received an award for Washington State Intervention Specialist of the Year. She also received a National Award recommended by the State Superintendent of Public Instructions for the State of Washington for work with College and Career Planning for students.

After retiring from the Seattle School District, she moved to California, where she continued in her Christian education and graduated from a four-year course in the School of Ministry.

Nova and Linda continue doing ministry work together as husband and wife, with each being a good help meet for the other.

Dr. Nova Dean Pack

Introduction

Jesus was concerned that money pursuits entice a person's soul, and when it becomes an obsessive-compulsive lifestyle, the person can become a convert of the evil god of mammon. Jesus said in Matthew 6:24, "No man can serve two masters: for either he will hate the one and love the other; or else he will hold to the one and despise the other. Ye cannot serve God and mammon."

Wikipedia reveals that the word "mammon" comes from the Aramaic word māmōn, which was a loanword borrowed as Mishnaic Hebrew, used as "mammon," with the common meaning of money. Aramaic māmōnā was an emphatic form of the word māmōn, meaning riches, income from businesses, or proceeds from sale of assets. "Māmōn" was also a loanword borrowed by the Canaanites from the Syriac dialect. Māmōnā referred to a Syrian deity, god of riches; and therefore, encompassed money or riches, but usually not wealth, as wealth are reserved to things created by God, such as land, precious metals, precious stones, livestock that procreate, and crops that grow. "Māmōn" is transliterated from Aramaic that also means money or riches. The earlier history of the Aramaic was present throughout the Canaanite languages, including the Philistines. Some scholars cite māmōn as the name of a Syrian and Chaldean god, like the Greek god of riches, Plutus. Most all the cultures outside Israel at the time the Bible was written, and before, worshipped "Māmōn" as the god of materialism, finances, economy, riches, and money, and this is the only false god or idol that Jesus specifically named that competed with God Almighty for worship by people who dedicated their lives to seek it, work for it, and acquire safety, control, freedom, romantic attractiveness, and personal magnetism when in their possession.

Personality Traits of Money

Albert Barnes, an American theologian in the 1800s, stated in his *Notes on the New Testament* that mammon was a Syriac word for an idol worshipped as the god of riches (Biblecommenter.com. Retrieved 03-20-2014). Thus, mammon or money can have false god-like characteristics to temporarily fulfill people's soulish needs, so, in essence, they sometimes unknowingly worship mammon who is the god over money. Mammon was the only demonic spirit that was in competition with Almighty God. Mammon or money controls most people's lives.

If you know a Believer who sees money as his source for his existence, and ask him, "Can you go with me on a missionary trip to bring the gospel of God's Kingdom and repentance and remission of sins to people in a third world country," his response may be, "I will have to hear what the money says." This is a sign that money to that person has taken on one of the obsessive-compulsive Personality Traits of Money disorders that are addressed in this book.

Believers began to use the word "mammon" as a pejorative, as the word in Matthew 6:24 was interpreted in context with Jesus' preceding words in Mathew 6:19-21, where Jesus admonished, "Lay not up for yourselves treasures upon earth, where moth and rust doth corrupt, and where thieves break through and steal: (20) But lay up for yourselves treasures in heaven, where neither moth nor rust doth corrupt, and where thieves do not break through nor steal: (21) For where your treasure is, there will your heart be also."

Thus, Jesus was contrasting the kingdoms of this world where people are engaged with seeking money every day versus the kingdom of heaven that Believers are commanded to seek first along with God's righteousness each day. Also, Jesus contrasts Believers serving Almighty God, the Creator of both heaven and earth, where giving and receiving motivated by agape love, is the Kingdom of God's economy versus people ignorantly serving the god of mammon or money that is the means of exchange in buying and selling transactions here in the fallen world's economy.

The heart in the soul is where the library of your beliefs is stored, and where your Will functions. Paul said in Romans 10:9-10, "That if thou shalt confess with thy mouth the Lord Jesus, and shalt believe in thine heart that God hath raised him from the dead, thou shalt be saved. (10) For with the heart man believeth unto righteousness; and with the mouth confession is made unto salvation." Righteous or unrighteous beliefs are where your heart and Will are, and this is the problem in believing in money for your financial needs instead of God in Christ Jesus as your Provider (Matthew 6:33; Philippians 4:19).

An act, whether good or evil, is the external manifestation of someone's Will in the heart. How does a sinful act get to that level of consequential harm and destruction? James writes about the five stages of sin, where the Personality Traits of Money could find a beginning and progression. James 1:14-15 says, "But every man is tempted, when he is drawn away of his own lust, and enticed. (15) Then when lust hath conceived, it bringeth forth sin: and sin, when it is finished, bringeth forth death."

First, sin begins with a desire that entices your soul through lustful temptation. Second, the evil temptation of lust gains consent of your heart and conceives. Third, sin is born and has its own authority and power and sinful lust and influence grows. Fourth, sin grows like a weed, and sin becomes a habit of lust of the eyes, lust of the flesh, or pride of life and is always present and spreads as cancer into your heart, mind, and emotions. Fifth, the sin enslaves you like an addiction, becomes a part of your personality, and produces consequential death.

Money begins as a temptation, and it takes you through the five steps towards the act of sin unless you resist the devil, resist the fallen world, and resist the lust of the flesh, lust of the eyes, and pride of life, which all are enhanced by money. Resisting the devil, James 4:7 says, "Submit yourselves therefore to God. Resist the devil, and he will flee from you." Resisting the temptations in the world, 1 Corinthians 10:13 says, "There hath no temptation taken you but such as is common to man (in the world): but God is faithful, who will not suffer you to be tempted above that ye are able; but will with the temptation also make a way to escape, that ye may be able to bear it." Resisting the sins of the flesh, Romans 8:13 says, "For if ye live after the flesh, ye shall die: but if ye through the Spirit do mortify the deeds of the body, ye shall live."

Personality Traits of Money

How do you stop the law of sin and death when money is used to sin, as the sin is the exercise of your Will in your heart? Victory from the sin of serving mammom or money becomes a decision in your heart in exercising your will to be righteous by submitting to God in Christ and not to be sinful by submitting to the desires of the flesh, the popular ideas of the fallen world, or the lies of the devil and his kingdom of darkness.

Romans 8:2-10 says, "For the law of the Spirit of life in Christ Jesus hath made me free from the law of sin and death. (3) For what the law could not do, in that it was weak through the flesh, God sending his own Son in the likeness of sinful flesh, and for sin, condemned sin in the flesh: (4) That the righteousness of the law might be fulfilled in us, who walk not after the flesh, but after the spirit. (5) For they that are after the flesh do mind the things of the flesh; but they that are after the spirit the things of the spirit. (6) For to be carnally minded is death; but to be spiritually minded is life and peace. (7) Because the carnal mind is enmity against God: for it is not subject to the law of God, neither indeed can be. (8) So then they that are in the flesh cannot please God. (9) But ye are not in the flesh, but in the (born again) spirit, if so be that the Spirit of God (Holy Spirit) dwell in you. Now if any man have not the Spirit of Christ (Jesus' resurrected humanity Spirit), he is none of His. (10) And if Christ be in you, the body is dead because of sin; but the (born again) spirit is life because of righteousness."

Galatians 5:17 says, "For the flesh lusteth against the (born again) spirit, and the (born again) spirit against the flesh: and these are contrary the one to the other: so that ye (heart in the soul where your Will resides) cannot do the things that ye would."

Thus, Jesus used the word "mammon" (money) in the context of a derogatory word meaning to not only denounce the person's service given to mammon or materialism, finances, economy, riches, or money, but also to describe the person's service to mammon here on earth as having no eternal reward. Jesus explained that an obsessive-compulsive service to mammon was a heart issue that interferes with a Believer's belief of and seeking an intimate relationship with the Godhead and Jesus' humanity nature. That which you seek daily to enrich soulish safety, control, freedom, romantic attractiveness, personal magnetism, or other soulish enhancements to replace seeking first the Kingdom of God and His righteousness and serving Jesus Christ as Lord, can result in serving an idol.

A BELIEVER ENGAGED IN OBTAINING MONEY FROM OTHER CHURCH MEMBERS MUST BE REMOVED FROM THE CHURCH COMMUNITY UNTIL HE REPENTS

Paul said in 1 Corinthians 5:11, "But now I have written unto you not to keep company, if any man that is called a brother be a fornicator, or covetous, or an idolater, or a railer, or a drunkard, or an extortioner; with such an one not to eat." There are three words in this scripture that relate to the problems people have with money, i.e., covetous, idolater, and extortioner. In 1 Corinthians chapter 5, Paul instructs the Believers in the Church in Corinth, and thus all Believers, how to deal with and respond when other Believers engage in actions that are blatantly sinful.

In 1 Corinthians 5:2-5 Paul's guideline is to politely remove the blatant sinner from the community of Believers UNTIL he is repentant and turns back to God, and then he may join the community of Believers again. Paul wrote in 2 Corinthians 2:7, "So that contrariwise ye ought rather to forgive him, and comfort him, lest perhaps such a one should be swallowed up with overmuch sorrow." Regardless of the blatant sin, if it may harm other Believers in the community, the removal until true repentance is the right decision. What is the reasoning behind removal of the blatant sinner who has an obsessive-compulsive Personality Trait of Money? Removal protects the community from being a victim or becoming caught up in sin, themselves. Yet, the removal objective is always to lead the Believer to counselling, repentance, soul transformation, and restoration back into the community. 2 Thessalonians 3:14-15 says, "And if any man obeys not our word by this epistle, note that man, and have no company with him, that he may be ashamed. (15) Yet count him not as an enemy, but admonish him as a brother." Paul says in Galatians 6:1, "Brethren, if a man be overtaken in a fault, ye which are spiritual, restore such an one in the spirit of meekness; considering thyself, lest thou also be tempted."

Personality Traits of Money

MONEY, RICHES, AND WEALTH

MONEY: Money is the means of exchange in each country. You exchange money for food, shelter, clothing, transportation, education, entertainment, investments in riches and wealth, and blessings from God in return for tithing and giving. Yet, money has an avarice love side to it that can enslave you into this world system. Also, money is used to enhance various obsessive-compulsive Personality Traits that are the subject of the comprehensive study and topic of this book. Money is controlled by the principality of the kingdom of darkness called mammon.

RICHES: In the parable of the four soils in Matthew 13:22, Jesus says that riches are deceitful: "He also that received seed among the thorns is he that heareth the word; and the care of this world, and the deceitfulness of riches, choke the word, and he becometh unfruitful." Mammon controls money and riches. Proverbs 11:28 says, "He that trusteth in his riches shall fall: but the righteous shall flourish as a branch." Investments in riches merely return to you a percentage, normally under ten percent. Anything above ten percent could be usurious if it is a Note that someone owes you, or it could be a ponzi scheme. Investment in riches is where you hand the other party your money, and he or a business entity delivers to you a piece of paper, such as a contract, a promissory note, a government bond, stocks, or an insurance product. If you turn over your decisions regarding investments in riches by first praying, hearing from God to acquire faith, and being led by the Holy Spirit, God will bless your investments in riches. Proverbs 10:22 says, "The blessing of the LORD, it maketh rich, and He addeth no sorrow with it."

WEALTH: Proverbs 13:22 says, "A good man leaveth an inheritance to his children's children: and the wealth of the sinner is laid up for the just." Deuteronomy 8:18 says, "But thou shalt remember the LORD thy God: for it is He that giveth thee power to get wealth, that He may establish His covenant which He sware unto thy fathers, as it is this day." Any investment in wealth never loses its value down to zero, but also regularly multiplies. Wealth are what people call "hard assets," or I call wealth assets created by God. Wealth assets are land and buildings (Psalms 24:1), silver and gold (Haggai 2:8), cattle (Psalm 50:10), crops planted (Matthew 13:8), and family-owned businesses (Luke 2:49). For example, land or buildings on land normally appreciates in value. A cow that has a calf in nine months is a one-fold return for the animal owner's investment. A kernel of corn as a seed will multiply a hundred-fold of seeds in return. A business that has one thousand dollars as initial capitalization on January 1 will normally generate income of a hundred-fold gross return equal to one hundred thousand dollars by December 31. Thus, wealth assets are better than riches because they are God created, multiplies by God's principles, and the investor exchanges his money for hard assets, and not have to trust others.

You need to be careful when you transfer the nature of a wealth asset as land in exchange for money. In Acts 5:1-11, Ananias and Sapphira were husband and wife, who owned land. They announced that they were going to sell the land and give all the proceeds to the new, infant Christian Church. They sold that which was wealth and turned it into money. Suddenly, the insidiousness of the spirit of mammon took over and joined itself to their sin of pride of life. Peter asked in verse 3, "Ananias, why has Satan filled your heart to lie to the Holy Spirit and keep part of the price of the land for yourself." Ananias and Sapphira withheld a portion for themselves when they said they brought all the proceeds of the sale of the land to give to the work of the ministry. Peter said, "While it remained unsold, was it not your own? (It could have been passed down as an inheritance). And after it was sold, was it not in your own control? Why have you conceived this thing in your heart? You have not lied to man but to God" (verse 4). The Holy Spirit caused the immediate death of Ananias and Sapphira for lying about keeping some of the money from the sale of the wealth asset (verses 5 &10). Notice that Peter said that the temptation of Ananias and Sapphira to hold back some of the money came from Satan, and Peter said that the temptation was conceived in Ananias and Sapphira's hearts, not their minds, nor their emotions because their hearts was where their wills reside.

Ananias and Sapphira did not have pure hearts. They had pride of life in their hearts. Ananias and Sapphira were seeking "position" by buying that position in the newly formed church. They saw Barnabas, a Levite Jew like John the Baptist, was elevated to a high stature after Barnabas sold his land and brought the proceeds and laid them at the Apostles feet as a donation (Acts 4:36-37). However, the prerequisite that Barna-

Personality Traits of Money

bas had for giving that Ananias and Sapphira did not have, was a pure heart. Barnabas name of Joseph was changed by the Apostles to Barnabas which means the "son of encouragement." Barnabas was later elevated to the office of apostle (Acts 14:14), and he and Paul went on missionary trips to various Gentile cities where he and Paul defended the Gentiles against the Judaizers.

WHEN DEALING WITH TEMPTATIONS OF MONEY, THE BELIEVER NEEDS
TO HAVE DISCERNMENT WHETHER THE TEMPTATION IS COMING
FROM THE EVIL SPIRITS, THE FALLEN WORLD, OR YOUR OWN FLESH

Realistically, as a Believer, you must engage the world's financial system to exist. Satan will see your avarice love of money that makes you think in your mind, feel in your emotions, and believe in your heart that normality demands you act to fulfill your obsessive-compulsive Personality Trait of Money. Satan will discern what activates you to sin and will tempt you. When you have an obsessive-compulsive Personality Trait of Money, then Satan will send his evil spirits to lie, defraud, falsely promise, and will tempt you with the lust of the flesh, the lust of the eyes, and the pride of life. If you have any obsessive-compulsive Personality Traits of Money, you will be vulnerable to temptations of evil spirits. The evil spirits will know what soulish button to push.

Let me give you an example. If you live as a youth without a father because of divorce or death, then your soul will hunger for a father figure who you will trust and want to be with him in his business and investment because you want a father-child relationship with him. He will ask for a little bit of money to get started, then more money, and then much more money, and "we just need this much to finish the project, and you and I together will become rich. We make a great team." Sound familiar? Then, the "fatherly figure" calls you and says, "I must leave because my sister, mother, or brother is extremely sick; and I must return to Brazil to be with her or him. Don't worry, I can keep things going from there for a while." Within ten days, you discover his phone is disconnected, and he has no forwarding address. Later, you learn that he is a con artist, where several counties, states, federal government, and international agencies have questions they want to ask of him. You did not have God's wisdom. You believed the man was sincere; you genuinely thought that he treated you as his son. He conned you, took your money, and you will never see him or your money again.

How do I know this? It is because I, personally, am that victim. I was young, only thirty-one years old at the time. Up until that time, I lived in an institution called education, then in an established law firm, and in the end the con man caused me to be at the verge of bankruptcy. You may think, "Why would anyone try to swindle a lawyer; he can sue you?" Yes, true. However, where is he? In what country? How many other people are his victims looking for him? Does he have any bank accounts or assets in the U.S.? When I met him, he was 78 years old, and I was a young lawyer at the age of 31. I had very little life experience regarding investment wisdom. He drank bourbon a lot. Other partners in the law firm had invested with him, and they lost money. He told them that he would pay them back as soon as his deals closed. My law partners did not warn me that he was a con artist. He kept telling me we were going to be extraordinary rich as his deal funded. He showed me contracts; I spoke to other men overseas who were part of the deal. Yet, there was no security for the money I invested with him. It was a scam. He was in poor health when he left California, USA, and he probably died within a couple of years. Romans 6:23 says, "For the wages of sin is death. ..." He most likely did not go to Brazil but rather some place where there was no tax treaty and no extradition treaty with the U.S.

To come to terms with my unwise choices that resulted in my horrific financial loss, I concluded that being a victim of fraud was my "tuition" paid to the school of "hard knocks." Why was it unwise? The investment was not a business, was without security, and required a lot of trust in the man who took my money. I did not do a background check on the fraudster. Neither did my law partners, prior victims of this con man, warned me about him based upon their own losses. It was hurtful to discover that my law partners were prior victims of this swindler, but it wounded me in my soul to realize that they failed to warn me of his proclivity to lie, hoodwink, and steal. They could have told me not to trust him, but they hoped this thief would succeed. I could not work at the law firm anymore, so I resigned and started my own solo law practice, which I have to this day.

However, my losses were my fault. I made the mistake to seek immediate riches in-

Personality Traits of Money

stead of long-term wealth. The problem is that I did not know at that time that the devil would come after me through all kinds of schemes. If I just learned one of the devil's approaches from the loss I suffered, that would teach me only about that approach the devil used in that transaction and relationship. Yet, the devil has a million other temptations to try to get me to fall. So, the negative experience did not teach me or give me wisdom from above.

I continued to make mistakes in my investments because I trusted people. It took me many years of trial and error that caused me many tribulations before I came to the realization that I lacked God's knowledge and wisdom. I finally came to the resolve that my only source of knowledge, wisdom, and understanding from above were to study God's word daily and be led by God the Holy Spirit. I finally repented and humbled myself, stopped investing my labor into deals. He has taught me to be a Biblitarian. I know the biblical principles that are in the Bible, but more than that, God has become my Father; and I hear His still small voice. I am led by the Holy Spirit in all that I do.

Today, I would never allow someone to take my money without security like real estate or other wealth assets. In truth, if the Holy Spirit told me to give all my money for a particular Kingdom project, and I discerned that He truly was instructing me, I would not hesitate. I do not have the greed, covetousness, or avarice like the Rich Young Ruler. I can sleep on someone's sofa or rent a spare bedroom. I have impeccable habits, and I live a godly life. I am married, and I live with my wife in her home, which is paid off, and our cars were purchased with savings, and our credit cards balances are paid in full each month. We both have monthly income. We are not rich, "But my God shall supply all our need according to his riches in glory by Christ Jesus" (Philippians 4:19).

Wealthy people invest in real property, businesses, and other wealth assets. I cannot disciple you to become a good businessperson or investor based upon my experience because it is knowledge and wisdom from the fallen world. On the other hand, what I have learned from the Bible is God's truth and wisdom. With my fifty plus years of law practice along with being a Pastor for over thirty-five years, I can use for your benefit. Much of the God's wisdom He has imparted to me I have written in this book and my book, titled Ministry of God's Business Servant.

As a pastor-teacher for over thirty-five years, I have acquired much spiritual wisdom, knowledge, and truth. God has economic principles in His word that are like gold nuggets, but then God transforms not only your mind but also your emotions and heart in your soul. Once you humbly submit to God and seek first His Kingdom and righteousness, you will find that in your heart you believe that He is the best Father, the Holy Spirit is the best teacher, and the Lord Jesus Christ, with His divine nature as God the Word, and His humanity nature as Lord, have already made the investment for you for your eternal prosperity here on earth (2 Corinthians 8:9; Philippians 4:19).

Every Believer needs to learn to discern the presence and operations of evil spirits that tempt him and devise schemes for his failure when he is daily in the commerce or operating a business in this fallen world. His soul must be spiritually transformed and submitted to God and the Lord Jesus Christ.

Satan is like a soap opera director, and he will send his demons to bring people in your life who you trust that will betray you because they did not care if they hurt you financially or in your soul. Satan will write a different script every time when he tempts you. Satan has his minions in government agencies like the FDA, which can have its employee send out an injunction that enjoins you from selling a particular health product after you worked hard to build a sales team. Satan can send his evil entourage to cause your bank to cancel your line of credit that you need for flooring cost to produce and move your products to the retail market. Satan has subordinates in the IRS that can cause you to have a tax audit or tax lien on all your assets. Satan, the master of bringing temptation, can cause his evil spirits to tempt a spouse to have an affair that causes a marriage covenant violation because you are working too hard in your career or business. Satan sets a trap for immature teenagers, especially Christian teenagers, to have illicit sex and get pregnant or cause to fall for temptation to consume illegal addictive drugs or alcohol that by the time the parents discover the rebellion, it is very costly and becomes a major problem that takes away the peace and joy in the family.

John 4:24 says, "God is spirit, and those who come to Him must worship Him in spir-

Personality Traits of Money

it and truth." Believers must come to God in His Kingdom with spirit, which means having "submissive hearts" to receive the grace, anointing, love, faith, and will of God as you encounter the fallen world system and people in need of salvation. After initial salvation, Believers must come to God in His Kingdom to acquire Jesus' Way, Truth, and Life. This means accepting in your soul the truth embodied in God's Son and the foundational laws and principles in God's Kingdom that are in His word and carry these truths as lifestyle wisdom for all whom you encounter with the gospel of the Kingdom (Matthew 24:14) and message of repentance and remission of sins (Luke 24:47). With truth and spirit combined, God releases His authority and power for His soulish transformed children to be financial ministers in God's Kingdom (Romans 12:6), penetrating the world system with the covenant relationship and promises of God. God has decided to move His Ekklesia and Kingdom also into the businesses and marketplaces, so He permeates the world with righteousness, peace, and joy in the Holy Spirit that manifests the Kingdom of God and His righteousness (Luke 2:49; Romans 14:17; Matthew 6:33).

God sends His grace, love, faith, authority, power, anointing, and provision to you, and every Believer, to work with your Vocations as a delegated king, priest, (Revelation 1:6), lord (1 Timothy 6:15), ambassador (2 Corinthians 5:20), and soldier (2 Timothy 2:3-4), as citizens of heaven here on earth (Philippians 3:20). So, through your spiritual Vocations, you can be a vessel through whom He will pour out an abundance to do His will and accomplish your assigned purpose here on earth as it is in heaven. 2 Corinthians 9:8 says, "And God is able to make all grace abound toward you; that ye, always having all sufficiency in all things, may abound to every good work." Thus, scripture says that "God is able." This means that God can exercise His sovereign Will when the spiritual matters being done as the Holy Spirit leads you to fulfill God's purposeful directives.

As you will see in the later chapters in this book, the personalities of people using money to fulfill their soulish needs, is using money which is manipulated by the demon-idol of mammon. Mammon is Satan's most effective evil spirit that is a principality which masquerades with God-like qualities to falsely convince you that he can supply all your needs from cradle to grave and from womb to tomb.

Dr. Nova Dean Pack

Satan invented Socialism as a philosophy for humanists who are deists or atheists to keep Almighty God out of their sovereign financial decisions. Socialism and Communism are economic or money philosophies where the government takes away freedoms in exchange for payment of money and providing food, transportation, childcare, and schooling to the citizens. Essentially, it is a form of "Plantation living" as slaves to the government. The god of mammon masquerades as being omnipresent, and its influence involving almost every economic transaction captivates people's minds, emotions, and hearts where the will resides in the soul. Socialism and Communism are government economic philosophies that promise to equalize the consequences that supplants the rewards for physical talent, mental engiftments, hard work, or the taking of risks of capital in business that creates jobs.

You must become knowledgeable of God's financial principles in the Bible. You need to become a disciplined biblitarian in your decisions pertaining to finances, businesses, investments, giving and tithing, sowing and reaping, and buying and selling. You should learn Satan's ways and his methods in furthering his kingdom of darkness and enslavement of people. Then, God commands you resist the devil for not only yourself, but also for your family, employees, and friends, and the devil has to flee (James 4:7).

Therefore, as a Believer who is submitted to the Godhead for transformation of your beliefs in your heart, you will be targeted by the evil spirits from the kingdom of darkness. Yet, you can overcome because "Ye are of God, little children, and have overcome them: because greater is He that is in you, than he that is in the world" (1 John 4:4).

The devil usually will attack you in three ways. First, he will connect you with rip-off artists who will by deceit steal your money or steal money from other people that you introduced to the swindler who will hold you responsible for the introduction. Second, Satan will withhold money from you by people who owes you money, and even if you file a lawsuit against them, they have no assets which can be taken to satisfy the judgment, or they go bankrupt. Third, Satan will flood you with too much money to properly manage and tempt you to divert your attention from the true riches, wealth, and prosperity available as you seek first the Kingdom of God and His righteousness.

Personality Traits of Money

Wikipedia's article, titled Mammon, states that "Gregory of Nyssa also asserted that Mammon was another name for Beelzebub.[Graef, Hilda (1954). The Lord's Prayer: The Beatitudes. Paulist Press. p. 83. ISBN 9780809102556]. In the 4th century Cyprian and Jerome related Mammon to greed, and greed as an evil master that enslaves, and John Chrysostom even personifies Mammon as greed. [Brian S. Rosner (28 August 2007). Greed as Idolatry: The Origin and Meaning of a Pauline Metaphor. Wm. B. Eerdmans Publishing. pp. 23–. ISBN 978-0-8028-3374-7]. During the Middle Ages, Mammon was commonly personified as the demon of wealth and greed. Thus Peter Lombard (II, dist. 6) says, 'Riches are called by the name of a devil, namely Mammon, for Mammon is the name of a devil, by which name riches are called according to the Syrian tongue.' Piers Plowman also regards Mammon as a deity. Nicholas de Lyra, commenting on the passage in Luke, says: 'Mammon est nomen daemonis' (Mammon is the name of a demon)."

Jesus preached more about money than Hell. Why? The reason is that people often try to use money to take care of their dysfunctional Personality Traits where they want to feel they are safe, be in control, have freedom, are romantically attractive, or possess personal magnetism, including a host of soulish thoughts, feelings, and other obsessive-compulsive behaviors. Yet, the Lord wants to use people who can be trusted and faithful to make a profit with money, which is a "very little thing" in God's eyes (Luke 19:17) to bring the wealth of the wicked into the hands of the just (Proverbs 13:22).

LUCIFER COMMITTED SIN IN HIS TRADING IN COMMERCE

When was the first commercial sin committed according to the Bible? Why does money have such an attraction for people? How can you know if you have a money problem? What does the "love of money" really mean? When and who committed the first commercial or trading sin as mentioned in Scriptures?

The first commercial sin was committed by the Archangel named Lucifer (Isaiah 14:12), who also was called Satan (Isaiah 14:12), serpent (Revelation 12:9), devil (John 8:44), prince of this world (John 12:31), prince of the power of the air (Ephesians 2:2), god of this age (Luke 4:6), angel of light (2 Corinthians 11:13-15), thief (John 10:10a), dragon

Dr. Nova Dean Pack

(Revelation 12:7), tempter (1 Corinthians 7:5), Beelzebub (Mark 3:22), a roaring lion (1 Peter 5:8), accuser of the brethren (Revelation 12:10), and other names.

Both Believers and unbelievers in the fallen world can be influenced by the temptations of demonic spirits, especially in the music and film industries, as Lucifer, himself before his fall was the music director in heaven with his musical instruments inside him.

Ezekiel 28:13 19 says, "Thou (Lucifer) hast been in Eden the garden of God; every precious stone was thy covering, the sardius, topaz, and the diamond, the beryl, the onyx, and the jasper, the sapphire, the emerald, and the carbuncle, and gold (Lucifer was the first rock star): the workmanship of thy tabrets and of thy pipes (musical instruments) was prepared in (inside) thee in the day that thou wast created. (14) Thou art the anointed cherub that covereth (had the anointing in music that played music around God's throne); and I have set thee so: thou wast upon the holy mountain of God (given great honor); thou hast walked up and down in the midst of the stones of fire. (15) You were perfect (without sin, with holiness, purity, and righteousness) in your ways from the day you were created, till iniquity was found in you. (16) By the abundance of your trading (sinful buying and selling he became very rich), you became filled with violence within (set up his own illegal money and riches cartel), and you sinned; therefore I cast you as a profane thing out of the mountain of God; and I destroyed you, O covering cherub, from the midst of the fiery stones. (17) Your heart (Lucifer started his own attempt at deification by believing in the superiority of his own false god-like characteristics) was lifted up because of your beauty; you corrupted your wisdom (which became wisdom of this world where there is envy and strife James 3:14-16) for the sake of your splendor; I cast you to the ground, I laid you before kings that they might gaze at you. (18) You defiled your sanctuaries by the multitude of your iniquities, by the iniquity of your trading; therefore, I brought fire from your midst; it devoured you, and I turned you to ashes upon the earth in the sight of all who saw you (future judgment execution into the Lake of Fire Revelation 20:10). (19) All who knew you among the peoples are astonished at you; you have become a horror and shall be no more forever." This was Lucifer's monetary avarice activity or illegal and deceptive trading that tempted him to sin and caused him to seek exaltation of himself to be as God Al-

Personality Traits of Money

mighty (Isaiah 14:13 14).

This fallen Cherub, Lucifer, through avarice, greed, and covetousness convinced one-third of the angels in heaven to join him in his commercial sin and rebellious against God (Revelation 12:3-4). Satan, Serpent, or Dragon brought deception in the Garden of Eden through fraud to tempt the first woman, who in turn convinced the first man because of his affection for her to eat the forbidden fruit from the Tree of the Knowledge of Good and Evil (Genesis 3:1-6). When the fraud and temptation worked against the first woman, and when the first man committed high treason against God, Satan was able to usurp from man the God given possessory rights to all the lands, vegetation, birds, animals, and fish in and on the earth. Satan took rulership over all commercial activity and the places of power in the world system. When the first woman and man sinned, the entire world fell under the spell and authority of this wicked and fallen Archangel along with his kingdom of darkness. By default, Satan became the prince of this world (John 14:30).

THE REVEALING OF EVIL BEHIND THE AVARICE LOVE OF MONEY

You will be illuminated with the spiritual origin of money in the next chapter and how it became a byproduct of the Tree of Knowledge of Good and Evil. The devil's evil commerce with money became the Forbidden fruit" that has been the continuous temptation to humankind thereafter. Satan appointed a special false principality called the god of mammon, which has captivated as an idol in the minds, emotions, and hearts of people in all the world.

The primary introductory scripture in this book as describing various personality traits defining soulish disorders regarding people's obsessive-compulsive relationship with money will be 1 Timothy 6:10, which says, "For the (avarice) love of money is the root of all evil: which while some coveted after, they have erred from the faith, and pierced themselves through with many sorrows." This scripture says that it is not money itself that is the root of all kinds of evil but the avarice love of money that enhances personality traits disorders in the soul that is the root of all kinds of evil.

Dr. Nova Dean Pack

In 1 Timothy 6:10, there is no separate Greek word for "love" in this scripture, as the word "love" was added in English. The Greek word for the "English phrase" in this scripture for "love of money" is "philarguria" which means "avarice of money." The avarice love of money is an ardent desire to obtain money to fulfill greed or covetousness, or a driving obsessive compulsion for security, authority, independence, romanticism, personal magnetism, or many other disorders or combinations thereof. These disorders become Personality Traits of Money in people who strive to obtain money, believing that money will fulfill their needs or will mask over their hurts. People who have obsessive-compulsive Personality Traits of Money seek positions of authority to wear masks to hide the evil they have in their souls. Those who have obsessive-compulsive Personality Traits of Money can be judges, lawyers, medical doctors, nurse practitioners, psychologists, teachers, principals, professors, social workers, and other professionals. These professional people operate in one degree or another in evil, so, their soulish thoughts, emotions, and hearts disorders behind their professional masks can hurt people because they have been given positions of authority to bless or harm people.

I encourage every Believer to read a great book by the author, M. Scott Peck, M.D. titled, People of the Lie (The Hope of Healing Human Evil), copyright 1983, published in 1998 as a Second Edition by Touchstone, a division of Simon & Schuster, Inc.

The Greek word "philarguria" comes from the root word "philarguros," which means "fond of silver." However, both Greek words are rooted in the Greek word "philos" or "phileo," which means "fondness" or "friendly." The Greek word "philarguria" also embodies the English meaning of "avarice love of money." The English word "avarice" has the root word "avar" within it, which means "blind." A person who is covetous of money is "blind" to the truth and "blind" to the snares that avarice, greed, and covetousness cause. A person who is blind to his Personality Traits of Money of using money to fulfill a particular soulish need is usually in denial of their disorder. The purpose why this book is written is to help people receive liberty from the bondage of avarice love of money.

The classic case in the Bible during Jesus' time here on earth as someone full of greed,

Personality Traits of Money

covetousness, and avarice was Judas, the betrayer and thief, who kept stealing money from the offering pouch (John 12:6) and eventually was driven to betray Jesus for thirty pieces of silver (Matthew 26:15).

It is the unlawful relationship with money, not money itself, which is the sin; and too much attention to money matters can lead one to seek money as an idol. Idol worship of money causes moral turpitude, and this insidious attachment to money opens the doorway to evil enslavement to a degree in the kingdom of darkness. People must earn money to exist, but people are not to prioritize their lives just to earn money. You must not fill your heart with the desire to obtain money. People must have money, but people must not allow money to have an undo importance in their lives.

What constitutes the love of money or avarice? What if you make business decisions with an unhealthy motivation to acquire money and spend money to fulfill a desire for security, power, independence, love, attraction, importance, fame, or any other soulish need? Does the fulfillment of these soulish desires drive someone to acquire money while neglecting relationships with family, friends, and even God? Again, the Bible says in the parable of the four soils in Matthew 13:22 and Mark 4:19 the "deceitfulness of riches." People put too much importance on money, so people are deceived in having a wrongful soulish attachment to riches. 1 Timothy 6:17 says, Charge them that are rich in this world, that they be not high-minded, nor trust in uncertain riches, but in the living God, who giveth us richly all things to enjoy."

Money issues are very complicated, and a particular activity may or may not become a driving obsession or compulsion that evidences a wrongful soulish attachment to money. Many examples will be given in the chapters which follow of famous persons in the world and in the Bible who abused money or who saw money as the fulfillment of a particular fracture or need in their souls. You may be able to see a little of yourself in these men and women of history.

You may go through your entire life without dealing with the issue of a wrong relationship with money. It may be a little problem, or it can totally consume most of your energy and time in life if you allow it.

Dr. Nova Dean Pack

Money itself is a reward for work completed or for wisdom exercised in investments. Anything that is a reward for certain behavior will be sought after by many. Similarly, money is used to pay for the necessities of life, such as food, clothing, transportation, and shelter. Therefore, money as a temptation will touch every person in our society.

Most people believe that somehow money solves all their problems. To seek safety from loss, be in control over things and people, seek freedom from authority, be romantically attractive to others, or have a magnetic attraction when you meet people, many people have established the acquisition of money as the most important goal in life. Most people believe that having more money is better than having less money. In fact, to a large degree money matters cause problems in marriages and businesses. Many businessmen and businesswomen suffer from "workaholism" because of their pursuit of money.

Today, most people think a person's net worth is based upon assets and liability statements and income and expense statements. In truth, in God's eyes net worth is the Believer's worthiness in how he is submissive, humble, and pursues intimacy with God and the Lord Jesus Christ, acquires wisdom, knowledge, and understanding from God's word, worships God in spirit and truth, seeks first the Kingdom of God and His righteousness for his provision, and exhibits agape love toward God, the Lord Jesus Christ, and other Believers in the body of Christ. In the world, the goal and philosophy are all about how much money people have. In the Kingdom of God, God's goal for His children is about the Believer's abiding faith, hope, and agape love, but the greatest of these is agape love (1 Corinthians 13:13).

Now, do you have a problem with money? You can find out right now. I invite you to copy and take the "Christian Money Beatitudes Test" which immediately follows this introduction. Answer the questions honestly and give yourself a score, which is explained at the end of the test but do not read how to score the answers as this will give you a false score. The test is a psychological test to reveal your thoughts regarding money; it is to help you, not degrade you, so be honest. You should take the test in private. I suggest that you copy the test from the book on separate pieces of paper, so

Personality Traits of Money

you can take the test again when you are done studying the illuminations found in this book. Also, taking the test in private by copying the test on separate pieces of paper will protect you from other people (such as your children) who may want to read this book. Do not let anyone see how you scored. I was honest when I took the test, and I failed, even though I knew the correct scoring results. I decided to get the monkey off my back regarding my pursuits of money. Thus, if you live in the Western First World countries, you should fail the test if you are honest because every citizen adopts the mores and cultural standards in each society.

Taking this "Christian Money Beatitudes Test" is like a wife who convinces her husband to go to a marriage counsellor to fix a few things she sees wrong in their marital relationship. The husband does not believe anything is wrong in the marriage. After a few sessions, the husband finally realizes there are things he does that are hurting the marriage, so he decides to change for the betterment of the marriage because he loves his wife. Yet, it is hard for the husband to admit his negative personality traits or behavior that is unloving toward his wife. The attitude of "Me Tarzan, you Jane," does not make for a good, loving marriage.

After you read this book, honestly take the "Christian Money Beatitudes Test" again; and more than likely you will receive a better score. Yet, do not feel condemned, but exercise your resolve and will to change. You must desire to change your ways and conform your actions to the principles in God's Word regarding your relationship with money.

Hosea 4:6 says, "My people are destroyed for lack of knowledge. Because you have rejected knowledge, I also will reject you from being priests for Me; because you have forgotten the law of your God, I also will forget your children." The word "knowledge" is the Hebrew word, "dahath," which is a derivative word from the Hebrew word "yada." "Yada" means knowledge through intimacy. Thus, the scripture could read, "My people are destroyed for lack of intimacy with Me, God. Because you have rejected intimacy with Me, God, I also will reject you from being priests for Me; because you have forgotten the law of your God, I also will forget your children." The opposite is also true. "My people have righteousness, peace, and joy by intimacy with Me, God."

Dr. Nova Dean Pack

Accumulating and having money may become obsessive-compulsive daily thought and desire. If acquisition of money consumes your time, energy, and thoughts, then look deep within your soul and understand what is the Personality Traits of Money that is causing you to experience a need to be safe, to have control, to experience freedom, to be romantically attractive, to have personal magnetism with others, or other soulish needs that you think, feel, or believe more money helps to fulfill. Personality Traits of Money can be caused by a fear of poverty, abandonment from death of parents or divorce, distress caused by rejection, hurt from negative teasing, bullying in school, humiliation for being poor as a child, or many other life's distresses, struggles, and disappointments. Money cannot heal you, and you have to be careful not to allow money to consume your life and thereby interfere with God's work in transforming your soul from carnality to spirituality.

Take the "Christian Money Beatitudes Test." It will be exceptionally good for you, and you will be enriched when you do. Even a medical doctor has you fill out a form to reveal your symptoms, your medical history, your weight, blood pressure, the medicines you take, so, he or she can properly diagnose you, make a sound prognosis, and prescribe a regiment of medicine, dietary changes, and exercises to make you well. You need a spiritual check-up in your life to ensure that you have health in your soul, so you can truly prosper spiritually. God desires you to naturally prosper financially and be in good health naturally even as your soul is transformed and prospers spiritually (3 John 2).

The first thing the good financial doctor should give you is the "gos-pill" to make sure you are saved; then prescribe a regiment of reading the word of God daily, even if it consists of memorizing two scriptures that are answers to your problems that you can repeat every hour of the day. Then, the Believer's financial doctor (such as your Pastor) should prescribe that your mind, emotions, and heart willfully pray and seek first the kingdom of God and His righteousness daily (Matthew 6:33). In so doing, make up your mind, become emotionally energized, and believe with your heart with faith in God for your provision, and not seek the idol of mammon as your financial source. God promises He will provide all your need according to His riches in glory by Christ

Personality Traits of Money

Jesus (Philippians 4:19).

Having God's riches by Christ Jesus is a better provision, both natural and spiritual, than a billion dollars in rental real property investments that are totally paid off, a billion dollars in Treasury Bonds, or a billion dollars in a liquid portfolio. Look at all the billionaires that are U.S. citizens. Look at President Trump, who has billions, but I personally have more righteousness, peace, and joy in the Holy Spirit than he does. My relationship with the Godhead and the Lord Jesus Christ is a far greater wealth to me than any of these billionaires have with money. Thus, keep this final preference in your life deep in your heart as this book shares with you the great truths that will set you free from the bondage of money.

Dr. Nova Dean Pack

Christian Money Beatitudes Test

Dr. Nova Dean Pack

Test

You need a spiritual check-up in your life to ensure that you have health in your soul, so you can truly prosper spiritually. God desires you to naturally prosper financially and be in good health naturally even as your soul is transformed and prospers spiritually (3 John 2).

1.) You find it necessary to put the acquisition of money ahead of other matters in life, including health, recreation, friendship, family, and church.

NEVER   ALWAYS

☐ 1   ☐ 2   ☐ 3   ☐ 4   ☐ 5

2.) Sometimes you purchase items you don't need or want just because they are a bargain on sale.

NEVER   ALWAYS

☐ 1   ☐ 2   ☐ 3   ☐ 4   ☐ 5

3.) You purchase cars, clothing, electronic devices or other things because they are status symbols.

NEVER   ALWAYS

☐ 1   ☐ 2   ☐ 3   ☐ 4   ☐ 5

4.) You feel guilty about purchasing necessities such as a new pair of shoes, a new suit, a new dress, a new television, even though you have sufficient money to do so.

NEVER   ALWAYS

☐ 1   ☐ 2   ☐ 3   ☐ 4   ☐ 5

5.) When you make a major purchase, you presume that the seller is trying to take advantage of you.

NEVER   ALWAYS

☐ 1   ☐ 2   ☐ 3   ☐ 4   ☐ 5

6.) Although you spend money grudgingly on yourself, you spend money freely, even cheerfully, on family, friends, or other Believers in Church, so they will like you.

NEVER   ALWAYS

☐ 1   ☐ 2   ☐ 3   ☐ 4   ☐ 5

Personality Traits of Money

Test

7.) You commonly say, "I can't afford it" regardless of whether you have sufficient funds or not in your bank account.

NEVER　　　　　　　　ALWAYS

☐ 1　☐ 2　☐ 3　☐ 4　☐ 5

8.) You pride yourself in always knowing to the dollar how much you have in your bank account and in your wallet or purse at all times.

NEVER　　　　　　　　ALWAYS

☐ 1　☐ 2　☐ 3　☐ 4　☐ 5

9.) You find it stressful to decide about spending money regardless of the amount.

NEVER　　　　　　　　ALWAYS

☐ 1　☐ 2　☐ 3　☐ 4　☐ 5

10.) You find it prudent to complain to a seller about his cost concerning almost every purchase to get the price lowered.

NEVER　　　　　　　　ALWAYS

☐ 1　☐ 2　☐ 3　☐ 4　☐ 5

11.) You emotionally feel better when you pay more than your share of a restaurant bill to make sure, so you are not indebted to anyone, or so no one thinks you are "cheap."

NEVER　　　　　　　　ALWAYS

☐ 1　☐ 2　☐ 3　☐ 4　☐ 5

12.) You tend to spend all the money you earn even though you have money left over after payment of normal bills at the end of the month.

NEVER　　　　　　　　ALWAYS

☐ 1　☐ 2　☐ 3　☐ 4　☐ 5

13.) You use money to control others because you feel that the guy who pays the money is the guy who is entitled to the decisions.

NEVER　　　　　　　　ALWAYS

☐ 1　☐ 2　☐ 3　☐ 4　☐ 5

Dr. Nova Dean Pack

Test

14.) You feel inferior to others who have more money than you do.

NEVER   ALWAYS

☐ 1   ☐ 2   ☐ 3   ☐ 4   ☐ 5

15.) You feel somewhat superior to those who have less money than you do.

NEVER   ALWAYS

☐ 1   ☐ 2   ☐ 3   ☐ 4   ☐ 5

16.) You believe that money can solve most all of your problems.

NEVER   ALWAYS

☐ 1   ☐ 2   ☐ 3   ☐ 4   ☐ 5

17.) You experience anxiety and become defensive when someone asks you how much money you have in your bank account.

NEVER   ALWAYS

☐ 1   ☐ 2   ☐ 3   ☐ 4   ☐ 5

18.) When talking about money or a business transaction with someone, you feel it is imperative to talk privately about the deal, even to the point of whispering the details.

NEVER   ALWAYS

☐ 1   ☐ 2   ☐ 3   ☐ 4   ☐ 5

19.) Your very first consideration in any buying transaction is the cost.

NEVER   ALWAYS

☐ 1   ☐ 2   ☐ 3   ☐ 4   ☐ 5

20.) You feel "dumb" when one of your friends purchase something for a little less than what you paid.

NEVER   ALWAYS

☐ 1   ☐ 2   ☐ 3   ☐ 4   ☐ 5

Personality Traits of Money

Test

21.) You actually dislike money and look down on people who you think boast of it.

NEVER   ALWAYS

☐ 1   ☐ 2   ☐ 3   ☐ 4   ☐ 5

22.) You believe a businessperson who has lots of moneymust have obtained it through "shady business practices."

NEVER   ALWAYS

☐ 1   ☐ 2   ☐ 3   ☐ 4   ☐ 5

23.) You believe that no one can get rich honestly.

NEVER   ALWAYS

☐ 1   ☐ 2   ☐ 3   ☐ 4   ☐ 5

24.) You prefer saving money rather than investing it.

NEVER   ALWAYS

☐ 1   ☐ 2   ☐ 3   ☐ 4   ☐ 5

25.) You don't like "long term" investments because you want to be able to get your money out because in the end times things can collapse quickly.

NEVER   ALWAYS

☐ 1   ☐ 2   ☐ 3   ☐ 4   ☐ 5

26.) You feel you can never truly retire because the amount you have saved may never be enough to live on.

NEVER   ALWAYS

☐ 1   ☐ 2   ☐ 3   ☐ 4   ☐ 5

27.) You feel money gives you a certain sense of security.

NEVER   ALWAYS

☐ 1   ☐ 2   ☐ 3   ☐ 4   ☐ 5

Test

28.) You feel people like other people who have money.

NEVER — ALWAYS

☐ 1   ☐ 2   ☐ 3   ☐ 4   ☐ 5

29.) You feel people look down on other people who are broke.

NEVER — ALWAYS

☐ 1   ☐ 2   ☐ 3   ☐ 4   ☐ 5

30.) You feel a person who has money is someone who should be able to give you sound financial advice.

NEVER — ALWAYS

☐ 1   ☐ 2   ☐ 3   ☐ 4   ☐ 5

31.) You would rarely ever take financial counseling from someone who is broke or has little or no assets, even though he or she is a biblical scholar.

NEVER — ALWAYS

☐ 1   ☐ 2   ☐ 3   ☐ 4   ☐ 5

32.) You tend to judge the quality of a person's worth based upon the amount of riches and money he has.

NEVER — ALWAYS

☐ 1   ☐ 2   ☐ 3   ☐ 4   ☐ 5

33.) You believe people who have money can buy influence they need to get ahead.

NEVER — ALWAYS

☐ 1   ☐ 2   ☐ 3   ☐ 4   ☐ 5

34.) You believe lawyers, doctors, and pastors say things just to get your money.

NEVER — ALWAYS

☐ 1   ☐ 2   ☐ 3   ☐ 4   ☐ 5

Personality Traits of Money

Test

35.) You believe tithing is not mandatory, but those people should just give cheerfully.

NEVER　　　　　　　　ALWAYS

☐ 1　☐ 2　☐ 3　☐ 4　☐ 5

36.) You believe pastors should not own a Mercedes, Rolls Royce, or a lake side vacation home.

NEVER　　　　　　　　ALWAYS

☐ 1　☐ 2　☐ 3　☐ 4　☐ 5

37.) You believe that most businesspeople commit "white collar crimes," but usually get away with it because they have the money to hire experts to camouflage their illegal activity.

NEVER　　　　　　　　ALWAYS

☐ 1　☐ 2　☐ 3　☐ 4　☐ 5

38.) You believe that people with money care less about people than those who are without money.

NEVER　　　　　　　　ALWAYS

☐ 1　☐ 2　☐ 3　☐ 4　☐ 5

39.) You believe that people with lots of money generally are serving mammon and are less godly than people who middle class or poor.

NEVER　　　　　　　　ALWAYS

☐ 1　☐ 2　☐ 3　☐ 4　☐ 5

40.) You want to become "financially free," so that you can spend your life serving God.

NEVER　　　　　　　　ALWAYS

☐ 1　☐ 2　☐ 3　☐ 4　☐ 5

41.) You believe people who have money also have prestige.

NEVER　　　　　　　　ALWAYS

☐ 1　☐ 2　☐ 3　☐ 4　☐ 5

Dr. Nova Dean Pack

Test

42.) You believe it is impossible to become rich unless you work hard and sacrifice your personal life.

NEVER   ALWAYS

☐ 1   ☐ 2   ☐ 3   ☐ 4   ☐ 5

43.) You believe if you have money, you do not have to admit to anyone that you have any faults.

NEVER   ALWAYS

☐ 1   ☐ 2   ☐ 3   ☐ 4   ☐ 5

44.) You continue giving to certain ministries because you believe that if you stop giving the particular Minister will not like you anymore.

NEVER   ALWAYS

☐ 1   ☐ 2   ☐ 3   ☐ 4   ☐ 5

45.) You believe that everybody has his "price," and all you must do to get the person to comply or agree is to find and pay his "price."

NEVER   ALWAYS

☐ 1   ☐ 2   ☐ 3   ☐ 4   ☐ 5

46.) You become anxious and worrisome when your bank account has a near zero balance.

NEVER   ALWAYS

☐ 1   ☐ 2   ☐ 3   ☐ 4   ☐ 5

47.) You find you are most comfortable, confident, and secure when you have more than enough money in the bank to pay your bills, able to go out to dinner, put aside money for a vacation, and money for Christmas.

NEVER   ALWAYS

☐ 1   ☐ 2   ☐ 3   ☐ 4   ☐ 5

48.) You feel uncomfortable every time an offering is taken at church.

NEVER   ALWAYS

☐ 1   ☐ 2   ☐ 3   ☐ 4   ☐ 5

Personality Traits of Money

Test

49.) You believe that what is "cheap" or "free" has little value.

NEVER ALWAYS

☐ 1 ☐ 2 ☐ 3 ☐ 4 ☐ 5

50.) You believe that if you are independently wealthy you will be free to do whatever you do and go wherever you go without anyone controlling you.

NEVER ALWAYS

☐ 1 ☐ 2 ☐ 3 ☐ 4 ☐ 5

Test

HOW TO SCORE YOUR TEST RESULTS:

Be honest in determining your score as this is a confidential test. To determine your score, add up all the numbers constituting your answers. A score of 100 or lower means you do not have a significant problem with money. A score between 101 to 135 means you have a moderate problem with money. A score between 136 to 170 means you have a profound problem with money. A score of 171 and above means you have a serious problem with money. Read certain personality traits that you believe you identify with and prayerfully be led by the Holy Spirit to transform your soul, so you no longer look toward money to influence or satisfy your mental, emotional and heart needs. After you read and study this book and seek pastoral counseling and submission to the transforming work of the Godhead that lives within you, then come back and take this test again. You will be surprised how much you have improved.

Personality Traits of Money

Dr. Nova Dean Pack

1
The Natural And Spiritual Origin Of Money

Personality Traits of Money

CHAPTER ONE

THE NATURAL AND SPIRITUAL ORIGIN OF MONEY

THE ROOT ORIGIN OF MONEY

The following scripture, 1 Timothy 6:10, will introduce several chapters where I discuss a particular personality trait that seeks money because of its primary relevance and as a point of reference as you read ideas presented. Again, 1 Timothy 6:10 says, "For the love of money (Greek - philarguria -avarice) is the root of all evil: which while some coveted after, they have erred from the faith, and pierced themselves through with many sorrows."

In this chapter, let us examine together the "root origin" of money. If you know from where something comes, you can know its attributes and characteristics. A dog is going to function as a dog because its parents were dogs. Fallen humans are going to act sinfully because they come from sinful parents, all the way back to Adam and Eve. People sin because they are inherently sinners; they are not sinners only because they sin. Thus, when someone is born again, their root origin has changed as they are now from the spiritual Last Adam and Second Man (Jesus Christ) instead of the natural First Adam and First Man who sinned (1 Corinthians 15:45-47). The devil is called the father of lies (John 8:44), and anything that comes from him can by nature tend to be deceitful.

Definition of the word "root" (American Heritage Dictionary) is 1). "The primary source or origin of a thing, or 2). The usually underground portion of a plant that lacks buds, leaves or nodes and serves as support, draws minerals and water from the surrounding soil and sometimes stores food."

One theory of the root source of money dates to antiquity to the sacrifice of animals, and the spiritual significance attached to money is the cause of much diversion, strife, avarice, greed, covetousness, and ungodly sense of importance.

Money can be used for good or evil. Money can be used to pay one's tithes and offerings to God, to buy narcotics, to feel safe, to acquire control and power, to increase freedom, or to pay for cosmetic surgery to look attractive.

In furtherance of this theory of the origin of money, it requires analyzing the source of money as the fruit from the Tree of the Knowledge of Good and Evil or the fruit from the Tree of Life.

MONEY REPLACED THE USE OF STRENGTH
AND SPEED TO ACQUIRE NEEDS AND WANTS

In primitive societies, amongst animals and in modern times amongst the unsaved business world, success and survival belongs to the most cunning, powerful, strongest, and swiftest.

In modern civilized society, money is not just used to purchase the things needed to survive, such as food, shelter, transportation, and clothing, but also is used for enhancement of one's safety, control, freedom, romantic attraction, personal magnetism, and many other soulish mindsets, emotions, and beliefs.

Therefore, people in civilized societies do not compete for the "game" (wild animal) to feed and clothe their families, but people do compete in the "game" to acquire money to buy the necessities of life for their families, to purchase products they believe beautifies their look and attraction, and to live a lifestyle in civilized society that enhances their sense of importance and stature.

TRANSFERENCE OF SPIRITUAL BLESSINGS OR CURSES OCCURRED FROM ANIMAL SACRIFICES, AS THE ROOT ORIGIN OF MONEY

God had ordained the sacrifice of animals as essential to pass to His people His covenant blessings. Blood sacrifices were essential for right standing with God, which sacrificial practices started after the fall of Adam and Eve.

Genesis 3:31 says, "Also for Adam and his wife the Lord God made tunics of skin and clothed them." Adam and Eve tried to cover their nakedness or sin consciousness with tree leaves, but God required covering by means of a blood sacrifice.

The covenant of love with God and redemption for sins committed required the sacrifice of innocent animals. This "substitutionary atonement" points toward the necessity of judgment upon the innocent to provide a covering for the guilty.

Under the New Covenant, we put on the crucified, resurrected, and ascended Christ Jesus and are clothed with Christ Jesus rather than with good works. We appropriate the blood of the Sacrificial Lamb (Christ Jesus) as the redemption for our sins and iniquities. However, it was Jesus' sacrifice and spilt precious blood on the Roman cross that brought the covenant blessing of eternal life. Romans 13:14 says, "But put ye on the Lord Jesus Christ, and make no provision for the flesh, to fulfill the lusts thereof."

What is important for this topic is that in the atonement through sacrificial animal practices, which continued until Jesus sacrificed Himself on the Roman cross, God "transferred" a temporary "spiritual forgiveness" to the participants. Even though the atonement for sins was only temporary; nonetheless, it allowed the Hebrew participants' spirits and souls who believed in the coming Messiah to stay in paradise in a righteous holding cell called Abraham's Bosom until Jesus Christ's sacrificial death went further than atonement to the point of redemption. Jesus, as Messiah, came to set captivity captive and set the captives free from the bondage of sin, iniquities, the fallen world, the kingdom of darkness, and the curse of the laws and the consequences thereof (2 Corinthians 5:21; Galatians 3:13; 1 John 3:8; Colossians 1:13).

After Adam and Eve's original sin, the religious sacrificial system was instituted through blood sacrifice of animals to pass God's spiritual righteousness to man temporarily until the coming of the Seed of the woman prophesied in Genesis 3:15, and as later manifested in the fullness of time as the Messiah's sacrificial death. Galatians 4:4-5 says, "But when the fulness of the time was come, God sent forth his Son, made of a woman, made under the law, (5) To redeem them that were under the law, that we might receive the adoption of sons." The word "redeem" is an economic word, and redemption was paid for by the sacrifice of flesh and spilt blood.

THE RELIGIOUS SACRIFICIAL SYSTEM WAS SEEN IN THE OFFERINGS OF CAIN AND ABEL

Cain's offering of the fruit of the ground was really the fruit of his own efforts and was his attempt at self-righteousness through works. Cain had a bad motive as Cain resented giving an offering to God since he felt it was the fruit of his hard work of growing crops; whereas, his brother Abel had less work because he simply led and watched over animals who he led to pastors and still waters (Genesis 4:3; Psalm 23:2). Abel was Shepherd like Jesus, but Cain was a farmer. Thus, Cain had a bad motive in his giving. Cain's poor attitude about giving was seen in Genesis 4:6-7, "And the LORD said unto Cain, 'Why art thou wroth? And why is thy countenance fallen?' (7) If thou doest well, shalt thou not be accepted? And if thou doest not well, sin lieth at the door. And unto thee shall be his desire, and thou shalt rule over him."

God accepted Abel's offering of an animal and Cains vegetable offering, so there was no need for Cain to feel cheated of a blessing from God. Leviticus 27:30 says, "And all the tithe of the land, whether of the seed of the land or of the fruit of the tree, is the Lord's. It is holy to the Lord." Money owed to God is holy in the spiritual realm when it is the tithed.

Abel's offering of the firstborn of his flock and his blood sacrifice properly transferred God's covenant blessing to him, but Abel also gave the "fat" of the meat. The fat was kept for cooking grease and to make soap. Abel also offered the fat which God did not require of Abel. Abel's offering pleased God because it showed Abel's thanksgiving heart. Abel adding the fat to his offering showed the motive of Abel to give more to God than was required to express the love he had for his Creator (Genesis 4:4). Offering is a heart issue, and Abel's pattern from the beginning is a sound principle to follow.

Life is in the blood, and the spilling of blood through animal sacrifices was necessary for temporary Atonement and continued life. Leviticus 17:11 says, "For the life of its flesh is in the blood, and I have given it to you upon the altar to make atonement for your souls; for it is the blood that makes atonement for the soul."

Under the Mosaic Law, the Israelite sacrifice religious order, life and blood of the sacrificial lamb or goat were killed and placed on the altar to cleanse the Temple while the sins of the people were placed upon the head of the escape goat by the High Priest temporarily to reconcile the Israelites with God and for the transfer of God's covenant blessings. The "transfer of God's covenant blessings" is centered around the sacrifice of life and blood on the altar.

God instructed the Israelites to bring Him five offerings. In Leviticus, there are five offerings that sum up God's requirement of sacrificial work and His bestowing mercy and grace to the then Israelites. The offerings are as follows:

- The Burnt Offering: A sacrificial animal was burned on an altar (except for the skin) to represent God's will. (Leviticus 1; 8:18-21; 16:24)

- The Peace Offering: The blood, fat, and kidneys of the sacrificed animal was put on the altar, as God and man can feed on the same offering. (Leviticus 3; 7:11-34)

- The Sin Offering: An offering for sins by the sacrifice of the buttock of the animal was burned outside of Israel. (Leviticus 4; 16:3-22)

- The Trespass Offering: An offering as a sacrifice for a person who unintentionally trespassed the Lord's law was burned. (Leviticus 5:14-19; 6:1-7)

- The Meal Offering: A handful of flour and oil was burned while priests eat the rest to offer God gratitude. (Leviticus 2)

The first four offerings required the sacrifice of animals as the offering, but the last "meal offering" was thankfulness and gratitude toward God. Jesus said in John 6:48, "I am that bread of (zoe) life."

The established ordinance of sacrifice of life and blood was culminated with the sacrifice of God's only begotten Son on the Roman cross. Jesus' suffering and crucifixion on the Cross eternally satisfied the requirements of God the Father which then allowed God's blessings, including eternal life, to be transferred to the Believer.

The Old Testament Faithfuls went to Abraham's Bosom upon death because they believed in the coming Messiah. Upon Jesus' death His spirit and soul went to Hades and to Abraham's Bosom to release the Old Testament Faithfuls, and took them to the Third Heaven, along with Paradise.

Alluding to Psalms 68:18, Paul said in Ephesians 4:8-10, "Wherefore He saith, 'When He ascended up on high, He led captivity captive, and gave gifts unto men.' (9) (Now that He ascended, what is it but that He also descended first into the lower parts of the earth? (10) He that descended is the same also that ascended up far above all heavens, that He might fill all things.)"

The truth is in the holy scriptures written by inspired men from God have the authority that man's ideas interpreting scriptures do not have. Thus, I want you to read some scriptures that reveal the truth how the avarice love of money is a spiritual stronghold under the idol of mammon. Yet, this demonic stronghold was a counterfeit of the truth, as money can be used for good instead of evil. Satan is the god ruler of the world money system, so Satan's demons are always lurking around to cause people to make money an idol. Money cannot redeem anyone. The redemption blessing started with the sacrifice of animals and was institutionalized under Mosaic law with the feast of atonement which is the great exchange between the sacrifice of an Atonement Lamb for the righteousness of God. We can follow the sacrifice of lambs and goats, and the High Priest laying his hands on the head of the scapegoat and leading the scapegoat for three days and nights to a wilderness. Sacrificial Lamb and the Scapegoat both represented Jesus taking the sins of mankind to Hades to rid the sin from the people and instilling their souls with the righteousness of God.

Jesus came from heaven (John 3:13) to be the Sacrificial Lamb and the Scapegoat once and for all that brought eternal redemption and eternal life that heretofore by the Atonement

Personality Traits of Money

sacrificial system of the Israelites under the Mosaic Law was only temporary year after year.

2 Corinthians 5:21 says, "For He hath made Him (Jesus' finite humanity nature) to be sin for us, Who knew no sin; that we might be made the righteousness of God in Him."

Hebrews 9:12 says, "Not with the blood of goats and calves, but with His own blood He entered the Most Holy Place once for all, having obtained eternal redemption." The Most Holy things in the Third Heaven is the Body and spilt Blood of Christ Jesus.

What is most important for this study is that redemption is an economic blessing as Believers were redeemed from being slaves to sin and the fallen nature of mankind. Every person was born with the sin principle in his body because of the sin passed down from Adam and Eve. Jesus redeemed us with His precious blood to set us free from the law of sin and death. 1 Peter 1:18-19 says, "Forasmuch as ye know that ye were not redeemed with corruptible things, as silver and gold, from your vain conversation received by tradition from your fathers; (19) But with the precious blood of Christ, as of a lamb without blemish and without spot."

There is a spiritual transfer of the sins of the people on the life and blood to cleanse the temple and through the High Priest sin was placed upon the scapegoat to remove the sins away from the people. This animal sacrificial system was terminated upon the sacrificial death of Christ Jesus. Jesus carried away Believers' sins when He went to Hades and threw Believers' sins vicariously in the bottomless pit. John the Baptist said in John 1:29, "The next day John seeth Jesus coming unto him, and saith, 'Behold the Lamb of God, which taketh away the sin of the world.'"

Hebrews 10:18 says, "Now where there is remission (complete eradication of sin as opposed to just a cover up atonement) of these, there is no longer an offering for sin."

Hebrews 9:7, 28 says, "But into the second part the high priest went alone once a year, not without blood, which he offered for himself and for the people's sins committed in ignorance. . . (28) Christ was offered once to bear the sins of many. To those who eagerly wait for Him He will appear a second time apart from sin for salvation."

Hebrews 10:14 says, "For by one offering He has perfected (transferred Christ's righteousness) forever those (Believers) who are being sanctified (continuously being spiritually matured through God's good works to and through the Believers)." See also Romans 12:1 2, Ephesians 2:10, 5:26, Philippians 2:12 13 and James 1:21.

Hebrews 13:12 says, "Therefore Jesus also, that He might sanctify the people with His own blood, suffered outside the gate." Jesus was the Sacrificial Lamb and the Scapegoat to carry away the sins of mankind to the bottomless pit in hell. Those who repent and believe with their whole heart in Jesus' sacrificial offering of Himself, that He justifiably was raised from the death, shall be saved, receive eternal life, have their names written in the Lambs Book of Life, and escape the eternal punishment in the Lake of Fire (Romans 10: 9-10; Revelation 20:15).

Things in the spiritual realm speak and have spiritual power and can be holy or unholy depending on what altar they are offered. Leviticus 17:12 says, "Therefore I said to the children of Israel, 'No one among you shall eat blood, nor shall any stranger who dwells among you eat blood.'" It was the blood itself that had the spiritual power inherent within to make atonement for sins or pass demonic power from idol worship.

Jesus had precious holy blood, with the blood type of Father God. Jesus' blood was applied not only to an earthly altar, but also to the altar of God in heaven, for redemption and remission of sins for all time to those who receive Him as Savior and Lord. (See Hebrews 9:12, 22). With the emphasis as pertains to the topic of this book, redemption and remission of sins is an economic covenantal transaction with God.

Genesis 4:10 says, "And He said, 'What have you done? The voice of your brother's blood cries out to Me from the ground.'" Blood speaks in the spiritual realm. Hebrews 12:24 says, "To Jesus the Mediator of the new covenant, and to the blood of sprinkling that speaks better things than that of Abel."

Hebrews 6:7 8 says, "For the earth which drinks in the rain that often comes upon it, and bears herbs useful for those by whom it is cultivated, receives blessing from God; but if it bears thorns and briers, it is rejected and near to being cursed, whose end is to be burned." The earth can be blessed or cursed. The earth is alive. The earth can be affected by prophecy. God instructed Jeremiah to prophesy to the earth. Jeremiah 22:29 says, "O earth, earth, earth, hear the word of the LORD."

Hebrews 4:12 says, "For the word of God is living and powerful, and sharper than any two-edged sword, piercing even to the division of soul and spirit, and of joints and marrow, and is a discerner of the thoughts and intents of the heart." God's Word is living. Matthew 4:4 says, "… It is written, Man shall not live by bread along but by every word that preceedeth out of the mouth of God."

Jesus' divine nature is the living God the Word (John 1:1) Jesus' humanity nature is revealed in John 1:14, which says "And the Word became flesh and dwelt among us, and we beheld His glory, the glory as of the only begotten of the Father, full of grace and truth."

The point of this discussion is that in the spiritual realm, created things, such as the tithe, which are innate in the natural world are alive or are holy or unholy in the spiritual world and are used to enter an economic covenantal transaction with God.

Even in the historical occult world of worshipping false gods, the sacrificial animal offering benefits or detriments were imputed to the beneficiary or offeror by eating the flesh of the animal.

Leviticus 7:18 says, "And if any of the flesh of the sacrifice of his peace offering is eaten at all on the third day, it shall not be accepted, nor shall it be imputed to him; it shall be an abomination to him who offers it, and the person who eats of it shall bear guilt."

Romans 5:19 says, "For as by one man's disobedience many were made sinners, so also by one Man's obedience many will be made righteous."

The Levite Priests and Aaron Priests in the Old Testament ate the animal sacrifice because

Personality Traits of Money

such eating was a necessary ingredient to transfer the covenant blessing from God to the Hebrew people.

Deuteronomy 18:1 says, "The priests, the Levites — all the tribe of Levi — shall have no part nor inheritance with Israel, they shall eat the offerings of the Lord, made by fire, and His portion."

Speaking to the Levite Priests and Aaron Priests, Moses said in Deuteronomy 12:27, "And you shall offer your burnt offerings, the meat and the blood, on the altar of the Lord your God; and the blood of your sacrifices shall be poured out on the altar of the Lord your God, and you shall eat the meat."

Symbolically, eating the bread representing the body of Jesus and drinking the grape juice or wine representing the precious blood of Jesus has a spiritual celebration of the blessings of remission of sins. Matthew 26: 26-28 says, "And as they were eating, Jesus took bread, and blessed it, and brake it, and gave it to the disciples, and said, 'Take, eat; this is My body.' (27) And he took the cup, and gave thanks, and gave it to them, saying, 'Drink ye all of it; (28) For this is My blood of the new testament, which is shed for many for the remission of sins.'"

John 6:48 58 says, "'I am the bread of life. Your fathers ate the manna in the wilderness and are dead. This is the bread which comes down from heaven, that one may eat of it and not die. I am the living bread which came down from heaven. If anyone eats of this bread, he will live forever; and the bread that I shall give is My flesh, which I shall give for the life of the world.' The Jews therefore quarreled among themselves, saying, 'How can this Man give us His flesh to eat?' Then Jesus said to them, 'Most assuredly, I say to you, unless you eat the flesh of the Son of Man and drink His blood, you have no life in you. Whoever eats My flesh and drinks My blood has eternal life, and I will raise him up at the last day. For My flesh is food indeed, and My blood is drink indeed. He who eats My flesh and drinks My blood abides in Me, and I in him. As the living Father sent Me, and I live because of the Father, so he who feeds on Me will live because of Me. This is the bread which came down from heaven not as your fathers ate the manna and are dead. He who eats this bread will live forever.'" In the spiritual realm, flesh and blood are "spiritual food."

Partaking symbolically with communion of the covenant blood and flesh of Christ Jesus, the Sacrificial Lamb of God sent from heaven (John 3:13), is God's provision for our remission of sins and unto eternal life. In this royal exchange with God, Believers become partakers of the divine nature (2 Peter 1:4), but Believers do not become divine or infinite like God. We receive the divine righteousness of God because Jesus vicariously took upon His humanity nature as the Sacrificial Lamb the sins of mankind. 2 Corinthians 5:21 says, "For He hath made him to be sin for us, Who knew no sin; that we might be made the righteousness of God in Him."

Redeem means to buy back, repurchase, to free from captivity by payment of ransom, to release from blame or debt, to remove the obligation by payment, the economic exchange for something of value, to atone, and to retrieve. Thus, money has a spiritual connotation as it is used to transact spiritual matters, such as offerings and tithes.

Knowing the spiritual significance of offerings of blood sacrifices for spiritual blessings, the devil caused money to come from the sacrifice of animals, and therefore money became an idol to be falsely worshiped. However, Jesus showed that His sacrificial blood has the true spiritual economic value to redeem mankind from infernal death.

Thus, redemption is an economic term in the spiritual and natural worlds, as Jesus' precious spilt blood was used to purchase us back by God, not gold or silver. In the spiritual realm, things other than gold and silver can be used in God's Kingdom spiritual economy. However, gold and silver can become holy if they are the "tithe." On the other hand, Satan as the original counterfeiter connected money with the sacrifice of animals to entrap people and confuse people to lead them away from the true meaning of the sacrificial blood.

Although we do not have to take of the Eucharist to receive salvation, the taking of communion is commanded to bring healing to our bodies, strengthening to our souls, bringing unity in the faith, and a recommitment as servant of Christ Jesus as His body and betrothed.

In the communion, Christians today receive the cup as a participation symbolically in Jesus' spilt blood and breaking of bread as a participation in His broken body. The communion meal spiritually reinforces Jesus Christ's act of joining us to Him and to each other as brothers and sisters in the Lord (1 Corinthians 11:24 32).

1 Corinthians 10:18 says, "Observe Israel after the flesh: Are not those who eat of the sacrifices partakers of the altar?"

Spiritual transfer of evil occurred in participating in ceremonies of eating the meat sacrificed to animals or in worshiping anything as an idol. 1 Corinthians 10:19 21 says, "What am I saying then? That an idol is anything, or what is offered to idols is anything? Rather, that the things which the Gentiles sacrifice they sacrifice to demons and not to God, and I do not want you to have fellowship with demons. You cannot drink the cup of the Lord and the cup of demons; you cannot partake of the Lord's table and of the table of demons."

Idolatrous sacrifices and worship are a direct confrontation with God and are an abomination. Therefore, one can bring God's wrath by worshiping any created thing as an idol. Exodus 20:3-5 says, "Thou shalt have no other gods before Me. (4) Thou shalt not make unto thee any graven image, or any likeness of anything that is in heaven above, or that is in the earth beneath, or that is in the water under the earth: (5) Thou shalt not bow down thyself to them, nor serve them: for I the LORD thy God am a jealous God, visiting the iniquity of the fathers upon the children unto the third and fourth generation of them that hate me."

Worshipping the god of mammon is worshipping an idol. Just as taking communion brings fellowship with Christ Jesus, eating meat sacrificed to idols brings fellowship with demons. It does not matter the U.S. says on its currency, "In God we trust." If we do not trust God when we have no money, how will we see God as our divine Source that brought the money to us?

No created thing, such as paper that is used to make money, is sinful or evil, naturally, since everything belongs to God Who created them (Psalm 24:1), including the gold and silver (Haggai 2:8). Also, when God created everything in Genesis 1, He "saw that it was good."

Personality Traits of Money

Deuteronomy 32:37 38 says, "He will say: 'Where are their gods, the rock in which they sought refuge? Who ate the fat of their sacrifices, and drank the wine of their drink offering? Let them rise and help you and be your refuge.'"

Deuteronomy 32:16 17 says, "They provoked Him to jealousy with foreign gods; with abominations they provoked Him to anger. They sacrificed to demons, not to God, to gods they did not know, to new gods, new arrivals, that your fathers did not fear."

Eating the flesh of meat sacrificed to idols and worship of pagan gods is more than mere superstition. Such activity submits the worshiper to demons. Leviticus 17:7 says, "They shall no more offer their sacrifices to demons, after whom they have played the harlot. This shall be a statute forever for them throughout their generations."

MONEY WAS CREATED OR CAME ORIGINALLY FROM THE PAGAN RITUALISTIC SACRIFICES OF ANIMALS TO IDOLS

With the pagan practices, the meat of the animal sacrificed to an idol, was given to partly to the idol god by burning, and the rest of the meat was distributed to the people who were chosen by the Priests to participate in the demonic ritual sacrifice to the idol. In the Greek and Roman cultures, a bull was generally the animal sacrificed, and its meat was eaten only by the most honored in society.

The portion of the bull eaten by the participants they believed transferred the characteristics of strength and heroism of the bull into the participants. The characteristics of the bull were "magically" (demonically) transferred to the participant. The bull's flesh and blood were thought to have "manna" or "magical powers."

Gary A. Anderson, Sacrifices and Offerings in Ancient Israel: Studies in Their Social and Political Importance, Atlanta: Scholars Press, 1987. Page 21, postulates that Canaanite and Mesopotamian religions utilized ceremonies of animal sacrifice as opportunities for "egalitarian festivals" in which the horizontal facet of primitive religion is apparent. In other words, in some cultures the sacrifice was not necessarily to their pagan god but more of a feast where the local community reaffirmed its collective societal uniqueness and history.

Receiving part of the sacrificial feast was a symbol of importance of citizenship. To be excluded from the sacrifice meant the person lacked importance in the culture or was ostracized from the community. The portion of the bull that each person received was indicative of his social rank.

As the community grew, and more and more prestigious citizens emerged, the number of the participants in the pagan ritual became too numerous to have enough meat to go around.

The occult priests and kings started giving participants coins or medallions to be hung around their necks as symbols and evidence of receiving the magical transfer of the strength or speed of the animal sacrificed. The image of the animal was usually on coins or medallions to facilitate the spiritual transfer.

Therefore, the origin of money was that the coins were handed out as magical charms from eating the sacrifice of animals to idols, and the possessors thought they had special spiritual power transferred to them.

Eventually, the coins or medallions replaced portions of meat sacrificed to idols as status symbols. These coins or medallions were given by the priests or kings as esteem and honor. They also symbolized the political or governmental service the individual made to the state.

The greatest honor received a gold coin or medallion, followed by next honored received a silver coin or medallion, and finally the last honored received a bronze coin or medallion.

The Olympics: The World History Encyclopedia, March 3, 2018, titled "Ancient Olympic Games," written by Mark Cartwright, says, "The Ancient Olympic Games were a sporting event held every four years at the sacred site of Olympia, in the western Peloponnese, in honour of Zeus, the supreme god of the Greek religion. The games, held from 776 BCE to 393 CE, involved participants and spectators from all over Greece and even beyond... The first Olympics were held from 776 BCE at the first full moon after the summer solstice (around the middle of July) in honour of Zeus. The winner of the first and only event, the stadion footrace was Koroibos of Elis and from then on, every victor was recorded, and each Olympiad named after them, thus giving us the first accurate chronology of the ancient Greek world. An Olympiad was not only the name of the event itself but also of the period between games. During a three-month pan-Hellenic truce, athletes and as many as 40,000 spectators came from all over Greece to participate in the Games at Olympia. Later, other games would be organized at other sacred sites such as Delphi, Isthmia and Nemea but the Olympian Games would remain the most prestigious. The Games started with a procession which went from the host town of Elis to Olympia, led by the Hellanodikai (judges) and on arrival at Olympia all athletes and officials swore an oath to follow the established rules of the competitions and to compete with honour and respect. The most important religious ceremony of the event was the sacrifice of 100 oxen, known as the hecatomb, at the altar of Zeus, carried out when the sporting events were over."

Thus, the original Greek Olympics were done to honor Zeus and ended with a demonic sacrifice to the false god.

The modern Olympic Games were reinstated in Athens, Greece during April 6-15, 1896, and on the medals the goddess of Victory seated with a rising Phoenix Acropolis in the background with an inscription was given to the athletes that won the top three positions in each competition. A similar practice of the occult practices of sacrifice of animals, today is the custom in the Olympic games where the first strongest or swiftest in various competitions is given a gold medal, the second strongest or swiftest is given a silver medal, and the third strongest or swiftest is given a bronze medal. It is considered a great honor today to receive one of the top three Olympian medals. These Olympian winners receive advertisement money to endorse athletic products.

Deuteronomy 4:15 19 says, "Take careful heed to yourselves, for you saw no form when the Lord spoke to you at Horeb out of the midst of the fire, lest you act corruptly and make for yourselves a carved image in the form of any figure: the likeness of male or female, the likeness of any animal that is on the earth or the likeness of any winged bird that flies in the

Personality Traits of Money

air, the likeness of anything that creeps on the ground or the likeness of any fish that is in the water beneath the earth. And take heed, lest you lift your eyes to heaven, and when you see the sun, the moon, and the stars, all the host of heaven, you feel driven to worship them and serve them, which the Lord your God has given to all the peoples under the whole heaven as a heritage."

THE ANCIENT KINGS IMPRINTED THEIR IMAGES, SEALS, OR OTHER EMBLEM ON MEDALLIONS THAT EVENTUALLY BECAME THE COIN OF THE REALM

Medallions were to be worn around the neck to transfer a portion of the king's "magic," "authority," or "power" to his Ministers to accomplish their delegated kingly authority. The medallion carried the king's authority and power over that area of governmental services which the political Minister was given responsibility.

The belief and practice were that the king's magic or power overflowed into or was transferred into the ministerial governmental office medallion. Thus, magic or power was granted to the person having the medallion. Likewise, the King would give his Minister to wear one of the King's "Insignia Rings."

The Medallions worn by political appointees of the King were to transfer His official government authority to them. In the classic Robin Hood 1938 Warner Bros. Pictures movie, titled, The Adventures of Robin Hood, starring Errol Flynn as Robin Hood, Earl of Locksley, and Olivia De Havilland, as Maid Marian, you can see the Medallions being worn. The villain was Guy of Gisbourne, played by Basil Rathbone. Prince John, played by Claude Rains, was the brother of King Richard who was absent from fighting in the Crusades. King John, influenced by the treasonous Guy of Gisbourne, convinces the Sheriff of Nottingham, played by Melville Cooper, to use harsh means to collect high taxes that became very burdensome to the poor Saxon citizens. After Robin, Earl of Locksley, killed the Norman men who killed his father, there was a price on his head. Robin escaped to Sherwood Forest and with his Merry Men steals from the rich and gives to the poor. Prince John sends out the Sheriff of Nottingham and ambush Robin and Friar Tuck who themselves were playfully fighting. Eventually, King Richard returns and sits on his throne, and Robin, Earl of Locksley is restored his lands by King Richard. The movie was one of my favorites of all time. In any event, the point is that the Sheriff of Nottingham, and other government appointees, wore the King's Medallion on a chain that was visibly seen in the movie that shows that the King's authority was transferred to the King's servants.

Portraits of prestigious people of a nation appear on local currency all around the world. In ancient Rome, the first coinage was minted in the late 4th century BCE. Early coins imprinted the heads of gods and goddesses on the front side, and the backside of the coin depicted animals, natural resources, symbols, and references to historical events. In 44 BCE the portrait of a living person, which was Julius Caesar, who declared himself a god, was imprinted on the front side of the coin, and on the back side depicted symbols, natural resources, animals, or historical events. Therefore, if a foreigner coming to Rome wanted to know what the god Ceaser looked like, the Roman citizen would hand him a Roman coin, and the picture of the Roman god Emperor was on the coinage of the realm. There was a spiritual transference of the spiritual false god authority of the Roman Emperor into the coin.

Jesus Deals with the Roman Coin when confronted by religious leaders: Mark 12: 13-17 says, "And they send unto him certain of the Pharisees and of the Herodians, to catch Him in His words. (14) And when they were come, they say unto him, 'Master, we know that thou art true, and carest for no man: for thou regardest not the person of men, but teachest the way of God in truth: Is it lawful to give tribute to Caesar, or not? (15) Shall we give, or shall we not give?' But He (Jesus), knowing their hypocrisy, said unto them, 'Why tempt ye me? bring me a penny, that I may see it.' (16) And they brought it. And He saith unto them, 'Whose is this image and superscription?' And they said unto him, 'Caesar's.' (16) And Jesus answering said unto them, 'Render to (the false god) Caesar the things that are Caesar's, and to (the true) God the things that are God's.' And they marveled at Him."

Jesus recognized there can be spiritual transfers of evil spirits in to idols and things, which will be discussed below. There can be spiritual transference to the sacrifice of idols. The Roman Emperor, Ceasar made coins with the face of Ceasar an idol.

EVENTUALLY, THE KING'S MEDALLIONS BECAME THE COIN OF THE REALM

The chains holding the medallions figurately were clipped off, and the medallions became the coin of the kingdom and usually with the King's facial picture or emblem, as the medallions already had been accepted by the citizens as symbols of prestige and of power.

The coins always would bear the king's image, and whoever had the coin, the King's magic, authority, and power were transferred to the holder of the coin just as the people were used to seeing the king's image on the medallions worn by his Ministers have their prestigious offices in government. This became known as the "coin of the realm."

Even today, in the U.S., and most every other country, the civil government generally uses the images of past Presidents or important persons on the paper and coin currency (the U.S.A. also uses the pictures of our founding fathers, such as on the $100 bill, which has Benjamin Franklin's image). However, this tradition has its roots in the belief that the king's magical power overflows into the currency, making the money important and acceptable for goods and services. The U.S. currency invokes a spiritual deity. It states, "In God We Trust."

SUPERSTITIOUS USE OF CHARMS, AMULETS, AND TOKENS

This superstition of wearing or using charms, amulets, and the use of coins and medallions taking on "magical" powers as symbols of prestige, importance, and authority is partly the reason why so much emphasis is placed on money today and in Scripture. These material things are especially sought by people with fractured personalities to satisfy their obsessive-compulsive Personality Traits of Money as you will read in greater revealing in the following chapters, which will be a great insight for you.

Although not seen as a cultist emblem, many Christians wear the Cross around their necks, and I must assume they are trying to let everyone know they are a Believer in Christ Jesus. Every Believer I fellowship with knows the cross around their neck will not save them or anyone else from the eternal lake of fire if they have not accepted Jesus Christ as Lord and Savior. Yet, when they look in the mirror and see the cross as a symbol of Jesus' death for them is a

Personality Traits of Money

good reminder of the most wonderful gift of eternal life bestowed upon them by their loving Savior. Also, wearing the cross like the medallions of authority from the historical Kings reminds others that we Believers are children of God in His royal family. The cross is a symbol of our Vocations in the Kingdom of God, which are the Lord's spiritual kings, priests (Revelation 1:6), lords (1 Timothy 6:15), ambassadors (2 Corinthians 5:20), and soldiers (2 Timothy 2:3-4), as we are citizens of heaven (Philippians 3:20). Believers must accept that neither the cross nor the fish sign has any inherent power whatsoever. My wedding ring has the cross imprinted in diamonds, and it simply is a reminder that I am married to my wife and the betrothed of Jesus at the same time.

When I pastored a church many years ago, I had a member that I noticed had an amulet, a rabbit's foot, which he clipped on his key chain. I finally asked him why he had the rabbit's foot, and he said, "It was given to me by my father before he died, and it was his good luck charm." I raised my eyebrows and lovingly kept staring at him and smiled. He said, "Oh my God; this is from the devil, isn't it? We don't believe in good luck charms, do we?" Without saying a word, he removed it from his key chain and handed it to me. I opened my arms and gave him a hug, and he said, "Thank you Pastor." Here was a young man out of ignorance who was wearing an amulet because it came from his father that he thought it would bring him "luck."

Farmers in the U.S. would hang a horseshoe on shed or barn for good crops, healthy cows, or for a prosperous year. Dating back to the Greeks, Sailors would take a coin and embed the coin or coins in various places onboard the ship to guard against it sinking. Some U.S. Amish people traditionally hang colorful, geometric hex charms on their barns to ward off wicked spirits. The Turkish people hang blue glass evil-eye charms to dispel bad luck. Four-leaf clovers are seen in Ireland, especially on Saint Patrick's Day. The Swedes use painted dala horses for good luck charms. Chinese put out golden toads. In ancient Egyptian they had Scarabs, which are beetle-shaped bugs that lay their eggs in a dunghill an roll it in a ball, which symbolized the Egyptian god Khepri who they believed rolled the sun across the sky each day at daybreak . Whether you grasp such good luck charms in your palm, wear them around your neck, or mount one near your front door these talismans or amulets are meant to provide a shortcut to a better future, a warding off evil spirits or malevolent forces who are from the kingdom of darkness, so do not use them.

There is a false Chinese ritual to cause money to come to you. They take a bowl and fill it with uncooked rice up to two-thirds full and set the bowl just outside their front doors. For 27 days, you put one or more coins in the bowl of rice and hide the coin in the rice and say affirmations of money coming into their lives. On the 28th day, you take the money out of the rice bowl, give 10% to charity and spend the rest on what they want.

Again, these charms, amulets, tokens, rituals should not be practiced by Christians because we are merely to seek first the Kingdom of God and His righteousness, and all things shall be added to us (Matthew 6:33; Philippians 4:19).

WE MUST CHOOSE WHOM WE WILL SERVE

Again, Matthew 6:24 says, "No one can serve two masters; for either he will hate the one and love the other, or else he will be loyal to the one and despise the other. You cannot serve God and mammon."

In Matthew 6:24, mammon or money is said to be a false god which would be a sin to serve. People still today unknowingly serve this false god of mammon or money. They give their whole lives to the pursuit of what this false god promises them for their loyal, committed service. The reason is that they see this god of mammon as fulfilling the soulish voids, disorders, or their Personality Traits of Money they have in their fractured souls. In the end, the god of mammon will leave them with great disappointment as the void inside their souls can only be filled by the only True Godhead and the Lord Jesus Christ.

Paul said in 1 Corinthians 8:4, 6, "As concerning therefore the eating of those things that are offered in sacrifice unto idols, we know that an idol is nothing in the world, and that there is none other God but one... (6) But to us there is but one God, the Father, of whom are all things, and we in Him; and one Lord Jesus Christ (Jesus' humanity nature), by whom are all things, and we by Him."

Again, 1 Peter 1:18-19 says, "Knowing that you were not redeemed with corruptible things, like silver or gold, from your aimless conduct received by tradition from your fathers, (19) but with the precious blood of Christ, as of a lamb without blemish and without spot."

The devil caused money to come from the sacrifice of animals, and therefore money became an idol to be falsely worshiped and with a false promise to make one's soul think, feel, and believe that money can make the person safe, in control, free from authority, romantically attractive to others, having a personal magnetism, and a host of other soulish stimuli. However, Jesus showed that His sacrificial blood, which had the only true spiritual economic value to redeem mankind and give mankind eternal life instead of infernal death.

Thus, the words redeem, or redemption is an economic term, except that Jesus' precious blood was used to repurchase our redemption, not gold or silver. In the spiritual realm, things other than gold and silver can be used in God's spiritual economy. However, gold and silver can become holy if they are the tithe or and offering. On the other hand, Satan as the original counterfeiter connected money with the sacrifice of animals to entrap people and confuse people to lead them away from the true meaning of the sacrificial blood of Christ Jesus.

The economy in the world is focused on "buying and selling," but the economy in the Kingdom of God is motivated by "giving and receiving." This difference is why Jesus took a whip to the money changers in the Temple yard (John 2:13-16) because it was the wrong venue for buying and selling, as it was God the Father's house of prayer where there should have been witnessing to Gentiles about the Lord's economy of giving and receiving, mercy, forgiveness, and love.

Jesus had no problem with being a good servant for the Master who made a profit in the buying and selling economy as Jesus taught this truth in both the parable of the Minas (Luke 19:11-26) and the parable of the Talents (Matthew 25:14-30) and other parables.

PROFANING THE IDOL OF MAMMON

Personality Traits of Money

AND SPIRITUAL WARFARE OVER MONEY

Tithing and giving offerings transfer money into God's Kingdom and profane the god of mammon. When you tithe and give offerings, they are always off the medium of exchange. This is why tithing is done with money, ten percent of what you earn, and offerings are above that amount.

In the Old Testament, when the medium of exchange was grain or animals, then the people would tithe those items. One bushel in ten was tithed to the Lord. The medium of exchange is used in the Satan's economic world system for buying and selling. When you tithe or give the medium of exchange, then you introduce it to fruit of the spirit, which is love, joy, peace, longsuffering, gentleness, goodness, faith, meekness, and temperance (Galatians 5:22-23). The fruit of the spirit manifests in the Kingdom of God, and by giving and tithing for the work of God through His Church here on earth you make the god of mammon serve the King of kings and Lord of lords. Also, giving and tithing causes the money to be transferred from the system of this world into the Kingdom of God and subjected to the principles of the Kingdom, which includes multiplication.

By tithing and giving that which is used in Satan's world system, you subject the mammon spirit attached to it that says "love me" to the control of the Holy Spirit. You then can say, "No way are you going to control me. You are going to be under my feet, and I am going to profane you mammon spirit."

How do you profane the mammon spirit? You can profane idols in a temple in the false religions by going in and tearing down all the idols, and you thereby take away their spiritual properties, powers, and functions in people's lives.

By tithing and giving into God's Kingdom you transfer that which is used in the world system commerce of buying and selling and place it in God's Kingdom commerce of giving and receiving. Every time you tithe or give an offering into the work of the Lord, you profane the influence of the idol of mammon in your natural life. You say, "Money, you were designed by the prince of this world for buying and selling, but I am going to use you as a gift for the work of the only True God." In giving that which was meant for buying and selling, you can say, "Money you are under my feet. You have no control over me. I do not love you. I love God. I give you away because you have no hold on me."

Knowing that you are profaning the god of mammon should help you in your decision whether tithing and offering is calculated off your gross income or net income. If you hold any part back, you lessen the act of profaning the idol of mammon in the world and in your life. By tithing you can constantly profane mammon's subtleness and seductive spirit. Tithing and giving profane the god of mammon, so it is a form of warfare. Thus, Malachi 3:11 says, "'And I will rebuke the devourer for your sakes, and he shall not destroy the fruits of your ground; neither shall your vine cast her fruit before the time in the field,' saith the LORD of hosts."

Proverbs 13:22 says, "A righteous man leaves an inheritance to his children's children, and the wealth of the wicked is laid up for the just." Wealth is the inheritance that is passed on from generation to generation, i.e., houses, lands, gold, silver, livestock, businesses, and family relationships.

The nature of wealth is that it normally is in the hands of the unsaved and in the fallen world system, but God says that the wicked is gathering and collecting the wealth to give to him who is a good Believer servant of God. Ecclesiastes 2:26 says, "For God gives wisdom and knowledge and joy to a man who is good in His sight; but to the sinner He gives the work of gathering and collecting, that he may give to him who is good before God...."

Deuteronomy 8:18 says, "But thou shalt remember the LORD thy God: for it is He that giveth thee power to get wealth, that He may establish His covenant which He sware unto thy fathers, as it is this day."

Every Believer with the desire and anointing to spoil the enemy of this world system has to come to the resolve to build financial affairs and do business according to God's pattern revealed in Scripture, the resolve to expand God's Kingdom and the Body of Christ with the money earned and wealth accumulated, the resolve to conduct the business and financial matters according to God's word, the resolve to become a giving person who uses Godly principles of economics in all matters, but most importantly the resolve to do spiritual warfare to defeat the enemies of God to take back what belongs to God as the spoils of the enemy.

Jesus said in Matthew 12:28-29, "But if I cast out devils by the Spirit of God, then the kingdom of God is come unto you. (29) Or else how can one enter into a strong man's house, and spoil (diarpazo) his goods, except he first bind the strong man? and then he will spoil his house."

The Greek word diarpazo means a spiritual taking. This means that the taking is not taking a gun and robbing a rich man. It means to attack the forces of darkness as you are led by the Holy Spirit, and using His omnipotent power to acquire the wealth scriptures reveals in Proverbs 13:22, Deuteronomy 8:18, and Matthew 12:29.

Jesus said in Matthew 11:12 says, "And from the days of John the Baptist until now, the Kingdom of heaven suffereth violence and the violent take (harpazo) it by force (harpazo)."

Jesus said in Matthew 6:33 says, "But seek ye first the kingdom of God, and his righteousness; and all these things shall be added unto you."

When you "seek" first the Kingdom of God, it means you usually must engage in spiritual warfare against your own lust of the flesh, lust of the eyes, or pride of life, against the fallen world system, and against the kingdom of darkness. 2 Corinthians 10:3-5 says, "For though we walk in the flesh, we do not war after the flesh: (4) (For the weapons of our warfare are not carnal, but mighty through God to the pulling down of strong holds); (5) Casting down imaginations, and every high thing that exalteth itself against the knowledge of God, and bringing into captivity every thought to the obedience of Christ." "Casting down imaginations, and every high thing that exalteth itself against the knowledge of God and bringing into captivity every thought to the obedience of Christ" often speaks to the problem of need to repent of the carnality of your own soul.

Personality Traits of Money

The blessing and goal to attain in the Kingdom of God is the reward of righteousness, peace (from the warfare), and joy in the Holy Spirit (Romans 14:17). Romans 14:19 says, "Let us therefore follow after the things which make for peace, and things wherewith one may edify another."

1 Timothy 6:6-11 says, "Now godliness with contentment is great gain. For we brought nothing into this world, and it is certain we can carry nothing out. And having food and clothing, with these we shall be content. But those who desire to be rich (without seeking God first) fall into temptation and a snare, and into many foolish and harmful lusts which drown men in destruction and perdition. But you, O man of God, flee these things and pursue righteousness, godliness, faith, love, patience, gentleness."

Dr. Nova Dean Pack

Today's Mystical Or Spiritual Significance Of Money

CHAPTER TWO

TODAY'S MYSTICAL OR SPIRITUAL SIGNIFICANCE OF MONEY

THE SPIRITUAL ATTRIBUTES PEOPLE ATTACH TO MONEY

The mystical or spiritual attributes people attach to money dates to antiquity, but money has changed and multiplied in its importance in people's lives in the last three thousand years.

The sacrificial ritual with the animal or king's image imprinted on the medallion or coin has now become more complex.

The money vocation and priesthood in the world have expanded to include such professions as politicians, bankers, loan brokers, accountants, lawyers, judges, real estate brokers, stockbrokers, economists, financial advisors, and estate planners.

People in the world try to acquire the power of the person whose image is on the currency. Again, money is the medium of exchange in the kingdom of this world, whose commerce is buying and selling. On the other hand, the commerce in the Kingdom of God is giving and receiving.

Like the King or President, the person possessing money thinks he or she is endowed with great prestige and power under the world's standards. Because he or she has money, an otherwise insignificant, unimportant man or woman can command others to wait on him or her, prepare and serve him or her with scrumptious meals, shine his or her shoes, pour his or her drinks, or tailor by hand his or her expensive clothes.

Two twenty-dollar bills can often make a table in a filled restaurant suddenly appear. Five one-hundred-dollar bills can make one ticket appear for you at an otherwise sold-out Caitlin Clark at an Indiana Fever WNBA basketball game.

The power of money has been used to finance the recent wars involving Ukraine and Russia and Israel and Hamas, create empires, send Neil Armstrong and Edwin "Buzz" Aldren to the moon, maintain the Royal Family in Great Britain, build bridges and roads, employ medical doctors to research cures for cancer and heart disease, or donate to Franklin Graham "Samaritan's Purse" or donate to Tim Ballard's charity that rescues sexual abuse children.

The balance of power shifts based upon the lead currency being held by a specific country. The U.S.'s lead currency status is being challenged by BRICS, which is an intergovernmental organization comprising as of this writing of Brazil, Russia, India, China, South Africa, Egypt, Ethiopia, Iran, and the United Arab Emirates. The international balance of power today is shifting because of the wealth from Arab Oil to the commerce in the Pacific Rim countries.

Many wars have been fought over money matters. The American Revolution was sparked over both higher taxes and religious freedoms. Controversy arises over money and religion;

Personality Traits of Money

there seems to be a connection. The reason is that money has a spiritual side to it. The U.S. dollar has "In God We Trust" printed on it. Money originated from the sacrifice of animals and the worship of false gods or to transfer the quality of a particular animal.

Labor Unions were created to start a proletariat movement in the U.S. and Europe to fight for higher wages and employee working conditions.

Organized crime exists because unlawful people are willing to commit illegal activity for money.

Our Lord Jesus was betrayed for thirty pieces of silver. How much was thirty pieces of silver? The Bible does not say. However, there are references. The Bible does not say what the silver pieces were.

To explain the use of Judas' thirty pieces of silver, in Matthew 27:8-10, it says that the thirty pieces of silver were used by Jeremiah in fulfillment of Old Testament prophecy in Jeremiah 32:6-9 where a plot of land was purchased. But in the writer's second mention of the sum, the writer puts the thirty pieces into context, that of fulfillment of Old Testament prophecy of purchasing a land to bring back the scattered Israelites from around the world. Jeremiah 32:37 says, "Behold, I will gather them out of all countries, whither I have driven them in mine anger, and in my fury, and in great wrath; and I will bring them again unto this place (where the land was purchased by Jeremiah to fulfill a prophetic word), and I will cause them to dwell safely."

Matthew also referred to Zechariah 11: 12-13, "And I said unto them, 'If ye think good, give me my price; and if not, forbear.' So they weighed for my price thirty pieces of silver. (13) And the LORD said unto me, 'Cast it unto the potter: a goodly price that I was prised at of them. And I took the thirty pieces of silver, and cast them to the potter in the house of the LORD.'" Zachariah gave us the value for the field. When Zachariah wrote these words, the words "thirty pieces of silver" would be referring to the silver shekel which was the normal and acceptable weight for paying a price of land with silver, even since Abraham's time.

Genesis 23:15-19 speaks of the silver shekels used to purchase land that Abraham wanted to bury his wife, Sarah, saying, "My lord, hearken unto me: the land is worth four hundred shekels of silver; what is that betwixt me and thee? Bury therefore thy dead. (16) And Abraham hearkened unto Ephron; and Abraham weighed to Ephron the silver, which he had named in the audience of the sons of Heth, four hundred shekels of silver, current money with the merchant. (17) And the field of Ephron, which was in Machpelah, which was before Mamre, the field, and the cave which was therein, and all the trees that were in the field, that were in all the borders round about, were made sure (18) Unto Abraham for a possession in the presence of the children of Heth, before all that went in at the gate of his city. (19) And after this, Abraham buried Sarah his wife in the cave of the field of Machpelah before Mamre: the same is Hebron in the land of Canaan."

In New Testament times, the shekel was the value of about four drachmas (a Greek coin) or four denarii (a Roman coin). It would be in weight a little less than half an ounce of silver. It's value as currency would be the common wages for a laboring man for four days, or in today's value around $400 to $500. The 30 pieces of silver, then, would be worth around $12,000 to

$15,000 in today's sum.

Notwithstanding, there was another element involved. To pay for a slave girl gored by Ox cost thirty shekels (Exodus 21:32), and Joseph was sold by his brothers to the Ishmaelites for twenty shekels (Genesis 37:28). It stands to reason that the payment of thirty shekels was to free the betrothed of Christ, the church, from religious bondage and setting the female slave to be free from this fallen world. John 8:36 says, "If the Son therefore shall make you free, ye shall be free indeed."

In the world, people use sayings such as, "money speaks," "money opens closed doors," and "money can make the plain Janes beautiful." The Bible says the "blood speaks" and the "tithe is holy" in the spiritual realm. (Genesis 4:10; Leviticus 27:30). There is more than a "penny of truth" in all these sayings.

OFTENTIMES, MONEY IS SEEN IN THE FALLEN SINFUL WORLD'S EYES AS HAVING AN EVIL NATURE INHERENTLY

The truth is that money simply takes upon the characteristic or better, personality trait of the person holding the money. The same dollar may buy drugs one week, and on Saturday or Sunday it may be dropped in the offering plate at a person's religious persuasion.

The phrase "He is poor, but honest" seems to be an accepted truth in society. On the other hand, the phrase "He is rich, but honest" seems to be fiction.

Those who use illegal means to become rich seem to make the above statements have a certain degree of truth. A person who strives to "get rich quick" often must choose between the "money" and "virtue."

Ill-gotten money is referred to as "dirty money," "filthy lucre," or "black money."

Gambling games, which pursue money without working for it, have been given names such as "craps" or "poker."

FEELING GUILTY ABOUT ILL GOTTEN MONEY

Some rich families who feel guilty about their ill-gotten money work for the good of humanity to try to diminish their guilt as to how they acquired their riches.

Many of the world's great charitable and humanitarian foundations were established because of the guilt feelings of their founders.

For example, Alfred Nobel became very wealthy because of his invention of dynamite. He felt guilty for inventing such a destructive force that killed people. His brother was killed by a dynamite blast, which caused his father's stroke. Alfred Nobel's guilt caused him to set aside a fortune to award prizes each year to be given to those who have made valuable contributions to the "good of humanity and peace." His charity is the "Nobel Peace Prize."

Personality Traits of Money

THE INFLUENCE OR NEGATIVE ASPECTS OF MONEY HAS AFFECTED OUR CHRISTIAN HERITAGE TO SOME DEGREE THROUGH THE SO CALLED PURITAN WORK ETHIC

The Puritan work ethic can be summarized as affluence that comes through submitting to God's will, doing Spirit led hard work, obeying God's principles, and using God-directed wisdom from above that causes soul transformation over time instead of seeking a fad or new untried worldly innovations. The Puritans believed that good character came from hard work and submission to Godly principles of economics, and they believed that large sums of money and riches were permissible only in the presence of God's good character. Thus, the Puritans believed that man should not strive to engage in "get rich quick" schemes, as they are bad for the soul's maturation, which requires incremental, daily work for perfection of business skills with honesty, trustworthiness, lovingly helping others, generous to employees, regularly participating in fellowship with other Believers which is Christ-centered, giving to the community, and where the business activity meets the needs of the local community by practicing moral free enterprise.

For example, I surmise, without mentioning names, there are some younger people in this information age who have become extraordinarily rich very quickly, but they lacked the maturity and good character to handle the "deceitfulness of riches" under their sovereign control. In truth, some of these men or women are not following God's principles of economics, giving to charities, having souls that lacks humility, and having used their money to financially support ungodly ideas that are against the scriptures in the Bible, such as espousing abortion on demand as a form of birth control or going into debt to finance a Socialist agenda.

There was an injection of "Reformation Theology" in the American economic psyche in the 1600's through the Puritans. Part of the "Puritan tenets of faith" was the "Puritan work ethic." This Puritan work ethic played a major role in the Great Industrial Revolution of America. America's greatness economically was at its height during the Industrial Revolution which caused tremendous wealth in many industrial families such as the steel magnate, Andrew Carnegie, the automobile mogul, Henry Ford, the banking investor, J.P. Morgan, the oil tycoon, John D. Rockefeller, and the railroad builder, Cornelius Vanderbilt. These five Great Industrialists laid the foundation for America to become the riches free enterprise society in history. Before the Industrial Revolution, the United States was more of a second world country, with most people living in farming communities. These Great Industrialists ushered post-Civil War United States into the industrial modern era that outdid all European countries at that time. Notwithstanding, the Federal Government sued these monopolies under the Sherman Anti-Trust Act, but most of their families are still very wealthy.

Before the early 1900s, "work" was seen as a Godly virtue which caused maturation, good character, good parentage examples, and good citizenship. In those days, you worked to increase your talents, to become a mature person of character, to be a Godly person, to make a better life for your family, to have a family dynasty of several generations, and to be a respected voice in your city, town, and religious community.

The coming of liberal self-directed religious ideas in America. When Henry Ware was elected the president of Harvard Divinity School in 1805, he soon thereafter denied the biblical doctrine of the Trinity and became a Unitarian. Other New England Pastors followed suit and became Unitarians. Unitarians reject the Triune nature of the Godhead, but also stand for broad freedom and tolerance in religious beliefs.

Unitarianism paralleled the growth of the Eastern Transcendentalism in America, which was the belief that knowledge of reality to be applied in the secular world is derived from intuitive sources rather than from objective absolute truths found in the Bible. Transcendentalism was fueled in part by the writings and lectures of Ralph Waldo Emerson and Walt Whitman in the 1800s. By the 1830s there was a heightened view of the preeminence of man's reasoning over and above the objective source of truth being garnered from God's Word in both the Church and the secular world.

At first, the Unitarian teaching was a mixture of God's word and man's reasoning. As time went on, there became a demarcation where the Church divided with those who believe the Bible contains the inerrant word of God and those Unitarians who believe that man's reasoning was the pathway to truth because men were basically good, and they merely need to practice that goodness. The Unitarian teachings were popularized in the New England States and many Politicians, especially those graduating from Harvard University, who professed the belief that the government should be deeply involved in socialist government economics and the eradication of social injustices. These Unitarian teachings continued into the 1960s and have become embedded in the Democrat Liberal party. These aberrant ideas of a new Christian view of environment and social injustice as the real culprit, not sin, has permeated much of liberal political ideology today and other anti-biblical practices.

As a result of the Unitarian teaching that sounded like Socialism that was becoming accepted by the Christian Union workers who wanted more pay and less working hours, and other benefits for workers, the Puritan work ethic was being challenged. Socialism and Communism were being considered as favorable to the working class, so there was a clash between the Great Industrialists and the workers. Through the Great Depression Franklin Roosevelt championed government infusing money into the economy to help poor people, establishing a social welfare program for the poor, and instituted Social Security for the elderly as a retirement (which later became a tax). Thus, in the early 1900s in the U. S. there was a popular concept of the workers' "escape from problems" and going to a "work free" Third Heaven. The elite used this to sway the Christians into a more liberal theology, which became the Liberal, Socialist, and Democrat party platform to attract votes at election time. Thus, Liberalism and Socialism came from the Social Gospel, taught in the Sunday School classes that spread from the teachings of the Unitarian Church, rather than telling the people that the origin of the teachings came from the Socialists/Communists teachings of Marx and Lenin. Later, these liberal, Socialist precepts started also being taught in secular schools, so the religions of "humanism" became a popular idea, especially with secular Politicians.

In Torcaso v. Watkins, (1961) 367 U.S. 488 became a Supreme Court case from the appeal from U.S. District Judge W. Brevard Hand, who wrote "The most important belief of this religion is its denial of the transcendent and/or supernatural: there is no God, no creator, no divinity." Judge Hand continued. "By force of logic, the universe is thus self-existing, completely physical and hence, essentially knowable." In his opinion, Judge Hand defined humanism as a religious belief system that holds that "everything is knowable." "Whenever a belief system deals with fundamental questions of the nature of reality and man's relationship to reality, it deals with essentially religious questions." He held, "A religion need not posit a belief in a deity." Furthermore, Judge Hand wrote, "Teaching that moral choices are purely personal and can only be based on some autonomous, as yet undiscovered and unfulfilled, inner self is a sweeping fundamental belief that must not be promoted by the public schools." Judge Hand concluded, "For the purposes of the First Amendment, secular humanism is a religious belief system, entitled to the protections of, and subject to the prohibitions of, the religion clauses [of the First Amendment]. It is not a mere scientific methodology that may be promoted and advanced in public schools. In conclusion, why should secular Humanism be allowed to be taught in school, as it indeed is a religion." In the U.S. Supreme Court decision, Justice Hugo Black stated in his opinion in footnote 11, "Among religions in this country which do not teach what would generally be considered a belief in the existence of God are Buddhism, Taoism, Ethical Culture, Secular Humanism and others." Thus, secular Humanism taught in schools and as the predominate belief amongst Democrat Liberal members of Congress, is a religion. Its predominance in educating our children in schools is a major cause of anti-biblical beliefs in American culture and that of European cultures.

Some Christian Church pastors started teaching an "economic evangelism" and "foundational teaching" that began in the early 1900s and continues today, especially with the Word-Faith Teachers. The Church leaders' teaching started the congregations began to view in a deeper way that work was a curse and the "ultimate pleasure weekend" was the goal of the acquisition of money and riches. It was taught that tithing and giving to the church or ministry was what was required as a prerequisite for prosperity, not hard work and the continued education and enhancement of skills in the workplace. To attract members into church this work-free heaven anemic sermons were preached from the pulpits in churches. Thus, there developed a social gospel that man was basically good, so there was no requirement of repentance to turn yourself away from the philosophies of this world and simply call upon the name of Jesus as Lord to be saved.

Then ministers started focusing on changing the environment and ridding society of social injustices without the need of repentance of sins. Some ministers who espouse this social and economic equality of consequences taught that the state and federal government were responsible for cradle to grave, womb to tomb, support of people in society. These ministry teachers started saying that equality in society is to be the focus where there must be equal consequences and guarantees and not just equal opportunities.

The truth is that the Bible teaches inequalities based upon natural born talents and rewards based upon hard work, humility, and faithfulness toward God and His kingdom. For example, not everyone can dunk the ball in a basketball game. A person who cannot dunk the basketball will not be signed as a professional player for the Boston Celtics, Chicago Bulls, or Los Angeles Lakers. The top salespeople should be paid more than those who sell less. This is why many professions, such as insurance agents and real estate agents, are paid on commission. If you work hard but do not sell a home that a client owns, the owner of the home does not owe the real estate agent a commission.

In Communist countries, the citizen's definition of economic freedom is "the government pays for my schooling, childcare, public transportation, health care, cell phone, rent, groceries for me and my family, etc." The economic freedom in Communist countries means that the citizen does not have to compete for livelihood. In both the parables of the talents and minas, Jesus taught that those servants who multiplied the talents or minas for the Master were considered faithful, good stewards, but the one who hid the talents in the ground or hid the minas in a handkerchief was chastised and lost his job. The servant's talents were taken away from him and given to the one who multiplied the talents, and the servant's minas were taken away from him and were not worthy of being a ruler over cities. (see Matthew 25:14-30; Luke 19:11-27).

Any short cut to the top is deplored by the traditional Puritan work ethic since that limits the development of character that is matured over time with life experiences and submission to God's principles of morality and servanthood. Character in the Bible is most important to withstand the temptations which one who has a large income, or many riches, are subjected.

Therefore, from the Puritan or biblical point of view, the speculator, gambler, or "get rich quick" methods of acquiring riches are unbiblical because it does not allow maturity through incremental daily problem-solving, using sound business planning, savings, R&D, and trying to capture a market share of the products sold or services rendered. These sound business principles have their origin in the Bible, and they are long run planning and thinking. God's purpose of business is to make faithful servants, where these attributes of maturity, humility, and faithfulness can be used as servants in God's spiritual Kingdom. In other words, God uses work after initial salvation in the marketplace to make disciples of His Kingdom. (For a greater in-depth teaching, see Dr. Nova Dean Pack's book, Ministry of God's Business Servant)

On the other hand, the extreme religious teaching, contrary to biblical truth, that also developed in the Church was the saying that "money is inherently evil" was inaccurate as well. 1 Timothy 6:10 correctly says, "The love of money (avarice) as being the root cause of all evil," and this scripture is the foundation addressed as the theme of this book.

Another movement fostering an anemic economic teaching in America was "Neo-Orthodoxy," which is a subjective application of the word of God that is personally relevant to the Believer. The Bible is not seen as having separate authority as the Book containing absolute truths from God, as under "Neo-Orthodoxy," all truth is relative to the Believer. For example, this anemic or aberrant teaching misapplied John 1:14 where the Word became flesh or personality and dwelt among us as meaning that truth is now subjective and based upon one's inner, subjective experience. This is one of the prevailing beliefs not only in the secular, fallen world, but also in a few denominations in the Christian Church. Thus, they believe that truth is derived from how they personally think, feel, and believe about things; and their untransformed souls are their guiding authority, not absolute truths embodied in God's Word.

Thus, these teachers present that giving to others is secondary and depends on how a Believer personally thinks, emotes, and their personal beliefs, as giving is not a mandatory lifestyle. They believe that truth depends on how it is relevant to them and relevant as applied to their life, personally, not biblically. They believe that morality is relative and is based upon each person's circumstances they are encountering in the world. Since they believe there are no absolutes, then everyone can develop their own personal mores, morals, and truths. The problem is that without God's principles and biblical truths, there are no divine restrictive guidelines of thought, feelings, beliefs, or behaviors. These lies from the devil take

Personality Traits of Money

away God's sovereignty over people's lives regarding money, lifestyles, standards of right and wrong, and relationships because there is an absence of God's wisdom, truths, principles, agape love, and zoe life. These fallen man's ideas make unbelievers and Believers rebellious and unrepentant. These people do not admit and repent of sin and turn to God, but they turn to the philosophies in the world to acquire their standards of ideas, beliefs, and behaviors.

The false principles of promoting one's inner self instead of turning around back to God and submitting to the transformation of one's soul as mandated in such scriptures as Romans 12:2 make for an unloving and lack of caring Believers in Church, and especially in the fallen world. You cannot create in you a born again spirit, and you cannot transform your own soul. After initial salvation based solely upon the sacrificial, substitutionary work of Jesus, the ongoing work of God's continuous transformation of the Believers' souls require Believers' daily submission to God. Philippians 12:12-15 says, "Wherefore, my beloved (already born again Believers), as ye have always obeyed, not as in my presence only, but now much more in my absence, work out your own salvation with fear and trembling (being submissive to the Godhead). (13) For it is God which worketh in you both to will and to do of His good pleasure (not your own self-centered pleasure). (14) Do all things without murmurings and disputings: (15) That ye may be blameless and harmless, the (righteous, holy, and loving) sons of God, without rebuke, in the midst of a crooked and perverse nation, among whom ye shine as lights (the Lord's luminaries) in the world."

Believers are given the narrow spiritual, holy, righteous, and loving path to walk in life. Believers are mandated to express agape love one to another (John 13:34-35), as the humblest servants, as the ones considered great (Matthew 23:11). Believers are commanded to seek first the Kingdom of God and His righteousness and not just seek prestige, money, riches, or anything that would be considered self-aggrandizement or merely of this fallen world absent of God and Christ's intimate relationships (Matthew 6:10, 33).

Believers are to submit their minds, emotions, hearts, and wills, which are the Believers' souls, to God the Father, who will prune the flesh out of the Believers' souls to produce more spiritual fruit (John 15:2). Believers are to submit to washing away the dirt of the flesh out of their souls and be sanctified and cleansed by the rhema word of God the Word, so they can be Christ's church without spot, wrinkle, or blemish (Ephesians 5:26-27). Believers are to submit to God the Holy Spirit, who will mortify the deeds of the flesh in Believers' souls, so Believers can experience more zoe life in their souls (Romans 8:13).

Many of the Liberal Theology Believers, historically and now, especially in the New England States of America, see that capitalism that seeks only profit as opposed to seeking the good of the lower working class has caused social injustices based upon unregulated greed, covetousness, and avarice. This idea of financial disparity has come into the foundational beliefs of some church denominations. They believe that it is the government's responsibility to support people from cradle to grave, or from womb to tomb, so there are equal consequences regardless of hard work by the faithful worker or the natural talents created by God. Again, this violates the principles taught by Jesus to reward those who work hard and are faithful in the Parable of the Talents (Matthew 25:14-30) and the Parable of the Minas (Luke 19:16-27).

Thus, many Liberal Theologians believe that government sponsored Socialism has a greater moral value than capitalism or even the moral free enterprise system recognizing man's granted sovereignty with humility and submission to God following biblical principles of economics. Socialist gospel teachers and politicians believe that because of the need for social justice, individual rights are justifiably supplanted in favor of the fulfillment of the masses' physical and personal needs. Confiscation of houses, buildings, and lands by the government is considered justified if it is for the good of the masses. They also believe that it is okay for local government to confiscate land through government eminent domain to collect greater sums of real property taxes for the government's increase in spending. Unfortunately, the money obtained often is spent to increase the salaries of government employees and acquiring more employees in government who will continue to vote back into office for the same politicians after each election.

Historically, many people proclaim that being affluent in the world implies an unlimited supply of money to spend on one's own personal appetites for housing, clothing, automobiles, prestige enhancement, and entertainment. Additionally, this creed and conviction that money is an unlimited source that has the mere "magical power" to give a person the thought, feeling, or belief of having safety from others, in control of others, freedom from others, or being attractive to others. God's soulish character development is based upon God's biblical principles, along with His guiding wisdom to invest in long term wealth in hard assets created by God with a strict bridle on spending. God's principles for wealth accumulation will last for at least three generations because He is the God of Abraham, Isaac, and Jacob, which represent three generations of prosperity that is the family blessing from God (Proverbs 13:22).

On the other hand, those who practice single-generation consumption without discipline on spending and to fulfill unbridled greed, covetousness, or avarice causes the soul to be dysfunctional, obsessive, compulsive, and becomes fractured that needs God's mending, renewal, and transformation. Believers, with obsessive-compulsive Personality Traits of Money, will not be good witnesses unto the Lord and His Kingdom, as unbelievers will think these Believers do not walk the Christian talk. Most people avoid other people with obsessive-compulsive Personality Traits of Money because they believe that rich people are in a different class, and they cannot keep up financially with them as friends. Rich people want to eat in expensive restaurants, live in affluent neighborhoods, drive luxurious cars, and take lavish vacations.

The Puritan or biblical perception is to place all things under the jurisdictional sovereignty, submission to, and limits of Almighty God. The Puritan Biblical precepts are to be led by the Holy Spirit, to stay humble, to be a servant to others, and to allow Christ to live His life in you and through you to minister His perfect agape love for others (Galatians 2:20). God resists the proud but gives grace to the humble (James 4:6).

FALSE ANCIENT ALCHEMISTS TRIED TO CHANGE CHEAPER METALS INTO PRECIOUS METALS TO ACQUIRE INSTANT WEALTH

Alchemists tried to use a blend of science, magic, and occult religious ceremonies to make gold out of lead. Alchemy is a demonic practice and invites the kingdom of darkness into your life, so avoid this practice completely.

Personality Traits of Money

The false theory of Alchemy is essentially that a metal can create riches by transforming that metal into a different metal of greater value. Metals such as iron have an almost unlimited supply, so if used by the alchemists to transform the cheaper metal into silver or gold, there would be an unlimited supply of wealth owned by the Alchemist. However, a major utility metal is Steel, which is made from iron ore. To make steel you have to remove the impurities, such as nitrogen, silicon, phosphorus, sulfur, and especially excess carbon which is the most important element to be removed from the iron ore to make steel. One can add to the iron ore alloys, such as manganese, nickel, chromium, and vanadium to produce different grades of steel.

Although no one has produced gold from lead, which if true would be an endless production of tremendous wealth, some people believe that money generates money or riches through interest and dividends where they do not have to manage or work. If a person has ten million U.S. Dollars and invested the money in a diversified portfolio of products from insurance companies, government securities, strip malls, consumer rental property, businesses, etc., and the money makes five percent per annum, the investor will earn five hundred thousand dollars per year as taxable income. Like the Alchemist, the investor thinks he has a perpetual never-ending supply of income to live on without having to manage or perform labor to earn it. The person would be rich by the world's standards. The principal of riches of ten million U.S. Dollars that initially were invested to make the earnings would never have to be touched. Conceivably, this income could go on forever generationally. However, money can lose its value, banks and insurance companies managing your investment can go bankrupt. The lack of wisdom is that you tie up your investment capital in purchased assets, so you have no money to invest when the Holy Spirit leads you to a better or more secure and productive opportunity.

Similarly, after you invest in real property, a state government can pass a law that you are forbidden to raise the rent (as it is still in effect in California) or forbid you as owner to evict consumer tenants for several years, as was done in California during the Covid-19 pandemic. Additionally, a city where the citizens pass an initiative to impose an extra real property transfer tax, called a "Mansion Tax". This was done in 2022 by the citizens' initiative in the City of Los Angeles. Under this Mansion Tax law, when the owner wants to sell his real property in the City of Los Angeles that has a value of five million dollars or more, he must pay an extra 4% Mansion Transfer Tax in addition to the County transfer tax, the real property tax, the escrow fees, and the real estate agent fees, which on a five-million-dollar piece of real property would cost close to $600,000 in selling costs. You may say, "Well, a five-million-dollar house is rare, so only a few rich folks will be affected." This is not true in California. Most homes in Southern California have a fair market value of close to one million dollars, and during a bubble they generally double in value. It is suspected the government will lower the minimum fair market value to capture the Mansion Tax from five million dollars to two million dollars and then eventually one million dollars. This means in the City of Los Angeles, a family having a modern track home valued at one million dollars will have to pay an additional forty thousand dollars to sell their home. If you have to pay 4% transfer tax, then the lending banks will not want to loan money for 80% of fair market value but will lower that mark perhaps to a loan for only 65% of the fair market value because in the event there is foreclosure of the real property, there may not be enough equity to pay off the mortgage loan after paying all the taxes and cause harm to the lending bank as well as the homeowner who loses his property. This will cause a reduction in values and cause poorer people never to be able to afford to purchase a home because they cannot produce the down payment of 35% of the fair market value of the home. Also, each City, County, and State in California, or in your state, most likely will start requiring the Mansion Transfer tax to be paid when a house of whatever value is sold.

Wealth can be lost through government involuntary takings. State and federal governments have passed laws to confiscate and cause forfeiture sale of the owner's real property, such as an apartment complex, if a tenant was arrested because of selling illegal drugs from his apartment if the owner knew that the apartment was being used as a drug house and did nothing about it. For example, California Health and Safety Code Section 11366.5 provides that it is a criminal act for any person who has under his or her management or control any building, room, space or enclosure, either as an owner, lessee, agent, employee or mortgagee, to knowingly: rent, lease or make available for use, with or without compensation, the building, room, space, or enclosure for the purpose of unlawfully manufacturing, storing, or distributing any controlled substance for sale or distribution. It's important to note that a criminal Prosecutor in California will only charge the owner with violating California Health & Safety Code, section 11366 in situations when the owner knowingly allowed people to sell or use controlled substances in a drug house, or the owner allowed other people to enter the drug house to conduct drug transactions. California Health and Safety Code, section11470(g) provides that the following is subject to forfeiture: "The real property of any property owner who is convicted of violating [Health and Safety Code] Section 11366, 11366.5, or 11366.6 with respect to that property." Thus, as owner, if you knew and turned a blind eye and allowed the apartment or house to be a drug house, you could be charged with a crime under Health and Safety Code, Section 11366.5 and your apartment complex can be subject to confiscation and forfeiture. If the California Prosecutors believe your apartment complex was known by you as being used as a drug house, the local Prosecutors can file a civil case pending your criminal trial, where the burden of proof is only by a preponderance (more likely than not) and take possession of your real property while the criminal case against you is pending. If you are convicted, the government can then do a forfeiture sale and take the proceeds from the sale and deposit the proceeds into the government's treasury bank account. Although you testify that you did not know that a drug house was in your apartment complex, the Prosecutors will present a case that you should have known; but you cannot cross-examine the jury what facts or law that they used to hold you guilty. As California, all states have pre-conviction confiscation laws during the pending criminal case and forfeiture upon a conviction. The federal government has similar pre-conviction confiscation of property laws while the owner's criminal case is pending and then a forfeiture sale upon the owner's conviction.

As the owner of a consumer rental property, you must take great steps screening your tenants before signing a lease, and you must make periodic visits to the tenant's residence for inspection and maintain proof of the tenant research and inspection dates of the premises at least every four months. If you are investigated but not charged with a crime with the first tenant conviction for maintaining a drug house, the next time a drug house is found in your apartment complex, the Prosecutors may charge you as an owner because you did not screen your tenant and did not make inspections of the apartment often enough. Remember, juries normally find the defendant charged with a crime guilty 90% of the time. This is one of the reasons why I avoid investing in consumer multi-dwelling rental properties. You normally do

Personality Traits of Money

not have this type of illegal activity involved with commercial property tenants.

Also, in 2005, in a case titled Kelo v. City of New London, 545 U.S. 469 (2005), the U.S. Supreme Court allowed a taking of property by a local government under eminent domain law to facilitate a private development that would pay higher real property taxes and business taxes to the city. The Court decided that the taking was justified for a better public use because the community would benefit from the economic development. A person's family home can be taken by the government, and all the government must do is pay the fair market value of the home without any consideration for the owners' emotional attachment to the home where they were born.

In the long run, the only secured investments are wealth assets, such as family-owned small businesses (Luke 2:49), commercial real property which has business tenants and not consumer tenants (Psalms 24:1), gold and silver coins (Haggai 2:8), diamonds, jaspers, pearls, and precious jewels (Revelation 21:18-27), and food and livestock land (Psalm 50:10-12). Wealth assets, or so-called hard assets, are better than riches, which are notes, bonds, stocks, annuities, other insurance products, where other people have your money, and they hand you in return paper riches, which can be defaulted, or the payors can file bankruptcy.

This attitude and motive that riches and money last forever is fostering single generation consumption. We can see single generation consumption among the new rich Arab oil families who lavishly spend their money as if it will never run out, even though oil is a limited fossil fuel.

According to Wikipedia, Adnan Khoshoggi, a Saudi Arabian businessman billionaire, who primarily was an arms dealer who brokered transactions, especially between the U.S. and Saudi Arabia, reportedly had an annual income over 500 million USD. His yacht was thought to be bigger than that of the late Aristotle Onassis. His yacht, the Nabila, was used in the James Bond film Never Say Never Again. After Khashoggi ran into financial problems, he sold the yacht to the Sultan of Brunei, who in turn sold it for $29 million to Donald Trump, who subsequently sold it for $20 million to Prince Al-Waleed bin Talal as part of a deal to keep Trump's Taj Mahal casino out of bankruptcy.

Oftentimes, people with obsessive-compulsive Personality Traits of Money think that since the money has appeared "magically," they have a "favored" position in the "eyes of fate" or some "higher' authority, such as the false religious god of mammon. Having money does not make you highly favored by God. Handling money properly is a prerequisite by God to promote you to be ruler over greater assets (parable of talents- Matthew 25:14-30) or ruler over cities to promote His kingdom (parable of minas-Luke 19:11-27).

If people are full of greed, covetousness, or avarice, then the people who have a wealth asset, like real property, frequently lose it because they exchange wealth for riches or money because they have not acquired the necessary knowledge, skills, and discipline to manage the wealth. This is why God's word says the wealth of the wicked is laid up for the righteous (Proverbs 13:22).

God instills character, morality, management skills, and strong work ethic in the Believers' souls before He gives the Believers a considerable amount of wealth assets to manage. God uses incremental problem-solving tasks, one problem at a time, as His method of maturation of Believers' souls. In other words, God's pattern is that complex businesses and investments are built upon simple things well done to aggregate into a larger thing or business that has greater utility and income production. God matures His children to transform their souls to have godly character, using God's laws of economics while being led by the Holy Spirit for the appointed season and time for a particular investment or business activity. God thinks in the long run, not the short run. God uses teleology and purposefully plans family wealth for at least three generations. God is the God of Abraham, Isaac, and Jacob, which constitutes God's three generations to produce and finish His spiritual plans and ultimate purpose for a select family in ministry.

MANY PEOPLE, INCLUDING CHRISTIANS, HAVE OBSESSIVE-COMPULSIVE PERSONALITY TRAITS OF MONEY IN THEIR SOULS AND THINK, EMOTE, AND BELIEVE THAT MONEY IS THE BEST ANSWER TO SOLVE THEIR PROBLEMS

Most people believe that if a little money will help make life better, then they believe lots of money always will increase more abundant life. There is an old saying, "I have been rich, and I have been poor; being rich is better." This is not true, as it is the false Personality Traits of Money that cause the person with the unhealthy soulish disorder to seek after money and think deep in their souls that their investments and businesses that make money, empowered by the evil spirit of this age, the god of mammon, are really the sources of their security, power, freedom, romantically attractive, and personal magnetism that is afforded to him and his family.

Deuteronomy 8:17-19 is God's warning, "And thou say in thine heart, 'My power and the might of mine hand hath gotten me this wealth.' (18) But thou shalt remember the LORD thy God: for it is He that giveth thee power to get wealth, that He may establish His covenant which He swore unto thy fathers, as it is this day. (19) And it shall be, if thou do at all forget the LORD thy God, and walk after other gods, and serve them, and worship them, I testify against you this day that ye shall surely perish."

Jesus said in John 10:10, "The thief cometh not, but for to steal, and to kill, and to destroy: I am come that they might have (zoe) life, and that they might have it more abundantly." It is God and the Lord Jesus Christ that increases your true eternal zoe life, not just psuche or natural existence in this four-dimensional fallen world, consisting of height, width, depth, and time. True zoe life is not in the abundance of things, but rather zoe eternal spiritual life is in Christ Jesus and the Kingdom of God. Jesus said in John 6:63, "It is the spirit that quickeneth; the flesh profiteth nothing: the (rhema) words that I speak unto you, they are spirit (pneuma), and they are (zoe) life."

Ecclesiastes 10:19 says, "A feast is made for laughter, and wine maketh merry: but money answereth all things." Money has a universal magnetism that draws people in the world into its system of commerce. Money may have temporary answers, but God through Christ Jesus has eternal answers for all your questions about zoe life in the natural and in the spirit.

The proper belief and attitude is found in Philippians 4:12, 19, which says, "I know both how to be abased, and I know how to abound: everywhere and in all things I am instructed both to be full and to be hungry, both to abound and to suffer need. . . (19) But my God shall supply all your need according to His riches in glory by Christ Jesus."

Personality Traits of Money

3 John 2 says, "Beloved, I wish above all things that thou mayest prosper and be in health, even as thy soul prospereth."

THOSE WHO HAVE THE OBSESSIVE-COMPULSIVE PERSONALITY TRAITS OF MONEY IS AN ILLUSION THAT MORE MONEY SATISFIES THEIR SOULS

For these people, money has become their idol, and making more money is often the time they experience contentment. Therefore, most worldly rich men and women say that it was the pursuit rather than the attainment of money and riches that brought the most fulfilment. Only God can bring true agape love and contentment. 1 Timothy 6:6 says, "But godliness with contentment is great gain."

Money cannot replace God Almighty in fulfilling the void that is present in an unsaved person's soul because an unsaved person is living in a fallen state below his spiritual potential. Once money is acquired, the person with the Personality Traits of Money realizes that money cannot fulfill his dreams, provide his soulish needs, take away his fears, or heal the fractures in his soul.

Money or mammon is the only idol or false god in the New Testament that Jesus said competes with the service to Almighty God (Matthew 6:24). There is nothing inherent in money that produces happiness, fulfillment, or purposeful living. You can be miserable with money or miserable without money. Many rich people are on antidepressants, and many poor people are also on antidepressants. The rich and poor can both be alcoholics. Only God through Christ Jesus can give Believers the (prothesis) purpose, (dunamis) power, (agape) love, (hodos) way, (alethea) truth, and (zoe) life which will fulfill the emptiness in Believers' souls during their lifetimes.

Instead of money filling a soulish vacuum, it creates a bigger soulish void. People expect too much from money. Anything that people use to try to replace the Lord God will leave people with empty souls without purpose or fulfillment. Many People have various Personality Traits of Money and have come to the false conclusion that money is the answer to their problems, needs, and desires.

People endow money with magical or mystical powers and feel betrayed and depressed when money does not live up to the panacea it was thought to have. The etymology of the word panacea originated from Greek mythology. It came from the Greek goddess Panacea who was thought to have a magic potion that could cure all diseases. Panacea comes from the dual word pan meaning "all" combined with the Greek word akos that means "cure." Later, English-speaking people started in the sixteenth Century using the Latin word designation Panacea, which is one of the Latin words obtained from the Greek. Panacea as a universal cure-all became a word that described any soulish illness in addition to as a cure-all for physical sicknesses. The relevance here is the word panacea is being attributed to money by many people who have the obsessive-compulsive Personality Traits of Money.

After my mother passed when I was ten years old, my siblings and I lived on a farm with our grandparents. When my brothers and sisters were minor children, our grandmother decided that all colds and running noses of children could be cured with the panacea Castor Oil.

Dr. Nova Dean Pack

When one child was sick with a cold, grandma would have us stand in line side by side; and we all were given a spoon full of Castor Oil. It tasted horrible, made us go to the bathroom, but we all said we felt better almost immediately; so, we did not have to take a second dose.

If one uses money simply as a tool to help one live, to help one perform his work or mission, and to be a better servant to others, one will not be disappointed with money but will appreciate it for what it can do. Do you work for money or does money work for you? This is an important question to answer. If you work for money instead of money working for you, then you may have in a degree one of the dysfunctional Personality Traits of Money that put too much importance on money, as money cannot solve all the splinters, hurts, disappointments, feelings of inferiority, fears of poverty, desires for control, seeking freedom, being attractive, having personal magnetism, or other self-reflective needs in your soul.

Some people have obsessive-compulsive Personality Traits of Money that spend most all their waking hours thinking about how to acquire more money and how to use money to fulfill their soulish disorders. Money hungry people are gluttons and act as if they are starving for money. Each dollar is perceived as if it is their last portion, and they must devour it before someone else does.

Money is symbolized as food. Money is compared to food because it is needed for survival. The money hungry person will often refer to money with such slang words as cabbage, lettuce, bread, dough, potatoes, cheese, or cheddar. Some foods resemble money. Cut the head of lettuce, and with its layers of green, it looks like crinkly arranged dollar bills. Slices of cheese and slices of bread resemble stacked dollar bills. In days gone by some would call different foods slang for money. "The basket of apples feels a little light." "I think you are a few eggs short." "Let's get out of here before the cops come and grab our clams." "I need for you to pluck some feathers off your chicken and pay me."

Different cultures have different foods that refer to money. Jews and Italians would say, "I need to get my hands on some cashola." Cashola came from the Italian food called "cassola." The Jews who were expelled from Sicily in 1492 moved to Northern Italy, and the Jewish exiles introduced cassola, which was ricotta cheese pancakes. Because they combined the two traditional types of foods–fried and dairy–the cassola pancakes became a natural Hanukkah dish for the Jews. The cassola pancakes stacked up looked like money.

Money is seen as the object which satisfies their cravings as food does for a hungry man. The unsaved person, or a saved person whose soul is not transformed, may have soulish craven-driven covetousness, greed, and avarice; and he often finds in his past the experience of people taking away his toys, depriving him of food, bullying him in school, or denying him of some other nourishment or material needs that satisfies his soul.

MONEY HAS BECOME MORE OF A MOTIVATION OF HUMAN
BEHAVIOR IN THE WORLD THAN GOD'S TRUE AGAPE LOVE
IT SHOULD BE THE OTHER WAY AROUND

Jesus brought agape love as the Godly motivating factor to encourage proper behavior, submission to God, seeking first the Kingdom of God and His righteousness, and avoid serving money as your idol. God's agape love can purify a Believer's soul and lessen the Believer's

Personality Traits of Money

greed, avarice, and covetousness for money and riches. Money attracts avarice love (1 Timothy 6:10), and riches are deceitful (Matthew 13:22).

Solomon said in Ecclesiastes 7:12, "For wisdom is a defense, and money is a defense: but the excellency of knowledge is, that wisdom giveth life to them that have it." The prophet Micah 3:11 had a sobering word regarding money instead of God Who is the leaders' true Source: "The heads thereof judge for reward, and the priests thereof teach for hire, and the prophets thereof divine for money: yet will they lean upon the LORD, and say, 'Is not the LORD among us? None evil can come upon us.'"

Unfortunately, the government elected representatives or bureaucrats throwing money at any social problem has the negative side that money often rewards those who are in that group of people who do little or nothing to solve their own money, homeless, or addiction problems. Money has a quality about it that reinforces the person to stay needy in the group who receives welfare. Therefore, the government's money hand-outs become a lifestyle of the mother with children without a father's help, the homeless, the impoverished, the drug addict, the alcoholic, and the mentally neurotic as they have little or no incentive to change their lifestyles to boost their sense of self-worth or being someone who is worthy of love from God or other people. They do not live, but merely exist. Only God's definition of zoe life is true living here in the world to achieve one's utmost potential in Christ Jesus. Jesus' admonition is that money or god of mammon is the spirit in the world that competes with Almighty Creator God. Again, Jesus implored His listeners that they cannot serve God and serve mammon (Matthew 6:24).

Government Socialist elected representatives and bureaucrats often overly tax the hard working and diligent, while the Government Socialist elected representatives and bureaucrats pay unemployed people who do not work tax free money. This practice does not make sense. The Bible in the parable of the talents and minas rewards the diligent hard-working servants and takes away the money handed to the lazy people who do not work and gives the money to the diligent and hard-working servants that produce a profit for the Employer.

A hand-out by the government managing taxes collected from the diligent and hard-working business owners and employees should never be a lifetime subsidy but should only be a temporary helping hand. A person who is not disabled should be required to work. A person who is injured on the job should be compensated and paid his salary until he recovers, but after recovery, then he should be required to go back to work.

A strong work ethic after initial salvation is a biblical principle in God's Kingdom. Paul said in 2 Thessalonians 3:10 says, "For even when we were with you, this we commanded you, that if any would not work, neither should he eat." Obviously, Paul was addressing laziness in the Body of Christ.

People in the world say that it is money that makes the "world go around." Whereas, in the Kingdom of God, it is the agape love that makes the "Kingdom of God go around." This difference explains much of Jesus' and His Apostles' teachings on money, God's perfect love, and God's Kingdom of righteousness, peace, and joy in the Holy Spirit (Romans 14:17).

It takes God longer to prepare a Believer for success to manage money as a "funnel" and not be stingy, too loose, or used for the Believer's own self-aggrandizement. It is quite easy to get puffed up when one receives a position of authority in secular business and is given a position of authority in the Church based upon his natural leadership qualities instead of his spiritual virtue and calling. When one has worldly wisdom and becomes puffed up, and then one brings that worldly wisdom into the Church community, even Believers naturally will equate worldly wisdom and Godly wisdom as being the same, but they are entirely different. It is exceedingly difficult for one to handle these areas of seemingly worldly success, and the insidiousness that comes with money that lessens God's Kingdom humility.

This is why one of the gifts of God the Father in Romans 12:8 is, "…he that giveth, let him do it with simplicity…." The word "simplicity" is the Greek haplotēs, which means, "with sincerity, without self-seeking, with generosity, copious bestowal, simplicity, with singleness of mind, not wanting anything in return."

Having the Romans 12:8 gift of giving without avarice, covetousness, or greed is a prerequisite to God pouring great wealth through you to build His kingdom and helping people truly in need here on earth. With a pure heart, God will empower you to obtain wealth from the fallen world and the kingdom of darkness; and He will make you a spiritual gift as a Giver in the body of Christ.

When God disciplines you to have a pure heart of giving money, He will cause great wealth for you to manage. He also will cause you to teach others to raise up other teachers with pure hearts regarding money, who will continue to raise up other teachers with pure hearts regarding money, and so on (2 Timothy 2:2). This could start an economic revival in the Lord's holy nation that is within countries throughout the world.

It all starts with hearts who give with haplotēs. When God has built a large Kingdom army of business men and women with pure, simplistic hearts when they give, He will send this Kingdom army of business leaders possessing the power to obtain wealth to tear down the gates of hell and bring the spoils of war back into the Kingdom of God to be used to fulfill God's will here on earth as it is in heaven.

Personality Traits of Money

Dr. Nova Dean Pack

3
Using Money For The "Safety Personality Trait Of Money"

CHAPTER THREE

USING MONEY FOR THE "SAFETY PERSONALITY TRAIT OF MONEY"

Main scripture reference: 1 Timothy 6:10 says, "For the love of money is a root of all kinds of evil, for which some have strayed from the faith in their greediness and pierced themselves through with many sorrows."

Firstly, the "Love of Money" means avarice for money to acquire safety, control, freedom, romanticism, magnetism, or any emotional or mental need fulfilled by money. In the principal reference verse of 1 Timothy 6:10, the word "love" in the phrase "For the love of money…." is the Greek word philargurio, which means here in this context, covetousness or avarice and comes from the root word philarguos, which means "fond of silver." However, both Greek words are rooted in the Greek word philarguria and embodies the English meaning of avarice or the "love of money." The English word avarice has the root word "avar" within it, which means blind. A person who is covetous of money is blind to the truth and blind to the snares that greed, covetousness, and avarice cause.

Secondly, the "Love of Money" also means the opposite of the "hate of money." The "love of money" means that money has become one's idol, trying to fulfill one's needs with money which rightfully can only be fulfilled by God.

DEFINITION OF OBSESSIVE-COMPULSIVE

I am using the words "obsessive" or "obsession" and "compulsive" or "compulsion" in describing people's soulish disorders regarding money with the following meanings. The words "compulsive" or "compulsion" means "resulting from, or relating to, an irresistible, uncontrollable, compelling, overpowering, overwhelming, or besetting urge or need." The words "obsessive" or "obsession" means "thinking about something or someone, or doing something too much or all the time, as being too impassioned, self-centered, egotistical, narcissistic, pompous, narrow-minded, stubborn, or zealous."

The obsessive-compulsive disorder regarding money described in the following chapters is an overwhelming thought, emotion, belief, and reaction without thinking about the consequences of the person harming themselves or other people with whom the person has affiliation or association.

The obsessive-compulsive disorders resist God from transforming the Believer's soul, which consists of the mind, emotions, and heart where the will resides. An obsessive-compulsive person often stays calm outwardly in appearance as long as the person has enough money to feel safe, to be in control, has freedom from authority, is romantically attractive, or has a magnetism with other people when the fear of losing money becomes a threat of loss. A person usually can restrain his obsessive-compulsive behavior when things and events in the natural are not threatening; but when he is soulishly vulnerable, he can seem out of control while losing his temper. The person with an explosive temper when he is threatened with loss of money can exhibit extreme anger that violates societal standards of soulish stability.

Uncontrollable anger by a person in your presence can be very intimidating, daunting, and alarming. The people with these obsessive-compulsive disorders regarding money sometime need deliverance from evil spirits but unquestionably need serious counseling to set them free. John 8:36 gives the answer "If the Son therefore shall make you free, ye shall be free indeed."

SEEK FIRST GOD'S KINGDOM AND HIS RIGHTEOUSNESS

The focus of all Believers must be Jesus' mandate to seek and serve first God, His Kingdom, and His righteousness, not just serve money because you cannot serve God and serve mammon at the same time (Mathew 6:24). Matthew 6:31-33 says, "Therefore take no thought, saying, 'What shall we eat? or, what shall we drink? or, Wherewithal shall we be clothed?' (32) (For after all these things do the Gentiles seek:) for your heavenly Father knoweth that ye have need of all these things. (33) But seek ye first the kingdom of God, and His righteousness; and all these things shall be added unto you."

Money is not a Believer's provision. A Believer's provision is from God Who is Creator and Sovereign Ruler of His Kingdom (Matthew 6:33; Philippians 4:19). When this truth becomes the foundation of your beliefs, and this truth becomes the gospel of the Kingdom that you preach (Matthew 24:14), along with preaching of repentance and remission of sins (Luke 24:47), then you will find the Lord's freedom from the devilish spirits tempting you with the idol of mammon or money. Money is something created by man, and whatever man creates can become an idol of worship. In God's Kingdom there are no idols such as money. In a pure sense, the economy of God's kingdom is giving and receiving and not buying and selling.

God the Father is Believers' Abba by adoption (Romans 8:15). Matthew 7:11 says, "If ye then, being evil, know how to give good gifts unto your children, how much more shall your Father which is in heaven give good things to them that ask Him?" Paul said in Philippians 4:19, "But my God shall supply all your need according to His riches in glory by Christ Jesus."

Thus, money by itself is not your provision. The word "provision" begins with the prefix "pro." "Pro" in the word "provision" means "support to send forward the vision," so, God supports you financially when you seek the spiritual Kingdom "vision" that God gave you as your ministry call for you to fulfill with a submissive Will in following the leading of the Holy Spirit, as you are God's image bearer here on earth (Genesis 1:26-28). As a Believer you have the vocation ministries as God's and Christ's Kingdom kings, priests of the order of Melchizedek (Revelation 1:6), Kingdom lords (1 Timothy 6:15), Kingdom ambassadors of Christ (2 Corinthians 5:20), and Kingdom soldiers (2 Timothy 2:3-4).

When Abraham decided to obey God and sacrifice Isaac, his son of promise, God stopped him by the appearance of a Ram caught in the brushes, which is a precursor of God allowing Jesus, His only begotten Son, to exercise His own free will to lay down His psuche life by being crucified on a Roman Cross (John 10:15).

Genesis 22:10-14 says, "And Abraham stretched forth his hand, and took the knife to slay his son. (11) And the angel of the LORD called unto him out of heaven, and said, 'Abraham,

Abraham:' and he said, 'Here am I.' (12) And He said, 'Lay not thine hand upon the lad, neither do thou anything unto him: for now I know that thou fearest God, seeing thou hast not withheld thy son, thine only son from Me.' (13) And Abraham lifted up his eyes, and looked, and behold behind him a ram caught in a thicket by his horns: and Abraham went and took the ram, and offered him up for a burnt offering in the stead of his son. (14) And Abraham called the name of that place Jehovah-Jireh: as it is said to this day, 'In the mount of the LORD it shall be seen.'"

"Jehovah-Jireh" is one of the many different names of God found in the Old Testament. Jehovah-Jireh is the King James Version's translation of YHWH-Yireh, which means "The LORD it shall be seen." Additionally, the statement "In the mount of the LORD it shall be seen" (verse 14), which refers to a future event on the same Mount Moriah, where God did not spare His only begotten Son, Christ Jesus, but "… delivered Him up for us all. . ." (Romans 8:32). In answer to Isaac's question, "… where is the lamb for a burnt offering? (Genesis 22:7)," Abraham's response in Genesis 22:8 was, "My son, God will provide Himself a Lamb for a burnt offering." Genesis 22:8 was prophetic when John the Baptist's exclaimed, "Behold the Lamb of God, which taketh away the sin of the world!" (John 1:29).

Jehovah-Jireh provided a sacrifice to save Isaac, and that action was a foreshadowing of the provision of His only begotten Son for the salvation of all Believers in the world. Isaac of the Old Testament could not save the Hebrew people. Yet, through Isaac, Jacob was born, through Jacob the twelve tribes of Israel were born, from the Tribe of Judah came the family of David, and from the family of David through the Virgin Mary who was the mother that birthed the Messiah, Jesus Christ. Jesus' humanity nature died on the Roman Cross to bring God's Kingdom and remission of sins for all who repent and believe that He resurrected from the dead and confess Him as Lord (2 Corinthians 7:10; Romans 10:9).

OBSESSIVE-COMPULSIVE SAFETY PERSONALITY TRAIT OF MONEY CAN CAUSE A DISTRUST OF OTHER PEOPLE

The reason why people have an obsessive-compulsive Safety Personality Trait of Money with a soulish imbalance attachment to or the use of money to receive a sense of monetary safety is because they distrust people, such as their employer, their spouse, businessmen, businesswomen, lawyers, judges, medical doctors, network marketing sales persons, pastors, or any other persons or institutions in society that seek money for payment of goods or services or even charitable donations.

This distrust can cause a fear of loss, and this fear of loss causes the person with the Safety Personality Trait of Money not to have loving and secure relationships, and eventually some divert their affection on money, which they falsely believe money can be trusted. 1 John 4:8 says, "There is no fear in (agape) love; but perfect (agape) love casteth out fear: because fear hath torment. He that feareth is not made perfect in (agape) love."

Because a person needs to trust others to maintain his soulish stability, the person who has the Safety Personality Trait of Money mistakenly puts his trust, security, and affection in money instead of God and other people, including his spouse and parents. He feels safer when he has a large bank account. When he decides to put his trust in money instead of God then he will suffer from a reduced amount of sleep and little peace. Genesis 4:8 says, "I will both lay me down in peace, and sleep: for thou, LORD, only makest me dwell in safety."

The person having the obsessive-compulsive Safety Personality Trait of Money is motivated by fear of loss or lack of enough money for his survival and wellbeing. Fear is the opposite of faith in God.

Revelation 2:10 says, "Do not fear any of those things which you are about to suffer." Proverbs 29:25 says, "The fear of man brings a snare, but whoever trusts in the Lord shall be safe."

A PERSON WHO USES MONEY TO MANAGE HIS SAFETY PERSONALITY TRAIT OF MONEY HAS AN UNSOUND MIND

Money or lack of money can cause a person to have an obsessive-compulsive Safety Personality Trait of Money that can cause an overreaction or an explosion of his temper. Again, a person who suffers from an obsessive-compulsive disorder does not think about the negative adverse consequences of being overly fearful of monetary loss. A person is free to make his own choices, however, he is not free to choose the consequences of those choices. Galatians 6:8 says, "For he that soweth to his flesh shall of the flesh reap corruption; but he that soweth to the Spirit shall of the Spirit reap life everlasting."

A person who has an obsessive-compulsive Safety Personality Trait of Money has a fear of loss about losing his livelihood, investments, and not having money, so, his saving money is more important than investing money. This person has an unsound fear and needs his mind renewed to trust in the Lord for his sustenance instead of the money in his savings. 2 Timothy 1:7 says, "For God has not given us a spirit of fear, but of power and of (agape) love and of a sound mind."

The Greek word for the phrase "sound mind" is sophronismos (pronounced so fron is moss). Sophronismos is a combination of the Greek words sos meaning safe and phren meaning the mind. The phrase "sound mind" means safe thinking.

The Safety Personality Trait of Money person that has an unusual need for the soul to feel safe sometimes is because he has been deprived by parents or others in authority of feelings of love, protection, and safety. He may suffer from a deep-seated fear of being abandoned.

A history of being hurt by people in authority is often the door to developing an obsessive-compulsive Safety Personality Trait of Money with fear of rejection and loss of money. The person who uses money as safety thinks, "If I have enough money, I will live with victory in safety, even if I am rejected by everyone." Fear of man and devoid of trust in God can lead debilitating fear of loss. Psalms 118:6 says, "The LORD is on my side; I will not fear what can man do unto me?"

As a Pastor and Lawyer, I have encountered people who have embraced the obsessive-compulsive Safety Personality Trait of Money who have encountered a near death experience or suffered some other physical deprivation. A childhood experience of accidentally being locked in an old refrigerator too long could be a repeatable nightmare of near-death experience and the feeling of being unsafe where having money is like having oxygen to breathe. Also, the experience of abject poverty causing a child to experience extreme hunger for days

Personality Traits of Money

at a time because the child lived in a third world country is a lifetime memory of unsafe physical deprivation. Similarly, if a child who was physically abused through beatings, sexual molestation, or not having warm clothing or shoes during winter, could trigger the Safety Personality Trait of Money to need to feel safer and secure from predators, weather changes, or disasters. A lifetime fear of rejection by others who have more money may have its origin of going to school as a child and being teased by other students for not wearing stylish clothing can linger into adulthood with working with other employees as an unsafe environment. Extreme lack or abuse as a child can make the adult have an obsessive-compulsive need to feel safe, and their minds think, emotions feel, and heart believes that money has the power to fulfill that need.

There are a lot of people in society with anger problems. It could be a so-called "Karen" that gets outrageously angry for not receiving what she thinks is improper service, or if she angrily confronts people who she thinks is parking incorrectly at a shopping mall. It could also be a supervisor at work who exhibits extreme outbursts of anger at times. This causes a passive individual to feel unsafe.

The scriptural advice of Jesus is seen in Matthew 18:21-22, which says, "Then came Peter to Him, and said, 'Lord, how oft shall my brother sin against me, and I forgive him? till seven times?' (22) Jesus saith unto him, 'I say not unto thee, Until seven times: but, Until seventy times seven.'"

The scriptural commandment by Jesus to "forgive" quite frankly can be difficult to internalize and to express. Many people hold deep grudges when they are offended or wronged, even if they are Believers. Grudges relate to a particular event, defamed or publicly shamed, and the victim discerns he has been wronged. His inner hurt is bad, so he will not forgive or forget those who wronged him. Holding a grudge and unforgiveness can lead to deep-seeded soulish anger that stops spiritual growth and maturity. The fact is everyone has been wronged in some way or another in their lives, but it is only rare that people develop an obsessive-compulsive extreme disorder that seeks money for safety. Forgiving other people of their wrongs will be liberating, and that is why Jesus said always forgive people of their sins. Believers have the vocation as Priests who have the ministry of reconciliation. This point is revealed in 2 Corinthians 5:18-19, which says, "And all things are of God, who hath reconciled us to Himself by Jesus Christ, and hath given to us the ministry of reconciliation; (19) To wit, that God was in Christ, reconciling the world unto Himself, not imputing their trespasses unto them; and hath committed unto us the word of reconciliation."

Whenever you work with people, or even have fellowship with other Believers, guard your soul until you get to know them and their inclinations. A fellow worker's proclivity to lose his temper makes it difficult to work with him. People who have grudges have triggers that can make them shoot bullet-like angry words. If you touch that area where they have a grudge, you can unknowingly trigger and receive an outburst of sudden verbal anger directed at you when you had never wronged the person. If this happens several times, it can cause you to feel the job has an unsafe work environment. You may not be able to quit your job, and you may have to lovingly confront the fellow employee or supervisor that his or her outburst of anger makes you feel unsafe, and that it causes you great distress that is affecting you physically and soulishly. This can develop into workplace unsafety, which is an actionable civil case under the law, and thus the supervisor's anger problem can cause a monetary loss to the employer. This should motivate the employer to chastise the supervisor to seek counseling to control his temper or be fired from his employment. The owner can personally be liable if he does not make the workplace safe for his employees.

Similarly, the church congregation you are attending may be an unsafe place, as you may find there are people who need anger management or spread defamatory untrue statements. You can meet with the Pastor and tell him or her that a particular church member has a temper and lost his temper at a fellowship meeting during a non-threatening conversation. The Pastor usually will have a counseling session with the Church member because he does not want any people leaving the church because someone else has a temper problem. The last thing the Pastor wants is that the community of Believers is not a safe place to fellowship. When people leave the congregation, there is a loss of donations, so any kind of anger problems in the congregation can affect the cash flow. Consequently, unsafe congregation meetings can cause a Pastor to feel unsafe for loss of donations and thus income when some Believers trespass other Believers' sense of peace. The same could happen if there is the sin of gossip amongst the congregation members. The unsafe feeling of loss of donations is a big motivator for the Pastor to preach a sermon on the sin of gossip.

If the employer, or the Pastor, who has themselves the obsessive-compulsive Safety Personality Trait of Money, their unsound minds may use money as a tool to fight against his fear of rejection, fear of loss of money, fear of loss of business or pulpit, fear of loss of magnetism by the members of the congregation, fear of humiliation, fear of ego infringement, or fear of not having enough income. The abnormal fear of loss can gravitate to the person developing an obsessive-compulsive Safety Personality Trait of Money.

Fear of monetary loss of income can become a paramount, overriding precondition to any financial decision by someone having the Safety Personality Trait of Money, which is an overwhelming need for monetary safety.

It is the degree of phobia or attachment to money to fulfill the need for safety that determines whether there is obsessive-compulsive behavior.

THE PERSON WITH THE SAFETY PERSONALITY TRAIT OF MONEY BECOMES ONE OF THE ROOT CAUSES OF WRONGFUL ATTACHMENT TO MONEY

The person with the obsessive-compulsive Safety Personality Trait of Money causes a distrust of others, and this makes it difficult for those who use money as safety to enjoy the luxury, ease, and leisure as normal reasons God prospers His children.

The person with the obsessive-compulsive Safety Personality Trait of Money causes the person's distrust of people to be transferred to the trust of money for his safety.

The obsessive-compulsive Safety Personality Trait of Money person that trusts in money, but not people, causes a false feeling of safety, which offsets a feeling of fear of loss.

The person with the obsessive-compulsive Safety Personality Trait of Money sees money as his safety blanket.

Personality Traits of Money

THE SAFETY PERSONALITY TRAIT OF MONEY IS SEEN IN THE "HABITUAL SAVER PERSONALITY TRAIT."

It is wise to save up money for emergencies, for capital to start a business, and to make a major purchase, such as a used or new car or a down payment on a house. These practices are sound financial expenditures and saving for those expenditures. However, when saving becomes an Obsessive-compulsive Personality Trait of Money, a consuming irresistible impulse, then a problem with money is evident.

The Habitual Saver Personality Trait compels him to put part of his paycheck in the bank to bring back the sense of safety to function normally to conduct other areas of his life.

The obsessive-compulsive Habitual Saver Personality Trait person derives emotional satisfaction in purchasing items at substantial savings. The primary focus of the Habitual Saver Personality Trait of money regarding any product or event is its cost, not its quality of craftsmanship.

An evening's dinner, recreational activity, or vacation cannot be enjoyed as a change of pace or an opportunity to relax and rest with the obsessive-compulsive Habitual Saver Personality Trait. The otherwise positive activity is experienced with stressful emotions because the cost of the expenditure is too burdensome of a thought by the Habitual Saver Personality Trait.

The person with the Habitual Saver Personality Trait will redefine sin to include any action which wastes time. He will quote people like Benjamin Franklin, who said, "Time is money."

The person with the Habitual Saver Personality Trait is fostered with lack of basic trust of people. Trust is the first stage of development toward maturity in having healthy relationships with others. This is why the person with the Habitual Saver Personality Trait needs to develop safe relationships, with people with pristine integrity, who are always on time to appointments, who have no debts or tax problems, and who are friendly with him unconditionally.

Oftentimes, the person with the Habitual Saver Personality Trait had childhood experiences where parents were divorced or one or both parents died. The Habitual Saver Personality Trait person sometimes distrusts even his own spouse, which distrust lessens as the years roll by into a long marital relationship.

In extreme cases, the Habitual Saver Personality Trait person cannot deal with the real world, which he believes is always after his money, so he increases his savings. He focuses his attention only on the size of his savings account. He looks at his savings account daily at times because it makes him feel safe.

During any pending crises, the person with the Habitual Saver Personality Trait will retreat into his protective fortress of money for safe thinking, safe emoting, and safe believing in his soul. Money is as a drug high, and the person with the Habitual Saver Personality Trait reaches a state of euphoria when he makes a new deposit. Then the euphoria leaves after a couple of days, so he may have a garage sale, sell a third car, gather cans and bottles, or find other things he can sell to acquire more money to add to his savings account. Sometimes, he will ask for overtime at work, or if he has a business, he will discount his products to create more cash that he can deposit into his savings account to obtain his money euphoria and the feeling of safety again. This pattern of adding to his savings account cycle is repeated over and over. People think he is smart by having a large savings account, but they do not understand that it is because he suffers as a Habitual Saver Personality Trait.

For the soulishly unbalanced Habitual Saver Personality Trait person, no amount of money will provide enough for complete safety. The fear of being without money, especially in his old age, never leaves him; and his obsessive-compulsive continues to amass greater savings because he has an insatiable hunger for monetary safety.

Unfortunately, those who do not have the Holy Spirit's discernment will not recognize the Habitual Saver Personality Trait as one who is driven by fear of rejection and fear of loss. Many people often will praise and look up to the Habitual Saver Personality Trait as a person who is thrifty and virtuously unattached to material things, since he does not have a fancy car, expensive clothes, and is not an extravagant spender. He normally eats at home to save money to avoid restaurant prices. The Habitual Saver Personality Trait person who expresses his phobia to feel safe through having a large saving account receive positive reinforcement with self-serving adages such as "a penny saved is a penny earned." However, normally the Habitual Saver Personality Trait person is a "penny wise and pound foolish" because he should be investing his money to earn money with his money.

The leaders in society who have the Habitual Saver Personality Trait are usually the bankers who believe they are more noble than those who are the less thrifty. Often, people who are driven by the Habitual Saver Personality Trait will seek out business or investment relationships only with others who are like minded.

The problem is that being "cheap" has its costs. The Person suffering from the Habitual Saver Personality Trait is not a consistent giver to people in need and normally suffers bad relationships. After the person with the Habitual Saver Personality Trait becomes born again, his soul needs to be transformed. He normally is not a consistent tither or giver in Church, and the devourer comes in and attacks generally his health, need for another car, or other unexpected expenditures, which depletes his savings.

The person who is the Habitual Saver Personality Trait eventually may not spend enough money to buy nourishing food and refuses to go to the medical doctor. He becomes fatigued from working long hours because his goal is to make more money to deposit into his savings account.

The person who is the Habitual Saver Personality Trait subjects himself to constant anxiety and tension and often develops psychosomatic diseases such as ulcers, headaches, high blood pressure, and allergies. His immune system often wears out early. The person who is the Habitual Saver Personality Trait regularly dies before or soon after retirement age, so he ends up not being able to spend his savings.

A famous example of someone who had the Habitual Saver Personality Trait was W.C. Fields. Because of his fear of being broke, and to ensure his privacy and his access to money wherever he traveled in Vaudeville, Fields opened hundreds of different bank accounts under assumed names, such as Figley E. Whitesides, Sneed Hearn, Ludovic Fishpond, Aristotle Hoop, Dr. Otis Guelpe, and Cholmonley Frampton-Blythe. These accounts were opened in almost every town where he traveled and varied from small sums to as much as $50,000. After his death on Christmas Day in 1946 only about 48 of the bank accounts were discovered. It is estimated that over $600,000 with its 1946 value was never recovered, which would be about $6.7 million in today's value. The money in these bank accounts was escheated to the state because they were unclaimed. [Commonplace Fun Facts. Wordpress. December 11, 2014]

THE SAFETY PERSONALITY TRAIT OF MONEY IS SEEN IN THE "SELF-DENIAL PERSONALITY TRAIT."

The person with the Self-denial Personality Trait has similar habits as the Habitual Saver Personality Trait and denies himself almost all pleasures of life. The person with the Self-denial Personality Trait sees a reward in "self-sacrifice" as it becomes a virtuous quality. The person with the Self-denial Personality Trait practices a form of asceticism.

The person with the Self-denial Personality Trait often purchases his food, shelter, clothing, and transportation strictly based upon the price, or he will not buy them. The person with the Self-denial Personality Trait sometimes has a "poverty mentality" and usually criticizes the "prosperity message" of some of the Word-faith Teachers. They normally choose a religious denomination which sees self-denial as a virtue, as self-denial is seen as "self-restraint" and "wisdom."

In Hinduism, renunciation of material things is the path toward enlightenment. Hindus beat the flesh, stick sharp sticks through their bodies, and give up all association of self to gain so-called enlightenment. Yet, spiritual self-denial is Hinduism, not Christianity. 1 Timothy 6:17 says to not trust in uncertain riches, ". . . but in the living God, who giveth us richly all things to enjoy."

The person with the Self-denial Personality Trait sees poverty as a form of godliness or one who suffers for Jesus. This is one of the belief virtues of "priests" in the Buddhist and Hindu religions. However, this false religious belief (that poverty is virtuous) has no place in the Christian truth as we are partakers of God's Kingdom blessings of prosperity because the Christian enters the economy of God of giving and receiving, loving, and servanthood.

Similarly, 2 Corinthians 8:9 says, "For ye know the grace of our Lord Jesus Christ, that, though He was rich, yet for your sakes He became poor, that ye through His poverty might be rich." Additionally, Galatians 3:29 says, "And if you are Christ's, then you are Abraham's seed, and heirs according to the promise." In proper balance, prosperity is directly related to spiritual maturity of the Believer's soul. 3 John 2 says, "Beloved, I pray that you may prosper in all things and be in health, just as your soul prospers."

The person with the Self-denial Personality Trait often puts off spending on himself under the excuse or reason that he is accumulating money for retirement, for a rainy day, or for an inevitable disaster.

The person with the Self-denial Personality Trait plays up his financial needs, hoping others will feel sorry for him and offer monetary assistance. Since he perceives his self-denial and austerity as virtuous, he believes others should reward him, compliment him, and promote them for his martyr like facade with his pretentious humble personality.

The person with the Self-denial Personality Trait seems to be caring, but he is very stingy toward others. He is judgmental and believes others would have enough if they just would not spend so much on their lifestyles. He often will say to others, "You are spending too much, and your maintenance is your downfall. You need to go on a strict austere budget if you want to get ahead in life. A penny earned is a penny not spent on non-necessities."

The person with the Self-denial Personality Trait is the one in church who demands strict budgets, votes "no" on any Church building expansion ideas, and always votes "no" to increase the Pastor's salary. Instead, he argues that people just need to "tighten their belts" and "learn to live within a budget." He might call all extra expenditures "self-indulgences."

The person with the Self-denial Personality Trait harbors hidden resentment toward those who have better things than he has, but he will not express his resentment. However, the person with the Self-denial Personality Trait has an awe and fear of those who are more affluent than him because he associates riches with power, authority, prestige, and influence.

The person with the Self-denial Personality Trait hopes to receive admiration and sympathy from people rather than scorn, contempt, or rejection. His goal is safety, and safety within the walls of his austere lifestyle. Since he acts as if he is satisfied with his meager existence, he believes he does not threaten others who have more money, power, and authority. Since he is always unthreatening, he has a sense that he will not be attacked and thus experiences a sense of safety in his perception of a rather dangerous world. He is like the animal who plays dead when an attacker comes around.

Since every servant needs someone to serve, those with the Self-denial Personality Trait often lend themselves to accepting gifts, subsidies, handouts, leftovers at church banquets or agape feasts, and no interest Christian loans. They tend to act like noble victims of an oppressive world.

Unfortunately, any activity such as church parties, church outings, and family fun times bring a certain degree of anxiety, stress, and a belief that the activity is a waste of money to the Self-denial Personality Trait person who does not like what he considers as selfish, soulish indulgence by the congregation. He may believe that a home Bible study should be run like a class and not have people bringing food for fellowship afterwards as he does not want to bring any food. He thinks that if he can fast one meal, then others should fast the meal as well and take what teaching they receive home with them and contemplate how it spiritually enriches their lives.

Normal pleasure times are a threat to the person with the Self-denial Personality Trait who has a self-imposed deprivation. Often, the Believer with the Self-denial Personality Trait will be the one serving the food to others, cleaning up the mess after the agape feast is over, straightening up the chairs, acting as the policeman to tell the children to keep the noise down, and encourage a solemn respectful gathering at all church group functions because the Believers are in the presence of the Lord and Holy Spirit. However, his work is not based upon true servanthood at all. His actions are merely an activity to cover up his deeper

Personality Traits of Money

self-denial which causes him not to enjoy himself at the Church social functions. He finds it stressful to have fun.

The person with the Self-denial Personality Trait thinks one of the best places he could live, and work, is like the Monks at the "Hermits of Our Lady of Mount Carmel" in Fairfield, Pennsylvania. These Hermit Monks live very austere lifestyles and are very dedicated to their faith. "Hermits of Our Lady of Mount Carmel" is sanctioned as a Roman Catholic diocesan religious community in full agreement with the Pope, and they practice the observance like the ancient Carmelite charism in its contemplative form. Although I do not question their sincerity, this is not the kind of fellowship practice that I find enhancing to my Christian beliefs.

The person with the Self-denial Personality Trait is not an overachiever and often suffers from low self-esteem and sin consciousness. He usually has no experience as to how the joy of the Lord can be anyone's strength (Nehemiah 8:10).

This person is not conducive to good family relations because he makes others in the family, especially the children, feel guilty about spending any money for self-indulgences. This person is depressing to be around, and certainly not the life of any party. Normally, children leave home as soon as they become adults because of the father's obsessive-compulsive Self-denial Personality Trait disorder.

THE SAFETY PERSONALITY TRAIT OF MONEY IS SEEN IN THE "BARGAIN CHASER PERSONALITY TRAIT".

There is usually nothing wrong in trying to obtain a bargain when you make your purchases. However, if there are hidden negative feelings about being satisfied by the Bargain Chaser, it can become an unhealthy, motivated compulsion.

Unless the bargain is exactly low enough based upon his set formula, the person with the Bargain Chaser Personality Trait will not buy. The Bargain Chaser Personality Trait person is always hunting for the right price. He is a fanatic for bargains, and money is fiercely withheld at the place of sale unless the item is cheap enough.

However, once the item found is cheap enough, the person suffering with the Bargain Chaser Personality Trait will buy it regardless of whether he needs it or not.

The person with the Bargain Chaser Personality Trait will comb through the rock-bottom sales in weekly flyers or newspapers, craigslist, e-bay, or any other online advertiser with reduced prices for products or services every morning or on another day when they are circulated or shown online. He will go around his neighborhood early on Saturday mornings to hunt for garage sale signs. He will get up and go to the garage sales that interests him or will just drive around for a couple of hours that he can get to on Saturday morning and buy things. Finding a good bargain always puts a smile on his face, and he can hardly wait to get home to show the great item he purchased for way below its value. Of course, these items sold at garage sales mostly are used furniture, tools, bicycles, exercise equipment, etc. and he purchases same "as is" without any warranties expressed or implied as to condition, merchantability, or fitness for use for the purpose intended. Thus, he ends up throwing his items he purchased into the trash.

The Bargain Chaser Personality Trait is sometimes a "coupon junky" and may be constantly cutting out coupons and placing them in envelopes to lessen the price at the grocery stores to obtain bargains when the stores have the products on sale to attract customers to come and buy other items as well that are not on sale. However, the person with the Bargain Chaser Personality Trait will only purchase the item on sale and leave the store.

The Bargain Chaser Personality Trait is convinced he saves money by buying bargains. Yet, the truth is that the person with the Bargain Chaser Personality Trait would save money if he does not purchase items he does not need or necessarily want.

If the person with the Bargain Chaser Personality Trait runs out of eggs, bread, butter, paper towels or anything else, he often will do without until he can buy the items at bargain prices at a sale.

Curiously, the person with the Bargain Chaser Personality Trait normally keeps accurate records of all the "savings" he receives from purchasing the bargain items, which he can show others his astute ability to negotiate bargains.

Unfortunately, the person with the Bargain Chaser Personality Trait never realizes that time is money and often will spend numerous hours and travel many miles just to buy a bargain product. He does not count the fuel costs or the wear and tear on his vehicle hunting down bargain items.

The person with the Bargain Chaser Personality Trait does not keep suitable time records, and generally he does not consider being on time a virtue. Time is not important – it is the best price of a product being sold that is important. Bad time habits are seen in every other part of his life. He is often late to his job or business, late to school, late to church, late to social gatherings, etc. The only time he is early is if being first at a garage sale or retail store sale means he gets the bargain.

Even if he is going to sell something, the person with the Bargain Chaser Personality Trait believes people will only be attracted to the price. He thinks, "If the price is right, they will buy from me even if I show my items for sale later than others at the garage sale." "Price is king" and "cash is king" are common expressions of the person with the Bargain Chaser Personality Trait. The only King that he should recognize that has the authority and power over life and death here on earth is God and Jesus, the King of kings.

The mind, emotions, and beliefs of the person with the Bargain Chaser Personality Trait is that he was deprived of some essential things as a child that gave him a sense of insecurity. The need for worthless personal property can become such an obsessive-compulsive urge that the only social interaction he treats important is the buy and sale transaction. He will say, "One man's junk is another man's treasure. People will buy anything if it is a bargain." That is true, at least about himself. Frequently, the person with the Bargain Chaser Personality Trait will make selling and buying things his career because it is an addiction.

The person with the Bargain Chaser Personality Trait normally comes from a house where a mother or father had died or dissolved the family unit by a divorce. He may also come from a family where those in authority were not demonstrative of their affection. In his family home, both money and friendliness were in short supply while growing up. Jesus would replace the void with His agape love. Whereas the person with the Bargain Chaser Personality Trait is trying to fill the void with money that is "saved" after each bargain transaction.

The person with the Bargain Chaser Personality Trait grew up learning to purchase items only if they were on sale at a retail store; they were used items for a bargain price at garage sale; or, they were items that are discounted at a flea market. The soulish disorder of the person with the Bargain Chaser Personality Trait manifests when he becomes an adult. And through hard negotiations he still tries to get more than his money's worth from every buy and sale transaction.

Unfortunately, the dividing line between the Bargain Chaser Personality Trait and the operation of an avarice disorder is often hard to see. It is the degree of the obsessive-compulsive disorder that the Bargain Chaser Personality Trait person exhibits in the pursuit of getting something for nothing that greed, avarice, or covetousness takes over. The obsessive-compulsive person's need for a buy and sale bargain transaction is a continuous temptation. Psychologists would simply call it an obsessive-compulsive disorder or a borderline personality disorder concerning the use of money.

The motivation of those with the Bargain Chaser Personality Trait is that he gains a sense of safety in proving to himself that he can survive longer than most other people and on less because he knows how to "stretch my dollar to make it go further." To this extent, he has a sense of superiority over others because of his shopping abilities and his prowess in negotiations. Also, he feels superior because others seek his advice in how to negotiate bargain purchases. He is good at buying used autos.

Interestingly, this Bargain Chaser Personality Trait disorder regularly is seen with those who are so-called "Preppers," who look for bargains to put in storage along with their other survival products to be prepared for any disaster that happens.

There is another negative side effect of the person with the Bargain Chaser Personality Trait. He learns to be a manipulator in his negotiations, and in so doing he can hurt people who desperately need the money because of a needed surgery, have no income because they lost their job, or they are desperate for money to pay rent, utilities, or fuel. He with the Bargain Chaser Personality Trait believes he can manipulate his environment and get more for his precious money.

Unfortunately, the person with the Bargain Chaser Personality Trait makes the mistake of focusing too much on the price instead of the quality of the merchandise; and when he does, he shortchanges himself. He also purchases things he doesn't need and ends up with a bunch of junk in his garage in storage.

The person with the Bargain Chaser Personality Trait becomes a victim of con men with the "big deal transaction" or the "get-rich-quick scheme." He often invests in false promises of others. Since the person with the Bargain Chaser Personality Trait is quite good with the art of negotiating a good deal, he is overly confident of his bartering ability. He can become a victim of a con artist who is better at negotiating, and who shows the person with the Bargain Chaser Personality Trait how he can get a house, a car, and recreation vehicles at unbelievable discount bargains that the person with the Bargain Chaser Personality Trait was "cheated out of as a child." The con man takes his money, and the person with the Bargain Chaser Personality Trait never sees the con man again.

The person with the Bargain Chaser Personality Trait is overly confident in his abilities and becomes overly prideful. He rejects sound judgment, wisdom, and helpful advice from his pastor, his spouse, his lawyer, his financial advisor, or his business friends. He often becomes a "sitting duck" as an easy target to lose his life savings.

Finally, the person with the Bargain Chaser Personality Trait gets the reputation of being cheap and sometimes causes others to withdraw from any friendly relationship. He reads the grocery receipt before he leaves the store and compares it with the prices on the items purchased. He questions the cost of items listed on a restaurant bill. He can be quite embarrassing. Also, people get tired or bored listening to the person with the Bargain Chaser Personality Trait whose main topic of conversation is always the bargain purchases he received. Among Believers, he comes off at times as having a too materialistic mindset.

THE SAFETY PERSONALITY TRAIT OF MONEY IS REVEALED IN THE "TREASURE COLLECTOR PERSONALITY TRAIT"

The person with the Treasure Collector Personality Trait accumulates numismatic coins, rare stamps, Tiffany belt buckles, historical guns, campaign buttons, baseball cards, antique clocks, famous paintings, vintage cars, and hundreds of other things that he finds interesting.

Having collectibles may be an innocent and enriching hobby, but collecting can open the door for a borderline personality disorder because of the person's obsessive-compulsive Treasure Collector Personality Trait in his soul in need of spiritual transformation.

It is the intensity of the desire and the extent the Treasure Collecting Personality Trait dominates the Collector's time, activity, and life determines whether the Collector has a problem that falls under the category of safety of money that manifests as a Treasure Collector Personality Trait.

Matthew 6:19 21 says, "Do not lay up for yourselves treasures on earth, where moth and rust destroy and where thieves break in and steal; but lay up for yourselves treasures in heaven, where neither moth nor rust destroys and where thieves do not break in and steal."

Matthew 12:35 says, "A good man out of the good treasure of his heart brings forth good things, and an evil man out of the evil treasure brings forth evil things."

The person with the Treasure Collector Personality Trait hoards collectibles as items of affection, precious items, and even is devoted to his collections. These collectibles often become idols that provide him with his needs and wants of feelings of safety as he gets older or loses his income.

In his past the person with the Treasure Collector Personality Trait may have been given toys

Personality Traits of Money

as a child by his parents instead of love and safety.

Occasionally, one can discover that the person with the Treasure Collector Personality Trait was an only child who had to spend many hours alone amusing himself. His only sense of identity was his interaction with his toys and later possessions.

Since the child's toys were his only connection that took away his loneliness, the person with the Treasure Collector Personality Trait continues to add to his collections and usually does not like to sell his collections because he thinks they really are providing him with love and safety. These are exhibitions of emotional or mental disorders. The transformation of his soul comes when his soul is replaced with the agape love that comes from God, Christ Jesus, and fellowship with mature Believers.

The person with the Treasure Collector Personality Trait is usually very competitive. His self-esteem and ego are usually transferred to the value of his treasure. If someone threatens to steal, questions his treasure's authenticity, or lessens his treasure's value, it becomes an indirect threat against the Collector himself, and he is offended and often loses his temper.

There was a certain person who had a lucrative business where he used part of the business income to invest in numismatic coins. This hobby of his became an obsession and compulsion. He and his wife sold the business on a large down payment and the balance paid on a long-term purchase agreement where monthly payments were made by the buyer, and the couple retired to the state of Tennessee, which had no state income taxes, to lessen the state taxes on their future income because California state income taxes were the highest in America next to New York. Eventually, the husband's obsession and compulsion of his treasure numismatic coin collection caused his focus to be on his treasure to protect it at all costs. After years passed, his treasure collection increased but he ignored his wife, and this caused his wife to feel unloved and neglected, so she filed for a divorce. His wife testified at their divorce hearings throughout the family law proceeding in Tennessee that lasted more than a year that her husband spent thousands upon thousands of dollars to acquire his numismatic coin collection that was his obsession and treasure that now were worth millions. The husband denied that such a numismatic coin collection existed, did not list the numismatic coin collection in his list of assets belonging to the marriage, even though prestigious friends testified at trial that they personally viewed the husband's numismatic coin collection and heard him say they were worth millions. With testimony of witnesses, the Judge made a judicial finding that the husband was lying, and the Family Law Judge ruled that the numismatic coin collection was worth millions and awarded the asset to the husband. The Family Law Judge awarded the home and the balance of the purchase price payments derived from the sale of their businesses to the wife. Yet, before trial, the husband disobeyed the court's order to present the numismatic coins collection to an appraiser and was held in contempt and spent time in jail. Yet, the husband was implacable and would not divulge the numismatic coin collection and kept denying under oath that he had purchased any numismatic coins. The wife at pre-trial hearings introduced a receipt where the husband purchased a numismatic antique gold coin from a dealer for an enormous price, but the husband said the wife just created a false sales receipt. Finally, an expert numismatic coin dealer testified at trial as to the value of such a complete set of numismatic gold coins in mint condition collection was worth, along with other coins he had, but denied having, which the Family Law Judge used as the value of the marital estate that was awarded to the husband.

Dr. Nova Dean Pack

The movie "Lord of the Rings," is based upon J.R. Tolkien's trilogy books, titled, The Lord of the Rings. The books introduce a very pitiful fictional character, named Gollum, who was first introduced in the 1937 book called "The Hobbit." Wikipedia says, "Gollum was a Stoor Hobbit of the River-folk who lived near the Gladden Fields. . .Gollum obtained the Ring by murdering his relative Déagol, who found it in the River Anduin. Gollum referred to the Ring as 'my precious' or 'precious', and it extended his life far beyond natural limits. Centuries of the Ring's influence twisted Gollum's body and mind, and, by the time of the novels, he 'loved and hated [the Ring], as he loved and hated himself.' Throughout the story, Gollum was torn between his lust for the Ring and his desire to be free of it. Bilbo Baggins found the Ring and took it for his own, and Gollum afterwards pursued it for the rest of his life. Gollum finally seized the Ring from Frodo Baggins at the Cracks of Doom in Mount Doom in Mordor, but he fell into the fires of the volcano, where both he and the Ring were destroyed."

Gollum wholly consumed the Ring's power. The Ring's power was very, very enticing, and Gollum was very addicted to the Ring and had to always have it as his companion. The Ring destroyed and imprisoned anyone who held the Ring. Gollum's whole life revolved around "my precious." Before meeting Bilbo the Hobbit, Gollum lived in lonely solitude with his only companion, the Ring. Thus, it is somewhat understanding why Gollum called the evil Ring, "my precious" because without possession of the Ring, Gollum had no meaning to his life. The fictional character, Gollum, reveals a good example of the possible ultimate destiny of the person with the Treasure Collector Personality Trait.

The person with the Treasure Collector Personality Trait usually joins clubs, and they develop a sense of purpose and avoid feelings of loneliness. It also gives the collector a sense of power and superiority when he has the best collection. He also usually has prestige for being an authority on the treasure collected, and others bring them their treasure for his valuation. Of course, if he wants to purchase the treasure collected, he will low-ball the estimated value and purchase it.

Furthermore, since the person with the Treasure Collector Personality Trait is accumulating things other than normal money, he is not considered a "miser" or "penny pincher," although there is little difference.

Unfortunately, collecting treasures is not just a fun hobby of the person with the obsessive-compulsive Treasure Collector Personality Trait, but is a matter of feeling safe that he can always rely upon if he needs money in the future. Yet, most Collectors die with their collections. If the obsession and compulsion is not brought in check, the acquisition and possession of the objects desired become more important than people or his own life, as he will want to leave this wonderful treasure to his children. The person with the Treasure Collector Personality Trait normally alienates his friends, family, and associates because his treasure generally comes up in every conversation and that is all he wants to talk about. He tends to withdraw completely from interpersonal relationships, as he is more attracted to the treasure that he holds in his hand instead of holding the hand of a loved one.

The person with the Treasure Collector Personality Trait ignites his thoughts, feelings, and beliefs of safety by holding and owning his treasure, but his fear of poverty can be a dysfunctional disorder that he is trying to remedy by his collectibles. Treasure collecting is the same

Personality Traits of Money

as collecting money, and these obsessive-compulsive people believe money is a wall of safety from any disaster, attack, or impoverishment.

THE SAFETY PERSONALITY TRAIT CAN BE EXPRESSED IN OTHER FORMS OF OBSESSIVE-COMPULSIVE PERSONALITY TRAITS OF MONEY WHICH DENOTE A SOULISH DISORDER WITH MONEY

The soulish disorder is that those people who put an excessive confidence and optimism on money serve an idol for their needs, which is a grave offense to God. Those with an obsessive-compulsive pursuit of money believe having copious amounts of money is a source of safety. Yet, this personality disorder of focusing their hope on money's safety and fortification can cause a whole derivative of other types of aberrant Personality Traits of money.

For example, the Safety Personality Trait of Money is revealed with the person having the "Regretful Personality Trait," who laments over the opportunities and deals that got away, and he spends his time thinking about a better life he would have had if the deals had been successfully consummated; and if he was paid the money he was promised.

Another example of the Safety Personality Trait of Money is revealed with the person having the "Undeserved Personality Trait," who continuously sets himself up to lose money because deep inside he believes he does not deserve it. The person with this soulish disorder believes that God does not want him to prosper. Yet, the person with the Undeserved Personality Trait sees a benefit of much worldly wisdom like a captain whose survived many storms in life. He thinks, feels, and believes he is strong because there are no threats of loss which he cannot overcome because of his experience as a survival of the many tempests. He really does not believe in his heart that he deserves to be rich. Yet, he is proud that he has the experience that weathered the storms of life, and he believes this experience makes him wise, which he can impart to other people. He believes he has learned from his failures.

This concept of worldly wisdom from weathering storms is like a young banker who desired to succeed in the banking business. He asked another employee who he could consult for wisdom and knowledge to put him on the path of success and promotion in the banking business. He was referred to Mr. Wiseman and asked him how he personally succeeded in the banking profession. Mr. Wiseman said, "Four words. Making good financial decisions." The young banker asked, "Yet, how do I get the experience to make good financial decisions?" Mr. Wiseman responded, "Four words. Making bad financial decisions."

However, a person cannot live long enough to gain all wisdom to become successful through trial and error or using the fallen wisdom of this world. There is a great distinction between wisdom from God as Creator and the wisdom derived from devils and from fallen creation. James 3:13-17 says, "Who is a wise man and endued with knowledge among you? let him shew out of a good conversation his works with meekness of wisdom (from God). (14) But if ye have bitter envying and strife in your hearts, glory not, and lie not against the truth. (15) This wisdom descendeth not from above, but is earthly, sensual, devilish. (16) For where envying and strife is, there is confusion and every evil work. (17) But the wisdom that is from above is first pure, then peaceable, gentle, and easy to be intreated, full of mercy and good fruits, without partiality, and without hypocrisy."

The problem with this self-imposed philosophy is that it is learning by experience alone instead of wisdom received from the Holy Spirit in each given transaction. The Holy Spirit can see in the future and knows where the pitfalls are and knows who is lying or telling the truth in their representations. The Holy Spirit helps you to point out the potential losses and benefits in a business or investment decision. Worldly wisdom is derived from eating the unwise four-dimensional fruit growing on the Tree of the Knowledge of Good and Evil instead of God's wisdom from eating the wise higher-dimensional spiritual fruit growing on God's Tree of Life.

God wants to bless His adopted children who are submissive, humble servants, who seek God's kingdom and righteousness where God's wisdom is stored. This requires the Believer's daily prayer and diligence of seeking wisdom from scriptures. Matthew 6:33-34 are not just inconsequential verses in the Bible but are the keys to God's blessings of prosperity. Matthew 6:33-34 says, "But seek ye first the kingdom of God, and his righteousness; and all these things (along with God's knowledge, wisdom, and understanding) shall be added unto you. (34) Take therefore no thought for the morrow: for the morrow shall take thought for the things of itself. Sufficient unto the day is the evil thereof." Believers cannot see in the future because they are restricted by time, but God can. Thus, seeking God, His kingdom, and His righteousness means you are seeking intimacy with God, along with His infinite attributes, which includes submitting to being led daily by the Holy Spirit in all that you do in this fallen finite world. The Holy Spirit will lead you while spiritually transforming your soul as God's spiritual Kingdom servant. The Holy Spirit will anoint you, empower you, and show you the way out of your tribulations and idolatry of money. 1 Corinthians 10:12-14 says, "Wherefore let him that thinketh he standeth take heed lest he fall. (13) There hath no temptation (Greek peirasmos- adversities) taken you but such as is common to man: but God is faithful, who will not suffer you to be tempted above that ye are able; but will with the temptation also make a way to escape, that ye may be able to bear it. (14) Wherefore, my dearly beloved, flee from idolatry (of money)."

A similar passage is seen in James 1:2-10, which says, "My brethren, count it all joy when ye fall into divers temptations (Greek peirasmos- adversities); (3) Knowing this, that the trying of your faith worketh patience. (4) But let patience have her perfect work, that ye may be perfect and entire, wanting nothing. (5) If any of you lack wisdom, let him ask of God, that giveth to all men liberally, and upbraideth not; and it shall be given him. (6) But let him ask in faith, nothing wavering. For he that wavereth is like a wave of the sea driven with the wind and tossed. (7) For let not that man think that he shall receive any thing of the Lord. (8) A double minded man is unstable in all his ways. (9) Let the brother of low degree rejoice in that he is exalted: (10) But the rich (unbeliever), in that he is made low: because as the flower of the grass he shall pass away. (11) For the sun is no sooner risen with a burning heat, but it withereth the grass, and the flower thereof falleth, and the grace of the fashion of it perisheth: so also shall the rich (unbeliever) man fade away in his ways. (12) Blessed is the (Believer) man that endureth temptation: for when he is tried, he shall receive the crown of life, which the Lord hath promised to them that love Him. (13) Let no (Believer) man say when he is tempted, I am tempted of God: for God cannot be tempted with evil, neither tempteth He any man."

The scriptural passage of James 1:2-13 has essentially eight affirmations and truths: First, the Believer is given wisdom from God to act and speak wisely in the hour of trial or ad-

Personality Traits of Money

versity. Second, that his trials are merely the trying of his faith and not punishment by God the Father because God, as a good Father, will discipline him for his betterment of having patience and deferred gratification, but not destruction (Hebrews 12:5-10). Third, God will not respond to the Believer's doubt in God's desire and power to rescue him and spiritually transform his soul, as God hates double mindedness. Fourth, the Believer needs to be like Paul who was content during times of abasement and times of abounding (Philippians 4:12-13). Fifth, the Believer needs to rejoice because of his exhibiting humility because he has faith that God will exalt him in due season. Sixth, that the prideful rich unbeliever who sees money as his protection and life abundantly will die away in the hereafter in total abject poverty eternally because he will be punished at God's White Throne Judgment. Seven, if the Believer endures the adversity, he receives the Crown of Life, which is authority in God's new heaven and earth when the Lord returns to earth with the New Jerusalem, along with the saints from heaven, to rule and reign with the saints throughout eternity here on earth (Revelation chp 20; Daniel 7: 14, 27; Revelation 5:10). God wants you to be an overcomer, so He can bestow on you the Crown of Life. Eight, God never causes adversity or temptation in your life as He is a loving and good Father, and He wants to bless you from heaven. James 1:17 says, "Every good gift and every perfect gift is from above, and cometh down from the Father of lights, with whom is no variableness, neither shadow of turning."

The source of temptation or adversity that the Believer will experience in life has three sources- a). the adversities that come from the reaping of the bad seeds sown from his own problem with lust of the flesh, lust of the eyes, and pride of life, b). the world's adversities from the stimuli, false philosophies, and four-dimension limitations of the fallen world, and c). the demonic forces adversities from the kingdom of darkness. These three sources of adversity are subject to the laws of sowing and reaping. Galatians 6: 8-10 says, "For he that soweth to his flesh shall of the flesh reap corruption; but he that soweth to the Spirit shall of the Spirit reap life everlasting. (9) And let us not be weary in well doing: for in due season we shall reap, if we faint not. (10) As we have therefore opportunity, let us do good unto all men, especially unto them who are of the household of faith." 1 John 5:19 says, ". . . the whole world lieth in wickedness." James 4:7 says, "Submit yourselves therefore to God. Resist the devil, and he will flee from you."

God wants to bless you with money, but He does not want money to possess you. Psalms 84:11 says, "For the LORD God is a sun and shield: the LORD will give grace and glory: no good thing will he withhold from them that walk uprightly." The Believer's prayer is the request in Proverb 3:27, which says, "Withhold not good from them to whom it is due, when it is in the power of Thine hand to do it."

THE BELIEVER IS TO OWN AND POSSESS MATERIAL THINGS, BUT THE BELIEVER IS NOT TO LET MATERIAL THINGS HAVE UNDUE INFLUENCE OVER HIM.

The best example in the Bible of a person who allowed material possessions to have control of him was the "Rich Young Ruler" (Mark 10:17 31). Jesus said to the Rich Young Ruler in Mark 10:21: "One thing you lack: Go your way, sell whatever you have and give to the poor, and you will have treasure in heaven; and come, take up the cross, and follow me." Jesus gave the Rich Young Ruler a test which revealed that money was his idol, which violated the first commandment in Exodus 20:3. The Rich Young Ruler could not let go of his material riches to follow Jesus, not even for eternal life. There is no doubt that had the Rich Young Ruler given up his material things, Jesus would have returned to him assets of greater value because Proverbs 19:17 says, "He that hath pity upon the poor lendeth unto the LORD; and that which he hath given will He pay him again."

When the Rich Young Ruler is told by Jesus to divest himself of his riches and give them to the poor, it was not in order to help the poor but because the Rich Young Ruler's act of giving to the poor would release a spiritual freedom to give an abundance of love that ennobles the Rich Young Ruler with God's true riches in becoming a Believer with godly character and agape love for the Lord and other Believers.

The Jews saw riches as a sign of God's favor and never thought that riches or great income could be a hindrance to one's relationship with God. Believers received through Christ Jesus the Abrahamic blessing, which includes the wealth of a spiritual life and wealth in the physical world (Galatians 3:14).

Mark 10:24 says, "How hard it is for those who have riches to enter the kingdom of God." However, the Lord did not say it is impossible. Proverbs 11:28 says, "He who trusts in his riches will fall, but the righteous will flourish like foliage."

The problem is that money has a built in immediate positive reinforcement for whomever will serve the idol of mammon. Likewise, the more you serve the idol of mammon, the more money you receive in the short run but not in the long run. People think money is the ultimate thing to have, and this is why investors sell their real property, sell a third expensive car, sell their gold and silver investment, or sell anything else they consider valuable to obtain immediate money. They believe they can buy anything with money, so money is the best thing to have. There are those people who hoard hundreds of thousands of dollars in their safes at their residence just to feel secure and protected. Some businesspeople keep at least fifty thousand dollars in their personal possession just in case the money in their bank accounts are taken to satisfy a tax lien, frozen by a Court-ordered prejudgment injunction obtained by a business owner who is being sued by another business owner for breach of contract, or money taken by an ex-wife because the businessman is behind in child support or spousal support.

However, you can read Psalm 37 where the illumination and wisdom are that in the long run, the money idol will turn on the evil person. Also, in the long run the wealth of the wicked comes into the hands of the just (Proverb 13:22).

Personality Traits of Money

Dr. Nova Dean Pack

Using Money For The "Control Seeking Personality Trait Of Money"

Personality Traits of Money

CHAPTER FOUR

USING MONEY FOR THE "CONTROL SEEKING PERSONALITY TRAIT OF MONEY"

Main scripture reference: 1 Timothy 6:10 says, "For the love of money is a root of all kinds of evil, for which some have strayed from the faith in their greediness and pierced themselves through with many sorrows."

Firstly, the "Love of Money" means avarice for money to acquire safety, control, freedom, romanticism, magnetism, or any emotional or mental need fulfilled by money. In the principal reference verse of 1 Timothy 6:10, the word "love" in the phrase "For the love of money…." is the Greek word philargurio, which means here in this context, covetousness or avarice and comes from the root word philarguos, which means "fond of silver." However, both Greek words are rooted in the Greek word philarguria and embodies the English meaning of avarice or the "love of money." The English word avarice has the root word "avar" within it, which means blind. A person who is covetous of money is blind to the truth and blind to the snares that greed, covetousness, and avarice cause.

Secondly, the "Love of Money" also means the opposite of the "hate of money." The "love of money" means that money has become one's idol, trying to fulfill one's needs with money which rightfully can only be fulfilled by God.

THE CONTROL SEEKING PERSONALITY TRAIT OF MONEY IS EXPRESSED IN BUSINESSES, THINGS, AND PEOPLE

Some aggressive unbelievers have the obsessive-compulsive Control Seeking Personality Trait of Money that use their riches to offset their hidden feelings of humiliation, scorn, rejection, and weakness. These people are masters at overcoming problems and never let anyone or any event stop them on their quest.

Often, people with the obsessive-compulsive Control Seeking Personality Trait of Money are taught by their parents or other authority figures in their lives that any sign of emotions or caring is a sign of weakness. Therefore, most people with the Control Seeking Personality Trait of Money repress normal, positive loving feelings and are rather cold, calculating, superficial, manipulative, and mechanical in their interaction with others. However, if their money is threatened, they suddenly explode with outward manifestations of repressed rage, and they instantly plan their attack against the person threatening their position of power and threatening to divest them of their money.

People with the Control Seeking Personality Trait of Money often become Gang leaders, Industrial Giants, corporate CEO's, Presidents, Congressional Politicians, Supreme Court Justices, Judges, Lawyers, Pastors, Popes, and Heads of Bureaucracies. While in these professions or political offices, they expect their controlling power to bring them money, other than their salaries, through speaking engagements, through given knowledge of special investment opportunities, and through becoming well known or famous. So, they retire from the office and obtain a book publishing deal, or they are paid to speak on cable news programs because of their public prestige. People who seek these positions want recognition as someone who is important. The problem is if they believe they are members of the elitist class of society, they often cannot be used mightily by God because of their lack of humility.

The people who have the Control Seeking Personality Trait of Money have as the root cause of their disorder the feelings of helplessness or humiliation they experienced as a child. They become hungry for authority and power, so no one can put them in a helpless situation again. They will not allow exhibiting of any sign of weakness in themselves, as they believe that weakness invites bullying. Some people who have the Control Seeking Personality Trait of Money overcompensate for their fear of bullying by becoming a bully themselves.

To justify his actions, the person with the Control Seeking Personality Trait of Money sees the world as a war zone, very hostile, and operates under the rule of survival of the fittest.

The individual with the Control Seeking Personality Trait of Money is in some degree operating with a sick soul, which has developed into an obsessive-compulsive Personality Trait of Money where he is compelled to use the acquisition of money to gain power and authority over other people to stop them from rejecting him as a weak person. People with this Control Seeking Personality Trait of Money must always dominate over every relationship and every personal and business transaction. The false need to be in charge is to combat the fear of other people.

Many leaders with the Control Seeking Personality Trait of Money see money as giving them power to maintain control and to handle their life tribulations and relationships. They think and believe if they have enough money, they can cover up their fear of being abandoned, fear of being abused, or fear of being labeled a loser. Individuals with the obsessive-compulsive Control Seeking Personality Trait of Money want to win, win, win. Failure is not an option.

GOD GIVES POWER TO GET WEALTH
NOT THE POWER JUST TO SEEK MONEY

It is the Lord that gives people the power (control) to get wealth. Many businessmen and businesswomen who are Believers work hard, but for some reason the wealth, riches, and money they seek seem to be out of their grasp.

Again, Deuteronomy 8:18 says, "And you shall remember the Lord your God, for it is He who gives you power to get wealth, that He may establish His covenant which He swore to your fathers, as it is this day."

2 Chronicles 25:8 says, "But if you go, be gone! Be strong in battle! Even so, God shall make you fall before the enemy; for God has power (control) to help and to overthrow." You cannot fight your battles with your own control, alone. If you are served with a major lawsuit, it could cost hundreds of thousands of dollars in legal fees to defend you, and your money is depleted. Your spouse could file for a divorce because you sacrificed your marriage for the business, and you lose one-half of everything you have accumulated with your money, riches, or wealth accumulated. The family law allows your spouse, who never worked in your business or contributed toward your investments, to receive half of your business, half value of your real estate, half value of your pension you worked for 30 years, half value of your IRA

Personality Traits of Money

accounts, and half value of your entire financial worth.

Money will disappear fast if you use it to fight for control when someone else has the same Control Seeker Personality Trait of Money as well. Personally, I have seen clients who substituted out their current attorney in a lawsuit and retained me. One had already spent $150,000 in attorney fees because he told his attorney, "I don't care how much it cost, I am not going to pay that man one nickel." That was music to his old attorney's ears. He paid me $2,500 and I had the case settled for $12,000 with the Plaintiff who filed the lawsuit against him. He first came to me with the lawsuit, and I told him he could settle the case for under $20,000. When he came back to me, he said, "I should have listened to you and saved a lot of money." Of course, the other attorney made most all the money, as I saw from the file where the other attorney fought everything, filing demurrers, motions to strike, questionable discovery proceedings, motions to compel discovery, and Summary Judgement, where most all had little to do with the trial evidence since it never went to trial. The relevancy is that when one person with the Control Seeker Personality Trait of Money sues another person with the Control Seeker Personality Trait of Money, then both parties want to win for winning sake alone, regardless of the cost. This type of case is music to both lawyers because they are going to be paid very handsomely to fulfill their client's desire to win when money is no concern.

Thus, learn from the teachings in this book, especially if you are in business, and you may be able to avoid costly lawsuits. In truth, it is best not to do business with people who have the Control Seeker Personality Trait of Money, as they can cause you all kinds of stress.

Lawsuits can cost hundreds of thousands of dollars. If you have a business, you need to maintain a legal fund to be able to immediately retain an attorney, which you already know and perhaps have retained to be available, because a Civil Complaint must be answered within 20 to 30 days from the date of service. Also, you need an enrolled agent with the I.R.S. or a tax attorney if they event of notice of an audit. Never speak to the taxing authorities directly, but have your representative, who you have signed a Power of Attorney to represent you. Let us look at some famous people and the cost of their litigation, especially those who went through a divorce or dissolution of marriage.

Reportedly, Bill Gates's divorce in 2021 from Melinda Gates was the most expensive divorce with Melinda paid $76 billion. Jeff Bezos's divorce in 2019 from MacKenzie Bezos was the second most expensive divorce with MacKenzie Bezos receiving $38 billion. Since her divorce in 2019, to her credit MacKenzie Scott (taking back her maiden name) has donated nearly $16.6 billion to various charities, including $2.2 billion in 2023 alone. Despite this, MacKenzie Scott remains the fourth-richest woman in the world.

Also, women celebrities have had to pay tremendous sums of money to their spouses upon divorce. For example, Madonna was ordered to pay her ex-husband Guy Ritchie reportedly between $76 million and $96 million (although the two agreed to keep the amount private).

As a lawyer, I must ask a legal question, "Why did not Bill Gates and Jeff Bezos, and all the others, require a Prenuptial Agreement before marriage to their spouses?" As they say in the South, "Bless their little hearts." I sincerely hope they all find true love and come to the knowledge of truth by accepting Christ Jesus as Lord and Savior if they have not already done so. Yet, there is nothing unscriptural about taking legal steps to protect your family estate that you accumulated in your working years.

SCRIPTURES FOR FURTHER TEACHING: Let us allow scriptures to teach us about the heart, riches, the anointing, submission to the Lord, being strong in the Lord, having sound minds, spiritual warfare, and other points of interest regarding the topic at hand.

Psalms 52:5-7 says, "God shall likewise destroy thee forever, he shall take thee away, and pluck thee out of thy dwelling place, and root thee out of the land of the living. Selah. (6) The righteous also shall see, and fear, and shall laugh at him: (7) Lo, this is the man that made not God his strength; but trusted in the abundance of his riches, and strengthened himself in his wickedness."

Psalms 62:10-11 says, "Trust not in oppression, and become not vain in robbery: if riches increase, set not your heart upon them. God has spoken once, twice I have heard this: That power (control) belongs to God (not by man over other people)"

Proverbs 10:22 says, "The blessing of the LORD, it maketh rich, and he addeth no sorrow with it." Proverbs 11:28 says, "He that trusteth in his riches shall fall: but the righteous (in God) shall flourish as a branch."

Psalm 68:35 says, "O God, You are more awesome than Your holy places. The God of Israel is He who gives (good) strength and power to His people. Blessed be God!" This scripture, and the many more like it should be your affirmation to trust in the Lord for your wisdom, knowledge, and understanding. Proverbs 3:5 says, "Trust in the Lord with all thine heart; and lean not unto thine own understanding."

Zechariah 4:6 says, "So he answered and said to me: `This is the Word of the Lord to Zerubabbel: "Not by might nor by power, but by My Spirit," says the Lord of Hosts.""

The phrase, "not by might" in Zechariah 4:6, above, is interesting. The word "might" is the same Hebrew word as "wealth" in Deuteronomy 8:17. The Hebrew word is chayil. The word in Deuteronomy 8:17, as here, refers to the "power (control) of accumulated goods." Here, the Lord is saying that the Temple will not be rebuilt by the forces of an army or through the physical control of the labor, but by the craftsmen with the "spiritual power" of the Holy Spirit, along with their artistic gifts.

Ephesians 3:7 says, "Of which I became a minister according to the gift of the grace of God given to me by the effective working of His power." God's authority and power extended to you will be all you need to be an effective child of God, an effective husband and father, an effective person in business, and an effective minister in your calling. Submitting to the Holy Spirit for His guidance and allowing Him to use His power in each situation builds your character along with your wealth. "For we know that all things work together for good for them that love God, to them that are the called according to His purpose" (Romans 8:28).

Ephesians 6:10 12 says, "Finally, my brethren, be strong in the Lord and in the power of His might (and not just the control of your own personality disorder). Put on the whole armor of God, that you may be able to stand against the wiles of the devil. For we do not wrestle against flesh and blood, but against principalities, against powers, against the rules of the darkness of this age, against spiritual hosts of wickedness in the heavenly places."

2 Timothy 1:7 says, "For God has not given us a spirit of fear, but of power and of love and of a sound mind." Having power or control shall not cause you to neglect being a loving person. Having control does not necessarily mean you have to have an unsound mind. It is when you cannot act unless you have obsessive-compulsive control over everything in a business, transactions, or church congregations. Yes, Pastors can have the Control Seeking Personality Trait, the same as any other person, but they should pray that God transforms their souls to rid of such soulish disorders.

THE CONTROL PERSONALITY TRAIT OF MONEY IS SEEN IN THE "MANIPULATOR PERSONALITY TRAIT."

The classic example of a person with the Manipulator Personality Trait in the Bible is seen in Jacob, the son of Isaac, the grandson of Abraham. The "birthright" meant "head of the family" who had a double share of the inheritance from his father because the first born had the obligation to finish what God called his father to do and what God is calling him to do for Israel and the Kingdom of God (Deuteronomy 21:17).

Although Esau was the firstborn of Isaac's twins, they were the same age, and Jacob had hold of Esau's heel during birth. Yet, Esau was considered the first born and was destined to receive the firstborn blessing of a double portion as his inheritance from Isaac. Genesis 25:26 says, "And after that came his brother out, and his hand took hold on Esau's heel; and his name was called Jacob: and Isaac was threescore years old when she bare them."

Esau had a lust for that which was immediate gratification at any cost. Jacob had the Manipulator Personality Trait and took advantage of Esau's weakness and tricked Esau to sell his birthright to Jacob for bread and bowl of pottage lentil soup. Genesis 25:31-34 says, "And Jacob said, 'Sell me this day thy birthright.' (32) And Esau said, 'Behold, I am at the point to die: and what profit shall this birthright do to me?' (33) And Jacob said, 'Swear to me this day;' and he sware unto him; and he sold his birthright unto Jacob. (34) Then Jacob gave Esau bread and pottage of lentils; and he did eat and drink, and rose up, and went his way: thus Esau despised his birthright."

Likewise, Jacob fraudulently manipulated Isaac, his father, into giving him the family's firstborn blessing. This meant that Jacob was fraudulently being transferred through the family blessing the bulk of the family's material property, aspirations, and the beneficiary of the covenant spiritual and material wealth promised by God. Again, under Hebrew law, the eldest son received double because he had the obligation to finish his father's work with half of his inheritance. Jacob even used God to further his selfish ambitions and took advantage of his own father's blindness to get his spiritual family blessing (Genesis 27:1-29). One of the marvelous changes of a man in the Bible came in the example when Jacob wrestled with the Pre-Incarnate Christ or Angel of the Lord, at Mount Peniel, and he received a special blessing. His name was changed from Jacob to Israel, which means "Prince of God" (Genesis 32: 22-30).

Since we are the body of Jesus' humanity nature, and since Jesus' humanity nature has the Firstborn blessing from God the Father, then as the body of Christ, Believers share the firstborn blessing of Christ since Believers are joint heirs with Him. Romans 8:17 says, "And if children, then heirs; heirs of God, and joint-heirs with Christ; if so be that we suffer with Him, that we may be also glorified together." Joint heirs with Christ mean we share in His heirship from God the Father.

What does joint-heirs mean? In the American Standard Version 1 Peter 3:7 says, "Ye husbands, in like manner, dwell with your wives according to knowledge, giving honor unto the woman, as unto the weaker vessel, as being also joint-heirs of the grace of life; to the end that your prayers be not hindered." Husbands and wives are entitled as joint-heirs to eternal life and will rule and reign jointly with Christ (Daniel 7:27; 2 Timothy 2:12; Revelation 5:10).

Colossians 1:18 says, "And He is the head of the body, the church: who is the beginning, the Firstborn from the dead; that in all things He might have the preeminence." Ephesians 1:20-23 says, "Which he wrought in Christ, when He raised Him from the dead, and set Him at His own right hand in the heavenly places, (21) Far above all principality, and power, and might, and dominion, and every name that is named, not only in this world, but also in that which is to come: (22) And hath put all things under His feet, and gave Him to be the Head over all things to the church (Ekklesia, kingdom assembly and kingdom army), (23) Which is His body, the fulness of Him that filleth all in all."

Finally, Matthew 28:18-20 says, "And Jesus came and spake unto them, saying, 'All power (authority) is given unto Me in heaven and in earth. (19) Go ye therefore, and teach (make disciples of) all nations, baptizing them in the name of the Father, and of the Son, and of the Holy Ghost: (20) Teaching them to observe all things whatsoever I have commanded you: and, lo, I am with you always, even unto the end of the world.'" Thus, Jesus shares His authority with Believers as His body and His disciples and Ekklesia, which is His Kingdom assembly and Kingdom army.

Although Jacob had his soul changed after he wrestled with the Angel of the Lord, there was a book written about a classic person with the Manipulator Personality Trait as described in the book titled, The Prince, by Nicolo Machiavelli, who acquired money to gain Political Control, and Political Control to get more money, to in turn get more money to get more Political Control, and so on.

The person with the Manipulator Personality Trait normally will only participate in situations where almost all the risks of failure have been eliminated. Although the person with the Manipulator Personality Trait appears to win in a competitive contest in business, he often has exploited many people and situations to gain an advantage. The people with the Manipulator Personality Trait will not play fair or by any rules.

The individual with the Manipulator Personality Trait believes he is not bound by any moral principles of behavioral restraint. Therefore, the person with the Manipulator Personality Trait is generally an unprincipled person.

When the person with the Manipulator Personality Trait receives salvation, he often brings with him this tendency of manipulation in the church fellowship because, although he is born again, his soul needs transformation and sanctification like everyone else. While the person with the Manipulator Personality Trait's soul is being transformed and sanctified in a

Personality Traits of Money

Christian fellowship, he can harm others in the fellowship; so, he needs to be in counseling and warned that any manipulative practices by him will not be tolerated. He must agree not to do any business or investment transactions with members of the local Church to which he belongs. If he violates this admonition, he should be warned but must repent.

Yet, if the person with the Manipulator Personality Trait continues soliciting people for money to put in an investment, then he must leave the congregation for a season. The Pastor should have lunches, personal Bible studies, and prayer time with him weekly for his recovery and transformation until he can be trusted not to solicit anyone in the congregation again. Galatians 6:1 says, "Brethren, if a man be overtaken in a fault, ye which are spiritual, restore such a one in the spirit of meekness; considering thyself, lest thou also be tempted. (2) Bear ye one another's burdens, and so fulfill the law of Christ."

The classic manipulation scheme perpetrated by Satan was done in the Garden of Eden when Satan deceived Eve to start the downfall of mankind by Adam and Eve's sins, so Satan could obtain their delegated possessory authority over the world and all animals, fish, birds, and vegetation (Genesis 3:1 14).

The person with the Manipulator Personality Trait is generally a fast thinker and talker who uses affinity of being of the same faith or other persuasion, exaggerated investment returns, flattery, get rich quick promises, letting someone have a responsible but inferior position to control him, and a host of other methods that brings the unsuspecting person under his control. The classic case in business or politics is inviting your chief opponent to be your Vice President.

The individual with the Manipulator Personality Trait will normally make his sales appeal to one's emotions, with ego enhancement words directed to the buyer.

For example, there is a technique of how a salesperson tells a customer that the customer cannot afford a particular product; and the customer gets insulted and buys the most expensive item just to prove to the salesman that the customer can afford it. This is a form of manipulation through attacking the customer's pride.

A person who suffers from an obsessive Manipulator Personality Trait often suffers from somewhat of a seared conscious and usually does not suffer guilt from making broken promises or conducting his manipulative practices.

Although once saved, an individual with the Manipulator Personality Trait is converted with a born again spirit, his mind, emotions, and heart in his soul was not born again and has to be transformed. The conviction of the Holy Spirit may bring remorse for bad manipulative behavior but not repentance, and the person with the Manipulator Personality Trait may not understand the difference. It may take years of counseling, reeducating, and confronting this behavior disorder before the manipulative habits are under control and the negative personality disorder is healed.

The person with the Manipulator Personality Trait may not think it wrong even after becoming a Christian to misrepresent his abilities in business or the quality of his product, to play off one person against another in Church politics; or to take advantage of loopholes in the law to gain more recognition, authority, or a quick result.

The individual with the Manipulator Personality Trait sees people as only winners or losers. Therefore, all their efforts, times, money, and energy are used to remain on top as the main winner, the most victorious, and the top man or woman. They must win at any cost, and often violate good morals and hurt other people.

The person with the Manipulator Personality Trait has a problem with servanthood and must be the boss where he or she can order others to act or work in executing his or her schemes, causing only his or her business to prosper, and is basically not interested in activating others in his or her business or ministry, as he or she sees them as potential competitors.

Normally, those with the Manipulator Personality Trait suffer from an exaggerated need to be recognized as winners and to feel superior over others to offset an underlying feeling of inferiority.

By and large, those who suffer with the Manipulator Personality Trait are rebels by nature and are teachable only to the point of not allowing anyone to touch their dysfunctional need to be in control. People with the Manipulator Personality Trait are trying to live up to the image of what their father or mother thought was successful. Routinely, the needs of the child that developed the Manipulator Personality Trait were rarely considered by his parents when he was young.

Typically, the individual with the Manipulator Personality Trait usually does not like practicing delayed gratification and usually does not finish college. He generally suffers from the need of immediate "impulse gratification" because as a child his rewards were given immediately or just forgotten. He was never trained to be patient, to work hard, or to trust in other people. In fact, the person with the Manipulator Personality Trait is often critical of others, from which he must be counseled and have his soul spiritually renewed by humbly submitting to the transforming work of the Godhead who lives in him as God's temple.

Controlling others like puppets gives the person with the Manipulator Personality Trait the feeling of importance by comparison. Also, his manipulative practices are a way to get even, seeking revenge for all the times he himself had been manipulated by others in the past.

The unsaved individual in the world with the Manipulator Personality Trait believes that other people whose emotional needs can be manipulated and used for control are weak and dumb and deserve to be watched over, told what to do, and need to become disciples of this fallen world in the rigors of his perception of a dog-eat-dog business realm. The unsaved individual with the obsessive-compulsive Manipulator Personality Trait sees people as mere puppets to be exploited.

Even after initial salvation, Believers still should submit to God to have their souls transformed to get the dog-eat-dog business world, its rules for existence, and work habits out of their minds, emotions, and hearts. Even after initial salvation, Believers suffering with the Manipulator Personality Trait enjoy living exciting lives and enjoy mingling with the top echelon of business and church leadership. However, rank-and-file relationships are usually strong initially, but dwindled rather quickly by him who has the Manipulator Personality

Personality Traits of Money

Trait. It is often the case that spouses and close friends suffer repeated indignities by those with the Manipulator Personality Trait yet remain loyal companions because the person with the Manipulator Personality Trait always seems to be a winner.

Loss of integrity, loss of meaningful relationships, and being manipulated by another person with the Manipulator Personality Trait are normally the downfalls of those suffering from this malady. Also, the individual with the Manipulator Personality Trait suffers from increased loneliness as he gets older as his distrust of people gets stronger and his relationships get fewer.

THE CONTROL PERSONALITY TRAIT OF MONEY IS EVIDENT IN THE "TYCOON PERSONALITY TRAIT"

While those with the Manipulator Personality Trait try to avoid hard labor by looking for shortcuts to wealth, the Tycoon Personality Trait are willing to work hard, are overly ambitious, and are very aggressive in negotiations and asset acquisitions.

Those that suffer with the Tycoon Personality Trait are very self-reliant, overly confident, and very independent in their decision-making practices. They fit the mode as over achievers and fit the definition as someone who is successful in the world.

Child abandonment, divorce, or death of parents are characteristic backgrounds of those with the Tycoon Personality Trait. The child learns self-reliance at an early age, and there are a few people who develop extreme self-reliance as the Tycoon Personality Trait.

The person with the Tycoon Personality Trait often develops an overestimation of his self-worth. Money is the standard by which he calculates his worth. Look at the billionaires in America and elsewhere in the world, and you can see the Tycoon Personality Trait in operation in the way they act and their self-worth.

Some with the Tycoon Personality Trait adhere to the Protestant work ethic and find Christianity's principle of hard work and the principle of prosperity as a blessing from God and very attractive ideas worth having as part of the foundations of their beliefs in their hearts.

Henry Ford, Frank Woolworth, Andrew Carnegie, John D. Rockefeller, and Cornelius Vanderbilt are some of the more recognizable great industrialists having the Tycoon Personality Trait in our American Industrial Revolution History. There are thousands of lesser people with the Tycoon Personality Trait who follow a similar pattern of behavior but do not obtain great wealth.

The person with the Tycoon Personality Trait fits well in American Society, for many of his qualities seem to have Christian virtue and American acceptance. The person with the Tycoon Personality Trait is always a leader, since for him following another is considered a weakness.

Those who exhibit the Tycoon Personality Trait are often very opinionated and dogmatic. They dislike having their decisions questioned and often display unhealthy tempers. The "Daddy Warbucks" in the comic strip or movie "Annie" is a typical character. This is not to say that the person with the Tycoon Personality Trait is evil, just controlling. Yet, without the businesspersons with the Tycoon Personality Trait, the U.S. would not have reached the financial stature with the greatest capitalist economy and its lead currency status.

Today, those who have the Tycoon Personality Trait would be persons like President Donald Trump, who is a large real estate holder throughout the world. Also, Nate Paul who is a 31 Year Old Texas Financial Tycoon with building a real estate empire and others that follow in this discussion.

California native Donald Bren is the wealthiest real estate baron in America, with an estimated net worth of nearly $17 billion, according to Bloomberg's Billionaires Index, including Bren's privately held real estate investment, Irvine Company, Orange County, is the largest landowner in California. Irvine Co.'s portfolio of properties exceeds 110 million square feet and includes office buildings, apartments, marinas, and hotels, most of which are in picturesque Orange County [Bren owns about 20% of Orange County, California.] Bren also has a footprint in Trump's native New York City as the majority owner of the New York Met Life building. Often these men's personal lives are difficult. For example, Bren has five children from three marriages and one courtship. [Sources: ABC News, Los Angeles Times; The Orange County Register]. These men tend to be big givers. For example, most of Bren's public persona revolves around his philanthropic endeavors, and his lifetime giving exceeds $1.3 billion. [Source: The Orange County Register]

Jeffrey Preston Bezos Jorgensen also is a very brilliant man who exhibits the Tycoon Personality Trait who was the founder, executive chairman, and former president and CEO of Amazon, which is the world's largest e-commerce and cloud computing company. He is now the second riches tycoon in the world, with a net worth of about US$205 billion as of April 5, 2024. He was also the riches tycoon from 2017 to 2021, based upon the reports of the Bloomberg Billionaires Index and Forbes. Bezos also founded the aerospace manufacturer and sub-orbital spaceflight services company "Blue Origin" in 2000. Blue Origin's New Shepard vehicle reached space in 2015 and afterwards successfully landed back on Earth; he flew into space on Blue Origin NS-16 in 2021. He also purchased the major American newspaper The Washington Post in 2013 for $250 million and manages many other investments through his venture capital firm, Bezos Expeditions. With his Tycoon Personality Trait Bezos uses his personal strength and control over his empire that keeps growing through the expenditures of large sums of money, business acumen, real property investments, banking resources, and very loyal smart people. However, Bezos has created an economic model that becomes a river of income and profits. He has the largest yacht in the world, and he spent billions to launch spacecrafts for just a short time just for the experience. With all his money, riches, and wealth, he still pays his employees that do the labor in all his warehouses of storing, packaging, and shipping to customers a little over minimum wage, which is wrong.

Colossians 4:1 says, "Masters (employers), give unto your servants (employees) that which is just and equal; knowing that ye also have a Master in heaven."

Another person who seems to have some of the Tycoon Personality Trait is Elon Reeve Musk, born June 28, 1971, in a somewhat wealthy family in South Africa. Wikipedia says that Elon Musk is a businessman and investor. He is the founder, chairman, CEO, and CTO of Space X; Angel Investor, CEO, product architect, and former chairman of Tesla, Inc. that

Personality Traits of Money

has created saleable and popular electric cars; owner, executive chairman, and CTO of X Corp.; founder of the Boring Company and xAI; co-founder of Neuralink and OpenAI; and president of the Musk Foundation, a non-profit organization. He has an estimated net worth of US$190 billion as of March 2024, according to the Bloomberg Billionaires Index, and $195 billion according to Forbes, primarily from his ownership stakes in Tesla and SpaceX. Reading his biography, Elon Musk, by Walter Isaacson is one of the best books about a man with the Tycoon Personality Trait. Musk had a tough life as a child, was beaten by bullies in school, but he isolated himself and read many, many books to educate himself and became far greater than those who bullied him. Without doubt, Musk is a genius innovator with a mind that never stops. He wants to colonize Mars because he fears that mankind will destroy the earth instead of taking care of it. He bought twitter partly because he wanted to keep the FBI from using twitter to silence those who have a conservative voice, such as Tucker Carlson, Alex Jones, and many radical others that people think that these people have something worthwhile to say.

Some of these people who have the Tycoon Personality Trait see and treat employees like military army personnel of different ranks, who are ordered to go forth with weapons of financial warfare to bring back the spoils of the business war. These Tycoons see the business environment as potential financial kingdoms to conquer.

For example, President Donald Trump, along with journalist Tony Schwartz, authored a best-selling book, titled The Art of the Deal, published in 1987 by Howard Kaminsky of Hachette. Donald Trump said in his book there were eleven things you must do to be successful: 1)Think big, 2) protect the downside and the upside will take care of itself, 3) maximize your options, 4) know your market, 5) use your leverage, 6) enhance your location,7) get the word out, 8) fight back, 9) deliver the goods, 10) contain the costs, and 11) have fun. His book reached the number one best seller in Mainland China.

The personality profile of the person with the Tycoon Personality Trait is the compulsive desire to overcome feelings of weakness, never allowing himself to be vulnerable to or dominated by others.

The people with the Tycoon Personality Trait characteristically have an unhealthy need not to be dependent on others, as they have a fear of being used make them cause others to be dependent on them. Loyalty to the person with the Tycoon Personality Trait is a commanded attribute that he expects from his employees and subordinates.

The individual with the Tycoon Personality Trait can be found in government bureaucracies, and his authority and power are based upon the number of employees he or she, as the department head, has under his or her control.

In Church government and denominational politics, generally the Pastor with the Tycoon Personality Trait measures success by the size and material riches of the church organization, size of the building, number of countries in which he has preached, and the number of other ministers who seek his advice concerning how to have a big Church like him. His emphasis is not solely hearing from or being obedient to God that motivates him, but how he is rated among other peers in the same Church denomination or non-denomination.

Dr. Nova Dean Pack

There is a special problem in America with professionals trying to counsel these people with the Tycoon Personality Trait. Much of why America is such a wealthy nation with its high per capita standard of living is because these people who have the Tycoon Personality Trait seem as American as apple pie.

Abraham Lincoln was born in a log cabin, lost almost every election, but finally became one of the greatest U.S. Presidents of this nation because he had this Tycoon Personality Trait. Without question, President Lincoln put the whole northern states under Marshal Law because the country was in a state of Civil War. With Marshal Law, the authority and control of President Lincoln was like a King.

Regarding President Lincoln's Christian faith, Wikipedia states: "Abraham Lincoln grew up in a highly religious Baptist family. He never joined any Church, and was a skeptic as a young man and sometimes ridiculed revivalists. He frequently referred to God and had a deep knowledge of the Bible, often quoting it. Lincoln attended Protestant church services with his wife and children. 'Especially after the death of his young son Willie in 1862, Lincoln moved away from his earlier religious skepticism.' Some argue that Lincoln was neither a Christian believer nor a secular freethinker. Although Lincoln never made an unambiguous public profession of Christian belief, several people who knew him personally, such as Chaplain of the Senate Phineas Gurley and Mary Todd Lincoln, claimed that he believed in Christ in the religious sense."

There can be somewhat of a negative, unhealthy side to those people with the Tycoon Personality Trait. They have a demanding lifestyle, a workload and driving demands of himself or herself and others working or living with him or her, that usually make for poor marriages and family relationships. The person with the Tycoon Personality Trait often will try to order his family around as he does his employees. "Don't walk in front of the T.V." "Children, clean your rooms." "Children, do your homework now." "Who took my newspaper?" "Children, I told you to make good grades, so why do you have this 'C' in your math class?" "Why can't dinner be ready at 5:30 sharp?" "Why can't you be ready to go to church on time?"

The person who has the Tycoon Personality Trait is sometimes, but not always, a tyrant to the whole family and expects the whole family to share with, be excited about, and center the family activities around supporting and working to fulfill his financial empire dreams and goals. Unfortunately, if the person who has the Tycoon Personality Trait has children, the children normally are somewhat dysfunctional. The children either put abnormal expectations on their own spouses and children based upon learned behavior, or the children become dropouts who reject everything for which the person with the Tycoon Personality Trait has as the foundation of his beliefs and goals. Sometimes, the children also develop this Tycoon Personality Trait themselves, and the family wealth continues to grow, such as in the case of Donald Trump's children.

Like those with the obsessive-compulsive Manipulator Personality Trait, those with the obsessive-compulsive Tycoon Personality Trait often never learn how to build lasting friendships and are often lonely as they become older. On the other hand, if those children who have this Tycoon Personality Trait work side by side with their father, then a family financial dynasty occurs; and the wealth is passed down generation after generations like the Rothschild family or Rockefeller family.

Personality Traits of Money

According to Wikipedia, "During the 19th century, the Rothschild family possessed the largest private fortune in the world, as well as in modern world history. The family's wealth declined over the 20th century and was divided among many descendants. Today, their interests cover a diverse range of fields, including financial services, real estate, mining, energy, agriculture, wine-making, and nonprofits." The Rothschild family dynasty historically has been known to be part owner or control of Central Banks of European countries and elsewhere.

According to Wikipedia, "John Davison Rockefeller Sr. (July 8, 1839 – May 23, 1937) was an American business magnate and philanthropist. He was one of the wealthiest Americans of all time and one of the richest people in modern history. Rockefeller was born into a large family in Upstate New York who moved several times before eventually settling in Cleveland, Ohio. He became an assistant bookkeeper at age 16 and went into several business partnerships beginning at age 20, concentrating his business on oil refining. Rockefeller founded the Standard Oil Company in 1870. He ran it until 1897 and remained its largest shareholder. In his retirement, he focused his energy and wealth on philanthropy, especially regarding education, medicine, higher education, and modernizing the American South. . . Rockefeller spent much of the last 40 years of his life in retirement at Kykuit, his estate in Westchester County, New York, defining the structure of modern philanthropy, along with other key industrialists such as Andrew Carnegie... Rockefeller was the founder of the University of Chicago and Rockefeller University, and funded the establishment of Central Philippine University in the Philippines. He was a devout Northern Baptist and supported many church-based institutions. He adhered to total abstinence from alcohol and tobacco throughout his life. For advice, he relied closely on his wife, Laura Spelman Rockefeller: they had four daughters and a son together. He was a faithful congregant of the Erie Street Baptist Mission Church, taught Sunday school, and served as a trustee, clerk, and occasional janitor. Religion was a guiding force throughout his life, and he believed it to be the source of his success. Rockefeller was also considered a supporter of capitalism based on a perspective of social Darwinism, and he was quoted often as saying, 'The growth of a large business is merely a survival of the fittest.'"

Rockefeller tried to marginalize his Tycoon Personality Trait by his faith in Christ Jesus, but he tried, whether successful or not, to be a godly man. Yet, he had a pull with his Tycoon Personality Trait with a belief in financial Darwinism where he believed that wealth acquisition is a result of the survival of the fittest. On the other hand, one can also see Rockefeller's extensive philanthropy. Thus, one can conclude that Rockefeller most likely was saved as a Christian based upon the history of his church attendance and large philanthropy foundation contributions to America and around the world.

One of the key soulish disorders of the person with the Tycoon Personality Trait is a subconscious desire to isolate himself from a self-perceived hostile, competitive, and unfriendly world. The world is viewed as a battleground, and the person with the Tycoon Personality Trait categorizes people as either enemies or allies. The person with the Tycoon Personality Trait often visualizes his ultimate residence as an isolated spot in a large castle like a mansion surrounded by acres of lawn or wooded areas with an eight-to-ten-foot protective wall and gates, with lots of modern security, along with armed guards. On the other hand, he may live in the city in a high tower that is totally secure. An exception is President Donald Trump who has an extraverted personality, and he enjoys the public life and running for President, but this characteristic is rare of those with the Tycoon Personality Trait.

The classic historical person with the Tycoon Personality Trait who sought isolation from the harsh world was Howard Hughes. Hughes was a billionaire hermit who apparently had a germ phobia, and he took great lengths to avoid any contact with germs. Towards the end of his life, rumor has it that he lay naked in bed in darkened hotel rooms, which were constantly cleaned to insure a germ-free environment. He wore tissue boxes on his feet to protect them. If someone around him became ill, he would burn his clothes. [American Psychological Association, July/August 2005, Vol 36, No. 7, print version page 102]

Matthew 16:24 26 says, "Then Jesus said to His disciples, 'If anyone desires to come after Me, let him deny himself, and take up his cross, and follow Me. For whoever desires to save his life will lose it, but whoever loses his life for My sake will find it. For what profit is it to a man if he gains the whole world, and loses his own soul? Or what will a man give in exchange for his soul? For the Son of Man will come in the glory of His Father with His angels, and then He will reward each according to his works."

Pastors with the Tycoon Personality Trait in churches who become leaders often work on creating followers rather than leaders and are good at persuading volunteers to work hard and to recruit other followers, but do not activate leaders under Ephesians 4:11-12, to equip the Believers for their Vocational work as God's kings, priests (Revelation 1:6), lords (2 Timothy 6:15), ambassadors (2 Corinthians 5:20), and soldiers (2 Timothy 2:3-4). Also, they do not train leaders under the guidelines of 2 Timothy 2:2, which is to teach others to become teachers to make mature disciples, who become teachers and so on.

Often, the American modern Church Pastor with the Tycoon Personality Trait distrusts any people meeting together outside of his supervision and control for fear that another potential person with a similar Tycoon Personality Trait will cause a church split. Regardless, the Church Pastor is mandated to discern and make leaders (not just followers). Every Believer has the same Kingdom Vocation, but each Believer has diversified gifts of the Godhead. The gifts of Father God are delineated in Romans 12:6-8. The gifts of God the Word are listed in Ephesians 4:11. The gifts of the Holy Spirit are 1 Corinthians 12:8-10. All these gifts of God the Father, God the Word, and God the Holy Spirit are for to serve others. Every Believer is to exhibit the fruit of the Spirit, which is love, joy, peace, longsuffering, gentleness, goodness, faith, meekness, and self-control (Galatians 5:22-23). A Believer's heart in his soul is required to grow these spiritual fruit trees that yield spiritual fruit for others. No spiritual fruit tree eats its own spiritual fruit; it is for other people.

Making disciples mean for the Pastor to make leaders, not just followers, that can be sent out into the marketplace, ordained as functioning apostles, prophets, evangelists, pastors, and teachers in businesses, and to send Believers into the local community as to fifty percent, and the other fifty percent into the counties, states, nations, and the uttermost parts of the world (Acts 1:8). The messages preached for initial salvation is both the gospel of the Kingdom (Matthew 24:14) and the repentance and remission of sins (Luke 24:47) because Believers must be born again to see the Kingdom of God and born of the water and the spirit to enter the Kingdom of God (John 3: 3,5).

Personality Traits of Money

THE CONTROL PERSONALITY TRAIT OF MONEY IS MANIFESTED IN THE "ROYAL BEE PERSONALITY TRAIT"

The man or woman with the Royal Bee Personality Trait always wants to control people, often through their conditional benevolent giving.

President Theodore (Teddy) Roosevelt exhibited the Royal Bee Personality Trait, with his boisterous personality, like President Donald Trump. People loved him or hated him. President Teddy Roosevelt said, "Speak softly and carry a big stick." This was in furtherance of the sphere of influence of the benevolent overseer Uncle Sam under the "Monroe Doctrine." In the foreign policy arena, Roosevelt won a Nobel Peace Prize for his successful negotiations and treaty to end the Russo-Japanese War. He also led the successful negotiations for the construction on the Panama Canal. After leaving the White House and going on safari in Africa, he returned to politics in 1912, mounting a failed run for president at the head of a new Progressive Party. However, on October 14, 1912, Roosevelt was on the campaign trail in Milwaukee, Wisconsin, when an assailant, named John Shrank shot former President Roosevelt in the chest. Roosevelt was not killed but went on stage to give his speech. The astonished audience, hearing the gun shot, were shocked and gasped as Roosevelt unbuttoned his vest to reveal his bloodstained shirt. He exclaimed, 'It takes more than that to kill a bull moose.' The wounded candidate assured them. He pulled out of his coat pocket a 50-page campaign speech with a bullet hole in it. Roosevelt continued. "Fortunately, I had my manuscript, so you see I was going to make a long speech, and there is a bullet—there is where the bullet went through—and it probably saved me from it going into my heart. The bullet is in me now, so I cannot make a very long speech, but I will try my best."

President Roosevelt, a Republican, embodied the Royal Bee Personality Trait. He was tough; he took charge, and he got things done. Roosevelt was born in a wealthy family, so he always lived with wealth. After President McKinley was shot and killed, Vice President Roosevelt took office, and he was challenged to deal with the bitter struggle with corporate employers and rank-in-file labor. President Roosevelt saw the equities and inequities on both sides of the struggle between business owners and the laborers. Although President Roosevelt saw that the Great Industrialists, massing outrageous fortunes through capitalism and deserved credit in their contributions of twentieth-century United States rising to an international prestige, he also concluded that labor in the United States were not given a square deal in wages, benefits, and working hours. Violence resulted, so Roosevelt used his presidential powers and persuasion to allow unions to develop. Roosevelt had a forceful and decisive relationship with business owners, laborers, financiers, and he persuaded Congress to pass laws to reform management and labor relationships.

To go after the giant corporate monopolies treating labor badly, and financially hurting competition by smaller companies, Republican President Roosevelt's used the Sherman Anti-Trust Act, which was sponsored by Sen. John Sherman (R-Ohio), and which was passed by Congress in 1890 and signed into law by Roosevelt's predecessor in office, Republican President William McKinley. The Republican-sponsored Sherman Anti-Trust Act was the first time Congress had passed a law aimed at prohibiting trusts and stopping monopolies where the super wealth generated went into the pockets of wealthy family trusts. Roosevelt caused Sherman Anti-Trust lawsuits filed by Roosevelt's Justice Department. President Roosevelt's administration sued J.P. Morgan's Northern Securities Co., a railroad conglomerate and the Federal Government successfully won the suit before the U.S. Supreme Court, and in a 5-4 decision, the Court ordered J.P. Morgan's Northern Securities Co. to be dissolved.

In 1911 the Supreme Court decided that Rockefeller's Standard oil was an illegal monopoly in violation of the Sherman Anti-Trust Act. Standard Oil was broken up into 34 different corporations, and many of these companies made Rockefeller's wealth grow even faster. These companies later became part of the Seven Sisters, who went into global petroleum production and became most of today's largest publicly traded investor-owned oil companies.

President Teddy Roosevelt also was a very resolute conservationist, setting aside two hundred million acres for national forests, reserves, and wildlife refuges during his presidency. As a Conservative, President Roosevelt believed that Conservatives should be the leaders in conservationism. At the same time, President Roosevelt was an enthusiast in hunting as a sport.

THE CONTROL PRACTICES OF THE ROYAL BEE PERSONALITY TRAIT

On a smaller scale, the individual with the Royal Bee Personality Trait uses financial rewards and punishments to control people. When a person does what the individual with the Royal Bee Personality Trait wants, the person is rewarded financially. When a person rebels, they are disciplined financially, such as cutting off allowances, taking the person out of a will, taking away the use of a car, or taking away charge cards.

The person with the Royal Bee Personality Trait often tries to play God, even though they may be conscious of the trespass of God's jurisdictional authority and kingdom rule. The person with the Royal Bee Personality Trait giveth and the taketh away based upon a reward and discipline system.

If her children or grandchildren obtain A's, they are financially rewarded by the individual with the Royal Bee Personality Trait. If the children misbehave, their allowance is taken away. Rewards and discipline are done with money. The employer Royal Bee Personality Trait likewise gives bonuses and pay raises much the same way. The employer with the Royal Bee Personality Trait pays money based upon obedience, not merit.

The church Pastor with the Royal Bee Personality Trait often will reward obedience and discipline disobedience by giving and taking away recognition of people and opportunity to minister in the church, or by allowing or disallowing someone to minister based on their obedience or disobedience. If the person with the Royal Bee Personality Trait is not the Pastor, she or he will try to control the Pastor, including the contents of his sermons, the programs, the size of the church, those in leadership, etc. by rewarding obedient behavior by the Pastor with large contributions or withholding contributions for her or his disapproval.

If the individual with the Royal Bee Personality Trait often is complaining about something, always wanting something done differently, and generally wanting people to appease her every complaint.

Personality Traits of Money

A classic Royal Bee Personality Trait character was Ms. Polly Harrington, played by Jane Wyman, who was the unmarried aunt whose family owned the town in the Disney Movie titled "Pollyanna," played by Haley Mills. The movie was set in 1910 historical period. Several scenes were shown where Ms. Harrington had the whole town under her control because most of the buildings where town folk businesses were operated were owned by Polly Harrington. Ms. Harrington was the biggest tither and giver to the Pastor in the town Church, so she felt she had the right to give the preacher the Scriptures to preach his hell, fire, and brimstone sermons to the town's people. Pollyanna's faithful and "happy thoughts" lifestyle changed the whole community, and she had a profound effect on her aunt, Ms. Harrington. The Preacher started listening to Pollyanna instead of Ms. Harrington who had the Royal Bee Personality Trait complex. In the end, Pollyanna changed the attitude of her aunt, who grew to love her. The whole town was changed by one person who saw God as the embodiment of love and goodness. 1 John 4:16 says, "And we have known and believed the love that God hath to us. God is love; and he that dwelleth in love dwelleth in God, and God in him."

Also, another movie which had the classic Royal Bee Personality Trait was Scarlett O'Hara in Gone with the Wind. Scarlet was played by a young actress, named Vivien Leigh, who was virtually unknown in the U.S. When the movie begins, Scarlett O'Hara is a teenager coming of age to find a man to marry. At age 16, her parents thought it was time for Scarlet to come out as a single woman desiring to marry; so, Scarlet surreptitiously presented herself as a delightful Southern Bell young woman, who was ready to be a submissive wife of any Southern wealthy man. Yet, Scarlet is vain, bossy, self-centered, and harshly orders servants. Scarlet has been spoiled by her wealthy parents. At the same time, Scarlet wanted to feel safe, and the family home "Tara" was her place of security, solace, and where she found her strength. However, Scarlet was innately intelligent and had the Royal Bee Personality Trait. Scarlet rejected the Old South's pretense of women's ignorance and helplessness. Scarlet was not like other genteel Southern women, and Scarlet rejected the standard weakness portrayed by Southern women just before the Civil War. Scarlet was a person who took control. She operated as the Royal Bee Personality Trait. Scarlet was in love with Ashley Wilkes, but he loved and married Scarlet's cousin, Melanie. Scarlet travels to Atlanta, Georgia, trying to start over after the death of her mother, but poverty became her reality. Melanie becomes pregnant, while Ashley rejects Scarlet's advances, but Ashley is gone off to war. Scarlet helps Melanie deliver her baby, but Melanie was not a robust woman like Scarlet's constitution. Scarlet takes care of her and brings her back with her to Tara. With the help of Rhett's (played by Clark Gable) wisdom and the theft of an old horse with a dilapidated old wagon, she, Melanie and her newborn baby, Scarlet's child, and housekeeper travel back to Tara. This was a nightmare trip. Scarlet grows in maturity as she becomes a servant and takes care of Melanie, her newborn, Scarlett's toddler son, and Prissy, her housekeeper. Scarlet is harassed by troops on both the North and South side. Scarlet and her family are hungry, wet from downpouring rain, are bitten by insects, and must traverse rough roads that made travel hard and treacherous during their twenty-five-mile journey to Tara. However, Yankee soldiers are possessing Tara. All valuables, gold, harvested crops, and livestock have been stolen.

The Civil War sweeps away Scarlet's privileged lifestyle which she enjoyed as a child and as a young woman, and the Southern genteel society had disappeared and was a mere memory. Scarlett left Atlanta destitute after Sherman's army marched through Georgia, and she becomes the sole source of strength for her family at Tara. Her character of privilege as a Royal Bee Personality Trait begins to harden as her relatives and the family servants look to her for protection from homelessness and starvation. Scarlett becomes a wise money-conscious businesswoman, tough, and took control of the dire situation. Her motivation was to ensure her family survives, and Tara stays in her possession, while other Georgian farmers who once had great mansions lose their homes. In the face of great hardship, the once spoiled Scarlett shoulders the troubles of her family and friends as a servant leader, but the near starvation and backbreaking, endless work in the fields changes her into a Royal Bee Personality Trait, an overcomer and survivor. She grows tough, durable, calculating, but loving to her family and those on her farm. An attack from a Yankee deserter forces her hand, and she shoots him in self-defense. She marries Rhett and they have a child that dies, and Rhet leaves her; but with her newfound confidence, she, her family, and servants will survive. She gained the idea that she was a lord over Tara which name came from the word Tara Ferma, a safe dry land where you can live, have food and water, and an income from forestry and planting of crops. Thus, even though Scarlet had developed a Royal Bee Personality Trait out of the need to survive, she protected her family.

People with the Royal Bee Personality Trait are survivors of tragedy, and their best days are when we see them rise up and overcome their trials and tribulations and thereby teach others to seek to be an overcomer in Christ Jesus. This was Scarlet in the movie and book of Gone with the Wind. The character portraying transformation of Scarlet's soul is a great story for women and men. Scarlet changes from a pampered daughter of a wealthy family to a woman who was a servant leader, helping and caring for her family and servants and many others during the Civil War. Her character as Scarlet is a great testament how she used her Royal Bee Personality Trait to become a great, caring person for others. The great script showed the Civil War matured Scarlet and brought out the best in her. Harsh times never last, but tough people survive the severity of the times when love for others motivates them to not give up.

1 John 5:4-5 says, "For whatsoever is born of God overcometh the world: and this is the victory that overcometh the world, even our faith. (5) Who is he that overcometh the world, but he that believeth that Jesus is the Son of God?"

Harsh times seem to bring out the best or worse in people, but during regular seasons the warmth of the Sun still causes the individual with the Royal Bee Personality Trait to control people who are beholden to them for the money he or she pays them. You cannot have the warmth and light of the Sun unless you accept storms exhibiting thunder, lightning, rain, and mud on dirt roads.

"Respect" is a key word in the conversation with someone who has the Royal Bee Personality Trait, and there seems to be a compulsive need to make other people feel not as important. The person who has the Royal Bee Personality Trait wears an invisible crown. Sometimes, women of Great Britain who have the Royal Bee Personality Trait will wear a hat that resembles the royal hats that the late Queen Elizabeth would wear, and many around her picked up her style.

However, underlying the obsessive-compulsive individual with the Royal Bee Personality Trait's disorder is anger and hostility for being hurt or humiliated during younger years. This dread of humiliation is often met with outbursts of anger and violent or radical behavior if there is any showing of disrespect. So long as there is obedience and respect, the anger of the person with the Royal Bee Personality Trait is repressed and the quiet, benevolent, even soft-spoken mannerisms are seen displayed again. Some men and women who have the obsessive-compulsive disorder of the Royal Bee Personality Trait will not receive, and in fact angrily reject any criticism of his or her actions or speech or are told that he or she has a rude personality and are too harsh toward others.

A person who has the Royal Bee Personality Trait is genuinely unforgiving. You cross him or her; you are his or her enemy for life unless a skilled intermediary intervenes. Unlike God and Christ who forgive, it is hard for a person with the Royal Bee Personality Trait to forgive someone who she thinks has trespassed her.

In Matthew 18:21-22, we see the issue of the importance of forgiveness, "Then came Peter to Him, and said, 'Lord, how oft shall my brother sin against me, and I forgive him? Till seven times?' (22) Jesus saith unto him, 'I say not unto thee, "Until seven times: but, Until seventy times seven."'"

Then, to further bring clarity to forgiveness, Jesus in Matthew 18:23-35 tells the parable of a King who grants his servant's request for forgiveness of the servant's debts. In Jesus' parable there are two debts that are owed, one very, very large debt owed to the King by the King's servant, and another much, much smaller debt owed to the Servant by a rather small income producing man. The King forgave his servant of 10,000 talents. A "talent" is a measure of weight, close to 130 lbs of silver denarii coins. One "talent" is equal to about 5,500 denarii silver coins. The king in the parable is owed 10,000 talents from his servant, which is about fifty-five million dinarii silver coins.

After the King's servant was forgiven of ten thousand talents of denarii silver coins, the servant left and found a fellow servant who owed him one hundred denarii. Since the fellow servant could not pay the King's servant, then the King's servant found him, knocked him on the ground, choked him, and decided not to forgive his debt, but called the police and threw him in jail and not let out until he paid the 100 dinarii. Other servants went to the King and told him what the King's servant, who had been forgiven of his large debt by the King, had done to the struggling servant who owed him the 100 dinarii. The King ordered his guards to bring the King's ungrateful servant before the King. Matthew 18:32-35 says, "Then his lord, after that he had called him, said unto him, 'O thou wicked servant, I forgave thee all that debt, because thou desiredst me: (33) Shouldest not thou also have had compassion on thy fellow servant, even as I had pity on thee? (34) And his lord was wroth, and delivered him to the tormentors, till he should pay all that was due unto him. (35) So likewise shall my heavenly Father do also unto you, if ye from your hearts forgive not everyone his brother their trespasses."

In the extreme borderline personality disorder, the person with the Royal Bee Personality Trait is seen to pattern her or his behavior as did Queen Jezebel of the Northern Kingdom, Israel. Jezebel was married to the wicked King Ahab. King Ahab wanted a vineyard near his winter house that was owned by Naboth. 1 Kings 21:3 says, "And Naboth said to Ahab, 'The LORD forbid it me, that I should give the inheritance of my fathers' unto thee.'" What Naboth meant was that trading or selling his ancestral property would violate the law and would be displeasing in God's eyes (1 Samuel. 24:6; 26:11; 2 Samuel. 23:17). Under the law, the Lord forbade Israelite families to surrender ownership of family lands permanently

(Leviticus 25:23–28; Numbers 36:7–9). Thus, Naboth declined Ahab's offer. King Ahab was incredibly sad for Naboth's refusal, but Jezebel, with her Royal Bee Personality Trait paid two false witnesses to testify that they heard Naboth blaspheme God and the King. Naboth was found guilty by the false evidence, so in judgment, the select people stoned him to death. King Ahab was free to take possession and ownership of the vineyard he wanted (1 Kings 21:13-16).

Similarly, Jezebel, with the Royal Bee Personality Trait, supported and fed all the prophets of Baal and Asherah to keep control of the spiritual leaders in her and Ahab's kingdom. Elijah said in 1 Kings 18:19, "Now therefore, send and gather all Israel to me on Mount Carmel, the four hundred and fifty prophets of Baal, and the four hundred prophets of Asherah, who eat at Jezebel's table." Jezebel set herself up against God's prophet, Elijah. Jezebel massacred many of the prophets of the Lord who were disobedient to her (1 Kings 18:4). She also tried to kill Elijah because he had called on the fire of the Lord to consume the burnt sacrifice and because he killed Jezebel's prophets of Baal. (See 1 Kings, Chapters 18 and 19).

Many people are attracted to the individual with the Royal Bee Personality Trait because of her or his apparent strength, authority, and protective qualities when the people are obedient. Therefore, people with the Royal Bee Personality Trait attract weak and insecure subordinates.

The individual with the extreme Royal Bee Personality Trait looks at subordinates as if they are sub-human without thoughts, feelings, and wills of their own. Generally, people with any ambition, self-respect, and a sense of their own destiny will leave the relationship with the person who controls people using money with the Royal Bee Personality Trait.

THE CONTROL PERSONALITY TRAIT OF MONEY WHO BECOMES A SERIAL THIEF IN THE "PONZI SCHEME PERSONALITY TRAIT"

CHARLES PONZI

The word "Ponzi" comes from a swindler named Charles Ponzi. Wikipedia says about Ponzi, "On November 15, 1903, Ponzi arrived in Boston aboard the S.S. Vancouver. By his own account, Ponzi had $2.50 in his pocket (equivalent to $85 in 2023), having gambled away the rest of his life savings during the voyage. 'I landed in this country with $2.50 in cash and $1 million in hopes, and those hopes never left me,' he later told a reporter for the New York Times. He quickly learned English and spent the next few years doing odd jobs along the East Coast, eventually taking a job as a dishwasher in a restaurant, where he slept on the floor. Ponzi managed to work his way up to the position of waiter but was fired for theft and shortchanging customers.

Wikipedia continues, "In 1907, after several years of failing to establish himself in the U.S., Ponzi moved to Montreal, Quebec, Canada, and became an assistant teller in the newly opened Banco Zarossi, a bank located on Saint Jacques Street started by Luigi "Louis" Zarossi to service the influx of Italian immigrants arriving in the city. By this time, Ponzi had a winning personality and spoke English, Italian, and French, which Zuckoff says helped him get the job at Banco Zarossi. It was at Banco Zarossi that Ponzi first saw the scheme of "robbing Peter to pay Paul" (which subsequently would be called a Ponzi scheme). Zarossi paid 6%

interest on bank deposits—double the going rate at the time—and was growing rapidly as a result. Ponzi eventually rose to bank manager. However, he found out that the bank was in serious financial trouble because of bad real estate loans, and that Zarossi was funding the interest payments not through profit on investments, but by using money deposited in newly opened accounts. The bank eventually failed and Zarossi fled to Mexico with a large portion of the bank's money."

Ponzi took over his wife's family's fledgling fruit company for a short time, but it failed shortly thereafter. In 1920, with only $150 to his account, Charles Ponzi promised clients a 50% profit within 45 days or 100% profit within 90 days, by buying discounted postal reply to coupons in other countries and redeeming them at face value in the U.S. as a form of arbitrage. A proponent of Ponzi's quick profit scheme promoted Ponzi as the greatest Italian of all time: "Columbus discovered America...but you (Ponzi) discovered money."

"In January 1920, Ponzi started his own company, called the "Securities Exchange Company" to promote the scheme. In the first month, 18 people invested in his company with a total of $1,800. He paid them promptly the very next month, with money obtained from a newer set of investors.

"Ponzi set up a larger office, this time in the Niles Building on School Street. Word spread, and investments increased rapidly. Ponzi hired agents and paid them generous commissions. Between February and March 1920, the total amount invested had risen from $5,000 to $25,000 ($80,000 to $380,000 in 2023 money, respectively). As the scheme grew, Ponzi hired agents to seek out new investors in New England and New Jersey. . . At that time, investors were being paid impressive rates, which subsequently encouraged others to invest. By May 1920, he had made $420,000 (equivalent to $6,400,000 in 2023). By June 1920, people had invested $2.5 million in Ponzi's scheme (equivalent to $38,000,000 in 2023). By July, he was approaching a million dollars per day.

"Ponzi began depositing the money in the Hanover Trust Bank of Boston (a small bank on Hanover Street in the mostly Italian North End), in the hope that once his account was large enough he could impose his will on the bank or even be made its president; he bought a controlling interest in the bank through himself and several friends after depositing $3 million. By July 1920, Ponzi had made millions. Some of his investors had been mortgaging their homes and investing their life savings. Most did not take their profits but reinvested. Ponzi's company, meanwhile, had set up branches from Maine to New Jersey.

"Even though Ponzi's company was bringing in fantastic sums of money each day, the simplest financial analysis would have shown that the operation was running at a large loss. As long as money kept flowing in, existing investors could be paid with the new money. This was the only method Ponzi had to continue providing returns to existing investors, as he made no effort to generate legitimate profits."

Ponzi was a serial thief with the Ponzi Scheme Personality Trait. Ponzi had no moral sense of right; he thought those who paid him money were just greedy people who wanted a fast profit. He believed that these investors should have known that this plan of his was too good to be true. Ponzi justified his actions because he was calling out people's greed. Yet, the poverty that he suffered was to be turned around. He became rich, important, and lived the life of the rich and famous temporarily.

These men with the Ponzi Scheme Personality Trait are devoid of any ethics, integrity, or remorse. John 10:10a says, "The thief cometh not, but for to steal, and to kill, and to destroy. ..."

Ponzi recognized there was a "get-rich-quick" mentality amongst normal people that is in the fallen world. Money has an insidiousness about it that attracts people to do even illegal acts to acquire it. Again, any "get-rich-quick" scheme avoids being first trained with managerial skills violates biblical foundational truths since "get-rich-quick" schemes are void in the incremental daily transformation of the soul for character development.

BERNARD (BERNIE) LAWRENCE MADOFF

The following facts were taken from Wikipedia and the film series, titled "Madoff the Monster of Wall Street." Bernie Madoff was the supreme serial thief known to mankind with the Ponzi Scheme Personality Trait.

Madoff was born on April 29, 1938, in Queens, New York City, to Sylvia (Muntner) and Ralph Madoff, who was an unsuccessful plumber and stockbroker. Madoff's family was Jewish. Madoff's grandparents emigrated from Poland, Romania, and Austria. After High School graduation, Madoff attended the University of Alabama for one year, but then transferred to and graduated from Hofstra University in 1960 with a Bachelor of Arts degree in political science. Madoff briefly attended Brooklyn Law School, but left after his first year when Madoff founded a penny stock brokerage in 1960, which eventually grew into Bernard L. Madoff Investment Securities, LLC. Madoff served as the Manager of the LLC until his arrest on December 11, 2008.

Bernie Madoff's wanted to become a successful stockbroker, so he studied hard to learn the buying and selling of penny stocks off the pink sheets, which can be very profitable, but one can lose it all in a flash crash, like it happened in 1962. In 1961, stocks had risen approximately 27%, with leading technology stocks such as Texas Instruments and Polaroid trading at up to 115 times earnings. Then, without warning, in 1962, during John Kennedy's Presidency, a flash crash occurred, causing stocks to plummet without the ability for investors to get out of the stock market fast enough. Madoff lost all the money he had from investors, equal to $30,000. Feeling despondent, Madoff borrowed $30,000 from his father-in-law and told his investors that through his wisdom, none of them lost their money.

However, Bernie Madoff studied how to successfully trade penny stocks off the pink sheets. He built a profitable penny stock trades business and built a profitable side business that provided clients with impressive returns (although they technically made nothing because it was a Ponzi scheme). Bernie and his brother Peter pioneered computerized trading and the consolidation of off-the-exchange markets which eventually led to the formation of NASDAQ for which Bernie would be on the Board of Governors.

Most all investors in Bernie's asset management were Jewish, and they trusted Bernie with millions and millions. The Security Exchange Commission has a special "Affinity Fraud." Affinity fraud is a misrepresentation of true investment facts and exploits the trust and

Personality Traits of Money

friendship that exist in groups of people who have something in common such as a common religious belief. Bernie Madoff committed affinity fraud because he primarily targeted Jewish people to be investors in his assets under management that was the Ponzi scheme. Some of Madoff's victims were enlisted respected leaders in the Jewish culture to spread the word about what later was revealed as Madoff's Ponzi scheme. Bernie Madoff's Ponzi scheme through Affinity Fraud bilked many businesses, individuals, and families an estimated $17.5 billion (or as much as $65 billion, including fictional profits), and also causing huge losses for banks and pension funds who invested in Madoff's unsuspecting Ponzi scheme.

With the obsessive-compulsive Ponzi Scheme Personality Trait, Bernie Madoff's firm became the sixth-largest Market Maker for S&P 500 stocks at the time of his arrest on December 11, 2008. Bernie Madoff had a front business which was his stock brokerage part of the business, as his public profile, but he did keep his asset management business for clients to be hidden because the latter was what he generated billions in dollars as he had the obsessive-compulsive Ponzi Scheme Personality Trait.

On December 10, 2008, Madoff's sons Mark and Andrew went to the FBI and informed agents that their father, Bernie Madoff confessed to them that the asset management unit of his firm was nothing but a massive Ponzi scheme, and that Bernie said the asset management unit was nothing but "one big lie." FBI agents arrested Bernie Madoff the next day and charged him with one count of securities fraud. The U.S. Securities and Exchange Commission (SEC) had conducted multiple investigations into Madoff's business practices but never uncovered the largest Ponzi scheme in human history. On March 12, 2009, Madoff pleaded guilty to 11 federal felonies because of the massive Ponzi scheme where his firm had over an estimated 50 billion dollars that they took from people.

Wikipedia says, "The Securities Investor Protection Corporation (SIPC) trustee estimated actual direct losses to investors of $18 billion, of which $14.418 billion has been recovered and returned, while the search for additional funds continues. On June 29, 2009, Madoff was sentenced to 150 years in prison, the maximum sentence allowed. On April 14, 2021, he died at the Federal Medical Center, Butner, in North Carolina, from chronic kidney disease."

Some of Bernie Madoff's famous victims of his Ponzi scheme were Steven Spielberg's Wunderkinder Foundation, Zsa Zsa Gabor, actors and couple Kevin Bacon and Kyra Sedgwick, Dreamworks Animation chief executive Jefferey Katzenberg, actor John Malkovich, Holocaust survivor Elie Wiesel, and broadcaster Larry King. Bernie Madoff had approximately 37,000 victims in his Ponzi scheme.

Several early investors and financial firms cashed out of Madoff's funds years before Madoff's arrest. The funds they received were not profits but came from newer investors' deposits with Bernard L. Madoff Investment Securities, LLC.

Appointed trustees have been searching financial depositories to locate, and through settlement agreements recover the loss funds held by a few of Madoff investors into the Ponzi scheme that were not profits earned but were later investor victims' monies deposited in Madoff's Ponzi scheme. One of those Trustees is the law firm of Irving Picard, who oversees the liquidation of Madoff's business, has successfully clawed back more than estimated $15 billion for the benefit of other victim investors.

Here is a list of a few largest Madoff investors who did receive money early on from Bernard L. Madoff Investment Securities, LLC. who were forced to return money back to compensate other victims of Bernie Madoff's Ponzi scheme: 1). Jeffrey Picower, $17.2 billion; 2) Tremont Group, $1.025 billion; 3). Kingate Funds, $860 million; 3). Thema International Fund, $687 million; and 4). Carl Shapiro & family trusts, $675 million.

SECURITY EXCHANGE COMMISSION'S
REPORT OF PONZI SCHEMES JUST IN 2023

The following is a quote of the Affinity Frauds and Ponzi Schemes that were prosecuted by the SEC in just 2023, so thieves with the Ponzi Scheme Personality Trait continue to this day. Most of these thieves with the Ponzi Scheme Personality Trait that rape innocent victims of their money are not reported by the victims, just like most physical rape victims do not report the violation.

"Affinity Frauds" and Ponzi Schemes
Based on investigations by Division staff, in fiscal year 2023, the SEC brought several actions against alleged fraudsters targeting various groups in affinity frauds and Ponzi schemes, including schemes targeting the Tongan American community, elderly church members, Spanish-speaking communities, law enforcement and first responders, and the Orthodox Jewish community.

Asset Freezes
The SEC's ability to obtain meaningful financial remedies and to return money to harmed investors may turn on securing an asset freeze at an early stage. Based on the Division's investigations, the SEC sought and obtained emergency relief freezing defendants' assets in numerous litigated cases, including:
• Against a Florida resident for allegedly operating a more than $100 million Ponzi scheme targeting the Haitian American community; and
• Against Miami-based investment adviser BKCoin Management LLC in connection with an alleged $100 million crypto asset fraud scheme."

THE CONTROL PERSONALITY TRAIT OF MONEY
AND THE CHRISTIAN PERSPECTIVE

Those with the Safety Personality Trait of Money, as discussed in the previous chapter, use money to withdraw from a seemingly hostile world, whereas those with the Control Personality Trait of Money use money to attack their seemingly hostile environment. Where the safety-oriented person responds out of fear, the control-oriented person responds out of anger with a desire to control people to avoid being attacked or to teach those who attack him will be met with a lion-like defense.

The Bible is clear that you should never use money as control to manipulate others. People are fearful of confronting the person with the Control Personality Trait of Money. They seldom give the Control Personality Trait of Money truthful opinions, so he that has the dysfunctional personality trait will not manipulate them or discipline them.

Personality Traits of Money

Genesis 1:26, 28 says, "Then God said, `Let Us make man in Our image, according to Our likeness; let them have dominion over the fish of the sea, over the birds of the air, over the cattle, over all the earth, and over every creeping thing that creeps on the earth.' . . . (28) Then God blessed them, and God said to them, `Be fruitful and multiply; fill the earth and subdue it; have dominion over the fish of the sea, over the birds of the air, and over every living thing that moves on the earth.'"

Believers have the same vocations, the same relationships with Jesus and God, but Believers have different spiritual gifts. Again, Believers' have the same vocations, being Jesus' servant kings, priests, lords, ambassadors, and soldiers in God's Kingdom. Believers' have the same relationship with Jesus as His body, betrothed, and eventual bride. Believers' relationships with Father God are as adopted children and are as members of the family of God. Similarly, every Believer has been mandated with servanthood dominion over the earth and over all the fish, birds, animals, and vegetation to care for them, but nowhere does it say that Believers have enslavement authority over other human beings. Yet, everyone lives in a world where there are authoritative people which Believers are required to submit to their authority, such as parents, teachers, pastors, police, judges, military officers, employers, and tax authorities, but Believers are never to submit to an abusive person with authority.

It is impermissible in the word of God (and under secular laws) for a spouse physically to strike the other spouse, as this is unbiblical prohibition and in the secular world criminal domestic violence. 1 Peter 3:7 says, "Likewise, ye husbands, dwell with them according to knowledge, giving honour unto the wife, as unto the weaker vessel, and as being joint heirs together of the grace of life; that your prayers be not hindered."

God mandates every Believer to be a humble servant, whether male or female, in the kingdom of God. Mark 10:42-44 says, "Ye know that they which are accounted to rule over the Gentiles exercise lordship over them; and their great ones exercise authority upon them. (43) But so shall it not be among you: but whosoever will be great among you, shall be your (humble) minister: (44) And whosoever of you will be the chiefest, shall be servant of all. (45) For even the Son of man came not to be ministered unto, but to minister, and to give his life a ransom for many."

Take a defensive action to protect yourself when you encounter people with Control Personality Trait of Money, so, you need to stop allowing these obsessive-compulsive Control Personality Trait of Money people to abuse you or control you with their money. Do not associate with these people until their souls are transformed, and they become loving and respectful toward you. Respect yourself because you have been made in the image and likeness of God. You can submit to Godly authority but not fallen world authoritative abuse. You have immense value in the Kingdom of God because, unlike angels, you are an image bearer of Jehovah Elohim, the Covenant Creator of everything, angels, and all humans. One of the ways to avoid evil is to get away from it. Resign your employment, resign off boards of corporations and non-profit charities, and leave the church community if the Pastor operates with the Control Personality Trait of Money. Life is too short to live or fellowship with someone who is abusive.

There is no right way to abusively dominate another human being. All people must allow their mission to be under God's mission. This is proper submission to God. Joining people with compatible missions does not give one the right to dominate the other.

Never use money as the control to buy a "religious office" to in turn "sell" to others. A ministering apostle cannot engift another apostle. A ministering prophet cannot engift another prophet. A ministering evangelist cannot engift another evangelist. A ministering pastor cannot engift another pastor. A ministering teacher cannot engift another teacher. The apostle, prophet, evangelist, pastor, and teacher are gifts, given by God the Word, not another human. Ephesians 4:7, 10-11 says, "But unto every one of us is given grace according to the measure of the gift of Christ. . . (10) He that descended is the same also that ascended far above all heavens, that He might fill all things. (11) And He (not man) gave some, apostles; and some, prophets; and some, evangelists; and some, pastors and teachers."

Acts 8:18 20 says, "And when Simon saw that through the laying on of the apostles' hands the Holy Spirit was given, he offered them money, saying, `Give me this power also, that anyone on whom I lay hands may receive the Holy Spirit.' But Peter said to him, `Your money perish with you, because you through that the gift of God could be purchase with money!'" Simon the sorcerer desired to use money to buy the office to impart the power of God to others. Although all that was in his heart was not stated, Simon thought God's power was worth lots of money. Simon had a compulsive Control Personality Trait of Money.

If the apostles would have received his "offering" to buy the ability to impart God's power to others, Simon would have sold this ability or office to others by having others give him offerings. He would have then duplicated the sin that Peter in the hypothetical would have done, but of course Peter did not take any money from Simon the Sorcerer. Fortunately, Peter was a great apostle of the Lord, and he rebuked Simon. There is a good chance that Simon learned his lesson from Peter's chastisement and went on serving the Lord properly without seeking control and power for his own self-aggrandizement.

The word "simony" was later used in church history as having the meaning of someone trying to sell or buy a church office, position, or influence (Acts 8:18-23).

Personality Traits of Money

Dr. Nova Dean Pack

5 Using Money For The "Freedom Seeker Personality Trait Of Money"

CHAPTER FIVE

USING MONEY FOR THE "FREEDOM SEEKER PERSONALITY TRAIT OF MONEY"

MAIN SCRIPTURE REFERENCE: 1 Timothy 6:10 says, "For the love of money is a root of all kinds of evil, for which some have strayed from the faith in their greediness and pierced themselves through with many sorrows."

Firstly, the "Love of Money" means avarice for money to acquire safety, control, freedom, romanticism, magnetism, or any emotional or mental need fulfilled by money. In the principal reference verse of 1 Timothy 6:10, the word "love" in the phrase "For the love of money…." is the Greek word philargurio, which means here in this context, covetousness or avarice and comes from the root word philarguos, which means "fond of silver." However, both Greek words are rooted in the Greek word philarguria and embodies the English meaning of avarice or the "love of money." The English word avarice has the root word "avar" within it, which means blind. A person who is covetous of money is blind to the truth and blind to the snares that greed, covetousness, and avarice cause.

Secondly, the "Love of Money" also means the opposite of the "hate of money." The "love of money" means that money has become one's idol, trying to fulfill one's needs with money which rightfully can only be fulfilled by God.

PEOPLE WITH THE FREEDOM SEEKER PERSONALITY TRAIT OF MONEY TRY TO AVOID SUBMITTING TO AUTHORITY

Those with the Freedom Seeker Personality Trait of Money desire to escape the bondage caused by those who dominate and control others. Often, these people with the Freedom Seeker Personality Trait of Money are the children of one of the Control Seeker Personality Traits. Their compulsion to be free and independent from authority is usually a reaction to the domineering parent's acts of attempting dominion over them.

When a person has a persuasion to be free when it is an overriding obsessive motivation, the use of money to achieve that goal becomes a compulsion that overrides every area of the person's life. He needs transformation of the soul.

The individual with the Freedom Seeker Personality Trait of Money often will use phrases such as, "Live and let live;" "I don't want anyone to tie me down;" "I am a free soul;" "I need my freedom;" "I need to do something to express my artistic talents;" "Work is a bummer;" "I need a job where I have the freedom to make my own decisions;" "I want a job with lots of paid holidays and vacations;" and "Hey! I am not going to be a slave to anybody."

Those categorized as having the obsessive-compulsive Freedom Seeker Personality Trait of Money work out of necessity, not enjoyment if it is a mundane job. They do seek employment if they can find it in those activities they may enjoy, which resemble more like a hobby than economic employment. They rarely want leadership responsibilities in the job or in social groups. They are very self-gratification oriented. They seldom work overtime, always take all their sick leave, often call-in "sick" on Mondays or Fridays to their employer to lengthen their weekends.

Those with the Freedom Seeker Personality Trait of Money drift into jobs as a salesperson where there are "no limits" placed on the amount of commission they can make. Also, they like jobs where there are no time requirements to be at work. They want to come and go as they please. They go from job to job, sometimes five jobs a year in sales. A vast number gravitate to network marketing sales to be self-employed to maintain their independence but earn some money to survive. They are satisfied to rent out a room from someone but can be late on their rent.

Many with the Freedom Seeker Personality Trait of Money go into business for themselves, so they do not have to take orders from anyone. They may play an instrument and play at churches for a stipend. They may establish their own ministry, so they can receive offerings from people. Yet, they often refuse to work hard to make the ministry successful. With laptops, tablets, computers, the Internet, new electronic devices, GPS, and robotics, they usually can work out of their residence or car, coffee houses, or in restaurants. The lifestyles afforded by the electronic age have facilitated the needs of those with the Freedom Seeker Personality Trait of Money.

Thus, those people with the Freedom Seeker Personality Trait of Money rebel against the 9 to 5 job routine, regimentation, employers giving them orders, and reject restrictions of any kind. They often go to the extreme in their actions, such as avoiding any activity which requires dependence on others, including marriage or children. He will resist or rise against authority, control, or tradition.

Job 24:13 says, "They are of those that rebel against the light; they know not the ways thereof, nor abide in the paths thereof." Also, Absalom rebelled against his father David and conspired against his father to be King of all of Israel, but in the end, Absalom died in battle because he was not chosen by God to be king like his father, David. (2 Samuel chps 15-19).

Freedom from daily drudgery work or from an overseeing boss is a non-intangible thing which people seek to acquire with money. These people want to chart their own destiny without any assistance or guidance from anybody, and often including God. The sin is they want to be self-made independent people, not God made submitted people. They want to be their own boss.

Those with the Freedom Seeker Personality Trait of Money try to "buy their time" to do what they want to do. They will negotiate an employment contract for more sick leave times, holiday times, and vacation times in exchange for a lesser salary.

These people have their own "Declaration of Freedom" and desire to pursue their "own thing." They admire the words in the song written by Paul Anka and first sung by Frank Sinatra, "I Did It My Way!"

The individual with the Freedom Seeker Personality Trait of Money expresses his or her obsessive-compulsive behavior usually through either a high degree of self-fulfilling activity or generalized attitude of rebellion toward all authority and reject living within a structured

Personality Traits of Money

environment full of rules and regulations, including even the institution of marriage.

The problem is that when the person with the Freedom Seeker Personality Trait of Money becomes a Christian, he often carries the rebellion or independence disorder into the Church governing hierarchy and does not submit to authoritative relationships or pastoral oversight. They jump on exciting new ideas that promise freedom from the daily routine. To their credit these people are often used as leaders by God to initially head up a new movement of the Holy Spirit. After the movement is started, the person with the Freedom Seeker Personality Trait of Money rejects God's authoritative leaders' oversight that he needs for discipline and maturation. When the person with the Freedom Seeker Personality Trait of Money refuses to submit to responsible character-building spiritual fathers and mothers in the Church, then he sometimes is asked to leave the Church because of his anti-authority behavior. The new "spiritual revivalists" or new "trend setters" eventually rebel against what they themselves started, even if at the beginning they were motivated by the Holy Spirit. Freedom Seeker Personality Trait of Money leaders usually end up not developing loyal followers that last, so they do not have those who continue to give into their personal ministry in their elder years. People who have the Freedom Seeker Personality Trait of Money usually die alone without close friends present.

In their defense, the individuals with the Freedom Seeker Personality Trait of Money are exciting, innovative people, who are not afraid to be a leader in the new movement to bring about needed change in the business field, in the Church, or in the local, state, or federal governments. To their credit, they are not stuck in a traditional rut. They are often the first to catch hold of a new idea or a new paradigm and the direction of the Holy Spirit is leading. They will think nothing is wrong in spending all the money they have to put into the new idea or movement. They sacrifice their security by giving most all their money toward promoting the new idea or movement they are involved, so, most will think they are giving just as a "cheerful giver" (2 Corinthians 9:7) and no one generally would conclude that they have a problem with handling money, a problem living within a budget, or maintaining a proper accounting system. They usually fail to hand out yearly donation receipts in church, and they have not kept accounts of the donors, or the donation amounts given to the ministry or church. They will surround themselves with supporters who have money to give into the ministry of this new idea or new movement. They will insist there can be no strings attached to the giving. The Freedom Seeker Personality Trait of Money initially will be the leader or in the leadership group and a recipient of some support, although they are not necessarily interested in massing large sums of riches as the Control Seeker Personality Trait of Money person does to build his own empire. However, like the Control Seeker Personality Trait of Money, they become out-of-touch elitists and wrongfully believe they know the direction of the movement of the Holy Spirit or know how to cure the ills of society. Giving credit where due, the Freedom Seeker Personality Trait of Money are highly intelligent, may read a lot, and normally pursue insatiable mental appetites for innovative ideas and trends. At the beginning, other people like their exciting leadership skills, as they are full of energy; and it is exciting to be around such a free personality. Eventually, when the new idea or new movement has become the norm and loses its excitement, or fails to reach an apex of support, the person with the Freedom Seeker Personality Trait of Money is back trying to find followers of the old idea or old movement who will financially support him.

What the Freedom Seeker Personality Trait of Money does not understand is the truth in

Ecclesiastes 3:1, which says, "To everything there is a season, and a time to every purpose under the heaven." God orchestrates the seasons and times, and the Freedom Seeker Personality Trait of Money leader normally does not know when God's season and time have come here on earth and when the season and time have changed. Normally, a season and time for a new idea and new movement lasts only about a decade until God believes that Believers here on earth have been discipled and taught what was the purpose for that season and movement.

The education system in most states and countries is set up for a season and time for its completion. In the U.S., students are scheduled to complete four years of high school to obtain a Diploma, complete four years of university to receive a BA degree or BS degree, complete additional two years post graduate to be awarded with a Master's degree. That is the ten-year full time education cycle that is set up in both the secular and religious education systems. A doctorate degree will take another three years to complete.

The number 10 represents divine order, God's law, or a period of testing. For example, the Ten Commandments were given to Moses by God on Mt. Sinai, and they represent how to live a righteous life, to find fulfillment, and the duties Believers owe to God, the day to fulfill our day of worship, duties to parents, actions for righteous living, and duties to our fellow man.

Likewise, tithing is the basic tax that God charges to give to ministers in the Church. Believers who tithe regularly and follow biblical laws of economics usually have lower debt, greater contentment, stronger families, and better spiritual fellowship with other Believers.

THE UNDERLYING SOULISH DISORDERS OF THE FREEDOM SEEKERS PERSONALITY TRAIT OF MONEY

The underlying soulish disorders of the Freedom Seeker Personality Trait of Money usually stems from the rejection of those he would normally be dependent upon that hurt him in the past. Therefore, the underlying motivation of the person with the Freedom Seeker Personality Trait of Money is avoid dependency of others as much as he can.

Soulish hurts involved with those who are the Freedom Seeker Personality Trait of Money are the fear of dependency, fear of grinding work in a dead-end job, and fear of responsibility because of the management of accumulated riches. Often, those who become rich that have the Freedom Seeker Personality Trait of Money do things subconsciously that are unwise to lose their accumulated money instead of seeking wise investment counseling. They become victims of those who promise high returns but take the money from him who suffers with the Freedom Seeker Personality Trait of Money. So, it is okay to pursue financial independence and freedom, but when it has become a compulsion, and you throw away your capital or savings on bad business deals, or listen and become victims to con men, it is a disorder that needs healing. You can find these Freedom Seeker Personality Trait of Money people who were once moderately rich but lost everything to con artists. The Freedom Seeker Personality Trait of Money people are usually incredibly talented, but they need to have someone else who is a licensed professional who is bonded and have errors and omissions insurance in the event of malpractice as trustees of their estates. Generally, if a person has the disorder as a Freedom Seeker Personality Trait of Money, and they become millionaires through the sale

Personality Traits of Money

of their talent as a writer, a singer, an actor, a playwright, or Inventor, when they earn great sums of money, they should have financial counselors that properly advises them how to invest and learn to live within a budget that matches their investment incomes. Those who suffer with a Freedom Seeker Personality Trait of Money usually do not want to give up their freedom to manage hard assets they own, such as real estate rental property. Thus, they must find someone who can manage his money, and there are a few good, honest, licensed, Professionals with errors and omissions insurance to protect against their malpractice.

The Freedom Seeker Personality Trait of Money person has a fear of dependency and has a real need to find someone who is dependable and trustworthy. God the Father, God the Word, and God the Holy Spirit indwells every Believer. The triune nature of the One Godhead and the Lord Jesus' humanity nature are the ones that will take care of his dependency needs, because they will genuinely love him. God will provide for his every need according to God's riches in glory by Christ Jesus (Philippians 4:19). God will instill in him wisdom from above that he can use to properly invest his money for his old age, but the biggest character flaw he has is the unwillingness to submit to authority.

In extreme cases, the individual with the obsessive-compulsive Freedom Seeker Personality Trait of Money is dominated by a rebellious soul which desires to escape from all authority but is not free at all. He, in fact, is in bondage to his own borderline personality disorder. This over-compensating personality disorder frequently manifests by seeking freedom from all authority and becoming a recluse and live "off the grid."

The classic example in the Bible of the rebellious Freedom Seeker Personality Trait of Money was Lucifer. This is why some Freedom Seeker Personality Trait of Money people get involved in evil or the cult or occult. They often will start a new religion; but it regularly is a cult or occult or seem to be with the foundation of Christianity but based upon aberrant theology. Sometimes, they start out with classic Christian doctrinal activity but justify the fractures in their souls by emphasizing some scriptures over others that may cause an imbalance. However, the fractures in their personalities cause deviation when the Holy Spirit's authority, encouraging unity, forgiveness, and love, but not necessarily conformity that often will lead to division. God loves diversity but not rebellion. God loves humility and not self-aggrandizement. The rebellious person with a Freedom Seeker Personality Trait of Money finds the work involved too limiting and soon will leave the organization or Church for what they think is the next great spiritual movement. They often activate a lot of people into their leadership callings, but they personally do not want the restrictive role that is demanded of leaders. They have charisma but not enough character to pastor a flock. True leadership demands one to be a servant of the many. This is contrary to the self-centered lifestyle of the individual with the Freedom Seeker Personality Trait of Money.

Lucifer's sin of lust of self-worship or covetousness of what rightfully belonged to God led to his sin of rebellion against God. Lucifer sought the importance of himself.

Isaiah 14:13 14 says, "For you have said in your heart: I will ascend into heaven (self-promotion), I will exalt my throne above the stars of God (self-exaltation); I will also sit on the mount of the congregation on the farthest sides of the North (self-enthronement); I will ascend above the heights of the clouds (self-empowerment), I will be like the Most High (self-deification)."

The same malevolent spiritual influence could try to deceive many Believers and non-believers into becoming self-centered, self-reliant, self-empowered, self-actualizing, self-directing, and they with their Freedom Seeker Personality Trait of Money become selfishness personified.

FINDING GOD'S TRUE FINANCIAL FREEDOM

You have heard some Believers saying, "When I get rich, I am going to spend my time pursuing the things of God." What they do not understand is that if you cannot spend time pursuing the things of God when you are down and out or poor, you will not do it when you become rich.

Unfortunately, the Believer with the obsessive-compulsive Freedom Seeker Personality Trait of Money would not do this, as they would continue to exercise deviant behavior to satisfy their borderline personality disorder to alleviate hurt in their fractured soulish personalities from overbearing parents, schoolteachers, bullies, military personnel, or ministers who have tried to bring character in their lives. They would seek a wrongful path to worldly freedom by constantly being stubbornly independent from Father God's rule and loving oversight. Yet, God disciplines every child He loves. Hebrews 12:6 says, "For whom the Lord loveth he chasteneth, and scourgeth every son whom He receiveth."

What happens if an obsessive-compulsive Believer suffers from the Freedom Seeker Personality Trait of Money? He will not become wealthy although he is saved but not transformed in his soul because God does not reward self-indulgence, stubbornness, rebellion, but rather rewards humility and submissiveness (Matthew 23:12). For the Believer's betterment through transformation of his mind, emotions, and heart where the will resides, consisting of the Believer's soul, God may strip him of his wealth, but then allow him to regain his wealth but by doing it God's way with God's principles of economics, love, and submissiveness.

Regularly, the riches of those compulsive Believers who suffer with the Freedom Seeker Personality Trait of Money stem from ill-gotten gain and the habits of doing business as the world did before the Believers were saved. In some cases, Believers bring unhealthy habits with them when they come into the body of Christ. The truth is that even when Believers are wealthy, they must remain submissive to and humble toward God and Christ Jesus. True contentment with riches and the enjoyment of true freedom come as the Believer seeks first the Kingdom of God and His righteousness (Matthew 6:33). Proverbs 10:22 says, "The blessing of the LORD, it maketh rich, and He addeth no sorrow with it." The Believer cannot experience true freedom until the Believer's soul has been transformed after initial salvation, and when he becomes submissive and obedient to God Who lives inside him, as the Believer is God's Temple (2 Corinthians 6:16; 1 Corinthians 3:16; Ephesians 2:21).

2 Corinthians 3:17 says, "Now the Lord is that Spirit: and where the Spirit of the Lord is, there is liberty." There is true freedom in God's Kingdom when the Believer becomes submissive, obedient to God, and adopts God's Kingdom principles, mores, morals, and ethical standards in doing business in the world; and then the Believer will be the recipient to God's wealth. Proverbs 13:22 says, "A good man leaveth an inheritance to his children's children: and the wealth of the sinner is laid up for the just."

Personality Traits of Money

The key to God's way of acquiring financial freedom is in allowing Christ's divine nature, God the Word, to bring the virtues of Christ's humanity nature to live with your soul as He does with your holy and righteous born again spirit (Galatians 2:20; Ephesians 4:24). You must come to the resolve that you allow Christ to live His life inside you. Galatians 2:20 is a major key in your soul's spiritual transformation: "I am crucified with Christ: nevertheless, I live; yet not I, but Christ liveth in me: and the life which I now live in the flesh I live by the faith of the Son of God, who loved me, and gave Himself for me."

The Believer should completely stop going to secular seminars, stop listening to internet people who say they are rich and will give you their secrets to acquire wealth because a lot of times these people are not Believers. They do not have the wisdom, truth, ways, and knowledge of God in their presentations. Once you are a child of God, you are God the Father's child by way of adoption (Romans 8:15), and by condition for receiving eternal life, you have consented to God the Father's discipline.

When you are content with what God already has given to you in your natural possession, then God will give you more. Hebrews 13:5 says, "Let your conversation be without covetousness; and be content with such things as ye have: for he hath said, 'I will never leave thee, nor forsake thee.' (6) So that we may boldly say, 'The Lord is my helper, and I will not fear what man shall do unto me.'"

How in a practical way does a Believer experience the liberty of Christ and His promised freedom, so the Believer can receive financial freedom? This is a complicated lifestyle change, but I will give a straightforward answer. You must submit to God for Him to transform your soul after initial salvation. 3 John 2 says, "Beloved, I wish above all things that thou mayest prosper and be in health, even as thy soul prospereth." The qualifying words here is "even as thy soul prospereth." Your soul's spiritual transformation by the Godhead is a condition to financial prosperity and health prosperity.

Romans 12:2 says, "And be not conformed to this world: but be ye transformed by the renewing of your mind, that ye may prove what is that good, and acceptable, and perfect, will of God." Again, when you become a Believer, as a condition of receiving eternal life, you have consented for the entire Godhead to live inside you with your born again spirit; and you have consented for the Godhead to transform your soul. Since God has your permission to transform your soul, then do not resist Him as He transforms your soul with the goal of making you a mature spiritual child of God and a mature servant in His kingdom. When you submit to God's transforming discipline, you can experience righteousness, peace, and joy in the Holy Spirit, which is in God's Kingdom. This is why the Lord's mandate in Matthew 6:33 says, "But seek ye first the kingdom of God, and his righteousness; and all these things shall be added unto you."

Do not be educated in foolishness regarding financial freedom by the principles presented by nonbelievers because they do not have the love of God, power of God, knowledge of God, or the grace of God working in their lives. God is Creator of the natural and spiritual worlds, and He owns the natural world system (Psalms 24:1), all the silver and gold belongs to God and every natural things that are precious here on earth (Haggai 2:8), and God created business because He is a business God, so His principles of operating business are the only ones to adopt (Luke 2:49). God is all knowing about how best His creation works, so the Holy Spirit is the best teacher you could ever have to learn the laws, principles, and truths that activate God's authority, power, love, and grace to come into your life as a Believer to prosper you in His natural creation. So, God wants to renew your mind, stabilize your emotions, and put into your heart a new foundation of beliefs that God wants you to have.

As a Believer you consented when you confessed Jesus as Lord to be disciplined by God the Father (John 15:2), God the Word (Ephesians 5:26-27), and God the Holy Spirit (Romans 8:13) to transform your soul from carnality to spirituality because the Godhead wants you to enjoy life with peace (Romans 8:6). Hebrews 13:9 says, "Be not carried about with divers and strange doctrines. For it is a good thing that the heart be established with grace; not with meats, which have not profited them that have been occupied therein."

Hebrews 12:5-11 speaks clearly of God the Father's discipline or discipleship training of a Believer's soul after initial salvation. "And ye have forgotten the exhortation which speaketh unto you as unto children, 'My son, despise not thou the chastening of the Lord, nor faint when thou art rebuked of Him:' (6) For whom the Lord loveth He chasteneth, and scourgeth every son whom he receiveth. (7) If ye endure chastening, God dealeth with you as with sons; for what son is he whom the father chasteneth not? (8) But if ye be without chastisement, whereof all are partakers, then are ye bastards (illegitimate), and not sons. (9) Furthermore we have had fathers of our flesh which corrected us, and we gave them reverence: shall we not much rather be in subjection unto the Father of spirits, and live? (10) For they verily for a few days chastened us after their own pleasure; but He for our profit, that we might be partakers of his holiness. (11) Now no chastening for the present seemeth to be joyous, but grievous: nevertheless afterward it yieldeth the peaceable fruit of righteousness unto them which are exercised thereby."

As part of God's discipline, the Believer has a duty of abstinence from the flesh's influence in the Believer's soul. Hebrews 13:9 says, "(Believers) do not be carried about with various and strange doctrines. For it is good that the heart be established by grace, not with foods which have not profited those who have been occupied with them."

Galatians 5:1 says, "Stand fast therefore in the liberty by which Christ has made us free, and do not be entangled again with a yoke of bondage."

John 8:36 says, "Therefore if the Son makes you free, you shall be free indeed."

Romans 8:2 says, "For the law of the spirit of life in Christ Jesus has made me free from the law of sin and death".

True freedom comes with relationship with Christ Jesus. "Where the Spirit of the Lord is, there is liberty" (2 Corinthian 3:17).

The prophet Samuel prophesied to King Saul in 1 Samuel 15:23 that: "For rebellion is as the sin of witchcraft, and stubbornness is as iniquity and idolatry. Because thou hast rejected the word of the LORD, He hath also rejected thee from being king."

Personality Traits of Money

THE EPIDEMIC IN THE U.S. OF THE THOSE HAVING
THE FREEDOM SEEKER PERSONALITY TRAIT OF MONEY

Again, Matthew 6:24 says, "No man can serve two masters: for either he will hate the one and love the other; or else he will hold to the one and despise the other. Ye cannot serve God and mammon."

I have been exploring deeply this obsessive-compulsive soulish disorder of those having the Freedom Seeker Personality Trait of Money because the U.S. is full of people with this destructive obsessive-compulsive personality trait. Hollywood actors, prize fighters, singers, those who develop beauty products, and so many people in network marketing, usually are freedom seekers. Yet, they focus their lives in seeking money to live like the rich and famous without working too hard because they want to live free. The problem with this pursuit is that it tries to ensnare the Believer to seek first freedom instead of seeking first the Kingdom of God and His righteousness and being a servant to God. The devil's goal is to tempt the Believer to serve the unrighteous mammon. In the parable of the minas, Luke 16:11 says, "If therefore ye have not been faithful in the unrighteous mammon, who will commit to your trust the true riches?"

Being out of debt, living under grace with God's covenants, providing support for family and the church community, seeking first the Kingdom of God and His righteousness, and being about your Godly vocation, are activities fulfilling God's will when money is invested, and businesses are started and operated using God's Kingdom principles.

The American Heritage Dictionary defines the word "freedom" as: "The condition of being liberated from restraints, especially the ability to act without control and interference by another or by circumstances: In retirement they finally get the freedom to travel."

The American Heritage Dictionary defines a similar word called "independent" as: "Free from the influence, guidance, or control of another or others; self-reliant: an independent mind. Providing or having sufficient income to enable one to live without working: a person of independent means."

Still, the foregoing definitions are too self-centered and do not mention the all-important requirement of a Believer's submission to God and seeking first His Kingdom and His righteousness. When a Believer with the Freedom Seeker Personality Trait of Money has an obsessive-compulsive yearning, and the Believer uses money to be anti-authority and independent to experience worldly freedom to the point of being rebellious, then this use of money for those reasons is a wrongful attachment to money and a wrongful detachment from the authority of God and Christ Jesus. Jesus gives the Believer spiritual freedom in his soul when he becomes a doulos for the Lord. Often, it is God's mercy to place obstacles that stop transactions to halt the Believer from falling into the world's financial system under the sway and control of the prince of this world.

The unsaved person with the obsessive-compulsive Freedom Seeker Personality Trait of Money is often remarkably interesting, thinks out of the box, and is sometimes eccentric. He has no strong attachments and remains mobile and free to move and entertain many diverse experiences. He often tries to live the lifestyles of the jet setters, rich and famous, and wins admiration from others, especially the nonconformists, other freedom seekers, or trend setters who have prestige in the natural world.

Other people who are motivated with the Freedom Seeker Personality Trait of Money may desire the liberty of living off the grid, growing their own food, receiving gifts from others, which as of this writing the donors can give a yearly gift up to $18,000 per year without any reporting requirement to the IRS or state taxing authorities. Other people who have the Freedom Seeker Personality Trait of Money may liberally teach people how to grow herbs and other healthy foods and teach how the manufactured foods are "poisoning" the consumers who buy food from the grocery stores. They often live in the woods or on a farm. They may have installed free solar energy, windmills, or solar operated generators with batteries to produce electricity. They may even earn a small income by selling art pieces but always earn less than the minimum to avoid having to file income tax returns. They choose to travel around by horse and buggy, or a three-wheel electric trike, but not a gas fueled small car that emits CO_2 gases that harm the environment. One problem that these people with the Freedom Seeker Personality Trait of Money may not consider is if they do not pay into Social Security, then they cannot collect Social Security later in life when they are older or feeble, unless they have been married to a working spouse who paid into self-employment tax.

There also is a problem area when a person with the Freedom Seeker Personality Trait of Money in his mind, emotions, and heart is impatient in obtaining freedom through self-actualization because self-actualization is a false religion. So, he may take great risks, seeking self-actualization at his own peril, to try to become financially free to be accepted as one of the rich and famous, one of the trend setters, or one of the artistic self-indulgers to his own financial impoverishment. Thus, often, the risks taken to enhance his own self-actualization lead to significant losses. Frustration, bitterness, and disappointments can lead to bankruptcy or an early grave if this personality disorder is very obsessive and overly compulsive.

The loss of money can lead to suicide by unbelievers when money has become their idol. Following the Great Recession of 2008, and the world economy almost crashing, came a spate of regulation and scrutiny brought by federal regulators and the government on U.S. and global financial institutions. During this period up to 2014, more than forty financial professionals, or bankers, committed apparent suicide.

The journalist, Michael Gray, of the Sunday Business Editor, New York Post, followed and reported these bankers or financial professionals who committed suicide. This included a banker from J.P. Morgan. Also, there were two Deutsche Bank bankers who the authorities ruled were suicides. For example, on January 24, 2014, in Bloomberg, it was reported by Laurence Arnold and Nicolas Comfort that William Broeksmit, an Ex-Deutsche Bank Risk Manager committed suicide by hanging in his residence, even though his personal life and business life seemed rock solid; but apparently, he was not able to handle the market decline and his failure.

Because the people with the obsessive-compulsive disorder Freedom Seeker Personality Trait of Money abhor any relationship which will tie them down, they sometimes come off as irresponsible and undependable. However, this is the wrong diagnosis, as it is not a case of slothfulness, but rather a desire to remain free from control.

Personality Traits of Money

You sometimes hear those with the Freedom Seeker Personality Trait of Money say, "Marriage is a great institution, but who wants to live in an institution."

Because every loving relationship requires the surrender of freedom for the betterment and fulfillment of others in the relationship, the person who has an obsessive-compulsive disorder with the Freedom Seeker Personality Trait of Money is usually unwilling to relinquish a portion of his freedom for intimacy. He sometimes will leave his children and spouse because he does not want to be tied down in the daily routine of raising children or having a continuous commitment to a family.

When the person with the Freedom Seeker Personality Trait of Money discovers that true freedom and liberty are gifts from God for those who repent and seek Christ Jesus as Lord and Savior and then submit to God to have their souls transformed, then he discovers the truth, but it may be too late to reconcile with his divorce spouse and abandoned children. Righteousness, peace, and joy is given by the Holy Spirit for whomever will seek first the Kingdom of God and His righteousness. Although it will take a serious and patient effort for reconciliation, Christ is the High Priest of reconciliation back to God (2 Corinthians 5:18-19).

USING MONEY TO FULFILL THE "PROTESTOR PERSONALITY TRAIT OF MONEY"

There are a lot of reasons why Christian Believers protest Socialism, big government, high taxes in America and in other countries. Protesting monetary indulgences seems to be a popular idea.

The U.S. is the world's greatest protest country, as we revolted against England, whereas other countries, such as Canada did not. What are the results of our protest? The U.S. is:

1 in drug addiction
1 in urban violence
1 in Western World in voluntary abortions
1 in Divorce
1 in teenage pregnancy in the Western World
1 in illiteracy in the Western World
U.S. Politicians to be re-elected cause the government to continuously vote to enlarge the debt instead of what is best for the citizens in the long run, as national debt is a hatred of citizens and their posterity.
U.S. Bureaucrats play politics in their actions and decisions to attack those with opposing political views instead of simply executing the laws passed by Congress and the President.

The Protestant Church movement has as its underlying root the protest of the Catholic Church. Now, we have thousands of Protestant denominations; so, we have multiplied the Popes we tried to avoid, and we call them Pastors or Ministers. Sometimes, you become what you protest.

The United States was founded on protest of King George III, as seen in the Declaration of

Independence, the American Revolution, and the U.S. Constitution.

Patrick Henry said, "Give me liberty or give me death."

Protesting is as American as apple pie. The right to redress our grievances before government, the right to assemble to protest, the right to freedom of speech, freedom of religion, and freedom of press are rights guaranteed in the First and Fourteenth Amendments of the U.S. Constitution. The U.S. has the Second Amendment guaranteeing that the citizens have the right to bear arms to protect themselves against government tyranny. There are only three countries that have the right to bear arms to protect the citizens against government tyranny, and they are the U.S., Guatemala, and Mexico.

Therefore, why is the Protestor Personality Trait of Money considered to be one of the underlying problems with mismanagement of money and causing soulish immaturity and obsessive-compulsive disorders and behaviors?

There are whole groups of people with the Protestor Personality Trait of Money who protest directly against money. They advocate Socialism or Communism and the equal distribution of wealth and over proportionate taxes against the wealthy. Things have changed, as now the Protestor Personality Trait of Money thinks it is perfectly okay to punish the industrious who invest and risk capital to build a strong business, while they reward those who do not work, especially who fall into several classes of victims in society. Victimization in society empowers the Protestor Personality Trait of Money.

In the "hippie movement" of the 60s and early 70s, those having the Protestor Personality Trait of Money reigned King among that generation, and they saw the money-hungry older generation as the cause of the world's problems.

Much of the "Jesus Movement" had the Protestor Personality Trait of Money leaders leading the communal lifestyles and brought the old teaching of the "virtue of poverty" strong in the church.

Many people with the Protestor Personality Trait of Money reject the normal 40 hour work schedules as a lifestyle and refuse to compete with those in the same profession, business, or trade because they protest being in the rat race of capitalism.

The commune lifestyle even entered the Jesus movement, with people communing together to "live off God's land."

The roaming, barefoot or sandals, wandering poets of the '60s were thought to be very "heavy," so, the Christian hippies became the itinerant evangelists, such as Lonnie Frisbee who played a significant role in the beginning of Calvary Chapel phenomenal growth and sprung forth the "Jesus Movement" from the late 1960s to the early 1970s.

The people, even some Believers, with the Protestor Personality Trait of Money came against the false teaching of inherent evils of money led a whole generation at first to reject the materialistic free enterprise economy built by our Founding Fathers and the Great Industrialists. 1 Timothy 6:10 refers to those who suffer from the love of money, not that money is

Personality Traits of Money

inherently evil, as the scripture says, "For the love of money is the root of all evil: which while some coveted after, they have erred from the faith, and pierced themselves through with many sorrows."

In fact, people with the Protestor Personality Trait of Money shunned the materialistic mindset in the U.S. and invited the false Eastern Religions into the United States, which rejected materialism and capitalism as evil in favor of spiritualism, which they taught was a higher state of consciousness, along with Socialism. Many of the "baby boomers" in America left these false religions and came back to follow Christ Jesus.

In Genesis 1, after God created the material, natural world, He said, "it is good." The Bible also says, first the natural then the spiritual (1 Corinthians 15:46). Thus, God created the wealth of the world for His Children here on earth for their sustenance and sovereignty, not for their impoverishment or enslavement.

The people with the Protestor Personality Trait of Money have had labels such as "hippies," "commune people," "flower children," and "Jesus freaks." Even today, after a week of wearing typical suit and tie or business dresses, you can see these "old Jesus freaks" of the "Jesus movement" wearing their casual clothes, sandals, brown loafers, and simple Levi dresses to church as a movement "dress code." Certainly not all these people of the 1960s and early 1970s have problems with money, but the influence of the Protestor Personality Trait of Money of the 1960s and early 1970s still prevails even today.

Many Socialist Activists see money and the free enterprise economic system as the oppressive manifestation of evil here on earth. These basic false precepts are expressed in the "isms" of the "new left" who believe in modernism and man's ability to fix man's own problems without God. Their internal thoughts, feelings, and beliefs are expressed in idealistic and humanistic pseudo concerns for the "underdogs" of society, irrespective of any sin involved on the part of the labeled "victims."

The leading philosophical idea exported from America is "victimization." If you want recognition, money, or favorable attention and financial help from the liberal left Socialist Democrats, be a victim. However, the problem is that the Socialist Democrat Bureaucrats of today think that money can solve most all the social ills of society, such as the homeless, social welfare, free education, health care, and the many other entitlements. These people with the Protestor Personality Trait of Money believe that people should be financially free to pursue their artistic gifts, while government should promote cradle to grave and womb to tomb support for everyone living in the country, including illegals. On April 24, 2018, journalists Dylan Matthews reported that far left Socialist Bernie Sanders proposed that the government should guarantee a job for every adult person living in the United States.

Some liberal rich movie stars, singers, and athletes from this era often lead the protests and cry for "green power," "save the whales," "protect Mother Earth," "promote Safe Sin" and "allow Abortion on Demand" because of "freedom of choice." Their mantra is, "Just do not tell me what to do. Do not put any burdens upon me. Give me financial support, and I will vote for you and keep you in office."

Freedom and liberty in the Kingdom of God does not mean God is okay with you exercising your freedom and liberty to sin, to hurt people, drink alcohol excessively, or take drugs. Even though you have initial salvation with eternal life, there are spiritual rewards and crowns that every Believer after initial salvation should strive to obtain. For example, the Crown of Life (James 1:12), the Imperishable Wreath (1 Corinthians 9:25), the Crown of Righteousness (2 Timothy 4:8), the Crown of Glory (1 Peter 5:4) and the Crown of Exaltation (1 Thessalonians 2:19) are special promises of authority bestowed upon special Believers to be used after God creates the new heaven and new earth when Christ and the New Jerusalem comes down from heaven (Revelation Chp. 21) and Christ sets up His throne in Jerusalem to rule and reign over the new creation and all the kingdoms of the world (Revelation 11:15). These special rewards for Christ's Kingdom servants are given by God for faithful work by the Believers led by the Holy Spirit while here on earth after initial salvation. In God's Kingdom, freedom and liberty mean that as a Believer you no longer are allowing the philosophies and ideas of the fallen world and the kingdom of darkness to cause you to stray away from God, the Lord Jesus Christ, and their Kingdom authority and mission here on earth.

When Believers with the Protestor Personality Trait of Money join the church congregation, they can be prior revolutionary activists, old hippies caught in a time culture, frustrated idealists, passive non-competitors, members of oppressed minority groups, anti-capitalists, anti-military, economic class structure dissidents, Christian economic Socialists, IRS dissenters, conspiracy promulgators, and many, many spoiled brats from the Dr. Spock lessons on parenting. They want "easy believism," "little personal responsibility," and "freedom from government intrusion."

These Protestors sometime stretch Jesus' precious grace without losing their salvation as a license to sin. Part of this wrong thinking is because most Pastors and Teachers preach that the purpose of accepting Jesus Christ as Lord and Savior is just to go to heaven, and working here on earth after initial salvation has no eternal purpose because you already have salvation. At best, this is an anemic teaching, and at worse is aberrant theology. Why? Because our future hope is not just to go to heaven, but to return with Christ Jesus to a new heaven and new earth, with the coming of the New Jerusalem and all the Saints that have passed, to rule and reign with Christ Jesus throughout eternity back here on earth (Revelation 5:10; 11:15). There is no ruling and reigning with Christ Jesus in heaven, but back here in the new heaven and new earth.

Revelation 21:1 says, "And I saw a new heaven and a new earth: for the first heaven and the first earth were passed away; and there was no more sea." Revelation 11:15 says, "…The kingdoms of this world are become the kingdoms of our Lord, and of His Christ; and He shall reign for ever and ever (back here in earth where there is a new heaven and new earth)." Revelation 5:10 says, "And hast made us unto our God kings and priests: and we shall reign on the earth." Daniel 7:13-14,27 says, "I saw in the night visions, and, behold, one like the Son of man came with the clouds of heaven, and came to the Ancient of days, and they brought Him near before Him. (14) And there was given Him (Son of Man and Son of God, Jesus) dominion, and glory, and a kingdom, that all people, nations, and languages, should serve Him: His dominion is an everlasting dominion, which shall not pass away, and His kingdom that which shall not be destroyed. . . (27) And the kingdom and dominion, and the greatness of the kingdom under the whole heaven, shall be given to the people of the Saints (Believers) of the Most High, whose kingdom is an everlasting kingdom, and all dominions shall serve and obey Him."

Personality Traits of Money

The people with the Protestor Personality Trait of Money unite as to what they are against. The 1960s Jesus movement allowed the worldly Protestors to be saved and come into the church; and many of them protested the "Christian Religious Establishment" that had been in existence about 1800 years as Catholics and since October 31, 1517, the day Martin Luther posted his protesting Ninety-five Theses on the door of a Catholic Church building at Wittenberg, Germany that started the Protestant Church revolution by the Holy Spirit.

Remember the Beatle's song? "Do you want a revolution, yea, yea. You know that you want to change the world." The people with the Protestor Personality Trait of Money are not satisfied with the world system or even a Christian moral free enterprise, as they normally prefer cradle to grave and womb to tomb financial support by a Socialist government allowing them more free time to drop out of society and protest the wrongs of the U.S. culture while they pursue their artistic, musical, or acting callings; or they just hide out off the grid without little societal interaction.

To the Protestor there is authority in the word "No." Many Protestors have joined likeminded protesting ministries throughout the Body of Christ. There was a time in the 1960s and 1970s when he who said "No" won the argument with little debate.

As an attorney at law, if a client consults me whether to join a business or investment, and if I say, "No, in my legal opinion, that may cause you a loss," I cannot be sued for malpractice, even if the person missed the opportunity that was profitable. Yet, if I as his attorney advise him that the investment sounds okay, and he loses his money, he can sue me for malpractice for what he called my professional "recommendation." I have learned to never recommend any investment. I do not have a license that is regulated by the Securities and Exchange Commission, but those professionals without a legal license cannot practice law like I do. I do not prepare income tax returns because I am not a licensed tax preparer, even though I know a lot about income, capital gains, gift, and estate taxes, as an estate planning attorney.

IN CHRISTIANITY, SEEKING POVERTY AS A FORM OF GODLINESS OR HOLINESS IS ABERRANT THEOLOGY

Many people in the world with the Protestor Personality Trait of Money have compromised their philosophical beliefs as they became older and sought businesses, high paying jobs, bought homes, and contributed to retirement plans. Many of them joined those business owners or employed workers who were working 60 hours a week.

In the world, Tom Hayden became a congressman. Timothy Leary became a highly paid public speaker.

Jane Fonda changed and apologized to the Vietnam Veterans for her going to Hanoi, North Vietnam during the Vietnam War in 1972 as a protestor against the war. Jane Fonda is an excellent actress and is the recipient of numerous accolades, including two Academy Awards, two British Academy Film Awards, seven Golden Globe Awards, a Primetime Emmy Award, the AFI Life Achievement Award, the Honorary Palme d'Or, and the Cecil B. DeMille Award.

However, the greatest award Jane Fonda received was when she became a Christian. She stated on June 10, 2009, in an article titled, About My Faith, "I am frequently asked about my faith. At the end of my marriage to Ted Turner I became a Christian. For several years prior, I had begun to feel I was being led. I felt a presence, a reverence humming within me. It was and is difficult to articulate. Today I think I know what was happening: I was becoming embodied, whole. I had spent 60 years dis-embodied, trying to be perfect so I could be loved. You can't be whole if you're trying to be perfect. Now, as I entered my sixth decade and with much work, I could feel myself becoming whole and I knew: This is what God is. I was stunned when I read in William Bridges's The Way of Transition, that in Matthew 5:48 when Jesus tells his disciples, 'You, therefore, must be perfect, as your heavenly Father is perfect,' it was a mistranslation of the Greek adjective teleios which actually means 'whole, fully formed, fully developed.' Jesus wasn't telling his disciples to be perfect like God, he was telling them to be whole, like God."

People mature and change over time, and they find life is not only to be protested but designed for them to make the best of it. When these people repent by rejecting the philosophies of the fallen word and turning around to accept Jesus as Lord and Savior, and they seek first the Kingdom of God and His righteousness, then they will find Jesus' abundant zoe life, true freedom, and liberty (John 10:10b; 8:36; 2 Corinthians 3:17).

In the world, people with the Protestor Personality Trait of Money confuse philosophical idealism with God's truth, and their philosophical fallen world idealism, where people want equal consequences, regardless of whether they work or whether they are not qualified for the profession, sport, or proclivity in a specific calling of God. To tell God that His creative rules of diversity is not the rules mankind will follow is a denouncement of God's truths. Most people with the Protestor Personality Trait of Money reap what they sow, which means they find many other people protesting the same ideas and ideals that make the people with the Protestor Personality Trait of Money think they are the ones with the "truth" while others are full of greed, avarice, covetousness, and are uncaring.

Some people with the Protestor Personality Trait of Money, who end up in the false religions are caught in a trap. The freedom they were seeking has become a non conformist turned conformist to a bad meditation rigorous lifestyle. All these false religions are nothing more than self-actualizing philosophies. They will not give their devotees eternal life. People cannot grant themselves eternal life. Hebrews 5:9 says, "And being made perfect, He (Jesus) became the Author of eternal salvation unto all those that obey Him."

PROTESTOR PERSONALITY TRAIT OF MONEY PEOPLE COME TO CHURCH

People with the Protestor Personality Trait of Money continue to come to church congregations to fuel a movement in church, often having a heart full of beliefs that support protesting money.

The protest of the Catholic Church has produced truly little unification amongst the Protestants. There are now more splits and denominations in the Protestant churches than ever was visualized by Martin Luther or any of the other Protestant leaders that followed. Most of the holidays practiced by Protestants were established by the Catholic Church, including choosing Sunday as the day of weekly worship instead of Saturday. The Protestant Ministers kept Sunday as the day of worship, listening to a sermon, and fellowship, even though Martin Luther and the other Protestant leaders held to the proposition that they believed in sola scriptura, which means belief in only what the scriptures say. Sola scriptura rejects any original infallible authority other than the Bible. So, why did Luther accept the change of the Sabbath to be Sunday instead of Saturday?

The Catholic Church leaders believe the Catholic Church priesthood is the government of God here on earth, and therefore the leader priests have the God-given authority to pass ordinances regarding religious matters. With this authority to legislate and change the words of the Bible, the Catholic Church priesthood leaders set forth the position that they had the authority as God's kingdom government here on earth to change the day of worship from Saturday to Sunday.

"Sunday is a Catholic institution, and its claims to observance can be defended only on Catholic principles. From beginning to end of scripture there is not a single passage that warrants the transfer of weekly public worship from the last day of the week to the first."-Catholic Press Sydney, Australia, August 1900. "Reason and common sense demand the acceptance of one or the other of these alternatives: either Protestantism and the keeping holy of Saturday, or Catholicity and the keeping holy of Sunday. Compromise is impossible." --The Catholic Mirror, December 23, 1893 [The Catholic Mirror is a Baltimore Roman Catholic weekly newspaper].

Notice that these statements were written by Catholic Priests who question the use of authority of the Catholic priesthood religious hierarchy to change scriptures.

Not only did the Catholic Church change the day of worship and fellowship, but the Catholic Church also made-up unscriptural innovative ideas to for people to donate more money. The Catholic church invented the concept of "purgatory," where Believers were allowed to pay indulgences to lessen the time that they and their loved ones' souls stay for a season of years before God allows them to enter heaven. Major charitable contributions were paid by wealthy Catholics, and the Catholic Church leaders financed wars and the construction of buildings, such as the St. Peter's Basilica in Rome and other magnificently built church buildings in Europe and throughout the world. Purgatory is a concept that wants Believers to accept that Christ Jesus' death on the Roman Cross was not enough work on His part for Catholic Church members to go to heaven, although they accepted Him as Savior and Lord.

The latest complaint of some Protestant Pastors is the protest of all the different denominations which were founded on some church practice disagreement that caused a "church split" needs to be resolved to bring unity in the church denominations. He who sows revolution sets off a protest idea that revolves and revolts against the original revolutionary idea (Galatians 6:7-8).

The current Catholic Pope is promoting for all the Eastern Orthodox churches and all the Protestant churches to reunite under the Catholic Church again, where the Pope is God's leading authority here on earth. Those advocates of this unification are out of touch with God's purpose of having "...a glorious church, not having spot, or wrinkle, or any such thing; but that it should be holy and without blemish."

Before the Catholic Church, Eastern Orthodox churches, and all the Protestant churches unify the body of Christ as His multi-Believers as betrothed and bride, the spiritual leaders and congregations must repent from religion, become humble, and set up twelve pure-hearted Apostles who are the government spiritual leaders throughout the world. These twelve pure apostles must wash themselves with the pure, unselfish, unself-centered word of God and are selected because of each of their humble servanthood unto the Lord, not their traditional religion. They must preach both the gospel of the kingdom (Matthew 24:14) and preach repentance and remission of sins (Luke 24:47) to every ethnic group throughout the world (Matthew 28:18-20; Acts 1:8). Jesus said in Mark 10:42-44, ". . . Ye know that they which are accounted to rule over the Gentiles exercise lordship over them; and their great ones exercise authority upon them. (43) But so shall it not be among you: but whosoever will be great among you, shall be your minister: (44) And whosoever of you will be the chiefest, shall be servant of all."

Matthew 19: 27-29 says, "Then answered Peter and said unto Him, 'Behold, we have forsaken all, and followed thee; what shall we have therefore?' (28) And Jesus said unto them, 'Verily I say unto you, That ye which have followed me, in the regeneration when the Son of Man shall sit in the throne of His glory, ye also shall sit upon twelve thrones, judging the twelve tribes of Israel. (29) And every one that hath forsaken houses, or brethren, or sisters, or father, or mother, or wife, or children, or lands, for My name's sake, shall receive an hundredfold, and shall inherit everlasting life. (30) But many that are first shall be last; and the last shall be first.'"

Thus, the first order of business of unification will be to dissolve the religious hierarchies of every faction and denomination in all the Christian churches. Whoever demands to be first or the chiefest among leaders is disqualified, so, the present Pope would not be one of the twelve end-time church Apostles because he wants everyone under his authority. The Holy Spirit will choose the humblest of all Believers. The Holy Spirit would choose some women. The Pope also wants all the Eastern Orthodox churches and Protestant churches to come underneath the Catholic Church and its authority over them. The fact that the Catholic Church history of changing scriptures because the Pope believes the Catholic Church is the government of God's kingdom here on earth also makes the Catholic Church disqualified to lead. The fact that the Catholic Church and several Protestant denominations teach as part of their creed that women are not qualified as Apostles, Prophets, Evangelists, Pastors, and Teachers, mean those denominations do not qualify to have one of their own to be one of the twelve ruling government leaders. Some religious leaders differ in baptism practices, and others do not believe that Apostles and Prophets are for today. Additionally, the Catholic Church still has purgatory and still preaches that good works are required to go to heaven. The Protestant Movement was founded on not recognizing purgatory or indulgences because they believe in justification by faith alone and believe that the crucifixion of Jesus on the Roman cross alone is sufficient work for eternal life, not by the Believer's own works lest he boast (Ephesians 2:8-9).

Yes, there is Ephesians 4:4-6, which says, "There is one body, and one Spirit, even as ye are called in one hope of your calling; (5) One Lord, one faith, one baptism, (6) One God and Father of all, who is above all, and through all, and in you all." It says there has to be one hope, one Lord, one faith, one baptism, and one God and Father of all.

Personality Traits of Money

In the Protestant churches, they do not call Pastors, "father" as a title before his name. There cannot be put a name of this new assembly of the Lord's Kingdom of Believers. God used the Jewish religious hierarchy in Jerusalem to fulfill God and Jesus' purpose of Jesus voluntarily laying down His natural psuche life of His body, vicariously taking on Himself the sins of mankind, so Believers can have the righteousness of God and vicariously taking on Himself the curse of the law by hanging on the cross to abolish the curse of the law for Believers to bring forth the Abrahamic blessing (2 Corinthians 5:21; Galatians 3:13-14).

Biblically, Genesis 1:28 and Galatians 3:28 say that women are equal ministers, with equal authority for dominion stewardship of God's earthy creation and have equal vocations as kings, priests, lords, ambassadors, and soldiers the same as men. Why has there never been a woman Pope? The Catholic Church and several Protestant churches have denominational prohibitions of women being Pastors, Elders, or Priests. Finally, all churches have to remove the racial and cultural practices of discrimination on Saturday or Sunday morning, where we have Black churches, White churches, Korean churches, Filipino churches, Hispanic churches, Chinese churches, Romanian churches, Russian churches, etc. In practice all of these church communities are built on the flesh and cultures of the congregations. This has to immediately stop. This practice is building the Ekklesia on the flesh, not Ephesians 4:1-6. God's healthy congregation is non-discriminatory of race, culture, or gender.

For a thorough teaching on the equality of women and men in ministry based upon scripture, and specifically the tradition of falsely interpreting scriptures to exclude women from being Pastors or Elders, I invite you read the author's book titled, The Great Bride Awakening.

Finally, I suspect that the Catholic Church may demand all the money in tithes and offerings must be deposited in the Catholic Church bank and investment accounts. The Catholic Church Pope really has no idea what he is saying and what it would take for his desire to reunite the Catholic and Protestant churches.

To start with, church Leaders and all Believers may unify with those that accept the Apostles' Doctrines that are enumerated in Hebrews 6:1-2, which says, "Therefore leaving the principles of the doctrine of Christ, let us go on unto perfection; not laying again the foundation of repentance from dead works, and of faith toward God, (2) of the doctrine of baptisms, and of laying on of hands, and of resurrection of the dead, and of eternal judgment."

Most all church leaders accept Ephesians 4:4-6 and Hebrews 6:1-2 as truths and mandates to follow. Yet, it is the man-made religious practices that often lack scriptural support, that have an over emphasis of one scripture over others, or that misinterpret some scriptures that bring about disunity. Some church leaders do not believe that gifts of healings, prophecies, wisdom, or other spiritual gifts like tongues are for today; and they do not believe that all Believers are Kings, Priests after the order of Melchizedek (Revelation 1:6; Hebrews chp 7), Lords (1 Timothy 6:15), ambassadors of Christ (2 Corinthians 5:20), or kingdom soldiers (2 Timothy 2:3-4). Other church leaders believe in water baptism by sprinkling or using a cup of water when a baby is brought before the Priest, while most Protestant church leaders wait until the child grows and has voluntarily confessed Jesus as Lord and Savior before baptism. Some church leaders practice in sprinkling of water to baptize while others believe in dunking under water for baptism. A very few churches believe in no instruments of music and all singing has to be acapella while other play musical instruments of keyboards, drums, violins, saxophones, guitars, choirs, orchestras, and singing as a big production.

All of these religious practices have something in common, and that is to continue these practices in order to keep the tithes and offerings to continue being donated by those who insist on these practices. Thus, these man-made practices that causes disunity draw donors every week to pay the church hierarchy to continue with these religious traditions. Jesus said in Mark 7:13, "Making the word of God of none effect through your tradition, which ye have delivered: and many such like things do ye."

In conclusion, it is the "religious practices" inside the church buildings that separate the Believers in the various denominations, contrary to scripture. I think all Believers have a little or a lot of protest in their hearts.

Yet, most denomination leaders share the same basic beliefs. There are fundamentals that all can believe who are Christians. For example, let me suggest the following creeds that are foundational for all Believers. "As Believers we believe in One infinite God the Father, God the Word, and God the Holy Spirit, and together as one God was the Creator of all things, both visible and invisible and spiritual and natural. We believe in one finite Lord Jesus Christ, the only begotten Son of God, begotten of the Father before the foundation of the world. Jesus is the Light of Light, has both a divine nature as infinite God the Word and a finite humanity nature as the only begotten Son of God, and His humanity nature is also a mortal Son of man. Jesus' divine nature and humanity nature are inseparably joined together but are distinguishable and not commingled. Jesus' humanity nature, coupled with His divine nature, God the Word, came down from heaven, was born of a virgin named Mary, born as King over all mankind. We believe that Jesus was crucified on a Roman Cross at the order of Pontius Pilate, and suffered, and was buried, and on the third day He rose again, according to the Scriptures. We believe those who repent, confess Jesus as Lord, and believe that Jesus rose from the dead on their day, are saved. We receive a born again spirit that is perfect and whole, does not sin, is righteous, holy, and is joined as one spirit with Christ's humanity nature, is a new creature in Christ, where old things have passed away and all things become new. Through Christ Jesus we are reconciled with God, have received eternal life, but we have souls that must be transformed to make us better servants to God. We will receive a resurrected new body like Jesus when Jesus returns in a new heaven and new earth and the new Jerusalem comes down from heaven onto earth. We believe that after Jesus was raised from the dead on the third day, He called His disciples to the Mount of Ascension, and there He ascended into heaven. Jesus' humanity nature now sits on a throne at the right hand of God as our Intercessor, King of kings, High Priest of priest of the Order of Melchizedek, and Lord of lords; and He shall come again with glory back to the new heaven and new earth to judge the living and the dead, whose Kingdom shall have no end. We accept that our eternal hope is that we, as Believers, will rule and reign with Christ here in the new heaven and new earth for all eternity. We believe in the Holy Spirit who manifested with power and jurisdictional authority on the day of Pentecost to start the Church age, whom we must follow, be taught, and be led in all things. We believe that after initial salvation, we should be baptized in water and the Spirit. We believe that our bodies are the temple of God, and believe that God indwells Believers individually, indwells Believers' corporate body in the local congregation, and indwells Believers in the universal body throughout the world. We believe that daily we are commanded to agape love each other and seek first the kingdom of God and His righteousness. We believe that the Bible was written by devout men who were inspired by God. These beliefs are the foundational beliefs that most all should believe. We believe that Jesus mandated Believers to preach both the gospel of the kingdom and preach repentance and remission of sins as the primary joint messages."

Now, let us look at some evil Protestors to show when the Protestor does not turn around and repent and accept Jesus as Lord and Savior but espouses a philosophy of humanism, fascism, or socialism that opposes God, Christ Jesus, God's Kingdom, and the body of Believers, the Ekklesia.

ADOLF HITLER WAS A PROTESTOR
PERSONALITY TRAIT OF MONEY

There are legitimate righteous Protestors historically, but also there are Protestors who are evil. One of those Protestors was a Nazi Fascist German Adolf Hitler.

Post WWI, at the end of 1923, the German Mark was worth practically nothing as the currency plummeted in value. In a matter of months prices rose to unimaginable levels, with people carrying wheelbarrows full of German money just to buy a loaf of bread or a quart of milk for the children. The hyper-inflationary spiral was fueled by a lack of confidence in the German Mark, the payment of war reparations, and oppressive government policies. The total devaluation of the German Mark caused catastrophic hardships for post WWI German citizens and the country's overall economy.

In Europe the exclusion of Jews from many trades and craft guilds began after the Roman Catholic First Crusade (1096–1099). During that time the Catholic clergy, the secular governments, and local trade and craft guild members promoted laws excluding Jews from the trades and craft guilds. Jews were forbidden to own land, so farming and sheep herding were not occupations they were entitled to pursue. The Catholic Church forbade Christians from charging interest for loans, but the prohibition did not apply to Jews. The prohibitions regarding trades, crafts, farming, and non-ownership of land, along with Christians not allowed to charge interest, led Jews into peddling, selling second-hand goods, pawn brokering, tax collecting, money exchangers, and money-lending; and these "Jewish trades" were considered "necessary evils" in society, including Germany.

The Insidious Protest Against Jews in post WWI in Germany: Antisemitism in post WWI Germany was fueled because of the struggle over lack of a valuable German Mark money to purchase necessities of life. Again, there were prohibitions regarding Jews being allowed to work in trades, crafts, and farming, along with Christians not allowed to charge interest, led Jews into peddling, selling second-hand goods, pawnbroking, tax collecting, money exchanging, and money lending. In post WWI during 1923 and onward, German people needed loans and needed currencies from other countries to purchase goods and services. Because the German Mark was worthless, Jews required hard assets security from non-Jewish Germans for any loans or to pay for foreign currency which did have value. Many non-Jewish Germans were using hard assets, including jewelry, cars, furniture, and anything of value as security for loans or to receive other foreign currencies, as Jews would not except the German Mark by itself because the hyperinflation was a daily and miserable life. Non-Jewish Germans wanted a group as the scapegoat to blame instead of their government, which had the power. The non-Jewish Germans surmised that the minority German Jews were the obvious choices to persecute, although most of the German Jewish citizens were suffering as well.

One can see how frustrating and difficult it was in Germany with the aftermath of WWI, and this shows how the avarice love of money is insidious and can be the root cause of all kinds of evil, including the hatred and blaming of a certain race, like the Jews, for a very bad economy that over time resulted in mass genocide of the Jews, Poles, Slavs, Russians, Eastern Europeans, Gypsies, and others as scapegoats to blame them for the reason of the financial suffering in Germany.

It may have been smarter at the time for the Jews not to involve themselves with taking German citizens family jewelry, cars, or even homes which can be sold as hard assets as payment for foreign money or as security or liens for loans. This made the German husbands and their wives furious that the Jews were prospering when they were giving away their family valuables, so, they could get foreign currency from the Jews for food and shelter for their families. The German non-Jews felt that Jews were greedy, and they felt the Jews should suffer like the rest of the Germans instead of taking advantage of non-Jewish German citizens during this economic crisis. On the other hand, not all Jews owned businesses, and Jews were indeed suffering like other non-Jewish Germans. In exchanging hard assets for foreign currencies and requiring hard assets for loans, the Jews thought they were just applying good business principles to make a secured investment to make a normal profit. Yet, an outcry against the Jews started, and it was a deadly protest.

The economically suffering non-Jewish German citizens were ripe for the Protestor Adolf Hitler, who had the Protestor Personality Trait of Money and who vehemently was against the Jews to blame them for the economic woes of German non-Jew citizens. Hitler's book Mein Kampf (German for My Struggle) included the following passage, which was representative of much antisemitism protest against Jews in Germany and Europe and even some in the U.S.: "The Jewish train of thought in all this is clear. The Bolshevization of Germany - that is, the extermination of the national folkish Jewish intelligentsia to make possible the sweating of the German working class under the yoke of Jewish world finance - is conceived only as a preliminary to the further extension of this Jewish tendency of world conquest.... If our people and our state become the victim of these blood-thirsty and avaricious Jewish tyrants of nations, the whole earth will sink into the snares of this octopus." Hitler's book, Mein Kampf, also protested any Slavs, Gypsies, Russians, Eastern Europeans, along with the Jews that were not descendants of the German "Aryan" race. Instead of accepting German citizens as a down-trodden defeated people, the Protestor Hitler and his evil men started the Aryan race religious concept as the superior German race that had as its philosophy to rid the planet of inferior races that culminated in exterminating of Jews, Poles, Slavs, Russians, Gypsies, other Eastern European nations, along with mentally challenged, and homosexuals. Hitler was determined to replace what he considered to be inferior races with the German Aryan race to make one new Aryan race that ruled the world.

Aryanism: Aryanism is an ideology of racial supremacy which views the supposed Aryan race as a distinct and superior racial group which believes they have the right to enslave and rule the rest of humanity. The Aryan religion is based upon the physical characteristic of people. The Aryan race, long extinct, were originally from Northern Iran and India and were light brown skin, not white skin as promoted by the Nazis. The Nazi symbol, the Swastika, was made like a religious symbol used as a holy symbol by Hinduism, Jainism, and Buddhism for centuries, but these religions were totally against killing of innocent people and against the genocide of entire races of people in other cultures. On the other hand, to the world, the German Swastika became a symbol of hate and evil, embodying painful and traumatic memories of the German Third Reich. The German Swastika is associated with genocide and racial hatred that the German leaders of the Third Reich justified the atrocities of the Holocaust, with German soldiers in concentration camps killing Jews, Slavs, Gypsies, Russians, Eastern Europeans, mentally challenged, and homosexuals, and anyone who protested the Third Reich. Thus, what started the Holocaust and the horrible crimes against humanity by WWII German Nazi Fascist government-sponsored genocide was triggered by the economic collapse of the German economy post WWI.

Nazi Fascism has been one of the harshest, most oppressive types of government philosophies known to man that took over all the infrastructure, education, religions, utilities, police, armies, youths, and every aspect within the nation of Germany in the 1930s-1940s. The Nazi Protestors became one of the most organized oppressors of history, based upon extreme economic antisemitism and falsehoods against different races of people by Nazi Germany, but which had some supporters in Europe and even in the United States.

After WWI the German Weimar Republic was looking to blame a group of people for the economic woes of its German citizens, so the government politicians promoted the false ideas that the rich Jews who handled the money exchanges and money lending were the cause of the German economy crashing, when the German non-Jews and German government officials should be repenting as a nation for its aggression in WWI to conquer other countries. The German non-Jews made the Jews to be scapegoats as causing the post WWI economic crisis that resulted in the German mark hyperinflation.

There were wealthy Jews living in Germany at that time, but most Jews were suffering impoverishment like the rest of the non-Jewish Germans. Historian Donald L. Niewyk noted that "by the end of 1923, the Berlin Jewish Community had established nineteen soup kitchens, seven shelters, and an employment information and placement office for the destitute Jews of the city. Other big-city communities did the same." [Facing History & Ourselves, "Who Is to Blame for the Inflation?," last updated August 2, 2016.]

Thus, most of the German Jews suffered just like the German non-Jews post WWI. Non-Jewish Germans refused to eat at the soup kitchens provided by the German Jews, and then non-Jewish Germans would not allow the German Jews to eat at their soup kitchens. However, the food shortage provided by the German government made the meals less satisfying. Many Germans owned land and could grow and sell crops. Yet, the German Jews did not own land. Because of the German Jewish communities, they gathered together and helped each other to survive.

Nazi Antisemitism after Hitler gained power: Wikipedia published an essay about Nazi antisemitism, titled, Economic Antisemitism, wherein it says, "Antisemitism and the persecution of Jews represented a central tenet of Nazism. In its 25-point Party Program, published in 1920, Nazi Party members publicly declared their intention to segregate Jews from 'Aryan' society and to abrogate Jews' political, legal, and civil rights. Nazi leaders began to carry out their pledge to persecute German Jews soon after their assumption of power. Adolf Hitler rose to power in Germany during a time of economic depression. Hitler blamed Jews for Germany's economic woes. From 1933, repressive laws were passed against Jews, culminating in the Nuremberg Laws, which removed most of the rights of citizenship from Jews by using a racial definition based on descent, rather than any religious definition of who was a Jew. Sporadic violence against the Jews became widespread with the Kristallnachtriots, which targeted Jewish homes, businesses, and places of worship, killing hundreds of Jews across Germany, including killing Jews in the newly-annexed Austria. The ideologically-antisemitic agenda culminated in the genocide of six million Jews of Europe, known as the Holocaust."

Americans Should Protest U.S. Auto Companies who were Nazi sympathizers. We citizens of America, especially those who had relatives disfigured or killed in WWII, should consider protesting the large auto manufacturers, consisting of Ford, General Motors, and Chrysler because they were Nazi Sympathizers and even made engines for the Nazi airplanes bombing England, and manufactured German troop trucks, and German Jeeps, etc.

The following is excerpted from a report printed by the United States Senate Committee on the Judiciary in 1974 regarding the U.S. auto industry as Nazi Sympathizers.

"The activities of General Motors, Ford, and Chrysler prior to and during World War II... are instructive. At that time, these three firms dominated motor vehicle production in both the United States and Germany. Due to its mass production capabilities, automobile manufacturing is one of the most crucial industries with respect to national defense. As a result, these firms retained the economic and political power to affect the shape of governmental relations both within and between these nations in a manner which maximized corporate global profits. In short, they were private governments unaccountable to the citizens of any country yet possessing tremendous influence over the course of war and peace in the world. The substantial contribution of these firms to the American war effort in terms of tanks, aircraft components, and other military equipment is widely acknowledged. Less well known are the simultaneous contributions of their foreign subsidiaries to the Axis Powers. In sum, they maximized profits by supplying both sides of WWII with the materiel needed for each side to conduct the war.

"During the 1920's and 1930's, the Big Three automakers undertook an extensive program of multinational expansion...By the mid-1930's, these three American companies owned automotive subsidiaries throughout Europe and the Far East; many of their largest facilities were located in the politically sensitive nations of Germany, Poland, Romania, Austria, Hungary, Latvia, and Japan...Due to their concentrated economic power over motor vehicle production in both Allied and Axis territories, the Big Three inevitably became major factors in the preparations and progress of the war. In Germany, for example, General Motors and Ford became an integral part of the Nazi war efforts. GM's plants in Germany built thousands of bombers and jet fighter propulsion systems for the Luftwaffe at the same time that its American plants produced aircraft engines for the U.S. Army Air Corps....

"Ford was also active in Nazi Germany's prewar preparations. In 1938, for instance, it opened a truck assembly plant in Berlin whose "real purpose," according to U.S. Army Intelligence, was producing 'troop transport-type' vehicles for the Wehrmacht. That year Ford's chief executive received the Nazi German Eagle (first class).

Personality Traits of Money

"The outbreak of WWII in September 1939 resulted inevitably in the full conversion by GM and Ford of their Axis plants to the production of military aircraft and trucks.... On the ground, GM and Ford subsidiaries built nearly 90 percent of the armored "mule" 3-ton half-trucks and more than 70 percent of the Reich's medium and heavy-duty trucks. These vehicles, according to American intelligence reports, served as "the backbone of the German Army transportation system."....

"After the cessation of hostilities, GM and Ford demanded reparations from the U.S. Government for wartime damages sustained by their Axis facilities as a result of Allied bombing... Ford received a little less than $1 million, primarily as a result of damages sustained by its military truck complex at Cologne...

"Due to their multinational dominance of motor vehicle production, GM and Ford became principal suppliers for the forces of fascism as well as for the forces of democracy. It may, of course, be argued that participating in both sides of an international conflict, like the common corporate practice of investing in both political parties before an election, is an appropriate corporate activity. Had the Nazis won, General Motors and Ford would have appeared impeccably Nazi; as Hitler lost, these companies were able to re-emerge impeccably American. In either case, the viability of these corporations and the interests of their respective stockholders would have been preserved." [Extracted from Bradford C. Snell, American Ground Transport: A Proposal for Restructuring the Automobile, Truck, Bus and Rail Industries. Report presented to the Committee of the Judiciary, Subcommittee on Antitrust and Monopoly, United States Senate, February 26, 1974, United States Government Printing Office, Washington, 1974, pp. 16-24.]

THE PROTESTOR KARL MARX AGAINST CAPITALISM

Another example of some having a Protestor Personality Trait of Money was Karl Marx, with his theories of Socialism or Communism, which protested the wealth, capitalism, religion, and royalty of the country. Communist leaders forced atheism as a religion on its people and became extremely oppressive, militaristic, and degraded the human worth for the higher worth of the social whole. "Marx believed that a truly utopian society must be classless and stateless. (It should be noted that Marx died well before any of his theories were put to the test.) Marx's main idea was simple: Free the lower class from poverty and give the poor a fighting chance. How he believed it should be accomplished, however, was another story. To liberate the lower class, Marx believed that the government would have to control all means of production, so that no one could outdo anyone else by making more money. Unfortunately, that proves to this day to be more difficult than he might have realized" [Alia Hoyt "How Communism Works" 25 February 2008.]

Karl Marx with the Protestor Personality Trait of Money did not believe in the sovereign identity of each individual. Marx wrote, "It is not the consciousness of men that determines their lives but, on the contrary, their social being that determines their consciousness." In other words, the collective group defines who humans are, not their individualistic creation by God. Early in his life, Marx, with his Protestor Personality Trait of Money wrote, "The human essence has no true reality." Marx was an atheist when he was a child, and he remained an atheist the rest of his life. Marx protested both the Jewish and Christian religions (and all other religions). Marx wrote, "Religion is the opium of the people."

Vladimir Lenin, another theorist with the Protestor Personality Trait of Money wrote in his The Attitude of the Workers' Party to Religion, "Religion is the opium of the people: this saying of Marx is the cornerstone of the entire ideology of Marxism about religion. All modern religions and churches, all and of every kind of religious organizations are always considered by Marxism as the organs of bourgeois reaction, used for the protection of the exploitation and the stupefaction of the working class."

As a man with the Protestor Personality Trait of Money, Marx was an atheist, did not believe in God, and did not believe each person was created in the image and likeness of God. Marx saw two groups in any economic system that did not have Socialism as its philosophy of government. At the top of the economy are the small minority Bourgeoisie, who are the capitalists and ruling class who own the means of production and monopolize riches and wealth. At the bottom in the non-Socialist culture are the Proletariat who are the working-class majority. The minority Bourgeoisie exploits the Proletariat working class whose labor makes the riches and wealth for the Bourgeoisie. Marx wrote, "This set of economic circumstances combined with environmental determinism means that the Bourgeoisie are conditioned to one set of truths about what's reasonable and good while the Proletariat are conditioned to an opposite set of truths about what's reasonable and good."

Marx protested that a Proletariat earning a living while working for a salary with a business or acting as a middleman was an unjust and exploitive aspect of capitalism. Because many Jews were employed in occupations that Marx considered "non-productive," he had a special criticism for Jews as capitalist and blamed Judaism for the exploitation and alienation of workers or Proletariats.

God does not reward people for rebellious behavior that violate His kingdom principles, but He does forgive them. People cannot make their decisions based upon the fact that their actions are sanctioned by political correctness to be acceptable and worldly fallen good instead of God's good based upon His Kingdom principles.

Normally, temporary rewards given to Protestors escalate the protest and the great gap between the parties widens, resulting in more division instead of acceptance of eternal truth of conciliation.

Part of the backlash of what is called the "fatherless generation" is that the older generation started listening to the younger generation for answers and guidance regarding new ideas, new technologies, new communication devices, and how to use social media, without first consulting the Lord of how these devices often are full of temptations and instruments of sin. Young people often set the styles in hairdos, clothes, music, automobiles, housing, and moral values, and the fifth-grade level television sitcoms, as the new generation. Those in the younger generation are in school learning computers, electronic advancements, and all new ideas. It seems that the younger generation always protest against the older generation who have much wisdom from the life mistakes they have made.

In church congregations, the younger generation Protestors against the older generations set the clothing styles, music, teachings, and the kind of pastoral care expected because the church leaders want to bring the world into the Church to attract people by making them feel comfortable with the church congregation fellowship and environment. However, the biblical approach is to fire up the younger generation to take the truths of the Bible to evangelize the unsaved and transform Believers in the world instead of the other way around.

The Protestors who are anti-establishment, with the Protestor Personality Trait of Money, with their rebellious attitudes, often bring agendas which eventually become acceptable new church tradition. Politicians study these church traditions and trends to attract voters and pass regulations or laws that appeal to the church members. Yet, if these traditions and trends become law but are not biblical, they can increase national debt, taxes, entitlements, military expenditures, and restrictions in every other area of citizens lives. In fact, the Unitarian church leaders who accept the LBGT agenda has become the Protester's request for a "new moral base" for biblical laws regarding morality standards and the definition of marriage and the family.

THE BLACK PASTORS RIGHTFULLY PROTESTED TEENAGE PREGNANCIES OUTSIDE OF MARRIAGE AS SIN

When Black Pastors in the inner cities accepted and endorsed Planned Parenthood in their church communities, and when they were told that Planned Parenthood was teaching and providing contraception without revealing that it included abortions on demand, they unknowingly sanctioned death of innocent humans still in their mother's wombs. However, abortion on demand became a church acceptance by agreeing that a child in the womb was not a viable living human being, which infiltrated into liberal politics of the Democrat economic Socialists and so-called Progressives. Progressives come from the word "progress" or movement forward for the betterment of people. How is killing innocent babies in the wombs of mothers constitute progress for humanity? This is especially true now when less children are being born than is needed to replace the older next to die generation, as most all the older generation most likely will die the next 20 to 30 years, or sooner?

A LEGITIMATE PROTEST OF NOT HAVING BABIES IS NOW A TOPIC OF INTEREST IN THE U.S.

In an article written by Linda Carroll and Shmard Charles, M.D. dated January 9, 2019, titled, Americans Aren't Making Enough Babies To Replace Ourselves, they stated, "Government researchers did not offer an explanation, but experts cited factors including changing economics and fewer teen pregnancies. Americans are having fewer and fewer babies; a new government report finds. In fact, we now aren't birthing enough babies to replace ourselves. For the population to reproduce itself at current numbers, the 'total fertility rate' needs to be 2,100 births per 1,000 women of childbearing age over their lifetime, researchers for the Centers for Disease Control and Prevention said in their report, . . . the latest data show a current rate of just 1,765.5 per 1,000, or 16 percent below the number needed to keep the population stable without additions through immigration. The total fertility rate has been declining steadily for seven years, but the numbers for 2017 represent the biggest drop in recent history. The rate for 2016 was 1,820.5; for 2015, 1,843.5; and for 2014, 1,862.5. The CDC offered no explanation for why the American fertility rate is dropping so precipitously. Experts say the decline isn't due to a single cause, but rather a combination of several factors, including changing economics, delays in childbirth by women pursuing jobs and education, the greater availability of contraception, and a decline in teen pregnancies. The trend seen in the United States is also seen in much of the developed world, including Western Europe, said Dr. John Rowe, a professor at Columbia University's Mailman School of Public Health. One crucial factor driving this is the changing roles of women in society, Rowe said. 'In general women are getting married later in life,' he explained. 'They are leaving the home and launching their families later.' But there is no guarantee that things will work out as planned."

The experts' reason we are behind in the birth rate includes changing economics and fewer teen pregnancies. What the experts are really saying is not fewer teenage pregnancies, but they should have said fewer teenage births because teenagers see abortion of the baby in the womb as a form of birth control. Abortion is not a form of birth control; it is the killing of a developing human being.

God wants Believers to protest the homicide of unborn children. God considers abortion murder by hire because the mother hires a medical doctor to kill the baby in her womb. The "hit man" is the medical doctor that commits the murder of the unborn baby. Let us consider the growth of the unborn baby in the womb.

Fertilization: About fourteen days after the first day of a woman's last period, her ovaries release an egg. If a man and woman have sex a few days before or after the woman's egg is released, a sperm can fertilize her egg. Fertilization happens in the tubes that connect to the woman's ovaries with her uterus. These are the fallopian tubes. The fertilized egg is the beginning of the human being.

Embryo and Placenta: The fertilized egg attaches to the lining of the mother's uterus and begins to grow into the embryo and placenta. The embryo is the part of the fertilized egg that is the human being baby. Although medical doctors call it a fetus starting at about ten weeks, it is a living immature child that is growing in the womb. A one-year-old child is not called a non-human just because the child is growing and cannot care for himself. The Placenta develops from the fertilized egg but does not become part of the baby. It is an organ that provides nourishment to the growing embryo.

Umbilical Cord: One side of the placenta is attached to the inside of the mother's uterus. After a few weeks, the umbilical cord grows out of the other side of the placenta. The umbilical cord connects the embryo to the placenta. The baby is alive because the baby produces blood, a distinct blood different from the mother. The baby is a definite separate life from the mother with his own blood type. Life of the body is in the blood (Leviticus 17:11), and the blood from the embryo moves through the cord into the placenta. In the placenta, the embryo's blood picks up oxygen and nourishment from the mother's blood. Then the oxygen and nutrient rich blood of the mother moves back through the cord into the baby. Right after the baby is delivered, the placenta comes off the mother's uterus and is delivered. The placenta is then called the afterbirth.

Amniotic Sac: The amniotic sac develops and surrounds the embryo baby. It fills with fluid for the baby to float and grow in. This fluid helps protect the baby from injury while it is growing in the mother's womb.

The Baby's Continuous Development in the Womb: In five weeks, the baby's heart starts to beat and most of the organs begin to develop, along with the brain and spinal cord. In ten weeks, the baby is considered a fetus, and in two more weeks (twelve weeks), most of the organs of the baby are formed. In two more weeks (fourteen weeks), doctors can determine whether the baby is a girl or boy. In two to six more weeks (sixteen to twenty weeks), the mother can feel the baby moving inside her womb. In another four weeks (twenty to twenty-four weeks), the baby has a good chance of surviving outside the mother's uterus in the event of a premature birth. Afterwards, until birth the baby's lungs continue to develop until near the time of delivery.

The baby's brain continues to develop throughout pregnancy and during the first year of life after birth. The fact is that after birth the baby's brain continues to grow and develop. Therefore, the immaturity of the body of the baby should not be grounds to excuse the killing of the baby. Otherwise, infanticide would become legalized homicide.

Birth control is stopping the seed of the man from entering and fertilizing the egg of the mother. Abortion is the killing of a human being that already is alive and growing in the womb of the mother. The mass killing of live human beings growing in the womb is genocide or infanticide. Again, the fact that the baby's body is growing in the womb should not be grounds for excusing the homicide of the baby human. Why? The reason is the baby continues to grow for an average of sixteen to eighteen years after birth. The fact that the baby is not fully mature at any stage of the baby's growth does not nullify the fact that the baby is a living human being and should enjoy Constitutional rights to life. The excuse of the pro-abortionist is that abortion is justified because of economic reasons of support since every baby born can be put up for adoption and relieve the mother of the obligation to support the child.

THE BABY IN THE WOMB ALREADY HAS AN IMMORTAL SOUL FROM GOD

The abortion protagonists only consider the physical body of the growing baby in the womb. What about the soul of the baby growing in the mother's womb? The baby in the womb has a developing brain in his body, but the soul of the baby has a mind, emotions, and heart where the baby's will exists that God put in the baby's body at conception that is involve in the baby's physical growth. If there is a still birth and the baby's body dies in the mother's womb due to an accident, the soul leaves the baby's body and returns to heaven. A human being's soul in the body is part of the definition of life, and when the mortal physical body dies, the soul leaves the body. Have the pro-abortionists not considered the baby's soul in their decisions to justify killing the physically unborn?

The physical body of the baby that is growing in the womb is alive and has a living soul that was placed there by God and has a unique personality along with certain natural adamic gifts given by God. A child's innate intelligence has nothing to do with the brain in the body but has to do with the unique quality of the mind in the soul. Abortionists speak about the viability of the physical body of the baby without mentioning that the baby growing in the womb has a mind, emotions, and heart as the baby's soul that is facilitating the growth of the baby's physical body. The mother does not have to think about each step of the development of the baby's body in her womb; the baby's soul in the human body that is growing in the mother's womb is growing because God planted the soul in the fertilized egg of the mother. The baby's innate intelligence is in the baby's soul and is what is causing the baby's body to grow. The soul of the baby causes the body after the child's birth to continue to grow until the child becomes an adult. Afterwards, the adult child's human soul continues to bring health to his body throughout the human's life. 3 John 2 says, "Beloved, I wish above all things that thou mayest prosper and be in health, even as thy soul prospereth." From the date of conception until the date of death, the body's health is dependent upon the health of the human's soul.

Every doctor knows that when the body dies, the soul leaves the body and goes to heaven or hell. The body decays back to dust. That is what happens at death. What happens at conception. This is when the soul comes into the egg that has just been fertilized. You can have a deadly disease and your body is dying. After your soul leaves your body, medical doctors can keep the body functioning by machines, but you are dead because your soul has left your body. After death the King James Version in Matthew 25:46 says, "And these shall go away into everlasting punishment: but the righteous into life eternal." In the Revised Standard Version, and others, state Matthew 25:46, "And they will go away into eternal punishment, but the righteous into eternal life." The body decays to dust, so this is a reference to the spirit and soul leaving the body.

The abortion advocates never call the baby in the womb a human being with a living soul. Their whole attention is on the baby's developing a physical body. They call the baby's body an embryo and then fetus, as if those words mean that the little physical body growing inside the womb is not yet a human being with a living soul. God creates a special soul in each baby the moment the egg is fertilized by the seed of the man, and the baby's will is in the baby's soul and the baby's soul facilitates the growth of the body, not the mother's soul and body. The baby's soul is what causes the baby to incrementally grow his eyes, ears, nose, hands, feet, heart, lungs, kidneys, stomach, intestines, brain, and his other organs.

Psalms 127:3 says, "Lo, children are a heritage of the LORD: and the fruit of the womb is His reward." Jeremiah 1:5 says, "Before I formed thee in the belly I knew thee (soul); and before thou camest forth out of the womb I sanctified thee (soul), and I ordained thee (soul) a prophet unto the nations." Elizabeth, who was pregnant with John the Baptist, said in Luke 1:41-44, "And it came to pass, that, when Elisabeth heard the salutation of Mary, the babe leaped in her womb; and Elisabeth was filled with the Holy Ghost: (42) And she spake out with a loud voice, and said, 'Blessed art thou among women, and blessed is the fruit of thy womb. (43) And whence is this to me, that the mother of my Lord should come to me? (44) For, lo, as soon as the voice of thy salutation sounded in mine ears, the babe leaped in my womb for joy (joy is an expression of the soul).'"

Since the baby in Elizabeth's womb was a prophet, the baby's soul in Elizabeth's womb knew that the baby growing in Mary's womb was the prophesized Messiah. The baby physically growing in Elizabeth's womb in the baby's soul became excited and exercised his will to cause his little body to leap. This was the baby's soul exercising his will, not Elizabeth's soul exercising her will. John the Baptist's soul before birth was created by God as a prophet of God.

If abortion was legal in Jesus' time, and Elizabeth being an older lady, and if she decided to abort the baby because she was too old to raise the baby, then she would have killed the greatest prophet of the Old Testament. How many prophets in her soul have been killed in America by the infanticide in mothers' wombs, oftentimes with the excuse of the mother that she did not have an income to take care and raise the child? How many mothers do not realize and accept that the baby in her womb is a living soul; otherwise, the body of the baby would not be alive. How many medical scientists that had a cure for cancer in her soul sent by God have been killed in America by the infanticide in mothers' wombs? How many great authors that had a literary skills in her soul sent by God have been killed in America by the infanticide in mothers' wombs? How many great musicians with an opus in his soul sent by God have been killed in America by the infanticide in mothers' wombs? How many great teachers with the gift of teaching in her soul sent by God have been killed in America by the infanticide in mothers' wombs?

It is very important that women who desire an abortion understand that a viable soul is in the baby in her womb, and she will be hiring a medical doctor to do the killing. God the Creator made Jeremiah and John the Baptist with prophetic souls when they were yet in their mothers' wombs. Genesis 2:7 says, "And the LORD God formed man of the dust of the ground and then breathed into his nostrils the breath of life; and man became a living soul." The body of the human comes alive only when he has a living soul. If the baby's body is alive, so is his soul. Thus, the killing of a baby living in a mother's womb is killing of a living, human soul. This is murder, not just aborting fetal matter based upon immature body parts.

Neither abortion doctors nor abortion clinics personnel ever tell the pregnant mother that the baby growing in her womb already has a living soul since the baby's soul directs the body of the baby to live and develop inside of the pregnant woman. Instead, do abortion doctors and abortion clinics personnel often use monetary facts or arguments to convince the young pregnant mother to kill the baby in her womb? This question should cause an investigation. If this is true, then the pressure could go like this, "Do you have sufficient income to properly raise this baby you are bringing into this cruel world?" The teenage mother usually will says, "No!" To use the lack of money to justify killing a human spirit, soul, and body in the womb of a mother. The soul in the baby in the womb is born with eternal life, but whether the soul accepts Jesus Christ as Lord determines whether the human will die and live with Christ and the Godhead or will burn infernally in the Lake of Fire. The abortion clinic's personnel using an monetary argument to kill another human being is the insidious use of the god of mammon to assist in killing another human being. God created a new soul the moment the mother's egg is fertilized by the father's sperm, then the mother and father together have already brought a living soul into this world because the essence of the baby is his living soul (although the baby also has a spirit joined to the soul that is in a coma until he is born again).

As an alternative of sanctioning the killing of the unborn living soul as a form of depopulation (birth control), the law should be changed requiring the mother to give birth to the child with a living soul and putting the baby up for adoption. This would increase the population that is now decreasing, as mankind is causing its own destruction through people deciding not to have children, deaths by abortion on demand, deaths by continuous wars, and deaths by man-made pandemics. If a woman is raped and has a new soul growing a body in her womb, then why kill the baby? Make it a death penalty for the rapist instead of the death penalty for a new soul and body that did not participate in any crime. By raping of a woman and impregnating her and causing her to kill a living soul in her womb by abortion makes the rapist an accessory before the homicide of the living soul in the rape victim. Needless to say, if a woman kills the baby in her womb through abortion, then there is an unlawful homicide as far as the rapist is concerned, so the rapist is also guilty of the murder by hire. Under the abortion rights defenders have the false belief that the right to abortion is a form of self-defense because the baby can "ruin" her life. Yet, self-defense legalizes the killing of an attacker. The baby is not attacking the mother. Also, the argument is, "The woman owns her own body, so she has a right to get rid of a life form who is like a germ feeding off of her." The baby is not a germ attacking the mother. The baby is not an enemy at war against the mother.

Abortion advocates' legal reasoning is a mere fiction under the law. If the woman has a right to her own body, then why is it illegal for a woman to inject heroin in her blood. If the woman has a right to her own body, why is it illegal for a woman to be a prostitute in most states? If the woman has a right to her own body, why is it illegal under family law to sentence a woman to jail if she refuses to work and does not pay child support? If the woman has a right to her own body, why is there a family law that says that she must submit to involuntary servitude to care for the child after the child is born until the child is an adult? If the woman has a right to her own body, why is it against the law for a woman to attempt to commit suicide? If the woman has a right to her own body, how can countries, like Israel and Switzerland, require women to join the military as an adult? Thus, it is an injudicious and imprudent argument that a woman can kill a baby in her womb using the false theory that a woman has a right over her own body. Women, you are committing murder through abortion in the eyes of God. If you are saved, you will meet your son or daughter in heaven after you die, and you will have to explain to your child why you killed him or her while growing in your womb in violation of the "Unborn Victims of Violence Act" as discussed below. By federal law and most state laws following the "Unborn Victims of Violence Act" states that if an unborn child in the womb is killed during a murder or violent crime, or attempted murder of the mother, the killing of the unborn baby is a separate murder homicide. To clarify that a rapist is a murderer of the unborn living soul may require an amendment of the "Unborn Victims of Violence Act." However, I would hope that the raped mother should seriously consider that the living soul in her womb is an innocent human being with a living soul and do not compound the violence by the mother hiring a medical doctor to kill the living soul in her womb. Christ never committed a crime, never sinned, never did anything wrong, yet the raped mother must be Christ like and not kill the innocent living soul in her womb. Which is worse, the rapist raping the woman, although horrible, or the mother and a medical doctor killing an innocent unborn living soul in her womb.

Abortion makes no sense. If a hunter accidentally kills a cow that the hunter mistakenly thinks is a deer, and the bullet goes through the womb and kills the growing calf, in most states the hunter must pay the owner for two cows because a cow is a cow by law at conception. The baby cow could only be in an embryo state in its physical growth in the womb, but it is still a cow, not just fetal body parts of a cow. So, a baby, made in the likeness and image of God in the womb is not a human being at conception?

Every human being, even a human baby growing in the womb, is an image bearer of our Triune Godhead, even at the time of conception because the image is not only the baby's body, but also the baby's soul and spirit. Humans are triune beings. 1 Thessalonians 5:23 says, "And the very God of peace sanctify you wholly; and I pray God your whole spirit and soul and body be preserved blameless unto the coming of our Lord Jesus Christ."

Personality Traits of Money

Again, the federal and most states passed the "Unborn Victims of Violence Act," which said that if an unborn child in the womb is killed during a murder or violent crime, or attempted murder of the mother, the killing of the unborn baby is a separate murder homicide in addition to the mother. A highly profile murder case involved Scott Peterson, who was married to Laci Peterson who was pregnant with their unborn child, Conner. Laci and Conner disappeared on December 24, 2002, from the couple's home in Modesto, California, after which Scott reported her missing. The remains of her and their unborn son, Connor, were discovered in April 2003 on the shores of San Francisco Bay. Subsequently, Scott was arrested and charged with two counts of murder. In November 2004, he was found guilty of the first-degree murder of Laci and the second-degree murder of Conner. In this case, baby Conner under the "Unborn Victims of Violence Act" was considered a human being at conception.

However, if a drunk driver kills a pregnant mother, the drunk driver is guilty of only one homicide of involuntary manslaughter because in that case the baby in the womb is not a human being at conception or while in the mother's womb.

What kind of twisted illogic are these laws concerning the unborn human baby?

IT IS THE SEASON AND TIME THAT CITIZENS PROTEST THE NATIONAL DEBT AND LET THEIR VOICES BE HEARD

The demonic spirit behind abortion is the same spirit connected with the national debt; it is the hatred of our posterity, our children. The national debt will not be paid by the politicians. Who is going to pay the U.S. national debt? The current national debt is nearing $35 Trillion and grows about $1 Trillion every 100 days, and is growing over $3 billion, 333 million every 24 hours. The U.S. has the fastest and largest growing debt of any country in the world. The politicians must hate our children and our posterity to the thousandth generation because we will never be able to pay off our national debt through income taxes collected, as our income taxes are not enough to pay the current cash flow commitments, and the U.S. always has a serious deficit in the budget every year.

In Washington D.C., there are 435 elected House of Representatives, 100 elected Senators, 1 President, and 9 U.S. Supreme Court Justices. These 545 politicians in Washington D.C. make the decisions for the rest of us living in the U.S. This is what a small church has as a congregation. We are governed by an oligarchy. These 545 people are derelict of their duties to protect our nation and our posterity from impoverishment by this run-away national debt.

Why are citizens not voting to elect politicians who vote to stop deficit spending, take steps to pay off our national debt, stay out of police actions the elected politicians do not want to call wars, and lessen the expenditures of government. As a people, the citizens have the freedom to elect the right politicians to save our country. Satan and his demonic principality called mammon has deceived the citizens of the U.S., and the devil is smirking at us just like he did in the Garden of Eden when he deceived Eve to eat the forbidden fruit of the tree of the knowledge of good and evil.

Upon a people's repentance, God can forgive debt owed by Believers in the world, and God will have a plan to forgive the national debut of His holy nation within Believer's secular country. God said in 2 Chronicles 7:14, "If my people, which are called by my name, shall humble themselves, and pray, and seek My face, and turn from their wicked ways; then will I hear from heaven, and will forgive their sin, and will heal their land." Although this scripture was directed by God to the nation of Israel, the direct descendants of Abraham, 1 Peter 2:9-10 says, "But ye are a chosen generation, a royal priesthood, an holy nation, a peculiar people; that ye should shew forth the praises of Him who hath called you out of darkness into His marvelous light: (10) Which in time past were not a people, but are now the people of God: which had not obtained mercy, but now have obtained mercy." The United States, or any other secular country, is not the nation of Israel of old when 2 Chronicles 7:14 was pronounced by God. We Believers within every secular nation is the holy nation of God and the focus of God's covenantal blessings.

Although God was speaking to the people constituting the nation of Israel who were direct beneficiaries of the covenantal promises that God had made with Abraham; nonetheless, God also has a better covenant with His only begotten Son, Christ Jesus. Hebrews 8:1, 6 says, "Now of the things which we have spoken this is the sum: 'We have such an High Priest, who is set on the right hand of the throne of the Majesty in the heavens. . . (6) But now hath He (Jesus) obtained a more excellent ministry, by how much also He is the Mediator of a better covenant, which was established upon better promises." Hebrews 12:24 says, "And to Jesus the Mediator of the new covenant, and to the blood of sprinkling, that speaketh better things than that of Abel."

Through Christ Jesus, God chose a new holy nation with a better covenant than He had with Israel. Again, 1 Peter 2:9 says, "But ye are a chosen generation, a royal priesthood, a holy nation, a peculiar people; that ye should shew forth the praises of Him who hath called you out of darkness into His marvelous light." Therefore, God through the sacrificial death of Jesus' humanity nature on the Roman Cross, God has created another covenant with a holy nation that has been created as the joint heirs of Christ Jesus (Romans 8:17).

Consequently, as Believers under a better new covenant can humble themselves, pray, seek God's face, and repent, then God promises to hear from heaven, forgive our holy nation of our sins, and will heal the land where we live. This is not a covenant between God and the United States of America, but a United Holy Nation of Believers that live in this land. In every country who have Believers constituting a holy nation in that country can appropriate the blessings of God promised in 2 Chronicles 7:14. The Promise Land now is not just the strip of land called Israel in the Middle East, even though it is a part of God's Promise Land, but now consists of the whole earth. Jesus said in Acts 1:8, "But ye shall receive power, after that the Holy Spirit is come upon you: and ye shall be witnesses unto Me both in Jerusalem, and in all Judaea, and in Samaria, and unto the uttermost part of the earth."

Consequently, even though the U.S. secular government does not have a special covenant with God as did Israel had, God does have a special covenant with the holy nation of Believers that Christ Jesus caused to birth with Believers' born again spirits. Therefore, indeed, the benefits and promises of God in 2 Chronicles 7:14 will bring about a blessing to the holy nation of Believers within countries throughout the world.

Yet, for now, we Believers, as God's spiritual holy nation within a natural secular nation, can be a major part of our debt cancellation for America by coming before God with repentant hearts seeking God's face, and God will hear from heaven, forgive us Believers as God's holy nation of our sins of complacency of voting in office the debt-making politicians, and God will heal our land wherever we live. It is time the politicians and bureaucrats running our secular governments humbly repent of this horrific national debt they voted to borrow on behalf of our nation. We, as citizens of God's Kingdom and as Christ's holy nation, need to humble ourselves and repent for serving the god of mammon almost unto annihilation and extinction.

Without question, Jerusalem is a very special place for Jesus the Messiah when He returns to earth after God creates a new heaven and new earth, and then God brings the New Jerusalem City where Jesus will have His eternal Kingdom Throne (Revelation 21:1-2). When Jesus returns, He will rule and reign with the saints throughout eternity (Revelation 5:10; Daniel 7:14,27). In the meantime, Jesus wants Believers to have His patience. Revelation 1:9 says, "I John, who also am your brother, and companion in tribulation, and in the kingdom and patience of Jesus Christ, was in the isle that is called Patmos, for the word of God, and for the testimony of Jesus Christ."

Hebrews 12:28 says, "Wherefore we receiving a kingdom which cannot be moved, let us have grace, whereby we may serve God acceptably with reverence and godly fear."

THE WRONGS OF THE SOCIALIST POLITICIANS WHO THINK MONEY IS THE ANSWER TO ALL PROBLEMS

The U.S. Socialist Politicians must start using sound business practices instead of acting like the big Socialist Mother to the world and here at home. The U.S. Socialist Politicians seem to only care about the people that live now who will continue to vote to keep them in office, which is short-term thinking instead of long-term planning. The Socialist Politicians are inviting illegal immigrants to come from bankrupt Socialist nations into the U.S. to increase those voters who will continue to vote for Socialist Politicians instead of Biblitarians who believe in the principles that God promulgated as truths in the Bible.

Why does not the U.S. Treasury collect the tremendous sums from other countries that owe debts to the U.S. and reduce the national debt? The reason is that the U.S. lent money to the same countries that also purchased U.S. Treasury Bonds from the U.S. It appears that the U.S. owes slightly more to the countries that invested in U.S. Treasury bonds then the debts owed those same countries to the U.S. If the U.S. forgave these countries of their debts owed to the U.S. while these countries forgive the U.S. debt owed to them for purchasing U.S. Treasury bonds.

Why did the U.S. Politicians and Treasury Department do this? On the surface this makes no business sense whatsoever. This violates the standard lender-debtor relationship. Being both a lender and debtor creates a conflict of interest. The U.S. and each of their debtor countries are lenders and borrowers of each other almost in the same amounts. The result is that the U.S. cannot collect the debts owed by these countries until the U.S. simultaneously pays off the Treasury Bonds they purchased from the U.S.

HERE IS MY PERCEIVED EXPLANATION OF WHAT IS THE PROCEDURE USED BY THE U.S. TREASURY AND FEDERAL RESERVE

If the U.S. wants to borrow money from the Federal Reserve, then the Federal Reserve requires the U.S. to issue its debt instrument called the U.S. Treasury Bond. The Federal Reserve lends the U.S. the money the U.S. wants for the U.S. Treasury Bond. The Federal Reserve sells the newly issued Treasury Bond it just received to the "buyer" that was arranged by the U.S. which is a country like Japan or China that owes the U.S. a major debt.

On the other hand, the U.S. could arrange a country like Iraq to purchase the U.S. Treasury bond. Iraq owes U.S. money for the war debt, which the U.S. can cancel a portion of the Iraqi war debt in exchange for Iraq canceling the U.S. Treasury bond as part payment by the U.S. In the meantime, Iraq's reserves look good by having its U.S. Treasury bond in Iraq's Treasury holdings. The Federal Reserve is made whole for the money it pays the U.S. Treasury by selling the U.S. Treasury Bond to Iraq. The U.S. no longer owes the Federal Reserve the money owed on the U.S. Treasury Bond because the U.S. Treasury now owes the money to Iraq instead. Iraq continues going further into debt to the U.S. for payment by Iraq for the cost of the U.S.'s military and U.S. government officials' presence in Iraq.

This scenario is why the U.S. is in an almost constant state of a police action throughout the world where the embattlement is financed by the U.S. to create a lender-debtor relationship with the host government. The U.S. Treasury and the Federal Reserve have this financial procedure going on all the time. This is why the Federal government does not want to stop being the Policeman of the world because of this scenario keeps the U.S. government with cashflow when in reality the U.S. is totally bankrupt. Although this scenario keeps the cash coming into the U.S. Treasury to pay current bills, the U.S. is losing in this game as the U.S. national debt keeps getting higher, equal to one trillion U.S. dollars every one hundred days. Even though it appears like the government is still operating with cash flow, the U.S. cannot stop the bleeding. The sale of more Treasury bonds is like a couple of pints of blood added to stop the U.S. from dying, but the wound has not been treated or sutured and the blood keeps pouring out of the body.

The only other way the U.S. can pay off the national debt is by paying off the money owed on the issued U.S. Treasury Bonds with a lesser valued dollar. However, if the U.S. Treasury and Federal Reserve devalue the U.S. dollar down to almost nothing, then the U.S. dollar would be basically worthless. Those countries who purchased U.S. Treasury Bonds must take the devalued U.S. dollar as payment in full to cancel the U.S. debt. There is no inflation or deflation connected with U.S. Treasury bonds in its language on the bonds. The U.S. Treasury Bond owner is paid in U.S. dollars based upon the value of the U.S. dollar at the time the dividend is paid, or the principal is returned. This scenario would cause the U.S. to no longer be the lead currency, and the U.S. would lose its stature in the world. Also, since no country would purchase the U.S. Treasury bonds again, then this would destroy the U.S. cash flow for spending on military and for Social Welfare. Is this what God wants to happen to the U.S. because the elected Politicians out of habit always have a deficit in its budget because they are Socialists who think about today and not tomorrow? There are not many long-run thinkers in the U.S. Federal Government.

THE PROTESTOR PERSONALITY TRAIT OF MONEY CONFUSES REBELLION WITH FREEDOM

Personality Traits of Money

Unfortunately, the people with the Protestor Personality Trait of Money confuse rebellion against authority with true freedom by knowing the truth of the Creator that is revealed in Scripture (John 8: 31-32).

The real protest should be against the kingdom of darkness, not against authority in the Kingdom of God. The protestor seeks freedom from the world, and that is why he protests the world. Jesus commanded that every Believer have the same agape love for each other as He had for them (John 13:34-35). The Believer and people in the world with the Protestor Personality Trait of Money often understand and have empathy for the protest by Cain, "Am I my brother's keeper?" (Genesis 4:9).

There is no such thing as a "liberated spirit" other than with the authority and power of the Spirit of Christ and the Holy Spirit. 2 Corinthians 3:17 says, "Now the Lord is the (humanity nature) Spirit; and where the (humanity nature) Spirit of the Lord is, there is liberty." Believers' born again spirits came from the Seed of Jesus' resurrected humanity nature Spirit (Isaiah 9:6; Hebrews 2:13; 1 Peter 1:23), is perfect or whole (Hebrews 12:23), does not sin (1 John 3:9), and is absolutely holy and righteous as the New Man (Ephesians 4:24), is a new creature in Christ (2 Corinthians 5:17), and is joined with the Lord's resurrected humanity spirit is one spirit (1 Corinthians 6:17).

With those scriptures in mind, Paul said in Romans 8:9, "But ye (souls) are not in the flesh (stimuli from the flesh's carnality), but in the spirit (stimuli from God's righteous spirituality), if so be that the Spirit of God (Holy Spirit) dwell in you. Now if any man have not the Spirit of Christ (Christ's resurrected humanity spirit giving birth to a Believer's born again spirit and joined together as one spirit, 1 Corinthians 6:17), he is none of His."

A Believer's soul can be attached to the Kingdom of God, to the kingdoms of this world through the body's five senses, or to the kingdom of darkness. "Who hath delivered us from the power of darkness, and hath translated us into the kingdom of His dear Son" (Colossians 1:13). No one is an island unto himself. Outside of Jesus, no one can be truly free or liberated. To be truthfully free living within Christ's "law of liberty" one must be a doulos or agape love servant of Jesus living in the Kingdom of God as a citizen of heaven and in God's colonial territory called earth.

This is what we have in American. The people have rebelled against God with their humanistic philosophies and misapplication of God's scriptures. Again, 1 Samuel 15:23 says, "For rebellion is as the sin of witchcraft, and stubbornness is as iniquity and idolatry." Godly change is what Christ's holy nation in America prays for revival, and conformance to God's biblical principles are prerequisites as repentance before the blessings of 2 Chronicles 7:14 become that change in America.

On the other hand, bringing about change without applying Biblitarian principles is stubbornness at least and dangerous at most that causes destruction of the moral base of our society. Those who do not follow God's biblical principles are in rebellion against God. They are not in God's Kingdom even if saved. They have joined the citizens and the fallen kingdoms of this world system that is ruled by the prince of this world, Satan, with his kingdom of darkness.

People who want freedom and who protest the world system to bring change can find their freedom, peace, and life in the Kingdom of God in God's Son, Christ Jesus. John 8:36 says, "If the Son therefore shall make you free, ye shall be free indeed."

A Believer receives Christ Jesus' peace between you and your God as Father and Creator. John 14:27 says, "Peace I leave with you, My peace I give unto you: not as the world giveth, give I unto you. Let not your heart be troubled, neither let it be afraid." 1 Timothy 1:7 says, "For God hath not given us the spirit of fear; but of power, and of (agape) love, and of a sound mind."

Continuous fear of the world authorities and the kingdom of darkness can make you soulishly ill with bad thoughts in your mind, which can lead to bad feelings in your emotions, and bad beliefs in your heart. Fear is an evil spirit, not the Holy Spirit or the resurrected humanity nature spirit of Christ Jesus, or your born again spirit. Believers can take comfort and solace in 1John 4:4, "Ye are of God, little children, and have overcome them: because greater is He that is in you, than he that is in the world." Romans 8:37 says, "Nay, in all these things we are more than conquerors through Him "(God in Christ) that (agapao) loved us."

Peace comes when there is a "peace treaty" signed. 2 Corinthians 5:18-20 says, "And all things are of God, who hath reconciled us to Himself by Jesus Christ, and hath given to us the ministry of reconciliation. (19) To wit, that God was in Christ, reconciling the world unto Himself, not imputing their trespasses unto them; and hath committed unto us the word of reconciliation. (20) Now then we are ambassadors for Christ, as though God did beseech you by us: we pray you in Christ's stead, be ye reconciled to God."

Personality Traits of Money

Dr. Nova Dean Pack

6 Using Money For The "Romantic Attraction Personality Trait Of Money"

CHAPTER SIX

USING MONEY FOR THE
"ROMANTIC ATTRACTION PERSONALITY TRAIT OF MONEY"

MAIN SCRIPTURE REFERENCE: 1 Timothy 6:10 says, "For the love of money is a root of all kinds of evil, for which some have strayed from the faith in their greediness and pierced themselves through with many sorrows."

Firstly, the "Love of Money" means avarice for money to acquire safety, control, freedom, romanticism, magnetism, or any emotional or mental need fulfilled by money. In the principal reference verse of 1 Timothy 6:10, the word "love" in the phrase "For the love of money...." is the Greek word philargurio, which means here in this context, covetousness or avarice and comes from the root word philarguos, which means "fond of silver." However, both Greek words are rooted in the Greek word philarguria and embodies the English meaning of avarice or the "love of money." The English word avarice has the root word "avar" within it, which means blind. A person who is covetous of money is blind to the truth and blind to the snares that greed, covetousness, and avarice cause.

Secondly, the "Love of Money" also means the opposite of the "hate of money." The "love of money" means that money has become one's idol, trying to fulfill one's needs with money which rightfully can only be fulfilled by God.

PEOPLE WITH THE ROMANTIC ATTRACTION
PERSONALITY TRAIT OF MONEY

In the Shakespearean Plays titled, "Two Gentlemen of Verona," "Henry V" and "The Merchant of Venice," Shakespeare said, "Love is blind."

Young teens think love is a "warm puppy."

In a movie of the 1970s, titled "Love Story," starring Ryan O'Neal and Ali McGraw, the famous line about love was, "Love is not having to say you're sorry."

All these above statements about love are earthbound and not eternal true romantic agape love as between Christ and His Betrothed and His future Bride.

I will advance the biblical definition what is true romantic love, which will stop the Hollywood, movie star, fallen world romantic love. The purpose is that money is often used to support and pay for this fallen world romantic love. People seek the fallen world romantic love, and they use money as the focus connected with the obsessive-compulsive Romantic Attraction Personality Trait of Money.

People who have the Romantic Attraction Personality Trait of Money enhance their physical looks, to be romantically attractive for reciprocal affection and for fulfillment of soulish needs. When these soulish needs become obsessive and compulsive, then those with the Romantic Attraction Personality Trait of Money decorate their bodies to make another person desire to be romantically involved with them. The problem is when this fallen world romantic obsessive compulsion monopolizes the person's mind, emotions, and heart it becomes an overindulgence that robs them of God's true agape love that has the unique grace and power to transform the soul from carnality to God's spirituality. Often, those who seek the fallen world romance get hurt because it is not true agape love where a husband lays down his life for his wife and the wife lays down her life for her husband.

What the person with the obsessive-compulsive Romantic Attraction Personality Trait of Money does is waste too much money on trying to look physically romantically attractive based upon the fallen world's offering of philandros friendliness, not agape love. Make-up, hair dye, anti-wrinkle cream, beautiful clothes, attractive hairstyles, going to the gym, losing weight, wearing expensive cologne, etc. are all okay until these things become an obsessive-compulsive disorder of your soul to make you feel good about yourself. Yet, this fallen world romance-type indulgences are to attract the wrong kind of person that God wants you to have. A person with the obsessive-compulsive Romantic Attraction Personality Trait of Money looks for the fallen world kind of philandros friendliness in all the wrong places, such as nightclubs, bars, and parties where sin abounds. It is okay to have a nice automobile, a comfortable house that you can afford, take time off to go to vacation resorts to rest and rejuvenate, going to plays, symphonies, fine dinners, and having family celebrations. Yet, if these activities cause you to go into debt because they become a lifestyle to attract someone romantically, then this would be the obsessive-compulsive Romantic Attraction Personality Trait of Money disorder that needs counseling and change in your perceptions. You must be taught the difference between false philandros friendliness love and what is God's true agape love. You cannot build a godly marriage just on philandros friendliness love.

Also, no one wants their physical unattractiveness to interfere with the preaching of the gospel or to interfere with being an acceptable witness for God to people in the world who only walk according to the knowledge of the flesh with sensory stimuli coming into the soul from the fallen world. A sign of the need for serious help is when you start living a lifestyle where a great percentage of your money is expended for "decorating" your physical body and existing with an expensive lifestyle to be physically romantically attractive to find a spouse. If you are going to find a godly man or woman, you will not find them in the nightclubs, bars, or parties in the fallen world. What you should do is focus on obeying God, being led by the Holy Spirit in using your spiritual vocation as kings, priests, lords, ambassadors, and soldiers, spiritual gifts of God the Father, God the Word, and God the Holy Spirit, and fruit of the spirit that God has given you to serve others and to seek a spouse that has a similar mature transformed soul.

Instead of allowing her soul to become spiritually beautiful, a spiritually immature Believer is captivated by the outward appearance of man because she has the obsessive-compulsive Romantic Attraction Personality Trait of Money to fulfill her fallen world romantic needs. When she goes broke paying for the beautification of her flesh to attract a man, then she will live a life of disappointment. The same with men who use the fallen world methods to attract a woman. When your life is a continuous dressing up of your body instead of working on submitting to God to spiritually beautify your soul, and this fallen world romantic attraction becomes an obsessive-compulsion, then you have a degree of the Romantic Attraction Personality Trait of Money.

Personality Traits of Money

What should a godly woman be looking for in a man she wants to be her husband. What should a godly man be looking for in a woman he wants to be his wife? 1 Peter 3:3-4, 7 says, "Whose adorning let it not be that outward adorning of plaiting the hair, and of wearing of gold, or of putting on of apparel;(4) But let it be the hidden man of the heart, in that which is not corruptible, even the ornament of a meek and quiet spirit, which is in the sight of God of great price... (7) Likewise, ye husbands, dwell with them according to knowledge, giving honour (paying tributes) unto the wife, as unto the weaker vessel, and as being (joint) heirs together of the grace of life; that your prayers be not hindered."

What is Christ Jesus is looking for as His betrothed and future wife is your beautification by having a spiritually transformed soul. Ecclesiastes 3:11 says, "He hath made everything beautiful in His (God's) time: also He (God) hath set the world in their heart, so that no man can find out the work that God maketh from the beginning to the end."

Sometimes, an unsaved person or a saved Believer deprived of love as a child, a person seriously hurt by a fiancé breaking the engagement, or a person crushed soulishly in a marriage that ended with divorce, often will use the Romantic Attraction Personality Trait of Money to search for someone else who is romantic to fill the person's loneliness and hurt of rejection. Yet, instead of being spiritually attractive, she mistakenly thinks that being physically attractive alone is the answer. There is a misplaced fixation to the belief that spending money to enhance physical attractiveness and to be sexually appealing will bring a good man in her life. Once Satan sees there is deception leading to confusion in this area, he will open a realm of darkness even more and cause the afflicted one to expend large sums of money to maintain this pretense of equating physical romantic attractiveness with God's beauty of spiritual soul maturity, like the Believers perfectly holy and righteous born again spirit (Ephesians 4:24). God has a time when your soul is most beautiful in His eyes (Ecclesiastes 3:11), and that is when your soul is spiritually mature that does not allow the lust of the flesh, the lust of the eyes, or the pride of life to dictate your actions and does not accept what the world claims as romance that is in the movies and love songs. The people acting in the movie or singing a love song are doing it for money, not because they romantically are in love with millions of people at the same time. They are just acting like they are romantically in love.

1 John 2:15-17 says, "Love (agape) not the world, neither the things that are in the world. If any man love (agape) the world, the love (agape) of the Father is not in him. For all that is in the world, the lust of the flesh, and the lust of the eyes, and the pride of life, is not of the Father, but is of the world. And the world passeth away, and the lust thereof: but he that doeth the will of God abideth forever." With this prevalent mentality, what happens when one loses his or her earning power and is no longer attractive according to the world's standards? Marriage vows are broken, business partnerships are breached, and some Christians start blaming God for their misfortune. Staying physically attractive can be an extremely expensive overhead to maintain, and if physical attractiveness becomes an obsessive compulsion, it can cause financial stress as compulsive gambling does.

Let us examine this human interaction or those with the Romantic Attraction Personality Trait of Money, so we can have a deeper understanding of the pitfalls to avoid. People often mistake a desire for "Hollywood romance" as "true love," but this not agape love, which is the God kind of love that He has with us, and we are commanded by Jesus to have for one another (John 13:34-35). Hollywood type of romance always comes with a price. To maintain this false belief in romantic maintenance, or overindulgence, thousands of dollars are spent on flowers, limousines, expensive dinner engagements, vacations, and expensive gifts. By itself, nothing is wrong if these things are given as expressions of true love for your spouse or your fiancé, and the giver has the money to spend without harming him or her financially. However, some have the attitude that, "If you love me, why are you not buying me flowers, new clothes, a new car, a new house, taking me to fancy restaurants, etc." The reason is the person might have been struggling in business, has had health problems, is being attacked financially by Satan, or persecuted for his or her giving extra offerings into ministry. It might be a temporary financial setback, paying legal fees for an unexpected lawsuit, or paying off the money owed in an unfortunate tax audit, which has lasted for five years. The person has not the natural God given talents to earn a large income. Consequently, to base one's need for "romantic attractiveness" trying to obtain a spouse who earns lots of money is sin and compulsive indulgence.

This Hollywood romance mentality is often expressed in poetry, is a preoccupation of teenagers, and the subject of scripts of movies, books, and soap operas on television. Yet, this is a false definition of love, as it is not God's true agape love. To be sure, romancing your spouse with philandros friendliness is itself not wrong, unless there is an unhealthy need to have romance to feel loved and to keep the marriage strong. True biblical love is agape, which is more than mere romance. It is a decision, a lifetime commitment, a marriage covenant with God, and a desire for your spouse's wellbeing over your own. This is agape love based upon covenant in God's kingdom.

The need to be truly agapao loved is a God-created need, and the sexual expression of this covenant agape love between a husband and wife is a God-commanded intimacy in furtherance of His command to be fruitful and multiply (Genesis 1:28). Yet, God has created this need for agape love to be fulfilled by God and the Godly relationship between a husband and wife, not some continuous Hollywood romantic weekend date. God created man to be recipients of agape love and to be givers of agape Love. In other words, God's true love is not a feeling, and it is not special thoughts toward someone. God's agape love is of God because God's very nature is agape love. 1 John 4:16 says, "And we have known and believed the (agape) love that God hath to us. God is (agape) love; and he that dwelleth in (agape) love dwelleth in God, and God in him." You cannot dwell in God without agape love.

When God created mankind in His image and likeness, as God's spiritual image bearers, He made man, both male and female, as His agape love creation. If a Believer does not express agape love to his or her spouse and other Believers (John 13: 34-35), then the Believer disobeys the Lord and does not fulfill the purpose for which he or she was born again. The lifestyle of giving and receiving agape love is a real need and mandate for personal and familial spiritual fulfillment and soulish maturation. Godly sex itself is described as, and should be restricted to, making agape love with one's spouse in the God-created institutions called marriage and family.

Man and woman, even before marriage, were made to be romantically in agape love with each other, for procreation, and with equal authority to subdue the earth. This romantic attraction between a husband and wife is to enhance the agape love that is a blessing from God because when agape love is present in the marriage, God is present because the very nature of God is agape love (1 John 4:16).

Personality Traits of Money

Let us explore 1 John 4:16 in context with other scriptures, "And we have known and believed the (agape) love that God hath to us. God is (agape) love; and he that dwelleth in (agape) love dwelleth in God, and God in him." Hebrews 11:6 says, "But without faith it is impossible to please Him: for he that cometh to God must believe that He is, and that He is a rewarder of them that diligently seek Him." There can be no expression of faith without agape love. Paul said in Galatians 5:6 that "… faith which worketh by (agape) love." Romans 10:17 says, "So then faith cometh by hearing, and hearing by the (rhema) word of God." Hosea 4:6 says, "My people are destroyed (Hebrew: damah, meaning, cannot speak God's words) for lack of knowledge (Hebrew: da'ath, from the Hebrew word, yada, which mean "intimacy"): because thou hast rejected knowledge, I will also reject thee, that thou shalt be no priest to me: seeing thou hast forgotten the law of thy God, I will also forget thy children." Hosea 4:6 should be read that "My people are made mute or speechless for lack of God's intimacy (expressing agape love)…." If you are not intimate with God, and do not have God's agape love in your soul, your soul cannot hear His spoken voice or rhema word, so you lack faith. Thus, without intimate agape love, you cannot have a working faith, which displeases God; and if God is displeased, then you are pulling yourself away from God. Yet, God agapao loves you unconditionally, so you can repent, which means turn around and come back to God.

Genesis 1:27-28 says, "So God created man in His own image, in the image of God created he him; male and female created He them. (28) And God blessed them, and God said unto them, 'Be fruitful, and multiply, and replenish the earth, and subdue it: and have dominion over the fish of the sea, and over the fowl of the air, and over every living thing that moveth upon the earth.'" Thus, the first man and first woman, and each Believer as descendants of the first man and first woman, were created equals and were equally commanded to replenish the earth, subdue it, and have dominion of God's creation, as Gods joint underrulers.

Genesis 2:18 says, "And the Lord God said, 'It is not good that man should be alone; I will make him a helper comparable to him.'" Since the original man was both male and female, the female that was taken out of man was "comparable" and "complementary" to him as his "other half or counterpart." The actual Hebrew reads, "LORD (Yehoval) God (Elohim) said (amar) not good (toub) man (adam) alone (bad) make (asah) helper (ezer) helper (ezer)." A "helper helper" or "helper aid" or "help meet" are really two words, and the King James translation of "helpmeet" is inaccurate. The second use of the Hebrew word, "ezer," denotes that the woman made by God was "ideally suited" or "fit perfectly' as the "complementary counterpart" of the man for the man's needs and the fulfillment of their joint purpose for being created in the image and likeness of God. The Hebrew word "ezer" comes from the Hebrew root word, "azar" which means "to surround in aid, to protect, to help, to succor, to nourish, to care for, to sustain, to minister to and to love." The Hebrew word "ezer" was never meant to justify the placing of the woman in a lower class of creation compared to the man, or unjustly subjugating her to enslavement or as mere chattel or a mere sexual object of the man. In fact, the Hebrew word, "ezer" is used throughout Scripture to describe God as the "Helper" of man. Surely, one would never relegate God to a lower class or "Butler" of man just because He was said to be a "Helper." For example, Deuteronomy 33:26 says, "There is no one like the God of Jeshurun, Who rides the heavens to help (ezer) you, and in His excellency on the clouds." Psalm 33:20 says, "Our soul waits for the Lord; He is our help (ezer) and our shield." Psalm 115:9 10 says, "O Israel, trust in the Lord; He is their help (ezer) and their shield. O house of Aaron, trust in the Lord; He is their help (ezer) and their shield." Psalm 124:8 says, "Our help (ezer) is in the name of the Lord, Who made heaven and earth."

Hence, if God, Himself, is called ezer, I do not believe that the use of the word signifies the placing of the woman in a lower position of servitude or honor than the man nor is she to be a "play mate" just to gratify the sexual urges of the man. If anything, the woman is to be a Christ like servant, just like the man, to fulfill God's redemptive order and plan as a couple God put together with a joint mission.

Genesis 2:22 says, "Then the rib which the Lord God had taken from man He made (banah) into a woman, and He brought her to the man." The Hebrew word, banah, also to means to build. In Genesis 2:7, the Scripture says the man was formed (yatsar) from the dust of the ground, but here the Scripture says God built the woman from the rib of the man. Genesis 2:18 says God would make (asah) woman. The Hebrew word asah means "making or providing something from substance that already exists." The Hebrew word, asah was used in Genesis 1:7 which says, "Thus God made (asah) the firmament and divided the waters which were under the firmament from the waters which were above the firmament; and it was so." The firmament was asah from things on the earth already in existence. God merely rearranged it and divided it so it would no longer be "without form and void." The word asah means "to make or provide order to the things in existence." Therefore, when God made the woman, He put man in his place and brought order, by a helper with whom he could have communion, companionship, support, and procreation. Man's complementary, comparable perfect helper was asah and banah to bring wholeness, order and completeness to the man and themselves as a couple with a joint mission from God. The woman was made and built as man's complement, not man's competitor. The woman was to be man's helper to fulfill their joint God-ordained purpose. Accordingly, the woman was joined to the man in "submission" to be the best helper and support to fulfill mankind's God-ordained mission.

Thus, God created Eve from Adam's rib, to be made from flesh of Adam's flesh and bone of Adam's bone, and Adam had a "helper helper" chosen by God, Himself, to be also a receiver of Adam's agape love and a giver of agape love to Adam. Likewise, man and woman were created as receivers and givers of God's agape love. The wife is to respect and submit to her Godly husband, and the husband is to agape love his wife as Christ loves the church (Ephesians 5:25-26). All Believers, both male and female, are to submit to each other in agape love, and are to submit, respect, and have a reverent fear of God. Ephesians 5:21 says, "Submitting yourselves one to another in the fear of God."

Those who submit to God's redemptive order and plan are to have honor in God's Kingdom. One of the greatest examples of this submission with honor principle is in Ephesians 5:21 33. Those who submit are honored, not enslaved. Submission is a way of life for the Christian, both male and female, although it has become a red flag word because of men's subjugation of women, even in the Church, for centuries. In Ephesians 5:22 wives are told to submit to their husbands as unto the Lord Jesus Christ. Submission of the wife cannot be required by the husband, but submission is to be given freely by the wife based upon her loving trust in her husband's leadership. Therefore, submission by the wife in this Scripture passage is a reference to God's redemptive order and plan. Verse 23 says that husbands are marital spiritual heads over the wives the same way Christ is over the Church, as the Savior and intercessor of the Body of Christ in God's redemptive order. Christ's great agape love for His betrothed caused Him to substitute Himself to suffer on her behalf.

Therein is the pattern regarding the responsibility of the husband toward the submissive wife, which is one of substitutionary sacrifice for the wife's benefit and the fulfillment of their mission. In line with Christ's pattern, the "submission" in verse 22 was balanced and conditioned with the agape love" in Ephesians 5:25, which says, "Husbands, (agapao) love your wives, just as Christ also (agapao) loved the church and gave Himself for her." Christ laid down His life for His betrothed, and husbands are exhorted that this is the pattern as to how husbands are to lay down their lives for their wives. Men should start this practice even before they marry as Christ laid down His life as the example. Jesus died for His betrothed while she was yet a sinner (Romans 5:8) and before she, the Church, qualified to be His bride in all Her glory (Ephesians 5:27). Ephesians 5:28 says, "So husbands ought to (agapao) love their own wives as their own bodies; he who (agapao) loves his wife (agapao) loves himself." Being the "spiritual head" means that husbands are not to flesh out when dealing with the wives but are exhorted to be examples in the home in maintaining their bodies as the Temple of the Lord. This means the husband is to be the leader in the home in nurturing the wife and family with the fruit of the Spirit instead of the works of the flesh (Galatians 5:19 23).

"Work" preceded "marriage" in the Garden of Eden. In like fashion, men should get a job, business, or other income stream prior to getting married, so they can pay proper "tribute" or support to honor their wives. Paul concludes in Ephesians 5:33 that: "Nevertheless let each one of you in particular so (agapao) love his own wife as himself, and let the wife see that she respects (revere, honor) her husband." Honor and respect by the husband to the wife must return respect and honor by the wife to the husband. The principle is consistent in that agape love, submission, respect, and honor are to be expressed together. They go together like God the Father, God the Word, and God the Holy Spirit. The entire Godhead infinitely agapao loves, respects, and honors each other as they combined with infinite agapao love, respect, and honor as one God. A Believer is to agapao love, respect, and honor his spirit, soul, and body as one unique person as the image bearer of God. Likewise, every Believer is to agapao love, respect, and honor the spirit, soul, and body of every other Believer because he, too, is the image bearer of God.

1 Peter 3:7 9 says, "Husbands, likewise, dwell with them with understanding, giving honor to the wife, as to the weaker vessel, and as being (joint and equal) heirs together of the grace of life, that your (husbands) prayers may not be hindered. Finally, all of you (both men and women) be of one mind, having compassion for one another; love (philadelphos) as brothers, be tenderhearted, be courteous; not returning evil for evil or reviling for reviling, but on the contrary blessing, knowing that you were called to this, that you may inherit a blessing."

John 3:16 says, "For God so loved (agape) the world that He gave His only begotten Son, that whoever believes in Him should not perish but have everlasting life (zoe)." God's agape love, money cannot buy.

Again, the basic Greek root word for the verb love in each of the above passages, unless indicated otherwise is agapao (Strong #25). Agape (Strong #26) is a noun and the God kind of love as His agape love embodies God's personality. God's agape love is unconditional, unconquerable, undefeatable, benevolent and manifests His goodwill for every human, but especially every Believer. Agape was a new Greek word brought to earth by Jesus at the command of God the Father to be the grace, faith, and mercy of all Believers in their relationships with each other. 1 Corinthians 13:13 says, "And now abideth faith, hope, (agape love) charity, these three; but the greatest of these is (agape love) charity." Again, Paul said in Galatians 5:6 that even faith for spiritual matters works only by agape love, ". . . but faith which worketh by (agape) love."

Agape is a Greek word denoting God's unconditional and purest kind of love expressed toward mankind, which is a restored agape love, which is to reconcile and reestablish the close agape love relationship, but even a better relationship God had with man before the fall. Along with God the Father, God the Word, and God the Holy Spirit, with the Holy Spirit's jurisdictional authority during the Church Age, has come to live inside of redeemed man, who's born again spirit is the New Creature in Christ (2 Corinthians 5:17), part of the Second Man in Christ (1 Corinthians 15:47), and the New Man in Christ (Ephesians 4:24). In fact, our relationship is as adopted children of God the Father and joint heirs with Christ (Romans 8:15) and as the Bride of Christ (2 Corinthians 11:2), is a far, far greater relationship than that of a natural husband and wife.

Agape kind of love connotes oneness in both a husband and wife (Bride of Christ) relationship and their bloodline (children through the humanity nature precious spilt blood of Jesus) relationship. These two relationships are as close as is possible. However, throughout the New Testament this agape love is required of all relationships, such as the agape love between the shepherd and sheep (John 21:17) and the agape love between brothers and sisters in the Lord (John 15:17). In fact, this agape love must permeate the gifts of the Holy Spirit, faith, good works, giving, suffering, kindness, truth, endurance, forbearance, and all fruit of the Holy Spirit (1 Corinthians chp 13). In fact, the Lord commanded Believers to pursue agape love with each other (John 13:34-35). Thus, agape love is the Christian expression of love one to another, including a husband and wife.

Therefore, when love is referred to in the world as a "chemistry," a "romance," an "affinity," a "feeling," or a "physical attraction," it is a lower form of interaction by the fallen nature of man to try and recapture and fulfill the purpose for which man was created. Eros (sexual), and phileo (friend) are affections of a lower nature than agape love.

In the world, the lowest form of attraction or affection is pathos," which is interpreted as "lust." Romans 1:26: "For this cause God gave them up unto vile affections ("pathos"): for even their women did change the natural use into that which is against nature."

The only place in the New Testament where wives are specifically required to philandros love their husband other than with agape love is in Titus 2:4, which says, "That they admonish the young women to love their husbands, to love their children". The Greek word here for "love" their husbands is philandros, which comes from the root word philos meaning friendly or being fond of their husbands or spousal friendliness. This is the area where romance can be shown. However, the wife is also to love their children in the same verse, which is the Greek word philteknos, having the same root word of philos mean being friendly, being fond of the children, or maternally affectionate. So, in this context, the expression of love here is to perform the family duties in the office of wife and mother with a friendly affection. Likewise, the affiliation of husband and father is supposed to express friendly affection for both his wife and children, the same that the wife should express to her husband and children.

Personality Traits of Money

Without any exception, Hollywood romance is not agape love. Neither is pathos or lust. This philandros friendliness is the kind of everyday relationship God requires of a husband and wife to each other, but even more requires that spouses agape love each other. Agape Love between spouses is a decision to lay down one's own life for the other spouse and the family. Agape love is a decision to always support the other spouse through the good times and the bad times. Agape love does not cancel practicing philandros friendly romance affection. A spouse does not have to agapao love the other spouse only so long as he or she feels goose bumps. A wife and husband agapao love or exercise philandros friendliness with each other, even if the wife is dying of cancer, even if the husband loses all his money (or hair), even if one of their children dies, even if neither spouse's body is good looking anymore, or even if the husband suffers from E.D.

This is not to say a husband is excused from bringing his wife flowers, excused from taking her somewhere on a loving weekend and have times of refreshing, rest, and intimacy. These are normal social graces. This is not to say one spouse no longer must tell the other spouse that he or she agape loves him or her. A husband can open doors for his wife, take her to dinner and have intimate conversation, or invite her to attend a live theater performance or symphony. Most immature men think that going out to dinner is to get something to eat, but most women think that going out to dinner is for romance. Please do not misunderstand the Biblical teaching. Agape love is a wonderful, caring, and laying down your life for your spouse more than yourself; and it is designed by God to be a commitment for a lifetime together. Yet, many couples go through divorce, or their spouse dies, and they remarry. Then the process of intimacy, adjustments, getting to know each other, starts all over again. God understands and can bless a relationship that joins together to agape love one another and that seeks after Him. God is always ready to forgive sin, failures, and divorces because "There is therefore now no condemnation to them which are in Christ Jesus, who walk not after the flesh, but after the Spirit" (Romans 8:1). Similarly, 1 John 1:8-9 says, "If we say that we have no sin, we deceive ourselves, and the truth is not in us. (9) If we confess our sins, he is faithful and just to forgive us our sins, and to cleanse us from all unrighteousness." Living a life of repentance is required of every Believer, and this is not living a life of condemnation or self-abasement, but a submission with humility before Christ Jesus and our always forgiving and loving God.

Likewise, an intimate relationship between a husband and wife is improved by the two or three things they do not bring up in conversations. For example, negative jokes and teasing can be hurtful and the habitual use of teasing and negative jokes should be avoided between husbands and wives (and parents and children as well). For some reason there has developed in society a gender double standard about negative teasing. This trend says it is okay for wives during fellowship with others to verbally tease husbands to prove that women are "tough," but husbands are not allowed to tease wives in polite society as it is seen as being cruel and insensitive. As young teenage boys, they are frequently told to "man up," so many boys grow up as men having developed effective strategies and comebacks for covering up their hurts. Just because a husband laughs at a wife's demeaning comments of toughness, does not mean the husband is not a little hurt by the teasing, negative comments, or showing of disrespect if the husband is a Medical Doctor, Judge, Lawyer, Pastor, Professor, Teacher, wealthy Businessman, Author of great books, or any other trade or profession.

The true compelling romantic attraction between men and women Believers is spiritual, soulish, and bodily. The whole man and the whole woman as God's image bearers should be romantically attracted to each other expressing agape love, starting when they are engaged and continuing throughout the marriage. Genesis 1:27 says, "So God created man in His own image; in the image of God, He created him; male and female He created them."

God Created first Adam in God's likeness and image, having both male and female characteristics within. Therefore, the Creator has both male and female in unison. The first woman was taken out of the first man and was bone of his bone and flesh of his flesh (Genesis 2:18, 21-23).

Therefore, all creation and life of man itself came from the Creator where there was and is the unity of male and female. The man and woman were created when God "split" His Own Image in His creation into two separate persons   male and female.

Because it is in their creative design, a man and woman are moved toward each other in agape and philandros type of affection. The man and woman are drawn to each other in marriage not just to make babies to perpetuate the species, but to experience the roots of their original creation of being one body, both male and female. The very act of a husband and wife in procreating the miracle of a child is done only when the husband and wife become one. In this oneness of relationship between the spouses, they become the true image and likeness of God, which is the divine community or family. The triune nature of the Godhead shows that God is One, but His Oneness is expressed in His family, i.e., Father, Word/Son, and Holy Spirit. Likewise, Jesus' resurrected humanity nature is Believers' birthing spiritual Father of our born again spirits (Isaiah 9:6; Hebrews 2:13; 1 Peter 1:23). Believers' born again spirits are made perfect (Hebrews 12:23), do not sin (1 John 3:9), are new creation in Christ where old things passed away and behold all things become new (2 Corinthians 5:17), as the New Man are absolutely holy and righteous (Ephesians 4:24), and have delivered our born again spirit from the kingdom of darkness into God's kingdom of His dear Son (Colossians 1:13).

Again, in both the primal, spiritual, and individual experience of conception, life only originates when the male and female form the image and likeness of God in becoming one. The desire for spiritual completeness and to experience again the original image and likeness of God is the mysterious, involuntary, compulsive desire to unite romantically to return to that unique oneness of male and female in the original created man and thereby commune closer to God. One is not to take this truth and start some weird cultist practice with it.

Children are to see the image and likeness of God in the family relationship of their mother and father. In this union of husband and wife, or better by their creation participation names of father and mother, children are supposed to develop a relationship with God. In fact, Abraham's obedience or faith was his willingness to teach to his children and children's children the promises and covenants of God. Mothers and fathers are to "Train up a child in the way he should go and when he is old, he will not depart from it" (Proverbs 22:6). Lifestyles of mothers and fathers are to be as servants and loving witnesses of God, not just adult playmates of the children or sources of money to finance childish games and experiences.

Personality Traits of Money

In the spiritual dimension of living with his mother and father, the memory of the original created man is suppressed in the child. When the man becomes an adult, it is important that the man leave his mother and father, and go into the world, or wilderness, to fulfill his spiritual purpose of oneness with a wife. Genesis 2:24 says, "Therefore a man shall leave his father and mother and be joined to his wife, and they shall become one flesh." The marriage covenant requires the man to leave his mother and father and unite with his wife to participate with the Creator in the act of creation and spiritual and physical communion. This essential experience in forming the marriage relationship was seen by God and Israel in the desert, "...The love of your betrothal, when you went after Me in the wilderness..." (Jeremiah 2:2). From this marriage between God and Israel came the birth of the Messiah, Who in turn, as the Son of God, "left His abode" to find His bride "lost in the wilderness." The Church members collectively are the Bride of Christ. The Christian experiences the spiritual oneness with Christ and becomes a reconciled, born again, complete person who enters the family of God to fulfill the purpose and destiny for which he or she was created.

The awe, mystery, or fear of the sexual encounter is present in social interactions between men and women because deep within each of us is the primal knowledge that the sexual act involves an encounter with the living God who created us. Also, the Cross upon which Jesus died reminds us that when we encounter the fullness of God's Control, we are stripped of the safety of our own human Control. All the mandates and teachings of Christ was to agape love, give, be a servant, and to constantly diminish your own self for the benevolence toward others.

Thus, without the biblical true agape love being shared between a couple, they should not marry. If they are merely physically romantically attracted to each other, and a spiritual bond under the Lordship of Jesus Christ is not developed before marriage, they should not marry each other. If either couple are spending lots of money maintaining a romantic relationship, without a spiritual bond being developed, then they should not get married. The Holy Spirit wants people thinking of marriage to become spiritually minded, not carnally minded.

Romans 8:5-6 says, "For they that are after the flesh do mind the things of the flesh; but they that are after the Spirit the things of the Spirit. For to be carnally minded is death; but to be spiritually minded is life and peace." Colossians 3:14 commands, "And above all these things put on (agape love) charity, which is the bond of perfectness." Thus, to be perfect before the Lord, then you must live a life that always relates to people with agape love.

OBSESSIVE COMPULSION OF THE "SEXUAL ATTRACTION PERSONALITY TRAIT OF MONEY"

People who have an obsessive-compulsive Sexual Attraction Personality Trait of Money believe that sexual attraction is what attracts other people to them. The devil, and those totally entrenched in the fallen world run by the devil, do not agape love anyone. The devil has no physical body, so he cannot have a sexual relationship with mankind. However, he knows that humans in having babies create spiritual beings that could be an enemy of the kingdom of darkness and could potentially supplant his rule here on earth.

The devil has perverted sexuality from being a wonderful spiritual fulfillment by making the sexual act a purely physical, material, and lustful experience, which is interwoven with money, lustful soulish desires, and perversion of the sacred act of procreating with another spiritual being who both are created to be image bearers of God.

The devil has deceptively combined sex with money. Pornography is one of the largest industries in the world, with the center of production in Hollywood, California, USA. It is no wonder that the definition of love, romance, and lust have all been redefined by devilish influence in Hollywood to rob spiritual sexuality of its beautiful experience with God as the expression of the agape kind of love, and to fulfill the will of God.

Advertisers push this demonic perversion to make money by prompting lustful, perverted desire for sex with sensuous pictures of fleshy men and women and perverting God's created sexual attraction between a husband and wife with the purchase of material products. It is like Pavlov's dog, which eventually started salivating when a bell was rung, which experience was associated with being previously fed food.

If you present what the world considers to be a sexy person along with your product long enough, soon the customer will experience false romantic attraction or lustful arousal upon viewing the business product without the sexy person being there.

It is time that the Church leaders and Christians in the marketplace take a stand together to proclaim and teach that our romantic attractiveness must be disassociated with money and material or physical experiences and given to Christ. Ephesians 5:22 makes it clear we are to submit to one another because of our reverence for Christ. Also, Hebrews 4:12 says that the Word of God can divide the spirit from the soul and the marrow from the joint in the physical body.

In the world, the macho men of society are not the big muscle men on the beach. Being macho in the world means having money. In fact, women in the world see the attribute of an excellent job or good income stream as a very important attribute which attracts them to the men under observation.

Women and men are victims of the lustful perversion used to attract money, and in turn the associated false belief that a romantically attractive partner is one who has money. Romantic freedom came on the scene when the women entered the work force en mass. A man's obligation to support his family is a mandate from God, and there is nothing wrong in a woman making sure that a man will do his best to live up to this Godly mandate before she decides to marry him and have children with him.

The spiritual man does not allow himself to have the definition of his masculinity restricted to his physical attraction. The spiritual man finds his true masculinity when he humbles himself to the King of kings and Lord of lords and respects the Holy Spirit's anointing, whether it is upon a man or woman minister. By yielding his natural desires to the Godhead, the man submits his soul to the Godhead, and God the Father prunes the influence of the man's flesh from his soul (John 15:2). God the Word washes the influence of his flesh in his soul and sanctified his soul with the rhema word of God (Ephesians 5:26), and God the Holy Spirit mortifies the deeds of his flesh in his soul (Romans 8:13). Thus, the spiritual man receives true masculinity submitting to the indwelling all powerful Godhead.

Personality Traits of Money

Men and women both must be delivered from the world's concept of Hollywood Romance, romantic attractiveness, affection, masculinity, femininity, and spousal obligations as being associated with over spending for physical body decorations, the rich playboy image, machismo domineering, expensive cars, clothes, houses and all the other toys to make one more romantically attractive as displayed on T.V., movies, magazines, signboards, and every other media source.

No woman can confer manhood on a man. No man can confer womanhood on a woman. A wife's admiration, respect, and submission should be a result or consequence of her husband's true authentic God-centered manhood. The woman who uses her physical arousal abilities to attract or control a man is like the black widow spider who entices the male spider to copulate with her only to kill him afterward. The woman who entices the man through her physical charms will disrespect and enervate the man eventually because she knows he is spiritually weak. A husband who fleshes out on his wife will pay the price of loneliness in his later years of life.

Masculinity does not grow out of conquering or subduing the woman, but in allowing God to conquer and spiritually transform the soul of the man. Femininity does not grow out of the continuous enticing of the man with physical attractiveness. We must allow the Godhead to conquer and spiritually transform our souls. We all must focus our human willpower to submit to God's will, agape love, and virtuous character to be supreme in our lives.

We must enter the crucifixion of Christ to receive the resurrection life of Christ. We must not allow our natural desires of our flesh to be perverted and used to pulling on our purse strings or pulling on the purse strings of another we are trying to attract. We must allow Christ to live His spiritual, sinless, holy life in our souls, so, we can release His healing virtue to others that we are led to minister and serve.

Galatians 2:20 says, "I am crucified with Christ: nevertheless, I live; yet not I, but Christ liveth in me: and the life which I now live in the flesh I live by the faith of the Son of God, who loved me, and gave Himself for me." True agape love and true life begins when you start allowing Christ to live His life in you and minister through you.

Hebrews 11:6 says, "But without faith it is impossible to please Him, for he who comes to God must believe that He is, and that He is a rewarder of those who diligently seek Him." The man and woman of faith who are submitted to allow Christ to live His life in them and through them is the most attractive people in God's eyes.

Dr. Nova Dean Pack

Using Money For The "Personal Magnetism Personality Trait Of Money"

CHAPTER SEVEN

USING MONEY FOR THE "PERSONAL MAGNETISM PERSONALITY TRAIT OF MONEY"

MAIN SCRIPTURE REFERENCE: 1 Timothy 6:10 says, "For the love of money is a root of all kinds of evil, for which some have strayed from the faith in their greediness and pierced themselves through with many sorrows."

Firstly, the "Love of Money" means avarice for money to acquire safety, control, freedom, romanticism, magnetism, or any emotional or mental need fulfilled by money. In the principal reference verse of 1 Timothy 6:10, the word "love" in the phrase "For the love of money...." is the Greek word philargurio, which means here in this context, covetousness or avarice and comes from the root word philarguos, which means "fond of silver." However, both Greek words are rooted in the Greek word philarguria and embodies the English meaning of avarice or the "love of money." The English word avarice has the root word "avar" within it, which means blind. A person who is covetous of money is blind to the truth and blind to the snares that greed, covetousness, and avarice cause.

Secondly, the "Love of Money" also means the opposite of the "hate of money." The "love of money" means that money has become one's idol, trying to fulfill one's needs with money which rightfully can only be fulfilled by God.

PHILARGURIA LOVE IS CONNECTED WITH THE PERSONAL MAGNETISM PERSONALITY TRAIT OF MONEY

As we saw in the previous chapter, dating people and those who become husbands and wives often wrongfully seek the world's ideas of romantic philandros friendly love different from the Bible's agape love. Since agape love was emphasized more in the previous chapter, I am going to emphasize how money plays a part in this philargurio avarice kind of love of money with people who have the Personal Magnetism Personality Trait of Money.

Money is used by those who foster and support an obsessive-compulsive Personal Magnetism Personality Trait of Money, such as, "She had a million-dollar smile."

Many children have no concept of limits on the amount of money parents have since children in America normally receive whatever they need and want.

Since children constantly see parents reaching into their pockets or purses, pulling out money and buying objects, the parents' money supply may seem inexhaustible to replenish itself from the point of view of the children. So, the children assume that the money is there when the children want to buy something. Also, if children are denied, the children may think it is unfair that they did not receive what they want since the parents always get what they want. The children may develop the thought that the parents "do not love me" since they did not buy me what I wanted when they had plenty of money to do so. As a result, since children conclude that a parent's money is unlimited, a parent's refusal to spend money is often interpreted by the child as a withdrawal of parental love.

Personality Traits of Money

A child must eventually learn that there is a limited supply of money. How the child deals with the reality of a limited supply of money is often the door through which problems with money are developed. Does a child grow up and accept God's truth, or does the child develop an obsessive-compulsive personality trait that uses money for special magnetism to be popular, to be sought, or to be highly esteemed?

The child must learn that the giving or withholding of money has nothing to do with giving of love or withdrawal of love.

Unfortunately, those people who did not graduate from this stage develop problems in associating love with money.

MONEY BEING USED TO ENHANCE ONE'S SPECIAL MAGNETISM
CAN BE SEEN IN THE "DECEPTIVE GENEROSITY PERSONALITY TRAIT"

People having the Deceptive Generosity Personality Trait are seen to give money to win admiration, friendship, and loyalty.

The Deceptive Generosity Personality Trait sufferers are seen giving large tips to waitresses or bellboys just to get a smile or a friendly word. They make generous contributions in church "with the motive to obtain attention and accolades from the Pastor."

There is nothing wrong in and of itself making generous contributions in church if it is done without trying to receive special attention (or loyalty or special appointment) in return. Since the Church structure is a form of government, there are a lot of people trying to pay favors. It is called church politics.

GIVING AND EXPECTING RECIPROCATION

When you do someone a favor, do you expect him to reciprocate? As a Believer, you must accept that the economy in the Kingdom of God is giving and receiving, not buying and selling, and not doing a favor in exchange for a reciprocal favor. Luke 6:34 says, "And if ye lend to them of whom ye hope to receive, what thank have ye? for sinners also lend to sinners, to receive as much again."

Although the following scripture is often used to collect offerings in a church meeting, it really is a commandment on how to live with a heart of giving. Luke 6:38 says when you give freely without expectation of return, God sends back a return because you did not ask for one; "Give, and it shall be given unto you; good measure, pressed down, and shaken together, and running over, shall men give into your bosom. For with the same measure that ye mete withal it shall be measured to you again."

People with the Deceptive Generosity Personality Trait keep track of the money, the favors, the services they invest in someone, and eventually they expect a return on their investment. This is how the MAFIA works. When they do you a favor, you must accept the condition that in the future, they will want a returned favor from you that you may not want because the MAFIA demands reciprocity.

A person in the world, or a Believer in a church community with an untransformed soul, will agree to run you an errand because you are in desperate need, but in turn he will want you to run an errand for him even if he is sitting by the pool relaxing and it is not an emergency. Moreover, this person or Believer may mow your lawn when you are sick but will expect you to mow his lawn even if he is not sick. Furthermore, he may help you move your furniture from one house to the next when your promised help did not show up, but he will expect you to help him move even though he has lots of help.

As another example, he may help you get some products wrapped and mailed due to a time restraint in your business but will expect you to help him in his business for the same hours even if it is not an emergency. There are countless situations where this scenario is used. The problem is you will never know when this person with the Deceptive Generosity Personality Trait calls upon you to return the favor. Thus, he did not help you with agape love because what favor he bestows expect payment in return when he wants it regardless of whether there is an exigent circumstance or not.

After salvation, as a Believer you must join the church community with the resolve to honor and use the principles of God's kingdom and give freely without strings attached. When you give conditional gifts of your time, labor, friendship, or money, your focus will be on how soon you can receive your return benefit. The way of the Kingdom of God is to give yourself, your money, and your agape love with the motive of pleasing the recipient only without any expectation of return.

Parents with the Deceptive Generosity Personality Trait spoil their children to buy their affection. Why would parents do that? Parents with the Deceptive Generosity Personality Trait feel unlovable without money, and they have deep seated anger and hostility toward their own parents who withheld their money (interpreted as withdrawal of love by the now adult parent).

The person with the Deceptive Generosity Personality Trait may have a problem with another person who has expressed personal anger and hostile feelings toward him. The way the person with the Deceptive Generosity Personality Trait will try to win him over is by bestowing monetary or material gifts, such as tickets to a professional baseball, football, or basketball game. In payment for the sports tickets, he may request you vote in his favor at a meeting where both of you are co-members of a Homeowners Association, a Church Board, or a Corporate Board of Directors. This is how he who has the Deceptive Generosity Personality Trait obtains repayment for giving monetary, material gifts, or services.

Sometimes, children who grow up in orphanages suffer from the Deceptive Generosity Personality Trait. The orphan soon realizes that people who take care of him are being paid to do so, and thus there is a price placed on the affection bestowed upon the orphan. He learns love is not given freely, but instead love is something for which one must pay.

Regularly, those who have the Deceptive Generosity Personality Trait suffer as children wounded from abandonment, rejection, hostility, bullying, or being told they are second-rate.

Personality Traits of Money

A rich old man with the Deceptive Generosity Personality Trait thought that he could buy love and loyalty by giving a particular young attractive woman a very expensive diamond necklace on her birthday, along with throughout the year showering her with expensive vacations, a new car to drive, and sharing with her the lifestyle of the rich and famous. She accepted the man's proposal of marriage, and she promised she would love him, care for him, and stay loyal to him. The rich old man failed to insist upon a prenuptial agreement. However, in a couple of years of marriage, the husband became upset because the young attractive wife had now filed for divorce, and she wanted a multi-million-dollar divorce settlement. He concluded that, "She just married me for my money." He should not have been surprised because money was his magnetism that he used to attract her in the first place. He became enlightened that she married him for a season until she received what she really wanted, which was lots of money in the divorce settlement. The young attractive woman knew the old man was marrying her because of her physical attractiveness, not because he agape loved her. Both the old man and attractive young woman used fallen world friendly love that violated God's creative agape love that a husband and wife were to express one to the other in a lifelong covenant of marriage.

People who suffer from the Deceptive Generosity Personality Trait seek friendly love, not true agape love, and they sometimes wrongfully use money to prove they are generous but do expect a returned favor. The person who suffers from the Deceptive Generosity Personality Trait measures how much he is attracted to someone by the amount of money he spends on a gift for a special holiday, such as Christmas, Valentine's Day, or a Birthday. A man with the Deceptive Generosity Personality Trait leaves the price tags on the presents for Christmas, birthdays, or other celebrations to expect appreciation and affection from the beneficiary due to the amount of money he spent on her.

When money is used symbolically as attractiveness by the man with the Deceptive Generosity Personality Trait, he does not understand that the affection returned is not real either.

J. Paul Getty finally accepted the truth that his money could not buy another's love. He, unfortunately, reached this conclusion only after five divorces. Hundreds of women proposed to him. Getty knew his personal magnetism attractiveness was not because of his blue eyes. He responded to an interviewer, "The magnetism I exert is of another color   green." (Newsweek, July 26, 1976, page 56).

MONEY BEING USED FOR SPECIAL
MAGNETISM CAN BE SEEN IN THE
"FREE LOADER PERSONALITY TRAIT."

The Free Loader Personality Trait is someone who offers affection, entertainment, endearment, and devotion to a rich person in exchange for monetary support and gifts. The person with the Free Loader Personality Trait knows that a rich person will use his or her money as a special magnetism to attract him or her with the Free Loader Personality Trait. It is a symbiotic relationship where each of their needs are met. The rich person will agree to share their lifestyle with the person with the Free Loader Personality Trait. The person with the Free Loader Personality Trait will live in their home as a guest and partake and enjoy the rich person's wealth in exchange for the Free Loader Personality Trait person's affection, entertainment, endearment, and devotion.

Often, the person with the Free Loader Personality Trait will even enter marriage with the rich person to legitimize or cover up his or her ulterior motive.

These people who have the Free Loader Personality Trait are not prostitutes because they do not openly advertise their affection for money. The women with the Free Loader Personality Trait are called "Gold Diggers." The men with the Free Loader Personality Trait are referred to as "Gigolos."

If the rich buyer of this affection can afford the Free Loader Personality Trait person, who is selling his or her affection, it often goes undetected by others.

HISTORICAL FIGURES WHO ATTRACT THE FREE LOADER PERSONALITY TRAIT

According to Wikipedia, Barbara Woolworth Hutton used her money to attract handsome husbands who had the Free Loader Personality Trait. "Barbara Woolworth Hutton (November 14, 1912 – May 11, 1979) was an American debutante, socialite, heiress, and philanthropist. She was dubbed the 'Poor Little Rich Girl,' first when she was given a lavish and expensive debutante ball in 1930, amid the Great Depression, and later due to a notoriously troubled private life. Heiress to the retail tycoon Frank Winfield Woolworth, Hutton was one of the wealthiest women in the world. She endured a childhood marked by the early loss of her mother at age four to suicide and the neglect of her father, setting the stage for a life of difficulty forming relationships. Married and divorced seven times, she acquired grand foreign titles but was maliciously treated and often exploited by several of her husbands. While publicly she was much envied for her possessions, her beauty and her apparent life of leisure, privately she remained deeply insecure, often taking refuge in drink, drugs, and playboys…Barbara Hutton habitually married: 1). 1933: Alexis Mdivani, a self-styled Georgian prince, divorced 1935, 2). 1935: Count Kurt Heinrich Eberhard Erdmann Georg von Haugwitz-Hardenberg-Reventlow, divorced 1938, 3). 1942: Cary Grant, divorced 1945, 4). 1947: Prince Igor Troubetzkoy, divorced 1951, 5). 1953: Porfirio Rubirosa, divorced 1954, 6). 1955: Baron Gottfried Alexander Maximilian Walter Kurt von Cramm, divorced 1959, and 7). 1964: Pierre Raymond Doan, divorced 1966."

Similarly, Anna Gould, the daughter of the notorious robber baron, Jay Gould, was also a famous victim of those men who had the Free Loader Personality Trait. Arriving in New York penniless, Boniface, Count de Castellane with his Free Loader Personality Trait entered a partnership with another Frenchman to defraud Ms. Gould out of her money. Boniface, Count de Castellane married Ms. Gould, who then divorced her after spending 12 million dollars of her money. The fellow Frenchman received a percentage of the spoils through "loans," use of yachts, palaces, racehorses, and extravagant spending habits. (John Dollard, et al., Frustration and Aggression New Haven: Yale University Press, 1963, pp. 1 3.)

On a smaller scale the high school girls who suffer from the Free Loader Personality Trait only date the boys with the most expensive cars. The Free Loader Personality Trait is also seen in the college athletes from the ghettos who only date the rich sorority girls, and this includes the secretaries or mid level executives who act seductively around their bosses to

Personality Traits of Money

get a raise, promotion, or a date and hopefully a more intimate relationship with the person's money.

The individual with the Free Loader Personality Trait usually comes from parents who use money to bribe the child to be sweet, considerate, and affectionate toward his parents. The perceptive child learns to determine when a response of flattery, a hug, or smile will earn approval and often money from his parents. The parents normally say, "If you love me, you will not put your feet on the table." "If you really love me, you will not bring home such a bad report card." Such statements not only put guilt in the mind of the child, but also reinforce the idea that "love" is sold for a price. Thus, the child can develop the Free Loader Personality Trait to have a special magnetism to people with money, and they conform their actions to be attractive to rich people who use their money to buy affection.

Parents with the Deceptive Generosity Personality Trait who use money to gain their children's affection in turn develop children with the Free Loader Personality Trait. Receiving monetary rewards in the form of money and gifts from someone with the Deceptive Generosity Personality Trait reinforces the person with the Free Loader Personality Trait to sell their affection, entertainment, endearment, and devotion.

There are wives who consider themselves as "Trophy Wives," and they do not want to work as they have the Free Loader Personality Trait who are loving and loyal while the money is flowing their way. Yet, they seek a divorce the moment the husband loses his business or job, or when she finds someone else who has investment income and a steady cash flow that she can share or obtain to spend on herself.

In the church community there are subtle signs of a Pastor with the Free Loader Personality Trait. Occasionally, you can find a Pastor with the Free Loader Personality Trait that comes across as warm, friendly, compassionate, honest, and innocent or sophisticated depending on what a Congregant with the Deceptive Generosity Personality Trait wants in the form of attention. Although totally against scripture and pastoral ethics, there are people who take on the disguise of sincere, godly Ministers where their false and manipulative friendliness and desire to help is designed to attract people with money to become givers and tithers to them. Sincere Believers who desire to be around ministers want spiritual endearment and care and will donate handsomely for a "compassionate" prayer, a friendly ear, or a shoulder to cry on. Other rich people who have the Deceptive Generosity Personality Trait will pay lots of money in monthly tithes and offerings just to be part of the Pastor's or Minister's enter circle as the rich person want to become a Minister or Associate Pastor in the Church or Ministry. Sometimes, the rich person with the Deceptive Generosity Personality Trait becomes the largest donor to the Pastor who may have the Free Loader Personality Trait, and they both are sin. Both have ulterior motives for money and ministry position. The Pastor with the Free Loader Personality Trait without saying it holds out a carrot to sale a ministry position to keep the larger tither in his congregation, while the rich person with the Deceptive Generosity Personality Trait wants to use his money to buy his ministry position, which is the quick way of promotion into ministry. In the end, both cross the line and commit the sin of simony (Acts 8:18-23).

In the secular world, people with the Free Loader Personality Trait seek professions such as social workers, nurses, counselors, or even news reporters to attract rich people to befriend them and offer their affection, entertainment, endearment, and devotion in exchange for the rich people sharing their extravagant lifestyles.

Each of the professionals above is paid a salary or fee to serve the soulish needs of people who are affection and friendship starved. If being paid for their service motivates them to put on a false mask of compassion, friendliness, and concern, then the professional may have to a degree the Free Loader Personality Trait.

A divorce often occurs when the person with the Free Loader Personality Trait meets and marries someone with the Deceptive Generosity Personality Trait. For a season, they find themselves in a symbiotic relationship. At first, it must be like the early days of taking drugs, as the euphoria feels good. Yet, these obsessive-compulsive personality disorders eventually conflict, causing the spouses to realize that they are feeding the other spouse's personality disorder.

MONEY BEING USED BY THE FRIENDLY "AFFECTION THIEF PERSONALITY TRAIT"

Theft of friendly affection can be seen in many other areas, sometimes where no money is involved. The employer or supervisor with the friendly Affection Thief Personality Trait steal talent, work, and time from an employee by showing friendly affection, endearment, and hints of promotion, to the employee to work more hours or put in more effort for less or no pay. The employee becomes a victim of working overtime without payment of money.

The friendly Affection Thief Personality Trait exploiters can lead to complicated obsessive-compulsive disorders, and these people can open the door to a lifestyle of exploitation of employees through a show of friendly affection by smiling, telling an employee, "That's a nice dress you are wearing," Or if it is a female boss to a man employee, "What a nice suit you are wearing, as it makes your eyes stand out." Using friendly affection to convince employees to work extra hours at no charge is a form of theft and is done frequently in business.

Personally, I have had both men and women clients who take me, as a lawyer, to lunch, acting friendly; but sometimes they are trying to obtain free legal advice or for me to write a demand letter for them for small or no attorney fees, just for buying me lunch. That is a form of robbing me of my services. The same goes with people who want to obtain free advice from a financial planner or a medical doctor. It is a form of theft of services. Licensed professional services are the Professional's product in trade for compensation, and a client or patient trying to obtain free professional services is robbing the Professional of his or her knowledge, experience, and wisdom.

John 10:10a says that "The thief does not come except to steal, and to kill and to destroy..." A perpetrator stealing time and labor from another through friendly affection is still a thief. The individual with the friendly Affection Thief Personality Trait does not steal with true friendly affection but will tempt others with unmeaning words as a "symbol of friendly affection." He fakes friendly affection to steal valuable labor. He wears a friendly disguise, such as a smile, a wink of the eye, or a pat on the back, or a payment of a lunch for him and the Professional.

Personality Traits of Money

These perpetrators offering friendly affection in exchange for work or services never believe that friendly affection should come freely. They put out the idea that "If you want me as your friend, it will cost you." They falsely believe there must be a cost involved with friendly affection. So, if someone comes to the perpetrator with the Affection Thief Personality Trait offering true friendly affection without asking for something in return, the perpetrator becomes very suspicious and will not trust the person because their foundational belief is that friendly affection comes with a cost.

Typically, the Affection Thief Personality Trait perpetrator would not spend any time at all with a person who freely offers friendly affection without doing some kind of service for them. The Affection Thief Personality Trait perpetrators want affection at a cost. Even in their personal relationship, such as a spouse, the Affection Thief Personality Trait perpetrator wants someone who is hard to get, so when they receive their partner's friendly affection, they know it is valuable.

The perpetrators with the Affection Thief Personality Trait want to steal friendly affection. In high school, a girl perpetrator with the Affection Thief Personality Trait will purposefully go after another girl's boyfriend because it is stolen affection.

There is something about stolen things having an attraction to those who have the Affection Thief Personality Trait. Proverbs 9:17 says, "Stolen waters are sweet, and bread eaten in secret is pleasant."

Unlike the person with the Deceptive Generosity Personality Trait, who will pay or purchase the friendly affections from another, the perpetrator with the Affection Thief Personality Trait wants to steal the friendship without cost of commitment by him or her.

However, stealing affection is still theft because you are not entitled to receive that person's friendly affection. The scriptures make it clear in Ephesians 4:28, that, "Let him who stole steal no longer..." Friendly affection is not true agape love that you want in a Kingdom wife or husband.

The underlying personality of the people with the friendly Affection Thief Personality Trait is that they may pretend they do not "need" friendly affection, but then they steal it wherever they can find it to satisfy their need. They would rather have a short-term relationship instead of a long-term relationship. Why? Because they see that in the beginning of relationships people act properly during initial dating but eventually their true soulish disorders come out. After the first or second argument occurs, the person with the friendly Affection Thief Personality Trait terminates the relationship. The perpetrator's false friendly affection may have been exposed to her dating partner. Instead of seeking help, she ignores her maladies by avoiding a dating partner for a season. God brought the dating partner for that very purpose to reveal her malady because God wants her to come to Him to enjoy true agape love.

Until cured, the perpetrator with the friendly Affection Thief Personality Trait does not believe he deserves or is entitled to receive any true agape love from others because human beings are sinful, treacherous, deceitful like him and cannot be trusted. The perpetrator does not want his needs for true agape love to be made known to others, as it makes him vulnerable to rejection, hurt, and manipulation. He does not want to be exposed about his soulish disorder as an affection kleptomaniac.

Children who are shown friendly affection exclusively by payment of money by the parents can "learn" that friendly affection comes when money is used to purchase friendly affection. On the other hand, children who are denied friendly affection by parents withholding money or objects start stealing at an early age objects or money given which were used prior by the parents to show friendly affection. A lonely or unhappy child could start stealing pennies out of his mother's purse to feel his mother's friendly affection because that is how his mother showed him friendly affection. The theft gets more complicated as the child becomes a teenager and then an adult. He sometimes exhibits a friendly Affection Thief Personality Trait at work and with his dating experiences. When he is confronted by someone who truly loves him, he often feels uncomfortable and terminates the relationship. He really needs pastoral spiritual counseling to introduce him to God and Christ Jesus who he learns to trust with their never forsaking agape love.

If not cured, an adult person with the friendly Affection Thief Personality Trait thrives on the affection, affirmations, and admirations of people in authority and steals from others to gain it.

For example, a young church group leader having the Affection Thief Personality Trait may take a collection from Church employees and volunteers to purchase a birthday gift for the Pastor. He then will present the gift to the Pastor without informing the Pastor that it was from the whole church staff and volunteers to steal the Pastor's friendship affection and admiration for himself alone. The Pastor assumes the expensive gift is just from the young church group leader. The young church group leader goes back to his fellow workers and tells them, "The Pastor really appreciated the gift you gave him. He was really thrilled to have it. I just want to tell you what a great bunch of guys you are." This is the deceptive work of the individual with the Affection Thief Personality Trait.

An individual with the friendly Affection Thief Personality Trait will use the time, money, talents, and energy of others to gain friendly affection without any cost to himself. At the same time, he will always put himself in the position of delivering the gift or object of friendly affection that cost others dearly. The person who has an obsessive-compulsive disorder with the friendly Affection Thief Personality Trait appears often as one of the "good friendly guys" who is loyal to the team effort and who always is arranging with people to do something nice for someone else, like the Pastor. This is merely corporate politics in church. Obtaining recognition and "political" gain in church with the Pastor is why they appear so generous, friendly, and considerate.

However, the perpetrator with the Affection Thief Personality Trait cannot cope with any confrontations and will avoid meeting with people who want to confront him because the Church employee or volunteer suspected he did not contribute to the gift or service given to the Pastor. The Church employee or volunteer suspects the perpetrator with the Affection Thief Personality Trait just took credit for it. Yet, often the perpetrator with the Affection Thief Personality Trait is never confronted because most Believers rarely confront another person who sins because forgiveness and agape love are God's kingdom principles and a way of life for the Believers. Also, the Believer may think that if he confronts a person who did not commit the wrong, it means the accuser has the problem of distrust, gossip, or lack of agape love. Consequently, the friendly Affection Thief Personality Trait person rarely is confronted as the church community is an overly friendly environment.

The Affection Thief Personality Trait perpetrator who refuses to show friendly affection to others unless he steals it, violates God's commandment to actively seek agape love without conditions; and this restricts his soulish maturation and growth. Trying to take credit for something others have done normally causes the loss of those who want to be friends.

PATHOS AFFECTION IS NOT TRUE AGAPE LOVE

The pathos affection purchased with money is not true agape love. Romans 1:26 "For this cause God gave them up into vile affections..." (The Greek word for affections here is "pathos".)

The kind of pathos affection that is involved is seen in Shakespeare's play, "Romeo and Juliet." You would have to be mentally ill to commit suicide because of a need for this kind of pathos affection pathology.

People who are tired of bartering for pathos affection can instead find true agape love without charge from the Lord Jesus Christ and fellowship with mature Believers.

Romans 8:38-39 says, "For I am persuaded, that neither death, nor life, nor angels, nor principalities, nor powers, nor things present, nor things to come, (39) Nor height, nor depth, nor any other creature, shall be able to separate us from the (agape) love of God, which is in Christ Jesus our Lord."

People who gain pathos affection through theft, manipulation, deceptive generosity, or being a free loader with other people's money must repent and seek remission of sins before healing can begin in their souls. God is ready, willing, and able to transform these pathos affection people who have degenerate souls that are unbalanced and have not experienced true agape love from God, a spouse, or others in the Church community. True agape love requires repentance and submission to God, for God is true agape love (1 John 4:16).

There is no need to fear about your exposure leading to shame caused by your disorders in your soul. 2 Timothy 1:7 says, "For God has not given us a spirit of fear, but of power and of (agape) love and of a sound mind."

1 Timothy 6:17 says, "Command those who are rich in this present age not to be haughty, nor to trust in uncertain riches, but in the living God, who gives us richly all things to enjoy."

Dr. Nova Dean Pack

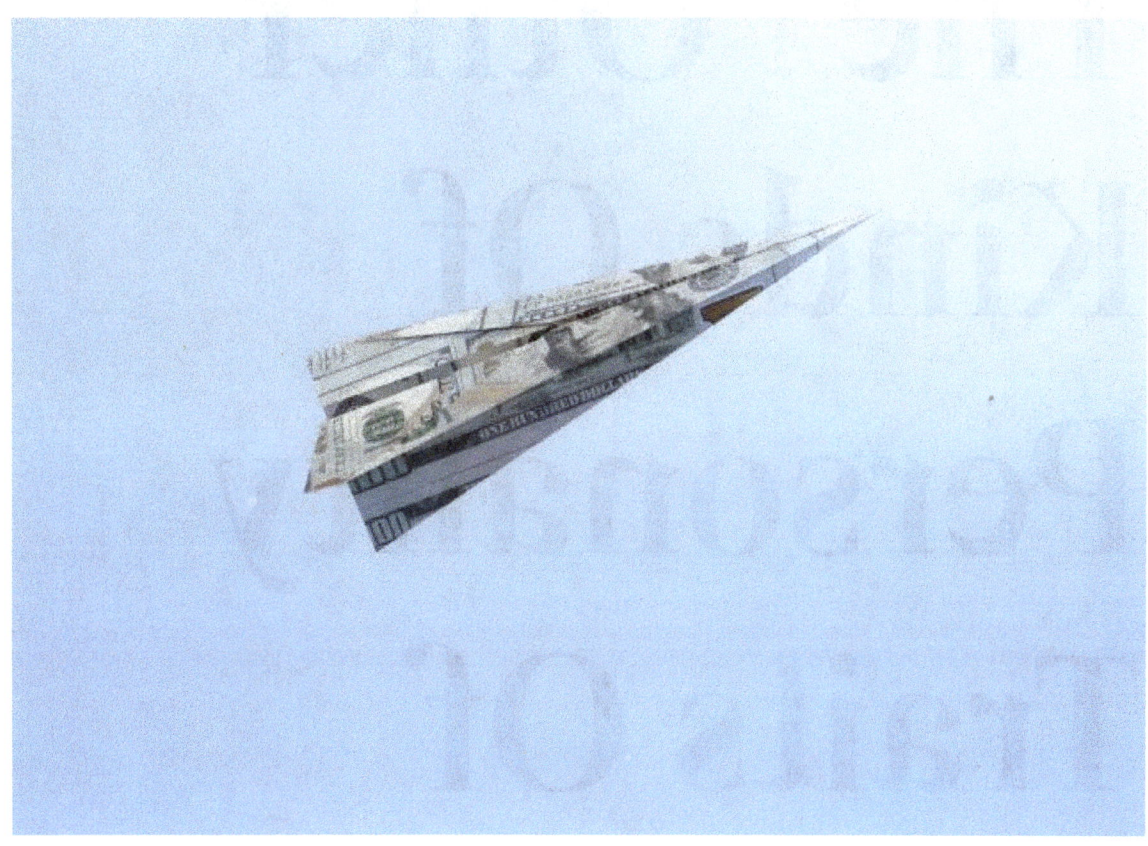

8 Money For The "Other Kinds Of Personality Traits Of Money"

CHAPTER EIGHT

USING MONEY FOR THE "OTHER KINDS OF PERSONALITY TRAITS OF MONEY"

MAIN SCRIPTURE REFERENCE: 1 Timothy 6:10 says, "For the love of money is a root of all kinds of evil, for which some have strayed from the faith in their greediness and pierced themselves through with many sorrows."

Firstly, the "Love of Money" means avarice for money to acquire safety, control, freedom, romanticism, magnetism, or any emotional or mental need fulfilled by money. In the principal reference verse of 1 Timothy 6:10, the word "love" in the phrase "For the love of money…." is the Greek word philargurio, which means here in this context, covetousness or avarice and comes from the root word philarguos, which means "fond of silver." However, both Greek words are rooted in the Greek word philarguria and embodies the English meaning of avarice or the "love of money." The English word avarice has the root word "avar" within it, which means blind. A person who is covetous of money is blind to the truth and blind to the snares that greed, covetousness, and avarice cause.

Secondly, the "Love of Money" also means the opposite of the "hate of money." The "love of money" means that money has become one's idol, trying to fulfill one's needs with money which rightfully can only be fulfilled by God.

MONEY IS USED TO SATISFY SEVERAL OTHER KINDS OF PERSONALITY TRAITS

The "Contentment Seeking Personality Trait of Money:" Some people seek money to be content where they are financially. A common statement is, "I'm not rich, but I am content with what I have." It is hard to attack this disorder because of scriptures as Philippians 4:12, which says, "I know both how to be abased, and I know how to abound: everywhere and in all things I am instructed both to be full and to be hungry, both to abound and to suffer need." Yet, taking this scripture in the extreme can be an excuse not to take steps toward economic stability.

The "Avenging Personality Trait of Money:" When the motive to get rich is to "get even" with someone who did you wrong, an improper motive exists. The plots of many movies have been modern day Robber Barons manipulating markets, setting up people in sting operations, and working long hours motivated by revenge. Romans 12:19 says, "Beloved, do not avenge yourselves, but rather give place to wrath; for it is written, 'Vengeance is Mine, I will repay,' says the Lord."

"The Knowledge Seeking Personality Trait of Money:" The acquisition of knowledge can become an idol or a sense of being better than others who have less knowledge. These people study every day to be the "answer man" that knows more than most others of a given subject.

The Bible encourages that you read and study your Bible. 2 Timothy 3:16 says, "All scripture is given by inspiration of God, and is profitable for doctrine, for reproof, for correction, for instruction in righteousness." The same Apostle Paul, who wrote 2 Timothy 3:16 also wrote a scripture to put his statement in balance in Romans 8:1 2, which says, "Now concerning things offered to idols: we know that we all have knowledge. Knowledge puffs up, but (agape) love edifies. And if anyone thinks that he knows anything, he knows nothing yet as he ought to know."

However, Paul also said that if a person had spiritual gifts and knowledge but had not agape love, in 1 Corinthians 13:2, which says "And though I have the gift of prophecy, and understand all mysteries, and all knowledge; and though I have all faith, so that I could remove mountains, and have not (agape love) charity, I am nothing."

Decades ago, I had a Pastor friend who spent over $20,000 in today's dollars collecting religious books and other kinds of books. He claimed his collection contained several religious books that were no longer available. In his acquisition of knowledge, he had acquired so many books that he had to rent two small houses side by side. One he barricaded and used as a private library to house his books, and the other he lived in it with his wife. Our many conversations often brought up the reason why he was trying to make extra money because he had an obsessive compulsion to buy more books.

"Many Other Personality Traits of Money:" Any soulish need being fulfilled with money can become an ungodly personality trait and often does capture the affection of the person looking toward mammon as his source of life. Again, Matthew 6:24 says, "No one can serve two masters; for either he will hate the one and love the other, or else he will be loyal to the one and despise the other. You cannot serve God and mammon."

MANY PEOPLE HAVE DIFFERENT COMBINATIONS OF PERSONALITY TRAITS OF MONEY

A person may use money to be safe, acquire control over people, romantically attractive, and have a magnetic personality to attract others, or pathos attractiveness at the same time.

Since every human being is different, a diverse combination of needs in the soul may occur at the same period in a person's life, and the person may try to use money to fulfill several needs to satisfy his obsessive-compulsive different personality traits.

As one gets older, one's financial needs, personal needs, and desires change, either for good or bad. When people grow older, some grow cranky, while others grow sweeter, some forgive everyone while others hate or distrust everyone. Older people often think people are always after their money.

At the same time, one's perception of money changes as one's soulish needs modify. When parents' financial responsibilities to support children daily are lessened, their stress level lessens, causing them not to be upset and anxious about money daily.

People's Personality Trait Disorders regarding money may change through various stages of life. They may use money to fulfill the need to have friendly attractions, then for control, then for freedom, and finally for safety, or in a different order of compulsion. Regardless, these all are Personality Traits that constitute soulish problems regarding money that can become an obsessive-compulsive disorder manifested as spiritual immaturity in the soul that is filled with carnality instead of God's spirituality. Romans 8:6 says, "For to be carnally minded is death; but to be spiritually minded is life and peace."

Although Jesus and Paul would disagree, Solomon said in Ecclesiastes 10:19 that "…money answereth all things."

Instead of being satisfied with what they have and can earn, while trusting God for their provision, countless people embrace the idea that money can heal all soulish wounds, can make them feel safe, can give them control, can pay for their freedom, can make them romantically attractive, or can enhance their personal magnetism. These people with soulish problems they are trying to nurture with money often seek more and more money to feed their phobias and soulish disorders.

The more these soulish injured people have the more they want because their phobias and soulish disorders cannot be cured with money. Money gives a temporary fulfillment of need, feeds the fears, but then the sense of fulfillment of their need fades rather quickly, even less than thirty days. They usually will take great risks for quick returns brought to them by con men resulting in their further loss of money. Repentance of the world's fallen philosophies about money, and submission to the entire Godhead for the transformation of their souls, is the only answer and cure.

Personality Traits of Money

Dr. Nova Dean Pack

Three Great Genius Inventors Who Were Denied The Wealth From Their Inventions

CHAPTER NINE

THREE GREAT GENIUS INVENTORS WHO WERE DENIED THE WEALTH FROM THEIR INVENTIONS

As a lawyer, I have found in my practice, and through historical research, that Inventors normally know only basic ideas about obtaining needed finances and legalities necessary to protect their inventions. Inventors are often Believers where God had created them with inventive minds and had engifted them with inventive ideas. I enjoyed associating with them. They usually are naïve and overly trustful with outsiders, as they just want their inventions to get to the consumers. They often do not have people interested in their inventions to sign nondisclosure agreements before they are shown the invention. Sometimes, they will hand the invention to an interested financier for him to validate the invention's authenticity with his "scientific expert." Where will the interested financier find another scientific expert of an invention when the only person in the world that knows the invention is the Inventor, himself?

There are evil people who have larceny and fraud in their hearts, and they may even disguise themselves as members of a particular religion that is represented as the same as the Inventor's faith to entice the Inventor to trust them. If they use their faith to defraud the Inventor of his invention, the S.E.C. calls that Affinity Fraud. I wrote about Affinity Fraud in a previous chapter regarding Bernie Madoff who conducted the largest Ponzi scheme in history and financially destroyed approximately 37,000 lives.

Sometimes, these people claiming to be Christian may be saved, but their souls need transformation. Being spiritually immature in their untransformed souls, they operate business using principles of the fallen world of Social Darwinism. As was said in a previous chapter, Rockefeller was a Believer and was a member of a church congregation, but he made the statement, "The growth of a large business is merely a survival of the fittest." Oftentimes, Inventors create things that help people; but then they have the task of convincing people that their inventions will fulfill their needs. Consumers rarely purchase things they do not understand. Also, most consumers do not examine or research products before they buy them, so they settle for the representations made in the advertisements and commercials. Afterwards, the consumer discovers that the product does not perform as advertised or represented. It is hard to obtain a refund from China.

Likewise, most Inventors do not realize that wealthy people become very prosperous because they sell to consumers the products that customers already want, so, there is no selling involved but merely taking orders. Bezos saw a need to help manufacturers to get their products to the consumers. He set up a company called Amazon, which developed warehousing and fast delivery of manufacturer's products and sold and delivered these products to consumers at home without the consumer having to experience buying the product at a shopping mall, and Bezos was considered the top two richest men in the world at one time. Amazon did not pay the manufacturer for its products until Amazon sold the products to the consumers. This was a genius idea, and Amazon really grew during the Covid-19 pandemic lockdown from March to August 2020, where people were buying through Amazon rather than stores. Convenience ordering products on Amazon, and with next day delivery, became a new way of shopping; and Bezos became extremely wealthy.

There was a government preference for electric cars, and people started buying electric cars. So, Elon Musk perfected the Tesla electric car that was better than any other electric car. He simply sold the car that people wanted. (Personally, I prefer a car that has both electric batteries, but also has gas fuel in the event I get stuck in traffic on a California freeway. Yet, Elon Musk with Tesla, and with his other businesses, at one time was the richest man in the world because he manufactured what consumers wanted to purchase.

Similarly, Rockefeller founded Standard Oil in 1870 and built refineries to refine crude oil into Kerosene and gasoline that the mass of consumers needed, and he became the richest man in the U.S., controlling 90% of all oil in the U.S. at its peak in 1900 which were used in lamps, to fuel ships, and later automobiles. (Rockefeller became wealthier after Standard Oil was divided up into various other companies by court order with the U.S. Attorney General filing a lawsuit under the Sherman Antitrust Act).

All of these men, along with several others became super wealthy because they found out what people wanted first and built their businesses to produce and deliver the products the consumers wanted. This is a strange idea for Inventors, as Inventors believe their ideas are revolutionary and that will make a major difference in humanity's wellbeing. The problem is it takes time to get a new invention into public confidence and usage.

THE INVENTION OF AUTOMOBILES TOOK CENTURIES TO CATCH ON BY CONSUMERS

Wikipedia writes, "Development of the automobile started in 1672 with the invention of the first steam-powered vehicle, which led to the creation of the first steam-powered automobile capable of human transportation, built by Nicolas-Joseph Cugnot in 1769. Inventors began to branch out at the start of the 19th century, creating the de Rivaz engine, one of the first internal combustion engines, and an early electric motor. Samuel Brown later tested the first industrially applied internal combustion engine in 1826. Only two of these were made. . . . The first modern car—a practical, marketable automobile for everyday use—and the first car in series production appeared in 1886, when (the German) Carl Benz developed a gasoline-powered automobile and made several identical copies. . . . From 1886, many Inventors and entrepreneurs got into the "horseless carriage" business, both in America and Europe, and inventions and innovations rapidly furthered the development and production of automobiles. Ransom E. Olds founded Oldsmobile in 1897, and introduced the Curved Dash Oldsmobile in 1901. Olds pioneered the assembly line using identical, interchangeable parts, producing thousands of Oldsmobiles by 1903. Although sources differ, approximately 19,000 Oldsmobiles were built, with the last produced in 1907. Production likely peaked from 1903 through 1905, at up to 5,000 units a year. In 1908, the Ford Motor Company further revolutionized automobile production by developing and selling its Ford Model T at a relatively modest price. From 1913, introducing an advanced moving assembly line allowed Ford to lower the Model T's price by almost 50%, making it the first mass-affordable automobile."

PUBLIC UTILITIES ARE LEGALIZED MONOPOLIES

Today, natural gas in homes and buildings for heating and cooking is provided by public util-

Personality Traits of Money

ities. The electric power companies that make and distribute to home alternating electricity are provided by public utilities. Why are these "utility monopolies" not broken up and allow competition, so consumers can have a choice. Monopolies stifle Inventors from creating a better product for the consumer. You may wonder why Oil Refineries who make gasoline for cars are not public utilities? They are a public need just like the power utility companies. Personally, I do not like public utilities who are legal monopolies; I trust in competition in a moral-based free enterprise economy in society. I find prices go down when there is competition, but prices rarely if ever go down in monopolies in each industry. You can see this happened in the cell phone industry. There are no longer long-distance phone bills because the telephone monopolies were dismantled. I am encouraged when people in various places are allowed to live off the grid and use solar, wind, and/or hydropower to produce their own electricity. Why cannot every homeowner in the city plan to live off the grid like the people in remote areas are allowed? When the government takes over all the industries, it squashes individual ingenuity and new inventions.

Fighting off jealous competitive Inventors who file a patent claim before the true Inventor and claiming they invented the product, avoiding temptation from financiers who have money offer to purchase the invention at a time when the Inventor is desperate for money, arguing with family who are tired of hearing about the invention and the poverty that they feel is an idol, or the ongoing task to find a person who has a good heart like me that wants the Inventor to have his invention reach the public consumer for the advancement and betterment of humanity.

In studying the plight of Inventors, one can see how 1 Timothy 6:10 is in full swing in the greedy mind of capitalists who take advantage of Inventors when they are down and out to buy their invention for a song. In my over fifty years of practicing business law with perhaps 5,000 plus business clients, at least 100 of which were Inventors, it is evil what the devil sends people to steal the invention what God gave to the Inventor for God's children to have a more abundant life.

I am going to write about three Inventors who were cheated out of the great financial returns because they invented something that had a profound impact on society where the invention was stolen or through legal process beat the true Inventor to the Patent office or simply could not get the proper backing to produce. People with money will try to steal something if they cannot buy it at the price they offered. Many Inventors have lost their invention when someone hires them to work in a laboratory or research and development department, when the Inventor creates something great, but now the business owner contends that he owns the invention because he was paying a salary to the Inventor as an employee at the time. These Inventors seem to always run out of money, abandon their invention for one season, and work for another, but their compulsion to work on their inventions is almost obsessive.

These three Inventors that I am examining their lives were all geniuses but suffered at the hands of others. They are Nikola Tesla, Tesla's grandson I call Niko, and an Inventor I named Neptune, with the last two being my clients at one time. I have not revealed their names for confidentiality purposes and their protection or that of their families. I believe Niko is still alive, but Neptune passed many years ago.

Dr. Nova Dean Pack

NIKOLA TESLA

Nikola Tesla (1856-1943) was a genius physicist and engineer. He was born in Smiljan, Croatia, which was then part of the Austro-Hungarian Empire. Tesla's father was a Serbian Orthodox Priest, while his mother managed their family farm. Tesla reported that he had visions of inventions, like the electric motor, which basic design is used throughout the modern world. Tesla never solidified through contract any rights for royalties, or the royalties stopped coming. Tesla did create dozens of inventive breakthroughs in the production, transmission, and application of alternating current electric power. He invented the first alternating current motor and developed AC generation and transmission technology.

Tesla's first invention he visualized the principle of the rotating magnetic field and developed plans for an induction motor that would become his first step toward the successful utilization of alternating current.

Though Tesla was famous and respected, he was robbed of his inventions that made others very wealthy. He was unsuccessful in converting his numerous patented inventions into long-term financial success—unlike his early employer and chief competitor, Thomas Edison.

In fact, Tesla first worked with Thomas Edison, but after Tesla invented a machine requested by Edison, Edison reneged on a bonus promised to Tesla on the pretense that he was joking about the bonus. Tesla immediately quit. Thomas Edison emerged as a leader in the field of electricity but tried to ruin Tesla's alternating current electricity invention as being too dangerous by demonstrating the killing of animals (including an Elephant) with the alternating current demonstration. Edison's work in electrical engineering and the creation of the incandescent light bulb in 1879 was his greatest invention for which he deserves great credit. Notwithstanding, he was ruthless against Tesla because Tesla's alternating current undermined Edison's direct currency business.

After coming to America, Tesla worked for both Edison and Westinghouse, but they eventually stopped paying him his agreed royalties for his inventions. Tesla and Westinghouse exhibited his invention of alternating electricity by lighting the 1893 World's Columbian Exposition in Chicago. Westinghouse then entered a partnership with General Electric and installed large alternating current generators at Niagara Falls that Tesla invented. Tesla invented the first modern power station for alternating current electricity, which continues to this day. Tesla should have received a percentage of the electricity being sold for the rest of his life and could have had a family legacy like the Great Industrialists, but he did not have a good business attorney or business consultant to negotiate such contracts.

I have found that with Inventors, the gratification of the invention itself is payment enough. In the 1890s Tesla invented many different things, such as the high-voltage transformer known as the Tesla coil, along with improved lighting, electric oscillators, and meters. Tesla also experimented with X-rays, invented the short-range radio communication two years before Guglielmo Marconi, and he received a Supreme Court decision postmortem declaring Tesla's invention of the short-range radio was first. And finally, to name just a few, Tesla successfully demonstrated a radio communication that controlled a boat traveling around a pool in Madison Square Garden.

Personality Traits of Money

Tesla lived his last decades in a New Yorker Hotel, occupying rooms 3327 and 3328, working in one hotel room on new inventions while living in the other hotel room. After years of living there, Tesla's physical health diminished because he would not eat properly. His mind was focused on his inventions. His obsession with the number "three" and fastidious washing were thought as just the eccentricities of Tesla being a genius. He spent his final years daily feeding the city's pigeons in the New York City parks and working on his ideas for inventions. Tesla died with very little money on January 7, 1943. Undoubtedly, Tesla was abused by financial backers like Edison, Westinghouse, and J.P. Morgan. People with money who are wealthy believed in the "strongest of the fittest" as their philosophy as they traverse the difficult transactions to become super wealthy. The problem Tesla had was he was dealing with very wealthy businessmen who wanted to steal his inventions and make the money without paying him or recognize him as the genius Inventor he was.

MY CLIENT NICOLA TESLA'S GRANDSON

As a lawyer, I had the privilege for a brief time to represent Nicola Tesla's grandson, whose name I will call "Niko." I will not reveal his name for his protection. What was amazing was his physical features looked like his grandfather. Niko was a Christian Believer. Amazingly, Niko had his grandfather's genius I.Q. and is an Inventor, mathematician, and physicist, who needed good legal representation for his protection. Niko was living in a somewhat rundown converted garage where he conducted inventive experiments in San Bernardino County, California. I would see him often and take him to lunch and slip him some money. Someone gave him this old Volkswagen, which he drove. Like most scientific geniuses, Niko's genius thoughts were hard to follow and way above my training, whereas my legal knowledge was beyond his training.

When I met Niko, he had created a motor generator that did not run by plugging it in an electrical outlet. It was about as close to perpetual motion that one could achieve. Before I met Niko, he entertained a couple of potential so-called investors, but they requested to take the machine with them to have an "expert" look at it for verification. If I had represented him, I would have asked, "Who is this expert? How could you find an expert that knew as much or more than this Inventor? My client and I will take the machine with us to your expert, and when we leave the meeting, my client will take his machine with him. Is that agreed?" This was a reasonable compromise on both sides, but they would not have agreed to this safe procedure because their idea was to steal Niko's machine.

Why Niko trusted them and allowed them to leave with possession of this fabulous machine, without a signed written bailment agreement and signed receipt of possession, along with copies of their driver's licenses, I do not understand. As I told him, "You will never see your invention again. I suspect they will take it to China to be manufactured there, and then the Chinese will steal it from them. The Chinese are very smart, and after discussion with them by their scientist, the Chinese will know they were not the Inventors." Therefore, that invention was stolen, and Niko never saw it again nor money from his ingenious invention.

The second invention Niko invented was lubrication that was not oil but biodegradable, nontoxic, lubrication inside the engine of a car that caused the engine to last longer and did not get dirty like regular petroleum oil. So, the oil did not have to be replaced (unless there were leaks in the engine) for the life of the car. I drained my oil and added Niko's lubrication, along with a friend of mine, who also put it in his car; and this invention oil substitute and it lasted and stayed pure. My car sounded better. I did have a small oil leak from my engine, so about every few months, I had enough extra lubrication to fill one-half quart into my car's oil reservoir again. Amazingly, there was no colored smoke coming out of my tail pipe. The oil replacement maintained its viscosity against internal friction of the internal engine parts. I thought this product could be manufactured with labeled plastic containers like oil or could be in the oil treatment section at automotive parts stores. The potential problem was that the oil products' competitors would hate the product, as over time Niko's product could cut heavily into their oil market. On the other hand, it would be an excellent product to sell multi-marketing as a car product along with their other products. Regardless, I thought this could be a saleable product. However, neither Niko, nor I, nor my and his friend, that also was a partner, had the money required to set up a manufacturing and marketing company. So, we had to look for investors.

There was a sophisticated financial firm who spoke serious interest in funding the manufacturing of this substitute oil for retail sales, located in Orange County, California. When we met them, I had them sign Nondisclosure and Non-competition Agreements. I did not charge any upfront attorney fees for my services, and I agreed to be paid only if and when we were successful with any of Niko's inventions. I worked on a contingency basis because Niko had no money. This meant that I would receive a percentage of net profits only if and when there were any.

The financiers had no capital themselves and were brokers that gave excuse after excuse. After many, many hours and my work and days and weeks went by without success, Niko received a job offer as a scientist in a laboratory. With good faith, I tore up my retainer agreement and gave Niko the freedom to continue his career as he saw was in his best interest, as he owed me nothing. After all, he was a brother in the Lord.

One thing Niko told me and then showed me was that he could prove that basic Algebra was inherently flawed. Of course I hated algebra, so I told him, "I knew that." Just kidding! On my White Board in my law office, he started writing algebraic letters, symbols, and numbers as genius mathematicians do, line after line. I stared at the board as he was writing, and I did not know anything about what he was doing. Eventually, he turned around and looked at me and said, "see?" I was like a deer at night looking at coming car lights. I said, "To be honest sir, I have no idea what you did in writing on my white board." Then he started pointing line to line at what he just wrote explaining his theory that algebra was flawed. So, I sat there and wondered how this genius standing in front of me can make money with this algebraic flaw discovery. That was my job. I did not have a clue.

The point that is relevant to this study is that most Inventors have no idea as to how to change their inventions into making money and how to keep their inventions from thieves. To his credit, Niko's inventions were to help people, and like his grandfather, he wanted to invent a machine to make free electricity. I have not spoken to him for years, but if he calls me, I would be honored to buy him lunch and have probably one of the most thoughtful and engaging conversations with this genius grandson of Nikola Tesla.

<u>Personality Traits of Money</u>

MY CLIENT AND DEAR FRIEND, NEPTUNE

"Neptune" was not his true name; this was a code word I made up to maintain his and his family's privacy. For example, a local newspaper reporter heard about Neptune and his invention and called him for an interview. His wife later told me that she whispered to him, "I don't think you should be speaking with that newspaper reporter with all the details you are giving her." Yet, he continued. In less than a week he was the subject of an article on the front page of the local section of the newspaper. His wife called me and told me about the article, which she has a copy for me. I said, "I will be there this Saturday." After reading the article, I said, "The article has already been printed, so there is really nothing we can do about it. No one contacted you after about six weeks, so I think that everything is okay." Then the next meeting, Neptune said, "I need to tell you that I got visitors in a black limousine. They appeared to me either Japanese or Chinese. There was an older man and a younger man, and the younger man spoke English while interpreting what the older man asked. I answered his questions, leaving out secret ingredients and just gave them the basics, and the young man interpreted my answers. The older man wanted to know if my water project was for sale. I told them 'No!' They thanked me for my time." I responded, "Now you see why I told you to not speak to any reporters because you do not know what thief or people will show up and try to steal your invention." Neptune died many years ago, and I want to tell the story of his and my experience together.

My client and dear friend, Neptune, outside of Jesus was the greatest man I ever knew. He was a genius but was somewhat eccentric. For example, he always wore denim Jeans, with the pant legs rolled up just at his ankles, wore a long sleave white dress shirt with the sleeves rolled up. He wore plain 1950's slip-on rockabilly style black boots that covered about three inches above his ankles, but his black boots always were polished and never scuffed. I never saw him wearing anything else in all the years I knew him.

With Neptune, you had to be invited to visit with him because he rarely spoke to strangers unless it was about his water project. He was a man who was serious most of the time; I never heard him laugh louder than a little chuckle, although he may have laughed often with his family. As Tesla and Niko's interest was primarily electricity, Neptune's interest was in taking water out of the air and liquifying it into enormous quantities for humanity at a low energy cost.

When I first met the Neptune's family in 1968, I worked part time while going to college as a clerk helper and knew Neptune's wife as a checker at a nearby grocery store. I was very polite and helpful at work, especially when Neptune's was pregnant with their last child. I made sure she had no heavy lifting. I was invited over to Neptune's family home for dinner, where I was told that the father (Neptune) was working on his water project in the back area of the house and would not be joining us for dinner. For a while, I thought that the family was kidding me about having a father or a husband. For almost a year, I did not see Neptune. Then, one day I came over to their home, and there Neptune was sitting at the kitchen table drinking a cup of coffee looking at me coming into his home. Growing up in the mid-west, I had impeccable manners, and his wife said I was going to college and was the politest and most helpful young man at the grocery store where she worked. He smiled at me and nodded his head in approval. Then he got up and walked back into the back area of his home without a word, and I assumed he had taken a break and was back to his private place to study or work on his water project. I asked his wife, "Does he ever talk?" She laughed, "Well, he must get to know you first, but even then, he wants the conversation to be about his water project. The kids are bored of the topic. If he did not like you, he would not have smiled and nodded his head." None of his family knew what Neptune's water invention was about, and neither did I; and it had no importance to me.

Becoming a regular friend of the family, I was invited by Neptune's wife at work to see whether I would like to travel with them to meet Neptune's cousin where Neptune built a hydroponic system that grew food without being planted in soil. Neptune told her he would like to show me his hydroponics system that he built. I had never heard of such a thing, but I was curious. After we arrived in San Luis Obispo and settled in at his cousin's house, Neptune invited me to see his hydroponics system where he and his cousin were growing large vegetables, which were going to be served as part of dinner that evening.

Having lived on a farm in Illinois as a child and young teenager, where we had three acres of vegetables growing in the soil each year, along with fruit trees, I was very inquisitive and asked a few questions as to how to grow vegetables without soil. Neptune grinned and was pleased that I was interested in his hydroponics system. Yet, he said something that later I remembered. He said, "There is so much more you someday will see." It was almost prophetic. In his provocative, soft-spoken voice Neptune continued with his scientific teaching of how hydroponics work as it is the water where nutrients are added without soil that grew those beautiful, large tomatoes and other vegetables, which were picked fresh to eat as opposed to the vegetables in the grocery stores that are picked when they are not ripe. That evening, these vegetables were served, and I can say they were the best tasting vegetables I had ever eaten. I will talk a little more about this hydroponics conversation later.

A year later, in the summer of 1969, at the age of 20, getting ready to drive to Cal State University Long Beach, Neptune finally asked me to sit down, have a cup of coffee, and have what I call a proverbial conversation at his kitchen table. He asked me questions in a very thoughtful way, as to what I wanted to be once I graduated from Cal State University Long Beach. I told him I planned to go to law school and become a lawyer. He showed a grin that was exceedingly rare because he was pleased. In his fatherly conversation with me, he encouraged me to continue my education, and advised me not to get married until I was finished with my higher education, "because you get married and start having children you will not finish your education." He told me that I had an aptitude to become a lawyer. His affirmation and encouragement stayed with me throughout my university years and law school. Two weeks later I started my junior and senior years at Cal State University Long Beach where in 1971, I graduated with a B.A. degree in political science.

In the winter of my senior University year, I applied and sat for the California Law School Admissions Test. I scored high marks and was accepted at several law schools. I decided to enroll at Pepperdine University School of Law (subsequently changed to Pepperdine University Caruso School of Law), which is accredited by all academia accreditation as a west coast "Ivy League Law School" in Malibu, California, with a Christian foundational base. However, Pepperdine University Caruso School of Law has a strong policy of non-discrimination of any faith and enrolls students of all faith, and even atheists. I received the best legal education there, so I highly recommend the law school. I graduated from Pepperdine University School of Law in July 1974, receiving a juris doctorate degree. I passed the California State

Personality Traits of Money

Bar exam the same year and became a licensed lawyer in December 1974. I started my own private law practice in December 1974 in Orange County, California.

Being remarkably busy with my education and starting my law practice, unfortunately, I lost track of Neptune. I was a business attorney, and a trial lawyer, and I taught as an adjunct professor at a local law school in Orange County. After about two years working from 60-80 hours a week as a lawyer and law school professor, I was looking to add something to my life that had more meaning than just working long hours a week without a great sum of money for my efforts.

In the middle of 1978, one of Neptune's daughters telephoned me at my law office, which shocked me. She said, "I found you in the yellow pages as I work for the Public Defender's office in Victorville, California, and I had to speak to an attorney in Orange County that was on our list as a referral when the Public Defender has a conflict case. You said you were going to be a lawyer and you did. I am proud of you. My father lives in Hesperia. I think my father was waiting for you to become a lawyer, so he can use you for his water project." I responded, "Wow, he is still working on his water project. So, your family moved to Hesperia. I remember you were still living in Oxnard when I attended Cal State University Long Beach because I went to visit your mother when she was hospitalized. Do you know what your father wants to talk to me about? Also, why move to Hesperia as that is a much smaller community than Oxnard?" She replied, "Well, he said he had to live in the desert because if his water project works in the desert where the air is much dryer and has less humidity, it can work anywhere. Dad has invited you to come to his home this Saturday, so can I tell him that you will come Saturday around 10:00 a.m.?" "Of course," I said, and I obtained his address.

I was excited to visit Neptune because I remembered in detail every conversation we had. I also was looking forward to seeing the whole family again. I drove on Saturday and arrived before 10 a.m. I did not want to intrude, but Neptune's wife saw me sitting in my car, and went outside to motion with her hand for me to come in. After the hugs with his wife, pleasantries with all the kids, who were there to greet me, they each shared what they were doing and where they lived. At about 10:30 a.m. Neptune gave them his look, so they said goodbye and left. His wife brought cups of coffee, and I sat down at the same kitchen table once again.

At this first water project meeting, Neptune became the learned Scientist-Inventor-Professor who asked questions like the Greek philosopher, Socrates. Having graduated from law school, and as a trial lawyer, I was used to the Socratic method of questions and answers to marshal the facts and narrow down relevant issues. Thus, Neptune's questioning me and my responding with answers did not make me feel uncomfortable. This is what Socrates did with his philosophy students. Also, Law school Professors used the Socratic method of teachings, and Jewish Rabbis often use this method of teaching as well.

Neptune preferred calling me by my middle name, "Dean," instead of "Nova." (My family members in Illinois call me "Dean" as well.) "Dean, what do you want to accomplish in your life?" "Dean, what do you think is the best thing you can do for people?" "Dean, what is the most important need for all humanity?" "Dean, is money the only motivation for your decision in accepting law cases?" "Dean, why do people congregate together when there is all of this cheap land out here in the San Bernardino County deserts?" "Dean, if I told you that I have invented a system that could help people and at the same time make more money than you could ever dream of having, would you be interested in helping me bring my utilitarian water invention to the world?" I thought to myself, "Well, Neptune you never ski on top of the lake, do you? You are a skin diver that wants to see what is deep down in the water where my soul resides."

Growing up as a Christian, I have always been a truth seeker and a servant of other people. Likewise, I always have been an altruistic person, so I told him about my Christian faith, and he accepted it as okay but that was not an issue he wanted to discuss. (When things get a little too personal, I always change the subject matter. I would "dodge the bullet," if you will.) That did not work with Neptune. He was pleased that the acquisition of money itself was not what caused me to get up every morning and go to work. I told him, "I try to do the best that I can for my clients. I work hard to represent my clients, and I have been successful because I am always prepared for every hearing when opposing lawyers are not as prepared. Some lawyers have three or four clients in different courts in the morning and the same number in the afternoon calendar, so they call the clerk of the Judge to put all matters on 'second call.' That meant the lawyer is representing more than one client in at least two different counties or court rooms. I never went to court with more than one client, and that is why during the week I am in court every day. I do my legal paperwork in the afternoon, but this work schedule has started affecting my health. Also, at night I have been teaching students at a law school for the last three years in Orange County, which I have given notice that I will quit at the end of the school year in the summer. I am separated from my wife, without a family and no children; so, I can work many hours, and I am young and can handle a heavy work schedule. I would be honored to begin something new and exciting, so my time here on earth is not wasted."

I always had a heart to do good and to help people, and I won almost all my cases for my clients because of my work ethic. I surmised that Neptune saw my tenacity, and he deduced I had an excellent work ethic in 1969 in our last conversation in Oxnard, California.

Spiritually, Neptune was raised a Catholic while I was raised a Protestant, but our spiritual differences were no barrier to the water project or our trusting friendship. To counter my affirmation as a Christian, Neptune said, "Dean, even Jesus who walked on water in a lake continuously had to know where the wells were located on his journeys on land because He and His disciples had to drink water every day." After we finished chuckling, I responded, "Well, you made a good point."

Now began the reveal of this man with the purest heart, a great Inventor, and an intellectual genius who self-educated himself in high physics, mathematics, chemistry, and engineering; and most importantly, he knew everything about water and people's desperate need for water. He said he invented a diaphragm made from special parts of cows that he could apply to any substance, like concrete or tile cylinders. He continued that he would spread the gel-like substance as a diaphragm on the exterior of the concrete or tile cylinders and then create a vacuum inside the cylinders. Nature abhors a vacuum, so the vacuum did not require on-going energy to work the water plant, so, it would pull pure $H2O$, without allowing any dirt, viruses, bacteria, or anything else that is in the air into the cylinders. The "flux factor" with the diaphragm was zero, which means only pure water molecule by molecule came into the cylinder. The pure water could be sucked out of the cylinder by an open and shut gate without releasing the vacuum. He said the engineering vacuum protection gate already has been invented. Then, he continued and said the pure water can be pushed into pipes that could transfer the water to a given destination, such as to operate a hydroelectric plant that is 800 plus feet below. This was his invention briefly.

Neptune continued his explanation with more details. Neptune told me how his water machine capturing water out of the air will make electricity at an exceptionally low cost. He said, "If we build a water plant on about one acre of land through something that looks like retrofit tubes on top of at least 800 to 1,000 feet above a hydroelectric plant would be best. The tubes will hold a vacuum, which engineering is already available, where there is space between the tubes in a disarrayed manner. The air flow should be at least between 5 to 10 miles per hour wind with about 20% humidity (which occurs most everywhere, even in the desert), so, volumes of air with water vapor can continuously pass around the tubes. The volumes of water vapor will be sucked into the tubes because of the vacuum inside. This size of the water from the air plant could produce one to two million gallons a day. Because of the vacuum, there is no need for continuous power to operate this water from the air production plant. All we would need is to have the front end of a jet engine to create the initial vacuum, and the closed and open gates will allow the pure water from the air to leave the tube without the tube losing its vacuum. Then, the water can be transported to water lines to continue to flow and pick up enough speed downward with waterpower to turn a turbine driven generator in a hydroelectric plant that makes electricity for citizens in businesses, schools, and houses. The pure water can be a water supply for people's homes, as the water is collected and stored in large steel containers."

Neptune taught me many things about human population and water, and the use of his water machine that took the water vapor out of the air, liquefied it, and stored the water in large steel containers to resolve the water shortage for humanity. Neptune said, "We do not have overpopulation, but an over distribution of population. All towns, cities, and people's homes must be near a water source because the human body cannot live more than three to four days without water." Neptune continued, "The value of land in the world depends on how close the land is to a water source. People drill water wells; they obtain water from rivers; they haul water from lakes to homes; they catch rainwater falling on the roof and captured in rain gutter and flowed into a cistern. Yet all the fresh rainwater originally comes from the rainwater in the air in the earth's hydro cycle. Every drop of water attaches itself around a particle of dirt in the air and that is what causes the water vapor to unify into a drop and gather weight, and that is part of the reason the rain drops fall to the ground."

He said, "Hydrogen and oxygen molecules go through my diaphragm without allowing any air, dirt, impurities of any kind; and the water which comes into the vacuum chamber is uncontaminated. Water is a the most attractive substance on earth. It continues to attract anything that is in the air. If you drink this pure water before it is in the environment for a while, then it could leach the minerals out of your body and harm you. Yet, this pure water is great for laboratories who need clean water to do experiments. One of the reasons that I moved to the desert here in Hesperia area is because the desert has less germs out here."

Neptune then invited me to his garage, where he had made a small prototype of his water out of air machine. It was a two-foot round tile tube, which was about eight inches in diameter, where on one end he had a see-through thick piece of round glass securely glued to the one end to block the vacuum from escaping. On the other end the tube was securely closed with a hose that sucked out the air in the tile tube to create a vacuum inside. On the outside of the tile tube was a gel diaphragm spread completely over the entire surface. He turned on the pump that created the vacuum inside the tile tube, and I watched through the glass that indeed the water came out of the air, passed through the gel diaphragm, and gathered into the tile cylinder. It was incredible. It was magic. Afterwards, we returned to the kitchen table, where he taught me how this machine on a larger scale would save money on people's water bills and would create money if a water source was created in the desert for a small community to be built.

We continued for about another six hours. I was happily soaking up information about Neptune's water from the air machine. I arrived home that night around 10 p.m. I could hardly sleep. This is the effect that happens after you have been in the presence of a genius. I came back the next weekend for more knowledge from my great teacher. I spent every other weekend with Neptune at his home month after month and year after year. All and all Neptune and I spent about eight years together working on his water project.

Neptune was a recluse. Yet, he was very engaging and articulate in conversation when speaking to people he wanted to speak with, but that number was few and far between. He did not like eating in restaurants; he would not stay overnight in someone's home unless they were relatives, but hardly ever did that. He did not attend social events, such as attending parties, going to theaters, attending sports events, and he avoided most everything other people engaged in as entertaining. Whenever he went somewhere, he normally had his wife drive. In all the years, he came to my house in Ontario, California only one time when we were driving to Arizona to meet U.S. House of Representative John Jacob Rhodes Jr. He did not allow his mind to be cluttered with everyday things, so, he could concentrate on his water project.

Neptune reminded me of our conversation when I was age 19 in 1968 in San Luis Obispo about the real purpose of the hydroponics that he developed. He refreshed my memory, when he said, "I asked you, 'Why do you think I made this hydroponics system all the way up here in San Luis Obispo since we did not live here to pick the vegetables when they ripened? The reason is I had no room in my house in Oxnard, but my experiment in hydroponics was to see the amount of water utilized to grow the vegetables and to determine if the water could be recycled and used again for conservation purposes."

Then he brought me back to our conversation in the present 1978 by continuing, "California is the largest State growing vegetables, and the farmers and ranchers are the largest users of water in the State. So, my interest in hydroponics is that its biggest advantage over soil growing is water conservation because the water can be used over and over to grow vegetables through a purification system similar to recycling of water in swimming pools."

In 1968 in San Luis Obispo, I picked up a larger than normal tomato grown through Neptune's hydroponics and responded, "I think the biggest advantage is you could grow one large hydroponics tomato to take the place of a dozen soil-grown smaller tomatoes and feed the world or at least lessen their grocery bill." Neptune ignored my response and said, "When growing plants in soil, the farmer must be very experienced to know how much water to pour around his plants. Too much water causes the plant's roots to be unable to get enough oxygen. Too little water and the plant can dry out and die. Also, constant watering the plants wastes water because the water not used seeps deeper into the ground around the plants and

Personality Traits of Money

does not conserve water. Hydroponics is about saving water." I knew in 1968 that Neptune was a great thinker and a very altruistic man. When we returned from San Luis Obispo, Neptune resumed his reclusive life in the back of his house. I did not speak with him until the summer of 1969.

In 1978 at my first meeting as a lawyer with Neptune, I finally understood the importance of water over food production, although both were needed for human survival. Neptune simply said, "You can last three to four weeks without food, but you can only last three to four days without water. Which is more important for survival, food, or water?" I responded with a lawyer-like answer, "I would say for immediate survival if someone were lost in a forest, it would be water, but in three weeks later, it would be food."

Neptune continued, "Historically all towns and cities were built around or near water sources, whether by freshwater lakes, artesian wells, springs, or man-dug wells to bring up water from the aquifers. Why is it that San Bernardino County, California, is the largest county in the world, and most of it is vacant desert when you drive less than an hour out of the city? The reason is all the people are crowded in the city to live near a water supply. Why is it that an acre of land in the city costs thousands of times more to buy than an acre of land in the desert? It is because of the water supply in the city and no water supply in the desert. Now, my invention that takes water out of the air in enormous quantities can bring water to the deserts and have the overcrowded population spread out, so, everyone has a house and a nice plot of land to live on. With my water invention, every single person on the planet could live on land the size of Texas. They can grow food with hydroponics, and drinking water will be abundant right out of the air. Then I can reverse my water system and make it produce air conditioning on every home at an exceptionally low cost because all you would pay electricity for would be the fan that blows the cool air through the ducts and vents."

My eyes opened wide and said, "Wow! We could buy some land in the desert, find investors to help you build your water plant to produce water, but what about electricity for the homes?" Neptune already thought it through with building homes in the desert, saying, "A hydroelectric power station is the least expensive to be built and to operate if you have a water supply, like a river or a dammed-up lake where the water falls over the dam can turn a hydroelectric turbine that runs the generator. Up here in the high desert, they have a hydroelectric plant where they use the lake water and the melting of snow to supply the waterpower to turn the turbine and generator. That is one of the reasons why I moved here. My water plant could be built on a big hill or a small mountain, and the water produced by the water plant can be directed into tubes that run down to the hydroelectric turbine with a force caused by gravity that would be as a fireman's hose shooting out water with great pressure enough to turn the turbine and generator that would create almost cost-free electricity after it is built. There are also windmills that can be erected because of the winds out in the desert that produce electricity. Yet, they do not produce water at the same time as my water from air system does. There are several people here in Hesperia who have erected windmills in their back yards that produce electricity. The point is with your knowledge as a lawyer, you could figure out the steps to build a Homeowners Association community in the desert, and I can design the water plant to power the hydroelectric station that already has been designed by others."

Neptune concluded, "We can change history the way cities determine the sites to build or expand cities which historically always had to be around a natural water supply under the ground. My invention takes the water from the air, not the ground. We do not have to find water, as it is all around us in the air. I have the machine to take the water vapor in the air and collect it as liquified water." I got excited and shook my head in affirmation and said, "Amazing. We can lower the cost of housing by building oasis communities in the desert and get paid handsomely for doing it." I had no idea how to start such a massive project, but it was euphoria thinking about something that was really helping people, and that was revolutionary, affordable, and good for people who could own a home in expensive California.

Later that evening, I was glad that I was reading my Bible daily, especially since I started in Genesis and was trying to go through the Bible in one year, which was a popular goal for many at that time. I remember reading about Abraham and his son, Isaac, where in the Bible scriptures talk about the water wells in the desert that they dug. Water wells in the Middle East deserts were protected by the owners of the land because water was critical, and families would have wars over the water wells if someone tried to still their water sources or if they built a water well on their land.

Genesis 26:19-23 32-33 says, "And Isaac's servants digged in the valley, and found there a well of springing water. (20) And the herdmen of Gerar did strive with Isaac's herdmen, saying, 'The water is ours:' and he called the name of the well Esek; because they strove with him. (21) And they digged another well, and strove for that also: and he called the name of it Sitnah. . . . (24) And the LORD appeared unto him the same night, and said, 'I am the God of Abraham thy father: fear not, for I am with thee, and will bless thee, and multiply thy seed for my servant Abraham's sake.' (25) And he (Isaac) builded an altar there, and called upon the name of the LORD, exand pitched his tent there: and there Isaac's servants digged a well. (26) Then Abimelech went to him from Gerar, and Ahuzzath one of his friends, and Phichol the chief captain of his army. (27) And Isaac said unto them, 'Wherefore come ye to me, seeing ye hate me, and have sent me away from you?' (28) And they said, 'We saw certainly that the LORD was with thee:' and we said, 'Let there be now an oath betwixt us, even betwixt us and thee, and let us make a covenant with thee; (29) That thou wilt do us no hurt, as we have not touched thee, and as we have done unto thee nothing but good, and have sent thee away in peace: thou art now the blessed of the LORD.' (30) And he (Isaac) made them a feast, and they did eat and drink. (31) And they rose up betimes in the morning, and sware one to another: and Isaac sent them away, and they departed from him in peace. (32) And it came to pass the same day, that Isaac's servants came, and told him concerning the (third) well which they had digged, and said unto him, 'We have found water.' (33) And he (Isaac) called it (the well) Shebah: therefore the name of the city (that developed around the well) is Beersheba unto this day.'"

Let me digest this scripture passage. Isaac retires, and he sets about digging a well for water for his wives, concubines, considerable number of workers, and the large herds of animals. He retreats from Abimelech's people who lived in Gerar and its suburbs, and he takes up his abode in the valley, or wady of Gerar. These wadys are the hollows in which brooks flow, and therefore they were well-watered and fertile parts of the country where crops can grow. Isaac has his servants dig again the old wells that Abraham dug that had been filled up by Abimelech's people and calls them by the old names that Abraham named. He digs two more new wells, but each time Abimelech's people claim they were theirs. So, Isaac gave them Hebrew names that meant "strife" and "opposition." When Isaac dug the first well, the herdsmen of

Personality Traits of Money

Gerar strive, claiming the water as their property. Isaac yields. He digs a second well, and they oppose once more, and he again yields. He now moves into a distinct region where the Abimelech people had no claim to ownership rights, so, Isaac dug a third gusher well that is not in the territory of Gerar, for which there is no contest. This third well, Isaac names "Rehoboth," which means "room" - a name which appears to be preserved in Wady er-Ruhaibeh, near which is Wady esh-Shutein, corresponding to Sitnah. "For now the Lord hath made room for us." Isaac's decision not to struggle with his neighbors' claim of ownership required faith because Isaac knew that God would show him where to dig for another well that will be a blessing not just for him but over time a whole city was built around the well as a water source.

The point of this passage of scripture that confirmed Neptune's teaching was that people in ancient times fought over water rights, and that the value of land increased abundantly when water was found on the land. When there was a great well, people moved there, and a town or city of people was built.

So, with Neptune, he concluded that the best thing he could do for humanity was to increase the water supply, not just the food supply. His conclusive logic was infallible. I finally saw my mistake at age 19 that Neptune was not concerned with growing larger vegetables with the hydroponics but was testing the hydroponics system to gain data that would encourage growing hydroponics food because it would reduce the consumption of water in comparison to the use of watering in the soil fields to grow vegetables.

Neptune was right in his conclusions, but in 1978 I was somewhat prideful as a young lawyer and highly educated. Neptune was a scientific and inventive genius, and I barely made Cs in college physics, chemistry, mathematics, and other scientifically based classes. I was a political science major, where I earned As and some Bs because I wanted to be a lawyer, not a scientist or a medical doctor. Political science is different and non-calculable because it is not a true science. This is why I received a B.A. degree in Political Science and not a B.S. degree in Political Science. Real scientists look at political science and ask, "Where's the formulas; where's the numbers; what purpose is political science if those who are in politics do not seek empirical data to discover provable facts?"

I told Neptune he is correct in saying that Political Science is not real science. U.S. Politicians seek compromise, not truth, and certainly do not seek empirical facts or using the sound economic biblical principle that debt is very bad. Politicians say and do things just to garner votes and compromise principles just to get something accomplished in the eyes of the voters. Politicians are not truth seekers in practice.

Truth, especially biblical economic truth, is not something Politicians use as guiding principles to follow. Most Politicians' ideas are speculative and experimental without any guaranteed outcome or provable researched outcome. There are many good men and women in Congress, but they learn the rules are that you must sell your vote by voting for other politicians' bill to get those other politicians to vote for your bill. This is the game that is the system of political science that must be learned and played to get anything accomplished for your constituents. The U.S. congress has very few principled Statesmen anymore. Politicians who are Statesmen normally resign after a couple of terms because they cannot deal with the lack of integrity, the manipulations, the cowardness, and the primary desire just to save their jobs by reelection.

For example, our national debt is short-term thinking and ignoring the long-term consequences of Politicians' actions of overspending that increases the national debt. Most Politicians must vote "yes" to borrow more money from the Federal Reserve by issuing new Treasure Bonds because there is always a budget deficit, and Politicians spend to buy votes and to maintain the U.S.'s leadership stature in the world. The result is that the national debt continues to increase, as the national debt is like a runaway train without an Engineer in control with the throttle wide open. The U.S. is the largest debtor nation in the world, and it is the fastest growing debt in the world. There will be a total crash in the U.S. economy; it is just a question of when, not if. If a Politician votes against using debt financing for government expenditures, then he or she is ostracized. The national debt is short-term thinking, not long-term wisdom. The national debt exists because politicians try to equalize consequences for people when God created people unique with individual different talents, and not everyone has the talents to be billionaires, scientists, doctors, lawyers, teachers, or professional basketball players. Also, the national debt is short-term thinking, not long-term wisdom, because we build our military for offensive attacks, not just defensive attacks. Why do the leaders in Washington D.C. think the U.S. should be the policemen of the world?

I HAVE TO TAKE A LITTLE RABBIT TRAIL BECAUSE WAR IS AN IMPORTANT TOPIC FOR EVERYONE

Here is what the U.S. Constitution says about Congressional responsibility regarding declaration of war, financing of war, and the time restraint of two years. Article I. LEGISLATIVE DEPARTMENT Section VIII, , Clause XI through Clause XIV says, "Clause XI: The Congress shall have power to: To declare War, grant Letters of Marque and Reprisal, and make Rules concerning Captures on Land and Water. Clause XII: To raise and support Armies, but no Appropriation of Money to that Use shall be for a longer Term than two Years. Clause XIII: To provide and maintain a Navy. Clause XIV: To make Rules for the Government and Regulation of the land and naval Forces."

There has not been a Declaration of War by Congress since WWII. Every war since then has been described as Police Actions and not wars. Firstly, one of the reasons is that if a War is Declared by Congress, then it invokes other Countries that are bound to join the War because of signed Treaties, such as NATO, SEATO, etc. There are Treaties also connected to military involvement by the United Nations. Secondly, by giving the power to declare war to Congress, then the Representatives and Senators should consult with their constituents as to whether the nation should go to war, where the constituents' sons and daughters will have to join the military and possibly die in battle. A declaration of war requires the consensus of the entire nation.

Yet, the President has powers as the Commander in Chief. Article II Section 2 of the U.S. Constitution, the Commander in Chief clause, states that "[t]he President shall be Commander in Chief of the Army and Navy of the United States, and of the Militia of the several States, when called into the actual Service of the United States." When can the President act as Commander in Chief when Congress has not made a Declaration of War? This issue is a source of conflict, and the Supreme Court has never had a case involving the powers of Congress versus the Powers of the President. The debate between scholars has been around historically without resolution. Some scholars contend that the Commander in Chief Clause confers expansive powers on the President, especially when there is an imminent attack facing the nation. Yet, other scholars argue that the Constitution does not define precisely the extent of those Presidential Commander in Chief powers.

Presidents Kennedy, Johnson, and Nixon committed U.S. troops and military weapons to the Southeast Asia conflict, primarily with Vietnam without Congressional approval, but in 1973 Congress passed the War Powers Resolution that halted the erosion of Congressional Power to participate in the decision whether to go to war, with the President being required to communicate to Congress the commitment of U.S. Troops within 48 hours. Also, the War Powers Resolution required the President to withdraw U.S. Troops from the conflict after 60 days if Congress has not granted an extension of the conflict.

Most Presidents have taken the position that the War Powers Resolution is unconstitutional because it treads on the President's powers as Commander in Chief. This is still an issue perhaps to be decided by the Supreme Court, but to date there has not been a case to bring to the Supreme Court. Yet, The War Powers Resolution grants the President with unilateral power to put U.S. troops in military action without prior Congressional approval. In practice, even though the War Powers Resolution exists, Congress largely approved of the President's action.

The Presidential powers were approved after the terrorist attacks of September 2001 which caused Congress to pass the Authorization for Use of Military Force against Terrorists (AUMF). While the AUMF did not officially declare war, the legislation provided the President with more authority upon which to exercise his constitutional powers as Commander in Chief. However, the U.S. Supreme Court explained in Youngstown Sheet & Tube v. Sawyer, 342 U.S. 579 (1952), during the Korea War, President Truman contended that he had national security powers on seizing privately owned Steel Company, where the employees had stopped working and conducted a strike, to make sure that production of steel was available for the Korea War effort. President Truman had ordered the Secretary of Commerce to take possession of and operate the steel mills in order to maintain steel production during the Korean War. The Supreme Court held that President Truman lacked either constitutional or statutory authority to seize the nation's strike-bound steel mills. The Supreme Court noted, however, that Congress could have had constitutional authority to do so and could have granted the Presidential power to confiscate the steel mill because of the war effort. Thus, when the President and Congress are in agreement, the Supreme Court would uphold the action by the President and Congress, as both branches have war powers.

BACK TO NEPTUNE: Continuous Wars and Political Science made no sense to Neptune. I told Neptune, "You are unequivocally right, as Political Science and continuous wars are not scientific nor logical. That's why lots of people in politics are lawyers. Political positions are nebulous as there are no infallible truths. All political positions have alternative arguments that make just as much sense as the opposing side. That is why there are Political Parties with Political Platforms in politics. Politics involves man's opinion about what ideas will work best to get votes to stay in power. There is no guiding truth in government, as Politicians do and say to get reelected. What is popular in society becomes Politicians' Platforms, regardless of whether they are unsound and not best for a country's future generation, like the national debt. Politicians just try out a theory to see if that theory works or not works to get them reelected. Politicians believe that lies are not untruths but are just political arguments to gain votes for a particular bill to become law.

It is the same with me arguing in front of a judge or jury trying to convince the trier of fact to accept my facts over the facts of the other party and his lawyer. So, every lawyer can use his legal training and experience to go into politics and immediately fit right in. Then, the fight is discovering what political leader has the power to bring your bill to a vote for passage. When you accept this, then you will know that a person with a pure mind and heart that wants to do good like you will be repulsed with politics and bureaucrats in either city, county, state, or federal governments.

Because Neptune did not understand politics and wars, which made no sense to him, he ended that part of our conversation, "Well, Dean, that's the reason why I have been waiting for you to become a lawyer like I encouraged you in 1969. I knew you would help me with my water from air project that I have invented, and I knew you would never do me wrong." I was astonished with Neptune's deferred gratification and patience waiting for me to become a lawyer.

Personally, Neptune's teachings, disclosures, and applications with his water from the air invention have never left me. I have been gifted from God with a great memory. Potable water availability is one of the most important topics for the preservation of mankind here on earth. I occasionally find articles on google, someone talking on youtube, or alternative social media about the shortage of water and plausible answers to resolve the inefficiency. I continue becoming knowledgeable in water conservation, and I particularly watch what California is doing for water management even when California has a very wet or drought winter. How much water is being captured in man-built wells and lakes, and how much fresh water just flows back into the Pacific Ocean and become salt water? Unfortunately, not enough fresh water is captured and conserved.

Here is what my research revealed. California's agricultural management and water management are closely intertwined. During much of the growing season in California for vegetables, fruit trees, almonds, and grapes, there is usually extraordinarily little rain. Nearly 80 percent of the water usage in California is by agriculture farmers that grow food and ranchers that water animals. So, California Department of Water Resources' largest user clients are farmers needing water for agriculture growth and ranchers needing water for their animals. The California Department of Water Resources holds the taps of dams and aqueducts delivering that water, and during severe droughts the water is cut off because there are close to 39 million citizens in California that also need water for survival.

Neptune had such accurate insights into the water plight needing resolution, as the population continues to grow in California. The new housing areas he projected would be expanded and built in new locations, raising the usage of water to be piped to that area. Neptune asked if the water "borrowed" from citizens and given to the farmers and ranchers would cause California to lose its greatest economic products sold since California's number one production is saleable crops? I responded, "I am not sure." For example, during the historic drought of 2011-2015, water deliveries to farmers and ranchers were cut drastically, and in some years stopped entirely. For ranchers, especially the thousands of milk cows and thousands of Black Angus cows, to keep their livestock watered and farmers to keep their crops growing, ranchers and farmers drilled wells and pumped record quantities of groundwater from the aquifers. The water supply in the aquifers dropped precipitously, so, in 2014, the California Legislators and Governor signed into law the first groundwater conservation regulations. This law established, among other things, the "California Sustainable Groundwater Management Act." This required watching what the farmers are growing because some vegetables require more water than others.

In our conversations in later months, Neptune also had statistics on how much water was being used to grow trees, and one of the problems with increased housing being built was they were primarily made of wood that had to be cut down that took away the oxygen production in the atmosphere. California people love their wood houses. Neptune saw that the most available metal on earth was aluminum, and the most available mineral available was sand and its silica. With aluminum you can replace wood studs and with sand and its silica you can produce glass instead of destroying our oxygen-producing trees. With aluminum and sand with silica, you can build communities and cities with modular homes, which sit on the ground that look like the wooden-built homes, but modular homes can be more fireproof and far less expensive to build. At that time in 1978, it was still difficult to obtain financing for modular homes, but before 1973, there was no financing available. "Stick housing" is the choice for construction of homes, but not so with commercial property. Fortunately, after 1973 financing for modular homes was becoming available if you had a history of good credit and had been on your job for years. It was much harder to obtain a loan if you were in your own business.

Neptune repeated that if we reverse the process of the water machine where water went the opposite direction through the diaphragm, it makes a very inexpensive air conditioning for a home, and this smaller machine would save a lot of money for the homeowner and be a better air conditioning system. This new, better, less costly form of air conditioning was perfect for the desert if one was going to build houses in the desert. That is what I and Neptune wanted to do, but it required arduous research, accurate planning, and finding investors; and those tasks were my assignments. Since I did not have a family, I worked around the clock. I stopped watching t.v., and I just practiced law and worked on Neptune's water project.

On one Saturday, I got up early and drove all the way to Barstow where I saw acres and acres of vacant desert land. I told Neptune, if I could raise the money to build a prototype of his water from the air system, and if we bought lots of acres of land out in the desert between Victorville and Barstow, or on the other side of Barstow, we could become builders of full community of homes, which would be a great financial blessing for people and be an income stream for us.

He inquired how did his water from the air machine would fit in? I asked him how much would it cost to build his water from the air plant to produce two million gallons of water a day on top of a small mountain that is about 800 feet above the flat land below? He started calculating with numbers on a sheet of paper (no computers in those days), and he was able to work the numbers quickly in his mind. Neptune said it would cost somewhere around seven to ten million dollars. So, I then asked how much would it cost to build a small hydroelectric power plant for 500 to 1,500 homes since we already have the water source from his water from the air plant to power the hydroelectric plant? He said that must be researched. I told him I would do the research and get back with him in about three weeks.

Dr. Nova Dean Pack

Plan for Developing Uninhabitable Desert Property with Neptune's water invention: I took a vacation from my law practice, and three weeks later, I said to Neptune, "I have been researching a plan that sounds interesting. I have done a lot of leg work, spoken to many people, and I have an accurate plan for building homes in the uninhabited desert. He looked pleased and smiled.

I said, "First, I contacted the office of California State Water Resources Control Board in Sacramento. The employee confirmed what you said that the electricity made by hydroelectric turbine generating is the cheapest form of electricity produced. He said, 'There are also wind turbines that can be utilized to create electricity. Additionally, there are solar panels being created that efficiently produce electricity.' I found out by calling Southern California Edison that the average household consumes about 10,500 kilowatt hours of electricity per year, which means about 29 kilowatts hours per day.

"If we start with building 500 homes, then that means we must produce 14,500 kilowatts hours per day for 500 modular homes. The cost to construct a hydroelectric plant would be from $500 to $1,500 per kilowatt hour. This means it would cost about $14.5 million to build the hydroelectric plant. However, other estimates for building a hydroelectric plant of that size are lower.

I continued, "Both the State of California and the Federal Government have grants and low interest loans specially for constructing hydroelectric power plants. For example, the U.S. Senate introduced in August last year (1977) to pay grants of $50,000 per year along with $50,000 loans each year. The details of the State of California grants need further research by me. Yet, we will have to obtain investors to help us pay for the building of the hydroelectric plant, but we will be able to return their investment from the sale of the homes. I will work on that.

"We could add windmills and solar panels systems that can also be used to create electricity. In fact, on part of our land, we can build a turbine wind farm and a solar farm, and the electric utility company has power lines along the highway where we can connect our electrical farms, but that must be negotiated, and a contract must be signed before we create the electrical farms. If we get hooked up and start selling the electricity, we produce the electrical back into the utility power grid; and Southern California Edison will pay us for the electricity we produce. This could be ongoing income in addition to the profit made from selling the homes on the property. I have contacted a contractor who knows how to build these wind and solar electrical power farms, but that contract I will have to negotiate and see the wind and solar farms he constructed for other people.

"In the last month I went to the County Recorder's Office to obtain owners of the ten landowners. I have spoken to all ten landowners who have together 500 plus acres between them that are next to each other, and each of them are willing to sale their desert land for a down payment of $200 per acre and a note for the remaining $200 per acre payable incrementally when we install the first homes, and they would be paid out of escrow. They each agreed not to have a deed of trust on the property because the homeowner cannot have a deed of trust before the bank's deed of trust. I told them we were considering building modular homes. One owner laughed and said, "What are you going to do, haul water to the land for the homeowners? What are you going to do to get electricity to the property as that could be expensive? Good luck with that. Yet, that is your business, not mine. I just want to sell my property because I have owned it for decades." Thus, we would have to raise the $100,000 for the down payment to purchase the land. What is interesting is there is are more than one 800 to 1000 feet high small mountains or large hills on the properties where we could build your water from the air plant, and we can build a small hydroelectric plant down below that will operate with the powerful water flow for its power source.

"I met with San Bernardino County Department of Planning, and they had little restrictions as to what we do in the desert that is far out and away from any city, so long as it did not become a dumping ground. So, the building of a modular home community is set if we can put all the pieces of the puzzle together.

"The San Bernardino County Department of Planning said a subdivision map where each one-quarter acre home would have its own Grant Deed would have to be prepared and approved. The Planning Department said that we would be on fast track because there would be little restrictions for compliance, and all we should do is hire one of the firms who create the legal descriptions acceptable to the County for each parcel and for the inclusion in the deeds of the common areas. The planning department gave me three names of firms that do that. We could transfer to every homeowner a fee simple grant deed, and an undivided right over the communal areas.

"Each modular home is made of strong aluminum and glass, which means we are not reducing the forests to build these modular homes. Each owner will have one-quarter of an acre, so they can have a garden if they want, or build a hydroponics system to grow vegetables if they want. We can teach them how to do that. We will have a few common areas, where there are places to meet, a swimming pool, a small gym, a small library, comfortable couches, and chairs in sitting areas, a small kitchen at each meeting hall, so, people can sign up for usage for a reasonable fee that is paid to the a Homeowners Association (HOA).

"I can write up a comprehensive Declaration of Covenants, Conditions, and Restrictions (CC&R) to be enforced by the HOA Board Members, elected by the owners to keep the new community free from harmful factors that decreases the value of the homes and maintains a safer environment. These homeowner restrictions would require only certain colored paints for the homes, no oil spills on the driveways, no junk cars, limited work on cars allowed, no harmful chemicals on the property that can be poison or can start fires, and the lawns must be properly maintained. If they want desert plants instead of green grass as a community standard, the HOA Board Members can send out a survey to the homeowners. If there is a violation of the CC&R, there will be proper warnings, fines, and then liens on the property for the work done if the HOA comes and does the work. There will be small monthly fees paid by each homeowner to maintain the shared areas and the streets. The common areas will include small parks with a covered outside eating area, where there is a barbeque pit, and children's playground, but the homeowners can bring their own charcoal or other natural gas grill. Everything will be maintained as a pristine friendly community. When the owners purchase their homes, they will be required to sign the CC&R. I can form a corporation for the HOA, with the Articles and Bylaws etc. of the HOA, along with the easements for the common areas that will have to be part of each of their deeds. It will be a lot of work, but it can be done. I can be the chairman of the HOA for 90 days or so and hold an election to choose homeowners on the board of the HOA. There are always some homeowners who like the leadership role of being decisionmakers. If we want, we could make the first homes to be 55 plus years old Seniors only, and the last two phases for individuals and families of any age with children.

"Once we have completed the first phase, the second phase can be walled off to protect the housing for those over 55 and above. The third phase can be decided later. We can duplicate this three phases plan, building new communities throughout the desert and creating little oasis communities for very affordable housing prices. The desert lands will be constructed not far from cities, where the residents can travel to find employment, schools, medical services, beauty parlors, larger grocery stores, clothing stores, car repair shops, etc. This would be a great project for the betterment of California. We can even encourage residents to use golf carts on the community streets in the area.

"We can build 1,500 homes, or more, with these 500 acres, with nice streets, and a gas service station and a small grocery store that outsiders can run and build and pay us land lease payments or pay to the HOA, along with the common areas and parks. The U.S. mail will be collected daily and delivered to the residences. There are telephone lines between Victorville and Barstow, so there will be no problem getting the telephone company to connect telephone lines in owner houses. People have VCR and VHS machines, and earlier last year (1977), Andre Blay of Magnetic Video Corporation came up with the idea of re-releasing movies on video cassettes. Twentieth Century Fox has now licensed movies to be released on VHS and the competing format Betamax through MVC. Thus, the residents will have good entertainment. They may be able to pick up UHF channels (this was before satellites).

"We can install septic tanks, hook the homes to the electrical power grid we are generating from the hydroelectric plant, connect to the homes the water supplied from your water from the air machine , all of which is underground, so there will be no power lines. So, our cost per modular home, in the ground with everything is about $25 thousand each, including the septic tanks, which is a discount because of the number of committed purchases with the factory, and these 500 modular homes will cost $12,500,000 total, but we will sell these homes and the land for $85,000 each but all that we build is one or two modular homes, and financing from banks that the homeowners obtain will pay the rest. This will be the best affordable and pristine modular home housing in the state. The streets and lights will cost $20,000, which again is discounted. The land will cost only $200,000. The sale of the land and the first 500 houses will generate $42,500,000. Our cost again to the factory that builds and installs the modular homes will be $12,500,000, with each house paid for from down payment and the loan taken out by the homeowner for the initial 500 homes. The cost of the water from the air plant will be $10 million and the cost of the hydroelectric station will be $14.5 million which all totals of the cost for the first phase to be $37,232,500. That would leave a net profit from the first phase to be $5,265,000, which we can share with the investors. Yet, all the investors' money would be repaid upon the sale of the homes, and they can enjoy greater profits in phase two and three.

"In total we have 1,000 additional homes to build where the land is already paid, our water plant and hydroelectric plants are already built, and there may be some upgrades expenditures on the hydroelectric power station, and more tanks to be filled for water storage at a

Personality Traits of Money

small cost comparatively. The second phase homeowners will have to pay $100,000 per home and net profits would be over $45 Million. The third phase owners will have to pay $120,000 per home, so there would be a net profit of over $55 million. This profit will be paid incrementally at the close of escrow of each house, and the ongoing monthly utility fees paid for much lower cost of electricity and water by the owners, creates an ongoing income stream for us. All total after all houses are built, will be a net profit that could reach $100 million.

This formula can be reproduced over and over. Once the first three phases are done, we need no more investors, and we can continue building small towns throughout the desert areas. Eventually, we will buy extra land and build a strip mall for every town, including a Bob's Big Boy type restaurant, a service station in a strip mall where stores can be there, along with a medical office that can take care of normal medical cold-like maladies. We also can invite a dental office to set up a branch office. These land development projects could make us billionaires, so then we would have more money than needed to start building your water project in third world countries like we talked about, as good potable water is the most needed commodity in the world. This work would take a lifetime, and we would never be finished. We would have to recruit like-minded people who have a passion to solve the water problem of the world.

Unfortunately, the people who were interested in investing the $10 million in the water from the air plant were not satisfied with what they were going to receive from the profits. They also demanded to own 75% of Neptune's water production invention, so Neptune said that percentage of ownership would take away his rights to decide how his water from the air plant would be developed and used, especially in poor third world nations. As a principled Inventor, Neptune could not in good conscience give away his altruistic plan to bring water to the world. The most Neptune was willing to give to them was 20%, with the stipulation that he and I would have authority of all decision-making regarding the distribution and use of Neptune's water from the air invention. He would never give away authority over his lifetime work. They rejected the 20% counteroffer.

That was pure greed on the exploiters' part. Unfortunately for them, we could have duplicated this housing formula all over the desert, and they could have received a $100 million or more, but they were greedy and had short term investment return ideas, not long-term investments for multi-generational wealth. Again, "For the love of money is the root of all evil: which while some coveted after. . . ." They destroyed a great deal. It was great for the homeowners. It was great for the landowners, and it was great for all concerned. Yet, the Inventor did not want to take the deal. I respected Neptune for turning down the offer, but I was depressed for a while because I had worked hard on that land development project.

No Protection by Patent: In one of our sessions, Neptune asked me about the protection that a patent of his water from the air invention would have? I asked him, "If someone came up to your water machine and merely took their fingernail and scratched the hardened gel substance that is the diaphragm, took the sample to a lab, and then added another ingredient, could they patent their new formula?" His answer was, "Yes!" Then I said, "Obtaining a patent was no protection against thieves."

I told Neptune the recipe formula for Coca-Cola syrup has never been patented. The Coca-Cola Company's formula for Coca-Cola syrup, combined with carbonated water created the company's popular and multi-billion dollar business was the cola soft drink. The recipe formula for the Coca-Cola syrup is a very closely guarded secret held in a vault. The Coca-Cola Company's formula for its Coca-Cola syrup was locked originally in a vault historically at Guaranty Trust Company of New York and later at Trust Company Bank in Atlanta, State of Georgia. After Neptune's death I discovered that on December 8, 2011, the formula for its Coca-Cola syrup was placed in a vault on the grounds of the "World of Coca-Cola" in Atlanta, Georgia, with the vault on public display. Thus, we both concluded that Neptune was to write out the formula and hand it to his children for safekeeping, which I believe he did. I, personally, did not want to know the formula, as I did not want to be tempted or accused of theft.

Placer Mine Gold Production: San Bernardino County, California has 103,023 mining claims on public land listed in The Diggings™. Most of these claims are closed, but the major problem to extract gold in a placer mine you must have lots of water, which out in the desert where there is gold, there is no water. However, with Neptune's water from the air plant, which we could construct a small water from the air plant at the mining site, then we could mine gold. Because we would be out in the desert, San Bernardino County would allow us to set up a gold extraction and gold smelting operation to refine the gold, put it in bars, or create our own gold coin. We could ship the gold miner bars to Johnson Matthey refinery, who can create or own gold coins like the Krugerrand, but they could have greater purity like the Canadian Eagle. The gold extraction and refinement could only be economical because of Neptune's water from air project.

Neptune's water machine could create money in the form of gold coins because water is required to mine gold. That was being planned after we got the first water from the air system built with the modular home community built.

The Saudi Arabia Deal with Neptune: Trying to obtain more validation for Neptune's water from the air invention, I was introduced to a top physicist from U.C. Berkeley. His physics department had a history of Nobel Prize winners, although he personally was not a Nobel laureate. I personally paid for his flight from Berkeley to Ontario airport, in Ontario, California. He said, "If I don't like him, or I think he is a want-a-be Inventor, I will charge you a fee of $500 for wasting my time." I agreed to that. I picked him up at the airport and drove him to see Neptune. After a brief introduction, and because of the time restraint, no time was wasted. This physicist, who I will not name, for his confidentiality, examined the scientific facts of Neptune's water from the air invention. I just allowed them to speak without interruption. This prestigious Berkeley physicist was told he could ask any questions he wanted to inquire of Neptune, and if he thought Neptune was mistaken in his work, his calculations; or if he thought that Neptune was a charlatan, then he had a right to come to that conclusion. He also was told by me that he could enter discussions with Neptune regarding higher math, physics, chemistry, engineering, or any subject he felt was relevant.

They spent about seven hours together just drinking coffee, as I knew Neptune would not share a meal with him. At the end of that first session, Neptune thanked the physicist for coming; and the physicist told Neptune that he would be back with further information and most likely further questions for Neptune to obtain more clarity. On the drive back from Hesperia to Ontario airport, the first stop was a local Diner because neither of us had eaten that day. While having a quick bite, I asked him his impression of Neptune. He paused for

Personality Traits of Money

a moment and looked at me and said, "He is the smartest scientist, physicist, and mathematician I have ever had the privilege of meeting. He knew more about the latest theories in physics than I knew, or anyone else at Berkeley for that matter. I was not disappointed, and I can tell he is a man of impeccable honesty and character. I believed everything he said, and I saw with my own eyes his small prototype machine that had the diaphragm on the tube, and as soon as the vacuum in the tube was made, the water started dripping inside the tube. It was fascinating to watch. Yes, I am impressed, and I will see what I can do for him." I responded, "So, I assume I do not owe you a fee for traveling to come and meet him." His emphatic response in laughter was, "I should pay you for introducing me to the smartest man I have ever met. He is a genius, and I don't know why he is not known. I was thoroughly impressed with not only his knowledge but his passion to help people regarding the world's water problem."

About two weeks later, I received a telephone call from the Berkeley physicist, who said he had a friend, a Saudi Arabia Prince he went to graduate school with, who is one of the ruling Princes under the then current King. He was not the Crown Prince (heir to the throne upon death of the King), but he had an important government position. He said he and the Saudi Prince took pilot training together and still are friends. He said he needed to speak with Neptune again. He said he would pay his own transportation cost this time. Days before the meeting, I spoke with Neptune, explained about the Saudi Arabia Prince's interest in Neptune's water from the air machine. Neptune invited the Berkeley Physicist to see him the forthcoming second Saturday, so I made the appointment with the Berkeley physicist for that date.

The Berkeley physicist arrived as scheduled, and I picked him up at the Ontario airport and drove him to Neptune's home. The second meeting that Neptune had with the Berkeley physicist was better than the first. The physicist said that he was relaying an offer from the Saudi Arabia Prince, whose jurisdictional authority included the holy city of Mecca, and that 1). Saudi Arabia would pay up to $2.00 to $5.00 a gallon of water produced if Neptune would build a prototype plant here in America that the Prince could bring his expert for examination, and that validated Neptune's invention. 2). If Neptune's water from the air plant indeed produced the water from the air moisture as represented, he would reimburse Neptune for the construction expenditure of the prototype in California, and 3). pay to have Neptune's water from air numerous plants constructed in Saudi Arabia.

Then Neptune said, "Since I was told that it was Saudi Arabia that was interested, I researched the nation's geography. Let me give you an idea to take back to the Prince. Near the western coastal area where the Red Sea is there are two mountain ranges on the Arabian Peninsula, with an elevation of about 6,900 feet high. The mountains wall drops abruptly on the western side toward the Red Sea, leaving the narrow coastal plain of Tihamah. However, on the eastern slopes of the mountains are not as steep and would be easier to build my water from air plants because of the better access. The eastern side is mostly desert, with Mecca toward the south and Median toward the north. What we can do is construct as many water from air plants as Saudi Arabia wants on top of these mountain ranges and allow the water from my water from the air plant to flow down the mountain on the eastern slope to empower hydroelectric plants, have the water stored in large steel storage containers, or have the water liquified from the air to go directly into the large steel storage containers without producing electricity if they want."

I interjected, "The problem with the proposal will be to find investors that will provide the capital to build the prototype water from the air plant out here in the desert in California, which will resemble Saudi Arabia." The Berkeley physicist assured us that could be a condition in the Contract.

Of course, at the time I was thinking about building the water from the air plant to provide water to the housing project in the desert land I had planned that fell through because of investor greed. By showing a Contract with Saudi Arabia to make these water from air plants to a new group would be security to make sure they will be paid. This was feeding two birds with the same bag of food. In principle, Neptune agreed, and I added so long as there were conditions in the Contract with Saudi Arabia that if sufficient capital was not raised to build the water from the air plant prototype here in California, then the Contract with Saudi Arabia would be null and void.

I found another group of investors that were interested, but I cautiously did not allow Neptune to sign any agreement with these investors until Neptune approved the terms of the Saudi Arabia Contract, including proper arbitration clauses in San Bernardino County, California under International Chamber of Commerce rules. In about 45 days, I received the Saudi Arabia Contract. It was very official looking written in English with even some Arab words at the top, seals, etc. The problem is it had a paragraph that Neptune was forbidden from ever building and selling his water from air plants to Israel. That paragraph killed the deal.

I tried through the Berkeley Physicist to convince the Saudi Prince and his kingdom government to make an exception to this contract because Neptune was bringing water to his country that has never been seen before. A lot of arduous work went into receiving a Contract proposal from wealthy Saudi Arabia, but Saudi Arabia's apparent hatred toward Israel was more important than water to the country.

As Christians, Neptune and I supported Israel, and I, personally, found it repugnant and unacceptable to exclude Israel. In the end, neither Neptune nor I wanted to approve the Saudi Arabia Contract, so the deal was dead. Because of religious and cultural prejudice that goes back between Isaac, born of Sarah and Abraham and Ishmael born of Hagar and Abraham is still a problem even though the half-brothers had the same Father Abraham.

A lot of work was done by Neptune and me (too much to list it all), but we had nothing to show from it except the experience and the passage of time. I was disappointed to say the least. Looking back at the time with Neptune, I wish a song that I love that was written by a great country singer, Larry Gatlin, who is a Christian brother, along with his brothers, who in 1997 wrote and sung a song titled "I've Done Enough Dying Today." Here is just the first verse.

> What will we do now? You tell me
> The hourglass is all out of sand
> How could love slip through our fingers
> And leave nothin' but time on our hands?
> And how will we live now? You tell me
> With parts of our hearts torn away

Personality Traits of Money

Just existing makes dyin' look easy
But maybe tomorrow I've done enough dyin' today

Hydrogen Peroxide Fuel made with Cheap Electricity: After I moved from Huntington Beach, California, to Ontario, California, to be closer to work with Neptune. I arrived at about 9:30 a.m. at Neptune's house, and I came to the Kitchen where Neptune was sitting. I helped myself with coffee, as I was now being treated like a relative.

I sat at the kitchen table, as I could see Neptune was going to be Socrates this morning. Neptune asked, "Dean, when you were driving up to Hesperia from Ontario this July morning, did you see the smog line." I responded, "Of course, yes, it's horrible and unhealthy." He continued, "So, have you thought about moving up here in Hesperia which has very little smog by comparison?" I responded, "Yes, it would be good for us to be closer, but my law office is in Anaheim, California, and it would take 2 ½ to 3 ½ hours one way to travel from here to Orange County to my office."

Neptune then got to the point he wanted to reveal. "Well in that case, through my water from the air plant and joined with an almost free-operating hydroelectric plant, I can take two electrodes and put them in my pure water and create H2O2, which is hydrogen peroxide. Hydrogen peroxide, without dilution like it is sold for medication, can be used as a viable clean fuel, and with some modifications can be used in the internal combustion engines. Being able to make H2O2 inexpensively, it would be economical. Also, H2O2 produces no waste chemicals but only water and oxygen that comes out of the tail pipe as opposed to gasoline where the exhaust is CO2, which is carbon dioxide and the primary cause of smog.

"Hydrogen peroxide can be an ideal energy carrier alternative to oil or hydrogen for automobiles. If you can get the people who want cleaner air to start using it, it will catch on and stop the CO2 exhaust coming out of the internal combustion engines which is bad for the environment, animals, and humans. You could do seminars and have the people send letters to their state representatives, and if the state representatives do not do it, then they say they will not vote for them in the next election. That is how you said politics work." I started laughing, and he smiled.

Neptune continued, "Besides, hydrogen peroxide is better than electric cars because of the traffic jams on California freeways during peak times. We have not invented good batteries yet. The main problem is batteries in electric cars will go dead when commuters get stuck in traffic. Hydrogen peroxide fuel will just stay in the car reservoirs and not dissipate, just like gasoline. Thus, hydrogen peroxide fuel would be better than battery run electric cars."

I responded with astonishment, "The things you come up with are amazing, and this idea just because you do not want me and people living in smog. So, based upon your comment about the exclusive electric car batteries dying sitting in a crowded freeway, could you design a system where there were both batteries and hydrogen peroxide to be the fuel to compel cars economically?" Neptune said, "Of course, I would have to set up two energy source systems and then . . . ." Quite frankly, I forgot the rest of what he said because it was a long reveal. Regardless, I could not get anyone interested in financing the hydrogen peroxide as fuel because we never contracted with anyone to finance the large water from air plant, which begins every one of Neptune's projects.

Dr. Nova Dean Pack

The Navy Ship Desalination Replacement by Neptune's Water from Air System: From Neptune I learned that desalination is used on many seagoing ships and also by countries in the Middle East where there is water shortages. Most of the modern interest in desalination on ships is focused on cost-effective provision of fresh water for human use. Along with recycled wastewater on the ship, it is one of the few rainfall-independent water resources. Desalination must distill 1,000 gallons of salt water to obtain 200 gallons of potable water for the sailors to use. There is a problem of longevity of the desalination plant because the salt in the salt water comes out by elevated temperatures that create a brine that clogs up the pipes which would have to be replaced on a ship. That is not an issue with Neptune's pure water production, as the pipes remain clean. A lot of the construction of ships with required desalination is very costly while the construction of the water from the air plant on the ship would be far less expensive and would not have to be replaced like the desalination plant. Neptune's water from the air system would look like part of the ship as it would be on the outside of the ship and would only be a fraction of the cost compared to the desalination plant.

Also, Neptune's water from the air plant is not down underneath where soldiers must live where heat from the desalination plant boiling water all hours of the day and night happens that makes the temperature hot, which must be cooled by costly air conditioning. Thus, Neptune's water from the air system would not use salt water but water vapor from the air and would produce more water than the desalination plant with much smaller ongoing maintenance without any heat radiating throughout the ship. The cost of ships built would be far less, which would save the Navy money. Also, a more proficient air conditioning system could be built on top of the ship by reversing Neptune's water from air system that would use only 10% of the electricity than regular air conditioning systems, just because only the fan blowers pushing the cool air through the ducts and vents would be needed. Overall, Neptune's water from the air plant on board the ship would be environmentally favorable and less expensive.

I contacted the Office of Naval Research, and after I was connected to the right person, and explained what Neptune shared, he said, "Obviously, the navy is always interested in innovation that is better, can cut costs, and in fact works. So, our department would have to see a prototype of your Inventor's machine taking water out of the air, along with his design on how his water from the air would fit on our Navy ships. We can give you the size and construction of one of our ships for your use. Of course, even after you present your invention, there is no guarantee that the Navy will buy your system because we would have the cost of renovating our current ships, and that cost alone could be prohibitive. If you want to present a proposal and make your prototype available for inspection, then you may have a chance of it being accepted."

I reported back to Neptune, and he and I both agreed to put the Navy Desalination Replacement deal on the back burner. Although there were other projects, we considered over the months that followed, Neptune called me and said, "I need you to come here, as I have something very important to discuss with you." If my memory is right, Neptune and I were in our seventh year working together concerning his water from air project.

Reconsideration: When I arrived on regular Saturday at his home, Neptune said, "Dean, get your coffee and sit down as I have something important to tell you." I chuckled and retorted, "You always have something important to tell me." He continued, "In all these years, we have not been successful in anything we have tried to do with my water from the air project. I am getting older, and you have worked without compensation for many years now. You have never complained and have been very faithful. I don't think I can ever repay you." I immediately responded, "You owe me nothing. Working with you all these years has given me satisfaction enough, a memory which will last me the rest of my life. You have motivated me beyond measure to fulfill my own destiny for the benefit of humanity. I learned from you to seek truth, and that is what I will do the rest of my life. I will find what is best for humanity and seek it. So, what is your plan?"

Unrelenting, Neptune said, "I am tired. I have symptoms of asbestos poisoning in my lungs taking a tow, and I have decided to give this water from the air system as a gift to the U.S. government for the benefit of the people before I die. I need your help to get my water system in the right hands. I am displeased that we have had no success collaborating with private parties. I am disgusted with people who do not have a heart to help humanity. These men only want the money my water from the air machine can make for them." I agreed with him, but I said, "On the other hand, these government bureaucrats are not pure public servants, as they seek government power and look constantly for better and greater salaried employment in the private sector. We must befriend a prestigious politician, a Senator or House of Representative that has been in Congress for many years to steer us in the right direction. The Federal government is a massive complex of bureaucracies with many agencies with the same vision or emphasis at taxpayers' expense. However, it is your invention. It's your decision. We will do it together. If you are going to give it away, then let us find a conservative that has a heart as a conservationist like us and let him direct us. Otherwise, we will never find the best place to present your invention." He agreed. Neptune smiled and was very pleased that I agreed with him.

Neptune and the U.S. Department of Energy Hydropower Grant Program: Neptune had been medically retired for years because of asbestos inhalation poisoning because he had worked in the air conditioning trade, and removal of the asbestos covering on ventilation ducts was inhaled and coated his lungs. However, he told me the air conditioning business is why he started thinking about the water from the air invention. He saw the amount of water that was collected in the condensation drip pan under the air conditioning as water vapor in the air accumulated just because of a change in temperature. He said it was like a glass of water with ice in it. There is condensation on the outside of the glass, and this is the concept of how his water from air gathers water.

Neptune water from the air invention is operated by the vacuum sucking in water molecules through a biological diaphragm which is far more efficient than just a change in the temperature in an air conditioning system. Also, using a difference in temperature causing the water vapor in the air to liquify would require lots of electricity to maintain air coolant; whereas, using a vacuum that sucked in the pure H2O through a biological diaphragm did not require very little ongoing energy after the vacuum is established.

After our research, we decided to contact U.S. House of Representative John Jacob Rhodes Jr., who was a Republican and was the minority leader from Arizona at that time. An appointment was made, and our travel to Arizona was fruitful. Representative Rhodes was impressed with the information, and Mr. Rhodes gave Neptune instructions to file an application for funding with the U.S. Dept. of Energy Hydropower Program, which was focused on technology assessment of a Small Hydropower system. Neptune prepared the applications, with his scientific explanations. Since it was the energy department, we presented the water from the air system to be placed on a mountain to allow the produced water to travel downward by force of gravity to a hydroelectric plant to turn a turbine to turn a generator to produce electricity, as that seemed to be the focus of the Department of Energy. Representative Rhodes sent a letter properly addressed to the sub-department head introducing Neptune's project and that he personally thought it should be given serious consideration.

Neptune's project graduated step by step upward until it went to the highest level where the head of the department made the final decision. This head of the department wrote a letter addressed to Neptune denying the grant on the grounds there was not a mountain high enough for Neptune's water from the air system to work as he needed a mountain higher than Mount Everest which is 29,032 feet high.

He missed the point altogether. Neptune's water from the air system would work at sea level even better because the air at sea level is maximum water vapor full unlike the thin air at the top of a mountain. It did not make sense that he would come to that conclusion, being a scientist, himself. In fact, if we could produce water to run a hydroelectric plant near the Pacific Ocean at hardly any cost, we could mine the gold that is in the ocean, which you can see when going swimming.

We contacted Representative Rhodes again, sent him a copy of the letter from the sub-department of the Department of Energy head denying Neptune's grant. He said that he would see what happened as he was shocked about the denial.

In a couple of weeks later, we heard from Representative Rhodes that the signatory of the letter had left the sub-department of the Department of Energy and was hired by Saudi Arabia to head up its Desalination Plants along the shoreline of the Red Sea.

The desalination plants had to be built along the shore of the Red Sea because it had to suck in the salt water from the Red Sea at a ratio of at least 1,000 gallons of salt water to produce 200 gallons of potable water. It would be impossible to pump the potable water over the mountains that were 6,900 feet high to bring potable water to the east side of the mountain range where the desert is. On the other hand, Neptune's water from the air system could be built on top of the mountains along the Red Sea, and the water could flow down the eastern side of the mountains to run hydroelectric plants without loss of any potable water which could be collected in large steel containers.

Neptune's water from the air system could produce enough water to make the desert on the east of two mountain ranges on the Arabian Peninsula, with an elevation of about 6,900 feet high to water agriculture crops and make the entire desert a garden spot with many oases, retreats, and abundance of water sources where cities could be built.

Again, greed and the avarice love of money for his own pocket made him deny the greatest water from the air machine ever built that used God's hydro cycle on earth to harvest the air of its water vapor to bring the water to the deserts in the world.

Personality Traits of Money

Dr. Nova Dean Pack

10 Why Some Stay Wealthy While Others Stay Poor

Personality Traits of Money

CHAPTER TEN

WHY SOME STAY WEALTHY
WHILE OTHERS STAY POOR

WHY THE RICH GET RICHER AND THE
POOR STAY POORER, AND HOW CHRISTIANS
NEED NOT BE BOUND BY STATISTICS

In 1925, F. Scott Fitzgerald wrote a short story titled The Rich Boy. In 1926, The Rich Boy was published in Red Book magazine and included what became a very popular collection of Fitzgerald's early short stories, titled All the Sad Young Men. In the third paragraph, Fitzgerald wrote, "Let me tell you about the very rich. They are different from you and me. They possess and enjoy early, and it does something to them, makes them soft where we are hard, and cynical where we are trustful, in a way that, unless you were born rich, it is very difficult to understand. They think, deep in their hearts, that they are better than we are because we had to discover the compensations and refuges of life for ourselves. Even when they enter deep into our world or sink below us, they still think that they are better than we are. They are different."

Ray Kroc became the owner of the McDonald's fast-food chain. Ray Kroc was a middle class man when he started and became very wealthy because he took advantage of a clever idea which was fulfilling a need to provide inexpensive food to primarily young people. McDonald's still directs its promotions to the young. However, what has made McDonald's wealthy is they have become large landowners. Therefore, it is the wealth of God, which is land, which has made one of the wealthiest businesses in the world.

Wikipedia states about the original McDonald's: "The original hexagonal McDonald's hamburger stand located at 1398 North E Street in San Bernardino, California, was demolished in 1953 and replaced by a building in the now familiar Golden Arches style. In an oversight, the McDonald brothers failed to retain rights to the McDonald's name when they sold the chain to Kroc and were forced to rename it "The Big M". It went out of business and was demolished in 1972, although part of the sign remains. The site of the original McDonald's was purchased in 1998 by Albert Okura, owner of the Juan Pollo chicken restaurant chain, for $135,000 in a foreclosure sale. Okura turned the property into the headquarters for his chain of restaurants and opened an unofficial McDonald's museum on the site, which, Okura refers to as the "historic site of the original McDonald's". Okura said though he did not intend to open the museum, an erroneous news story that mentioned he was planning on opening a museum gave him the idea; former employees and customers sent the museum many of the items on display."

Wikipedia writes about Conrad Hilton, the creator of the Hilton Hotel chain and the Hilton family: "The Hilton family is an American family that originally comes from Kløfta, Norway, and spans over four generations from New York City and Los Angeles. The family members hold varying degrees of power, wealth, and status as socialites in the United States. They are widely known for the Hilton Hotels & Resorts Group which was established by Conrad Hilton in 1919 when he bought his first hotel. The Hilton family is one of the world's most powerful and famous families and is worth over $14.2 billion.

"As a young boy, Conrad Hilton developed entrepreneurial skills working at his father's general store in Socorro County, New Mexico, which was partially converted into a 10-room hotel. This was followed by varied experiences, including a stint as a representative in New Mexico's first State Legislature, and a career decision to become a banker.

"It was intending to buy a bank that he arrived in Texas at the height of the Texas oil boom. In 1919, he bought his first hotel instead, the 40-room Mobley Hotel in Cisco, Texas, when a bank purchase fell through. The hotel did such brisk business that rooms changed hands as often as three times a day, and the dining room was converted into additional rooms to meet the demand. He went on to buy and build hotels throughout Texas, including the high-rise Dallas Hilton, which opened in 1925; the Abilene Hilton in 1927; Waco Hilton in 1928; and El Paso Hilton in 1930. The first hotel outside of Texas that Hilton built was in 1939 in Albuquerque, New Mexico. Today, it is known as the Hotel Andaluz. During the Great Depression, Hilton was nearly forced into bankruptcy and lost several of his hotels. Nevertheless, he was retained as manager of a combined chain, and eventually regained control of his remaining eight hotels.

"Over the next decade, he expanded west to California and east to Chicago and New York, crowning his expansions with such acquisitions as the Stevens Hotel in Chicago (then the world's largest hotel; it was renamed the Conrad Hilton), and the fabled Waldorf-Astoria in New York City. He formed the Hilton Hotels Corporation in 1946, and Hilton International Company in 1948.

"During the 1950s and 1960s, Hilton Hotels' worldwide expansion facilitated both American tourism and overseas business by American corporations. It was the world's first international hotel chain, at the same time establishing a certain worldwide standard for hotel accommodation. In 1954, Hilton Hotels bought The Hotels Statler Company, Inc. for $111 million, then the world's largest real estate transaction. In all, Hilton eventually owned 188 hotels in 38 cities across the U.S., including the Mayflower Hotel in Washington, D.C.; the Palmer House in Chicago; and the Plaza Hotel and Waldorf-Astoria in New York City, along with 54 hotels abroad. He later purchased the Carte Blanche Credit Company and an interest in the American Crystal Sugar Company, as well as other enterprises."

One of the richest men in the US, on his death in 1979 Conrad Hilton left the bulk of his wealth to the "Conrad N. Hilton Foundation," an international charity. Conrad Hilton wrote in His Last Will and Testament the following sentences:

"Love one another, for that is the whole law; the people of the world deserve to be loved and encouraged—never to be abandoned to wander alone in poverty and darkness."
"There is a natural law, a Divine law, which obliges you and me to relieve the suffering, the distressed and the destitute."
"Charity is a supreme virtue, and the great channel through which the mercy of God is passed on to mankind. It is the virtue that unites men and inspires their noblest efforts."
"As the funds you will expend have come from many places in the world, so let there be no territorial, religious, or color restrictions on your benefactions."
(From the Conrad N. Hilton Foundation website: https://www.hiltonfoundation.org/about/

Personality Traits of Money

history)

William Barron Hilton learned the hotel business from his father, Conrad Hilton, and he took over management of the Hilton Hotels Corporation. William Barron Hilton who died "… of natural causes at his home in Los Angeles, in his 30 years as chief executive officer built the Hilton brand into the best known, most successful, and most respected name in the industry. When it finally was sold in 2007, the Blackstone Group paid $26 billion for 2,800 hotels with 480,000 rooms in 76 countries. That same year, Hilton announced that he would leave about 97% of his estate, estimated then to be worth $2.3 billion, to the Hilton Foundation, an international charitable organization begun by his father, Conrad Hilton, the family patriarch, and founder of the hotel chain." (Los Angeles Times, by By Mike Kupper, Sept. 20, 2019)

IT TAKES MONEY TO MAKE MONEY

A simple principle of finance is that it is easier to make one million dollars when you have $100 million than it is when you are working to earn a living month to month.

Money earns money and people earn money, but money earns money when people are asleep. This is why the wealthy stay wealthy. Money makes money all the time. Yet, money as a commodity is not stable and is subject to inflation and currency revaluation changes.

Any business with moving parts can break down. People are moving parts, and they are the costliest parts of any business enterprise. People break down and do not show up for work, even though the business owner often must pay them anyway for sick leave. On the other hand, money properly invested does not break down in the general economic scheme of things, save a problem with inflation, such as the U.S. had during President Carter's term in office, in the fall of the stock market, or other economic recession, as in 2008.

It takes money to make money. Every idea must involve a good plan, a good market, good personnel, hard work, and proper money investment. Sometimes, you can create an asset through your ingenuity, as an invention or a betterment of an older invention, a new air conditioning system, an electric car, or a new and better cell phone.

Except for top executives in mega corporations, entertainers, and professional athletes, it is impossible to become rich working for a salary.

The truth is most wealth accumulation comes from investments rather than labor. The middle-class people put themselves to work while the wealthy put their money to work. Money earned by labor is taxed much higher than money earned by investments because the government wants to encourage investments. For example, businesses can deduct their rent as a business expense from their taxes, but regular working citizens cannot. If a capital asset held over one year is sold, the profit realized is taxed as long-term capital gains and not ordinary income.

The rich are admonished in 1 Timothy 6:17 19, which says, "Command those who are rich in this present age not to be haughty, nor to trust in uncertain riches but in the living God, who gives us richly all things to enjoy. Let them do good, that they be rich in good works, ready to give, willing to share, storing up for themselves a good foundation for the time to come, that they may lay hold on eternal life."

THERE IS A SIMILARITY BETWEEN THE VERY POOR AND THE VERY RICH WHO HAVE INHERITED MONEY AND ASSETS

The wealthy live from the income derived from their income producing investments while the extremely poor live off the family, friends, government, and sometimes crimes such as burglary instead of a job. Both groups have a disdain for challenging work and support themselves from unearned income that normally other people work for a salary.

Those who work for a living acquire on-the-job skills that those who do not work have not acquired. If the electricity suddenly is shut off in a home, the rich call for someone to come to fix it and stay in the dark or light candles waiting for a repairman to arrive. A middle-class worker simply goes to the fuse box and flips the switch back on. If a rich person gets into an accident, they call someone to come to her rescue. If a middle-class worker is in an accident, and the cars are drivable and no one is seriously injured, they simply exchange driver's licenses, insurance information, and telephone numbers, report it to their insurance companies, and the insurance companies through their adjustors handle it. Sometimes, rich parents have Nannys and Maids. If the baby starts crying, the rich mother often does not know what to do, so she calls the Nanny to take care of the child. A middle-class mother knows exactly what to do-check the diaper, see if the baby is hungry, or hold the baby because he just wanted to be held.

Sometimes, the poor teenager decides she doesn't want to raise her child and takes the child to grandmother, who raises the child. If she needs a ride, the poor person calls a friend, or takes a bus, so she does not need a car. If the poor person needs a doctor, she has Medi-Cal or Medicaid or the state agency in your state or country. If the poor person needs a place to live, she finds a Section 8 housing apartment paid by the State like we have in California or government paid housing in other states or countries. If she needs food, the state and family members provide her food without having to work for money to purchase food. The poor stay poor because they learn how to exist being poor.

The very wealthy and extremely poor are immune from having to "give up a need" to fulfill another need. The very wealthy who have obtained their wealth through inheritance, and the extremely poor, often lack the skills acquired through experiencing the stress in having to weigh various alternatives which the rest of us regularly experience in our everyday business and personal lives.

Without the risk of the consequences of failure facing a person, the person does not learn the seriousness of life. The very wealthy do not have to deal with the pain of making choices, whereas the extremely poor do not have the money to make choices. Therefore, both the wealthy and poor are immune from stressful decision making to maintain their sustenance daily.

Being wealthy or poor can have a crippling effect on people's maturity and growth as it dehumanizes the people involved and keeps them from God's discipline through daily incremental problem-solving that brings maturity needed to fulfill their purposes God has for them.

Personality Traits of Money

Many of the super wealthy and super poor are not servants at all and are easily offended, self centered, mildly depressed, bored, shallow in thinking, disinterested in work, weak on values, lacking in dreams and visions, and believing they are secure in the basic needs of life.

Wealthy people do not necessarily fit into any mode, and personalities do differ. Similarly, poor people cannot be categorized as having one personality type or mindset. Yet, they are both lazy. They have time to protest, to attend Education Boards to protest, protest climate change, protest with the MeToo movement, or any other types of issues.

CHARACTERISTICS OF THE RICH AND WEALTHY THAT SEEM TO KEEP THEM RICH AND WEALTHY IN THIS LIFE

Proper vision, with incremental steps to achieve the vision, and delayed gratification are three especially important ideas that rich and wealthy people have and practice.

A successful investor learns about trends to predict future market swings. This involves future planning and putting off immediate gratification for long term rewards.

God is an agrarian, so preparing the soil, planting seeds, watering plants, removing weeds, and gathering in the harvest can be used in business as biblical principles of the steps for prosperity. God's agrarian economic principles can be applied to any business or investment that have the status of being a wealth asset. The successful investor never spends his seed, but spends his time looking for good soil, for tilling, planting, watering, fertilizing, and weeding to obtain a bountiful harvest. He makes sure the crop is going to be sold during the harvest season. A good investor sets aside seed for the next harvest. A good investor never spends all his income earned, but increases his net worth because inflation is always present. Constantly, educating yourself with market trends, what products are selling, tax advantages or tax avoidance strategies that are available, and starting plans for investments in January and setting aside capital is wise unto your salvation and biblitarian lifestyle.

Rich people invest every year, sometimes in short-term investments but most of the time in long-term investments. Rich people pay for professional advice from Wealth Managers, Tax Attorneys, and Certified Public Accountants to avoid mistakes. Rich people always know the balances in their bank accounts. Rich people never hand over signatory authority to their checking accounts except by skilled, licensed, professionals with errors and omissions insurance.

These wise efforts based upon God's principles can be used by anyone having a business or investment. The successful businessperson invests in advertising to capture a market share to continue to increase the sales of the product or service. The successful businessperson has a research and development department to bring in new products. The successful businessperson finds a product or service that people want to buy, so there is little salesmanship involved, but just taking orders.

For the poor who are involved only in the acquisition of food, shelter, transportation, and clothing needs, it is extremely hard to think in the long term or in setting aside money for a business, a home, or other wealth investments. In the ghetto, survival is a day to day reality. The "mentality of the poor" is that "tomorrow is not guaranteed" and "five years in the future is unknown and unpredictable."

In contrast to the poor, the real needs of the rich can be met without any effort, so their time can be used to strategize to fulfill plans.

Also, the rich can afford to invest money in various ventures and wait for the highest return because they have the staying power and patience for the best time to sell.

THE GRUBSTAKE PRINCIPLE

Individuals who have become rich after starting with nothing but a "dream and a desire" are unusual. These individuals accumulated "grubstakes" when they were young at a considerable sacrifice, having a positive mindset of delayed gratification. Most people, especially poor people, who are not already rich do not want to sacrifice or to delay their wants through delayed gratification.

In order to acquire a grubstake by your own labor, you have to work two jobs, lower your standard of living, avoid entertainment expenses, avoid expensive gifts for Christmas or birthdays, have garage sales, sell the old third car you are not using, and maintain an older good running car that is paid off to avoid monthly payments. You can also buy and resell items on eBay or other internet markets to earn more money. Deposit all money that you do not use for monthly expenditures into a savings account. Within five years, you can have a grubstake of $50,000 to $100,000 to invest in a business or start flipping real properties, invest in properties at tax lien foreclosures, sell products through Amazon, etc. Obtaining a grubstake means sacrificing your desires to have what you want when you are young. Sacrifice must be a lifestyle, and deferred gratification is the key, along with long working hours and ingenious ways to increase your cash flow. This is why getting your grubstake must be accomplished when you are young and when you have the energy to do it and can live with a lower economic lifestyle because everyone expects you to have very few material assets. People brag about the things they have purchased, the entertainment they are enjoying, the places they travel to, and spend their money instead of saving a grubstake as future capital to invest.

Those who already are wealthy or rich have investment capital that is always readily available, and they do not have to sacrifice or restrict their lifestyles for a grubstake to invest in money-making ventures. This is why rich people have more than the rest of us. The problem is that I, like most people, did not have wealth accumulation counselors. One of the keys is to not allow people to put pressure on you to increase your lifestyle when you are young, but instead build the grubstake and develop the idea that this is best for you and your family. You will be pleased that you did this and later everyone else will think you are a genius, and they will be jealous that they did not do it themselves.

WEALTHY ROLE MODELS

Children learn to talk by "imitating sounds" they hear others make in their immediate environment. Children learn to walk by imitating movements by watching adults or other

Personality Traits of Money

children.

Most attitudes and values are learned by subconsciously internalizing those attitudes and values held by their parents and other significant adults in their lives. This is why the 5th Commandment of the Decalogue Ten Commandments in Deuteronomy 5:16 says, "Honour thy father and thy mother, as the LORD thy God hath commanded thee; that thy days may be prolonged, and that it may go well with thee, in the land which the LORD thy God giveth thee."

Children of the wealthy or the rich have wealthy or rich role models to emulate. They learn how to think and act like the wealthy or rich, and they associate with other wealthy or rich children. They are predisposed to marry a spouse who also comes from a wealthy or rich family, so the marriage creates greater riches or wealth.

An example is Prince of Wales William and Kate Middleton's wealth after William became the next in line for the Monarch. Reporter Becky Pemberton wrote in the U.S. Sun, U.S. Edition, published: May 14 2024, Updated: May 15 2024 the following: "Currently the Prince of Wales is the richest member of the Royal Family with a net worth of around a staggering £1.05 billion. The heir-to-the-throne even beats his dad King Charles III, who is worth £900 million, and it's all thanks to what he was given when he became monarch. Prince William became a billionaire when he took control of the 687-year-old Duchy of Cornwall estate from his dad following the Queen's death. Much of the estate comprises farmland, but it also includes homes and commercial properties, forests, rivers, coastline and around a third of the Dartmoor national park, which was once used for mining minerals such as tin and copper. Prince William was already wealthy after inheriting £10million from his mum Princess Diana and £7million from the Queen Mother, who died in 2002."

Children of the wealthy learn about business, investments, managing large sums of money, delayed gratification, avoiding con men and the various schemes designed to steal the money of the wealthy. Children pick up conversations at the dinner table or when their parents are speaking with other wealthy or rich people on the phone.

Children of the wealthy not only inherit the money of their parents, but also, they inherit the family attitudes and values that a wealthy person has.

For example, Howard Hughes inherited approximately $450,000 from his father when he was 18 years old, and he built an empire in the aerospace industry worth billions because he had acquired the business acumen of long run thinking from the environment created by his father.

Similarly, George F. Getty was among the oilmen who explored and developed Oklahoma's vast energy resources, and he made millions of dollars in business. However, George F. Getty was father of J. (Jean) Paul Getty, and learning from his father, J. Paul Getty made billions of dollars while using business principles of long run thinking for the accumulation of wealth. J. Paul Getty made a vast amount of his money in the oil industry. He learned the business as a child, following his father into the Oklahoma oil fields during summer break from school. J. Paul Getty at age 11 had his first oil strike. J. Paul Getty took over his father's oil business at age 30, but he already was fully experienced in wildcat drilling and the rudiments of managing an oil company because of his father's tutelage. In the late 1940s, J. Paul Getty successfully negotiated a thirty-year oil exclusive concession contract with Saudi Arabia and Kuwait to drill oil in the "Neutral Zone" between the two countries. J. Paul Getty piloted his corporation to become a global conglomerate that managed all aspects of oil production, from exploration to shipping, and became a multi-billionaire. In 1957, Fortune magazine named J. Paul Getty the "Richest Man in the World." With his fortune J. Paul Getty started seriously collecting art in the 1930s and became a lifelong collector and enjoyed the tax benefits of donating art to a non-profit organization he established. Today, The Getty Center in Los Angeles, California, houses most of J. Paul Getty's art collection but the Trustees continue to purchase fine art, paintings, and statues, which are some of the best collections in the world for the public to enjoy.

The Rockefellers, Du Ponts, and Fords perpetuated their family wealth from generation to generation by passing on successful attitudes and values to their posterity. Some of the industrial giants used Biblical economics to acquire great wealth. Rockefeller was a tither and giver. He handed out a dime to everyone he met after he recovered from a severe illness, claiming that he had heard from God to start giving away his fortune, less he dies. The more he gave, the more was returned to him, and his family kept receiving greater wealth. In fact, it was Rockefeller's influence alone which started the "March of Dimes" when he rode in his limousine and laid down dimes one after another for one-mile down Wall Street. These "robber barons" did a lot of things contrary to scripture, as well. In contrast, the models available to the poor are usually not wealthy, successful businesspeople.

The models available to the poor are failures as far as wealth accumulation is concerned in the abstract. This is why people who are in the middle class need to learn Biblical principles of economics, as God is the most successful business Person in His created universe; and He is our role model. We must be like Jesus, who said He must be "about My Father's business" (Luke 2:49).

AMBITION AND HARD WORK

The beginning of every wealthy family starts with someone who has a splendid work ethic. Then, if the next generation has the same work ethic, then that second generation continues to amass a fortune for the family dynasty. The result is a lasting wealth that continues from generation to generation.

With but a few exceptions, the Rockefeller and Kennedy families are ambitious, highly educated (a lot of lawyers and politicians) and have a penchant for hard, long hours work.

Among the wealthy, a compulsive drive to work to accomplish their goals is very common. Many enjoy work as others enjoy sports, hobbies, and other recreation. Work, more than money, seems to drive them. For example, President Donald Trump works around the clock; it is said he only sleeps two to four hours a night.

Challenging work alone will not make anyone wealthy. However, demanding work is primarily a characteristic of the middle and upper middle class rather than the super wealthy upper class, financially speaking.

Personality Traits of Money

"PROPINQUITY" - MEETING INFLUENTIAL PEOPLE

By attending the right schools, joining the right social clubs, and belonging to the right fraternities, the wealthy meet other wealthy people and develop wealthy friends. These wealthy friends share opportunities they have discovered and often invite their other wealthy friends to invest in the great opportunities. The greatest opportunities are kept secret for the super wealthy to share amongst the super wealthy class.

Associating with other people who have money and are making money stimulates friends to do the same.

A person normally marries amongst the people with whom he or she is associated. Therefore, normally, wealthy men marry wealthy women and vice versa.

When wealthy families marry each other, normally their financial empire increases. For example, a daughter of the wealthy Greek shipowner Stavros Livanos married another wealthy shipowner, Aristotle Onassis, while his other daughter married the wealthy Greek shipowner Stavros Niarchos. When Tina Onassis divorced Aristotle Onassis and her sister Eugenie died, Tina Onassis married her sister's ex husband Stavros Niarchos. The money stayed in the wealthy families.

POOR PEOPLE NORMALLY ASSOCIATE WITH OTHER POOR FAMILIES, BUT THERE ARE OVERCOMERS

In contrast, poor people associate primarily with other poor families. For example, the movie "Staying Alive," starring John Travolta, who played a character that tried to get out of the poorer culture through associating with a dance partner outside of his barrio.

Most poor people cannot escape and learn to tolerate their misfortune as painlessly as possible. Some poor people as children, dream of a being a medical doctor, lawyer, professor at a university, or a high school teacher and with their focus on their goal and deferred gratification, they become great men or women.

DR. BEN CARSON

For example, Dr. Ben Carson grew up as a poor child and teenager, but today he is a real-life overcomer and great man of God. According to Wikipedia, Dr. Ben Carson was a poor black boy growing up with his single mother and brother who lived in various places. At the age of eight, Carson dreamt of becoming a missionary doctor for the Seventh Day Adventists Church. Carson attended the predominantly black Southwestern High School for grades nine through twelve, graduating third in his class academically. In high school, he played the euphonium in band and participated in forensics (public speaking), chess club, and the U.S. Army Junior Reserve Officers' Training Corps (JROTC) program where he reached its highest rank—cadet colonel. Carson served as a laboratory assistant in the high school's biology, chemistry, and physics school laboratories beginning in grades 10, 11, and 12, respectively, and worked as a biology laboratory assistant at Wayne State University the summer between grades 11 and 12.

Carson's SAT college admission test scores ranked him somewhere in the low 90th percentile, which is a very high score. Carson says he could only afford the $10 application fee, so he applied and was accepted at Yale and was offered a full scholarship covering tuition and room and board. However, he was not pre-med but graduated with a B.A. degree in psychology in 1973. Carson graduated from the University of Michigan Medical School with an M.D. degree in 1978. Afterwards, Carson was accepted at the Johns Hopkins University School of Medicine neurosurgery program, where he served five years as a neurosurgery resident, completing the final year as chief resident in 1983. He then spent one year (1983–1984) as a Senior Registrar in neurosurgery at the Sir Charles Gairdner Hospital in Nedlands, Western Australia.

Upon returning to Johns Hopkins in 1984, Carson was appointed the university's director of pediatric neurosurgery. As a surgeon, he specialized in traumatic brain injuries, brain and spinal cord tumors, achondroplasia, neurological and congenital disorders, craniosynostosis, epilepsy, and trigeminal neuralgia.

While at Johns Hopkins, Carson figured in the revival of the hemispherectomy, a drastic surgical procedure in which part or all of one hemisphere of the brain is removed to control severe pediatric epilepsy. Encouraged by John M. Freeman, he refined the procedure in the 1980s and performed it many times.

According to The Washington Post, the Binder surgery "launched the stardom" of Carson, who "walked out of the operating room that day into a spotlight that has never dimmed", beginning with a press conference that was covered worldwide and created his name recognition leading to publishing deals and a motivational speaking career.

SOMETIMES, THE ABSENCE OF STRUGGLE BECAUSE OF WEALTH CAN CAUSE PSYCHOLOGICAL DISORDERS, INCLUDING SEVERE DEPRESSION

CHRISTINA ONASSIS

The rich and wealthy are not immune from severe depression. Writing for the "Greek Reporter," journalist Theo Ioannou wrote and published a piece on November 19, 2023, titled, "Christina Onassis: The Short Life of an Unhappy Heiress." He wrote, "On a warm, South American day on November 19, 1988, Christina Onassis, the golden heiress of the Onassis shipping fortune, died in a friend's house in Argentina at the age of thirty-eight. The only daughter and sole surviving heiress of Aristotle Onassis, Christina was supposed to live a sheltered and carefree life. Yet, all testimony from friends and staff around her point to a star-crossed and unhappy woman, haunted by family death and her unfortunate choices in love. She married and divorced four times in her life, and her struggles with her weight and drug use were widely known... Christina spent her life as a rich girl, living a life of almost unheard-of wealth and luxury. She spent thirty thousand dollars just to send a private jet to the U.S. to keep her stocked with Diet Coke. She even once ordered a helicopter to fly from Austria to Switzerland to retrieve a David Bowie cassette she'd left there. When friends said they were too busy to spend time with her, Onassis would give them cash—as much as thirty thousand dollars a month—to clear their schedules. She once told Peter Evans, who wrote

Personality Traits of Money

a biography of her father, that she liked to wear diamonds to breakfast. . . Diagnosed with clinical depression at the age of thirty, Christina had been living for some time on an array of prescribed drugs, but she also reportedly self-medicated with other drugs and used food as a way to deal with her demons. Her fourth marriage eventually also broke up. . . Though Christina's death was attributed to a heart attack brought on by years of drug abuse, her last moments have continued to be shrouded in mystery, another sad moment in the Greek tragedy of the Onassis family. She is buried alongside her beloved father, Aristotle, and her brother, Alexander, in the family cemetery on the Island of Skorpios."

Although Christina Onassis technically diagnosed as dying of a heart attack, her history of using "legalized" anti depressant drugs could have weakened her heart. Had she turned her life over to Jesus, she would not have had to suffer her depression that perhaps led to her early grave. Her death was sad, but it is not unexpected because she was not happy or content with her life. Having lots of money to spend does not guarantee contentment or happiness.

RICHES CAN COME BECAUSE THE PERSON IS IN THE RIGHT PLACE AT THE RIGHT TIME

The right timing factor cannot be over looked or underestimated. J. Paul Getty, Hugh Roy Cullen, Everette Lee De Golyer, and others who have made fortunes in oil give credit to luck for drilling in the right places.

W. Clement Stone, who accumulated over 400 million dollars selling insurance was blessed from the beginning by making two sales on his first day in his insurance sales career.

I knew of an attorney acquaintance in Orange County, California, who was working for the IRS. He found a "tax loophole." He quit his IRS job, waited for the requisite time to avoid a conflict of interest per his IRS employment agreement, and then sold the tax loophole for a yearly royalty of thousands of dollars with built in cost-of-living increases. What a great way to start out the beginning of each new year.

WHEN YOU ARE KNOWN FOR THE AMOUNT OF MONEY YOU HAVE, THEN IT CAN BECOME AN IDOL

The poor stay poor because they often see money as the answer to all their problems, which means money has become an idol, and they suffer the consequences of serving an idol. This is very subtle. Poor people work for money instead of having money work for them.

Mature people discover that money is not worth what it takes to obtain it. This is why unlike the rich or wealthy – few middle-class or poor people want to pay the price of sacrifice and delayed gratification to become rich. They do not want to be too restrictive with their spending and enjoying pleasures of life just to accumulate riches or wealth.

Some middle-class people take too big of risks and lose their investment capital and their seed money, and as a result they run out of money and time. Extensive research should be done before you invest. Never decide the same day that an investment opportunity is presented to you. Trust no one. Whatever the salesman represents, tell him you have to consider his proposal afterwards as you never make a hasty decision. Ask to speak to other investors. Check the presenter's and his company's names on the internet. Research the type of business or investment opportunity that is being presented and always read the negatives as well as the positives. Embellishment is the routine of the salesman. For each representation, ask the presenter how you can verify what he just said. If the presenter gets offended because you are messing up his sales pitch, then stop the presentation or excuse yourself and say you are not interested. Good investments have historical proof of profit.

Here is a good pattern. When Jesus fed the five thousand, after everyone had eaten, He told His Apostles to gather up all that were the leftovers, so nothing was lost. Jesus said in John 6:39, "And this is the Father's will which hath sent me, that of all which He hath given Me I should lose nothing but should raise it up again at the last day."

If you have been given the anointing to spoil to bring into the Kingdom of God the wealth and riches in the hands of the fallen world or the kingdom of darkness, then your duty is to gather up all the leftovers that came with that anointing, so, that nothing is lost as God wants to use that surplus anointing for the last day revival. What does this mean? If God decides to grant you wealth, then He first trains you how to handle that wealth, so nothing is lost because He has a purpose for you to use that wealth for His Kingdom.

For every Colonel Sanders who parlays a small chicken business into a fast-food chain called "Kentucky Fried Chicken," there are hundreds of thousands who go broke because they took for granted the anointing to spoil the Kingdom of darkness.

SIN OF GREED BY LUSTING FOR MONEY
CAN BE THE ENEMY OF WEALTH BUILDING

Although a few people get rich despite their greed, most greedy people remain poor. Greed is an attitude that you want more of what you already have, and covetousness is an attitude that you want what someone else already has.

The poor people are the biggest pursuers of lottery tickets, so millions of dollars are being invested in an extremely considerable risk by the poorer class of society.

FEAR OF LOSS STOPS PEOPLE FROM TAKING
NECESSARY RISKS TO BECOME WEALTHY

While greed causes people to gamble recklessly and take too many risks, fear causes people not to take necessary risks to become wealthy.

Fear leads to paralysis of decision and opportunities pass by people.

ENVY OF OTHERS CAUSES PEOPLE
TO COMMIT THE SIN OF COVETOUSNESS

The more value people put on money, the more envious they will be of those who have it. People who want to be rich try to live like rich people before they, themselves, are rich. In other words, people cannot become rich before they can afford to be rich. If people try to live like the rich people before they can afford it, they are committing the sin of covetousness

Personality Traits of Money

and the loss of their money over foolishness.

The Tenth Commandment of the Decalogue says in Exodus 20:17, "Thou shalt not covet thy neighbour's house, thou shalt not covet thy neighbour's wife, nor his manservant, nor his maidservant, nor his ox, nor his ass, nor any thing that is thy neighbour's." To covet what belongs to someone else is the sin of covetousness.

Many people stay poor because they increase their cost of living and lifestyles "to keep up with the Joneses" instead of investing their money to have wealth assets working for them in their older age and while they are asleep.

ANGRY PEOPLE CAUSE OTHERS NOT TO DO BUSINESS WITH THEM

A person who usually fails in negotiations is because he does not suggest to the other party his willingness to concede what the other party mostly wants in exchange for what he mostly wants. If the angry person does not get all he wants, he gets angry; then he becomes angrier when the other party pulls away in the conversation. Generally, the person's anger destroys the business deal and lessens his chances of becoming rich.

Phrases like "blind rage" or "consumed with anger" describes a man or woman who has suffered financial loss and is bitter about it and has not forgiven the perpetrator. Anger makes the intellect dysfunctional or ineffectual and not good in conversations with people who know the art of negotiations.

Proverbs 14:17 says "He that is soon angry dealeth foolishly. . . ."

Proverbs 19:19 says, "A man of great wrath will suffer punishment; For if you rescue him, you will have to do it again."

Proverbs 22:24-25 says, "Make no friendship with an angry man; and with a furious man thou shalt not go: (25) Lest you learn his ways and get a snare to thy soul."

LACKING SELF-WORTH CAUSES YOU NOT TO ASK FOR HIGHER PRICES OR HIGHER FEES

Many people's feelings of lack of worthiness make them not strive to be rich or wealthy. Some people with low self-worth mistakenly conclude it is caused by negative thinking about themselves. In truth, negative thoughts are a symptom, not the cause of lack of self-worth or low self-esteem. Some people misdiagnose themselves as having low self-worth when in truth they have low self-confidence.

Low self-confidence could be because of failure of deficient performance in jobs, or a belief that you do not have the skills to do a particular job, or that you failed at the last attempts at performing the same tasks.

In the person's soul, the mind thinks, the emotions feel, but the heart believes. Lack of confidence is the thinking of the mind. However, the lack of self-worth is of the heart because it is what you believe. Thus, the symptoms of low self-esteem are more difficult to transform because people believe what they conclude is true or factually correct.

Psalms 9:1 says, "I will praise Thee, O LORD, with my whole heart; I will shew forth all thy marvelous works."

Psalms 95:8 says, "Harden not your heart, as in the provocation, and as in the day of temptation in the wilderness."

Psalms 13:2, 5 says, "How long shall I take counsel in my soul, having sorrow in my heart daily? How long shall mine enemy be exalted over me? . . . (5) But I have trusted in Thy mercy; my heart shall rejoice in Thy salvation." Salvation is a heart issue.

King James version of Proverbs 17:22 says, "A merry heart doeth good like a medicine: but a broken spirit (ruach spirit or soul or emotional state depending on context) drieth the bones." God's Word version of Proverb 17:22 says, "A joyful heart is good medicine, but depression drains one's strength."

Proverbs 23:7 says, "For as he thinketh in his heart, so is he: Eat and drink, saith he to thee; but his heart is not with thee." The Hebrew word for "thinketh" is shaar, which means "to act as a gate keeper to allow things to come in or out." Your heart in your soul, or personality, can either be carnal or spiritual, depending on the beliefs that you hold. Out of the abundance of the heart the mouth speaks (Matthew 12:24). Beliefs in the heart are different than thoughts in the mind. The Hebrew word for "thoughts" of the mind is "machashaboh," which is a different word that means imagination, invention, plans, or ideas (see Isaiah 55:8 for example). The Will is in the heart where a person's library of beliefs is stored. This Hebrew word shaar is an action word that means a gateway that opens and closes to ideas, thoughts, inspirations, revelations, emotional enticements, and stimuli that effects the decision in choosing life and death, which is a heart issue. "Therefore, choose life, that both you and your descendants may live" (Deuteronomy 30:19) is the choice of opening up the gateway in your heart to the Kingdom beliefs that operate the law of the spirit of life in Christ Jesus, instead of the choice of opening up the gateway in your heart to the beliefs of this fallen world that operate the law of sin and death (Romans 8:2).

1 John 3:20-21 says, "For if our heart condemn us, God is greater than our heart, and knoweth all things. (21) Beloved, if our heart condemn us not, then have we confidence toward God."

A FALSE SENSE OF CONTENTMENT

A false sense of contentment or satisfaction with one's status quo causes some people to not strive to become rich or wealthy.

What is false contentment in life? Some people find contentment when they are under the influence of drugs or alcohol. Other people think they will find contentment when they move to a new location, a new state, a new house, drive a new car, obtain a new job, start a new business, or even begin a new ministry. The euphoria may be temporary because every person carries their soulish problems with them. Believers must submit their hearts to the Lord to transform the foundation of their spiritual beliefs that are in line with those in the Kingdom of God and His righteousness.

True contentment can only come from God. 1 Timothy 6:6 says, "But godliness with contentment is great gain." It is your heart that must be content. Your mind must be renewed (Romans 12:2). Your emotions must be stabilized (Isaiah 33:6). The foundation of your beliefs must be reformed and transformed (Ezekiel 36:26).

Psalms 13:5 says, "But I have trusted in thy mercy; my heart shall rejoice in thy salvation."

REPENT FROM SEEKING FIRST MONEY TO BECOME RICH AND FAMOUS

A new Believer's soul must be transformed from his unlawful proclivity of seeing that money as the answer to all problems. As said before, if a new member in church solicits money from other members in the church community, the Pastor needs to halt such activity and forbid the Believer from soliciting any person in the church congregation into any business or monetary investments. The Believer must repent and have his mind, emotions, and heart spiritually transformed away from the god of mammon. If the Believer continues to solicit and refuses to abide by the Pastor's admonition, then the Believer should be asked by the Pastor to leave the church community on condition that he is allowed to seek counselling from the Pastor for his soulish transformation.

It bears repeating that affinity fraud is a serious matter with the U.S. Security Exchange Commission (SEC), and if it sometimes occurs in the church community, and the Pastor knows about it, he could be subpoenaed to testify before the SEC, or its equivalent in the State government. However, the Pastor can have private meetings with the errant Believer for personal counseling and for repentance with the purpose of bringing him back into the community once his soul has been transformed. This soliciting money from people in the church community can be a very serious legal and spiritual matter, so the Pastor needs to be watchful but loving toward the recalcitrant Believer. He could be acting out of lack of knowledge that what he is doing is sin.

The Pastor must exhibit tough love, as it must be tough to protect the church community. The Pastor is the overseer of the sheep, so he must keep a watchful eye as to any business transactions that are being touted. The Pastor must ascertain whether he can counsel the Believer into repenting and turning his heart to God and seek first the Kingdom of God and His righteousness instead of money for his provision.

When I was pastoring my church community, I was very strict but loving. I did not like anyone trying to sell an old automobile to another Believer in the church community. I always sought righteousness, peace, and joy in the Holy Spirit, and I expected others to do the same. For example, if I wanted to get rid of a car, I gave the car to him. As a gift transaction, there could not be any bad feelings involved if the car needed repairs or stopped running after a year. When money is involved in any transaction between members of the church congregation, there can be bad thoughts, feelings, and beliefs afterwards with those involved.

THE BLESSINGS OF REPENTANCE

Jesus started His ministry after the temptation in the wilderness when he said in Matthew 4:17, "… 'Repent: for the kingdom of heaven is at hand.'" The first thing Jesus said in His declaration is "repent." Repenting is the key that opens the entrance into the Kingdom of heaven. We have this same timeless message today. "Repent: for the kingdom of heaven is at hand."

Mark also declares how Jesus started His ministry by saying in Mark 1:15, "The time is fulfilled, and the kingdom of God is at hand: repent ye and believe the gospel (of the kingdom)."

Repent means for the sinful, defiant Believer to turn around and begin thinking, emoting, and believing God's righteous kingdom principles instead of the fallen world's immoral business practices.

Jesus said to preach repentance and remission of sins (Luke 24:47), not only for initial salvation but for the ongoing spiritual transformation of the soul. Daily repenting and turning to God for cleansing of the soul to rid carnality is a way of life. Repenting is the precursor to humility. 1 John 1:8-10 says, "If we (Believers) say that we have no sin, we deceive ourselves, and the truth is not in us. (9) If we (Believers) confess our sins, He is faithful and just to forgive us our sins, and to cleanse us from all unrighteousness. (10) If we (Believers) say that we have not sinned, we make Him a liar, and His word is not in us." The Apostle John in 1 John 1:8-10 is addressing the Believers' souls because Believers' born again spirits are born of God with Christ's resurrected humanity nature Seed (1 Peter 1:23), does not sin (1 John 3:9), and the New Man (born again spirit) is absolutely righteous and holy (Ephesians 4:24).

Seeing money as an idol, Believers must repent for the remission of sin and for their souls to be in right standing with God to duplicate the relationship that the Believers' born again spirits already have.

If a person has a Manipulator Personality Trait, it is very hard to divorce himself from the idol avarice love of money because as a manipulator, he must keep his thoughts and actions secret from those he seeks to manipulate. Also, because the manipulator is inundated daily by social media with the philosophy of this world that uses money to entice disciples of the fallen world system headed up by the prince of this world (John 14:30). The individual with the Manipulator Personality Trait also can be influenced by a demonic spirit temptation, as Satan, himself uses manipulation and lies as a means of deceiving people to obey him. John 8:44 says, "Ye are of your father the devil, and the lusts of your father ye will do. He was a murderer from the beginning, and abode not in the truth, because there is no truth in him. When he speaketh a lie, he speaketh of his own: for he is a liar, and the father of it." Jesus directed His comments to religious leaders, who were not saved. Just because you are religious, know the Scriptures, and have a title in church does not mean you are saved and certainly does not mean you are spiritually mature in your soul, especially when your relationships are not governed by agape love. If you know you are born again, then you are saved; but after initial salvation, you still must submit to the spiritual transformation of your soul by the Godhead.

Having lots of money can be a blessing, or it can be an enemy of the transformation of your soul. A scripture that is regularly taught by some Church leaders is Paul's message in 2 Corinthians 8:9, which says, "For ye know the grace of our Lord Jesus Christ, that, though He was rich (when He was with God in heaven), yet for your sakes He became poor, that ye through His poverty might be rich." However, Paul who wrote 2 Corinthians 8:9, also balanced out his teaching with 1 Timothy 6: 9, 17-19, which says, "But they that will be rich fall into temptation and a snare, and into many foolish and hurtful lusts, which drown men in destruction and perdition…(17) Charge them that are rich in this world, that they be not high minded, nor trust in uncertain riches, but in the living God, who giveth us richly all things to enjoy; (18) That they do good, that they be rich in good works, ready to distribute, willing to communicate. (19) Laying up in store for themselves a good foundation against the time to come, that they may lay hold on eternal life."

THE BLESSINGS OF HUMILITY

Jesus never sought money or fame, neither did Paul or the other Apostles, save Judas. Jesus sought and lived the perfect sinless life, with perfect obedience and perfect humility before God the Father. Philippians 2:5-8 says, "Let this mind be in you, which was also in Christ Jesus: (6) Who, being in the form of God, thought it not robbery to be equal with God (7) But made Himself of no reputation, and took upon Him the form of a servant, and was made in the likeness of men: (8) And being found in fashion as a man, He humbled Himself, and became obedient unto death, even the death of the cross."

Jesus' humanity nature taught humility by teaching His disciples by word and to emulate His humility in His relationship with God. Jesus taught that if you are humble before God, He will exalt you. As your heart becomes a true servant with utmost humility, God grants you more authority. Jesus taught His disciples that the greatest among them was the servant of all (Mark 9:35). Jesus taught in Matthew 23:11-12, "But he that is greatest among you shall be your servant. And whosoever shall exalt himself shall be abased; and he that shall humble himself shall be exalted."

Peter reiterated the Lord's admonition in 1 Peter 5: 6, "Humble yourselves therefore under the mighty hand of God, that He may exalt you in due time (Greek Kairos- season)." Direct your heart to God and the Lord Jesus Christ and their Kingdom principles of life and you will experience life abundantly (John 10:10b). Jesus said in John 6:63, "It is the spirit that quickeneth; the flesh profiteth nothing: the words (rhema) that I speak unto you, they are spirit, and they are (zoe) life."

CONFESSION OF SINS IS DIFFERENT THAN REPENTING WHICH IS TURNING AWAY FROM SIN AND THE WORLD AND SEEKING GOD

Confession of sins is acknowledgement and admission. Confession can lead to salvation. Romans 10:10 says, "For with the heart man believeth unto righteousness; and with the mouth confession is made unto salvation." James 5:16 says, "Confess your faults one to another, and pray one for another, that ye may be healed. The effectual fervent prayer of a righteous man availeth much." Confession is a precursor to forgiveness. 1 John 1:9 says, "If we confess our sins, He is faithful and just to forgive us our sins, and to cleanse us from all unrighteousness."

However, repenting means turning around and going in the opposite direction. Repenting is like a Believer who lives in Los Angeles and decides to drive his car to San Francisco. He maps out his route, enters the on-ramp on the 405 Freeway, then merges onto the 101 Freeway; but when he gets to Santa Barbara, he repents and turns around and heads back home.

Thus, repenting means to turn around from your God-rejecting philosophy of existence in the world and your sinful practices and start living by seeking first the Kingdom of God and His righteousness (Matthew 6:33). The new Believer must turn around and reject the fallen world philosophies of godless humanity. The new unbeliever seeking salvation must repent of the world's materialistic selfishness, self-centeredness, and love of money to meet all his needs, by confessing Jesus Christ as Lord, believing that Jesus died on the Roman cross, but rose from the dead on the third day, and then start seeking first the kingdom of God and His righteousness. If he repents by turning to the Lord, then he will be born again and will receive eternal life (Romans 10:9; John 3:3; 2 Corinthians 5:17). Then the Believer is admonished in Matthew 6:33 to seek with his will in the heart of his soul the kingdom of God and His righteousness, and all things will be provided to him by God. The new born again Believer cannot stop with initial salvation, although he has eternal life, as God wants the new Believer to continue repenting daily and submitting to the Godhead for the transformation of his soul (Romans 12:2) by God the Father (John 15:2), God the Word (Ephesians 5:26-27), and God the Holy Spirit (Romans 8:13).

Let us in a deeper way examine the word "repent." The word "repent" has a special meaning. The prefix "re" means going back or turning around. The word "pent" is from the Greek word "penta" that means "five." Five is the number for God's grace, which means God's unmerited favor. Thus, repent means to turn around and come back to God's grace or unmerited favor. An example of the number 5, the Pentateuch is the first five books in the Bible, which are Genesis, Exodus, Leviticus, Numbers, and Deuteronomy. When you multiply 5 x 5, you get a total of 25, and this stands for "grace for grace." John 1:16 reveals this multiplication of grace, "And of His fulness have all we received, and grace for grace." When you sow grace, you receive a multiplication of grace in return.

Repent gets you closer to God. The word repent is like getting the room in the top floor of the hotel closes to God, which is called the "penthouse." It means returning and getting back on top closer to God and His unmerited favor. Grace means God's faith and agape love are given to you. This is where true Believers belong. Daily repentance is a way of life, but it is NOT the continuous guilt piled daily upon yourself. You are to invite God's grace in your life. Repentance is a prerequisite of receiving the goodness of God. Romans 2:4 says, "Or despisest thou the riches of His goodness and forbearance and longsuffering; not knowing that the goodness of God leadeth thee to repentance?"

Thus, repentance really means to decide to turn around, reject the world philosophies, and come back to God. Repentance does include stop sinning, but every Believer sins while their souls are being transformed, unlike the born again spirit that does not sin (1 John 3:9). The main thing that repentance does is the key to submitting your soul to God.

Confession of sins, alone, does not put you in permanent good stead with God, because God wants from your repentance. Repentance means rejecting the fallen world and the kingdom of darkness and turning and coming back to God. Confession and repentance of sins invokes God's faithfulness to forgive you of your sins. Yet, confession does not make you a better servant per se, but with repentance it does evoke forgiveness from God. Confession of sins, without repentance, may make you think, feel, and believe you are guilty. 2 Corinthians 7:9-10 says, "Now I rejoice, not that ye were made sorry, but that ye sorrowed to repentance: for ye were made sorry after a godly manner, that ye might receive damage by us in nothing. (10) For godly sorrow worketh repentance to salvation not to be repented of: but the sorrow of the world worketh death."

Romans 8:1 says, "There is therefore now no condemnation to them which are in Christ Jesus, who walk not after the flesh, but after the spirit." A good sense of guilt is not bad per se, but you should discontinue your heart believing in condemnation. You cannot stop sinning by your own fallen nature in your untransformed soul, but when you enter the crucifixion of Christ and allow Him to live His life in you and through you, then you will stop sinning because Christ is living His life in you, and He is not a sinner (Galatians 2:20).

THE OPERATION OF SIX LAWS IN ROMANS 7 & 8

A law denotes an established natural or spiritual rule having a cause and effect, an inclination and activity, and a principle and consequence associated with it. There is the law of God, the law of the soul, the law of sin, the law of the spirit of life in Christ Jesus, and the law of sin and death. God's laws are not God's judgments. Violating God's laws has built in consequences. Take the law of gravity for example. If you jump off a ten-story building and land on the sidewalk below, you cannot blame God for killing you because of the law of gravity. You died because you violated the law of gravity. Galatians 6:7-8 says, "Be not deceived; God is not mocked: for whatsoever a man soweth, that shall he also reap. (8) For he that soweth to his flesh shall of the flesh reap corruption; but he that soweth to the Spirit shall of the Spirit reap life everlasting." God grants every human the sovereign freedom to make their own choice decisions, but humans do not have the sovereign freedom to choose the consequences.

The first law in Romans is seen in Romans 7:22, which says, "For I delight in the law of God according to the inward man." This law of God is the written Ten Commandments, as expounded in Deuteronomy 5:6-21.

The second and third laws are delineated in Romans 7:23, which says, "But I see another law in my members, warring against the law of my mind (Greek-nous, meaning thoughts, feelings, or beliefs, so meaning is pertaining to the whole mind, emotions, heart where the Will resides) and bringing me into captivity to the law of sin which is in my members (flesh)." The sin principle lives in your mortal body, so when you die, your body decays back to dust from which was made from the beginning with Adam. Genesis 3:19 says, "In the sweat of thy face shalt thou eat bread (referring to the body and flesh), till thou return unto the ground; for out of it wast thou taken: for dust thou art, and unto dust shalt thou return." Your sinful body dies and decays away and does not go to heaven.

The law of the mind or soul is that the soul's daily nourishment is stimuli from either the spiritual realm brought to the soul by the born again spirit from God's Kingdom or the stimuli from the fallen world brought to the soul by the five senses of the body or flesh. Galatians 5:16-17 says, "This I say then, 'Walk in the Spirit, and ye shall not fulfill the lust of the flesh.

(17) For the flesh lusteth against the Spirit, and the Spirit against the flesh: and these are contrary the one to the other: so that ye cannot do the things that ye would.'" Romans 8:6-7 says, "For to be carnally minded is death; but to be spiritually minded is life and peace. (7) Because the carnal mind is enmity against God: for it is not subject to the law of God, neither indeed can be."

The law of sin operates in fallen mankind's body like weeds. Again, Romans 7:23 says, "But I see another law ... bringing me into captivity to the law of sin which is in my members (flesh)." You don't have to plant weeds, as they automatically grow. The law of sin is in operation in the fallen world and the body through the five senses takes in the sins of the fallen world and brings the sinful, fallen world stimuli, and false self-centered philosophies into the mind and the entire soul. Sin is everywhere in the fallen world, so you do not have to go to Satan's kingdom of darkness to learn about sin or to entertain sin because the fallen world is under the rulership of the evil prince of the world. Jesus said in John 14:30, "Hereafter I will not talk much with you: for the prince of this world cometh, and hath nothing in Me." If you do not seek righteousness, peace, and joy in the Holy Spirit, you automatically will be seeking the fallen kingdoms of this world.

The fourth law is written in Romans 7:21, which states: "I find then a law, that evil is present with me, the one who wills to do good." This fourth law was especially troubling to the Apostle Paul. This law we may call the "law of good and evil." It operates from the Tree of the Knowledge of Good and Evil. Whenever Paul tried to do good, he found that evil suddenly became present. Paul expounded how the law of good and evil works in Romans 7:19: "For the good that I will to do, I do not do; but the evil I will not to do, that I practice." This fourth law is the one that causes the Believer the most difficulty daily. The problem is there is God's good and there is fallen man's humanistic good. The "good" in the Tree of the Knowledge of Good and Evil is man's fallen humanistic good. Man's humanistic good grows on the same tree as evil grows. This is observed by Paul who says when he tries to do good evil is also present. In this sense, Paul is showing the difference between fallen humanistic good and God's eternal kingdom good, which he exemplifies in the two laws revealed in Romans 8:2.

When you try to be humble, pride will raise up its haughty head. If you do not try to be good, then pride does not appear. If you decide to not lose your temper, you find that you are losing your temper more than normal. If you try to be patient, you encounter circumstances revealing your impatience. When you try to be calm and restful, you become easily irritable and agitated. The more you try to live like the "new man," the more you live like the "old man." The law of good and evil works this way: the more you try to do good, the more you encounter evil. You must stop activating the law of good and evil. You are eating the fruit from the wrong tree. Stop trying not to sin. The secret is in Galatians 2:20, which says, "I am crucified with Christ: nevertheless, I live; yet not I, but Christ liveth in me: and the life which I now live in the flesh I live by the faith of the Son of God, who loved me, and gave Himself for me." The greatest submission is to enter the crucifixion of Christ and allow Christ Jesus, through His divine nature, God the Word, to substitute His humanity nature's, Lamb of God, with His sinless life for your sinful life. God's only begotten Son, Jesus as the Lamb of God, are sinless and express all goodness of God, not the humanistic good that grows on the Tree of Knowledge of Good and Evil. This is why Paul wrote in Romans 2:4, "... the goodness of God leadeth thee to repentance."

Personality Traits of Money

The fifth and sixth laws are expounded in Romans 8:2, which says, "For the law of the spirit of life in Christ Jesus has made me free from the law of sin and death."

Similarly, John said in 1 John 1:1-2, "That which was from the beginning, which we have heard, which we have seen with our eyes, which we have looked upon, and our hands have handled, of the Word of life; (2) For the life was manifested, and we have seen it, and bear witness, and shew unto you that eternal life, which was with the Father, and was manifested unto us." Jesus said in John 10:10b, "I am come that they might have life, and that they might have it more abundantly."

Romans 6:23 says, "For the wages of sin is death; but the free gift of God is eternal life in Christ Jesus our Lord." The law of the spirit of life in Christ Jesus brings freedom and more abundant life to the believer. Sin activates the law of death and puts the Believer in a consciousness of death where God's life is absent. This state can cause anxiety, depression, and hopelessness. When you repent by turning back to God, anxiety, depression, and hopelessness lessens or disappears.

Jesus said in John 8:36 that: "If therefore the Son shall make you free, you shall be free indeed." Since Believers have been given eternal life, the law of sin and death only operates temporarily but not infernally in the soul of the Believer. When Believers die and go to the third heaven and when Believers return to the new heaven and new earth, along with Jesus and the New Jerusalem, the law of sin and death no longer operate in their lives.

From the beginning of the creation of Adam, God warned Adam in Genesis 2:9,16- 17, "And out of the ground made the LORD God to grow every tree that is pleasant to the sight, and good for food; the tree of life also in the midst of the garden, and the tree of knowledge of good and evil…(16) And the LORD God commanded the man, saying, 'Of every tree of the garden thou mayest freely eat: (17) But of the tree of the knowledge of good and evil, thou shalt not eat of it: for in the day that thou eatest thereof thou shalt surely die.'"

After Adam and Even sinned, in Genesis 3:15 God promised to send the Redeemer. "And I will put enmity between thee and the woman, and between thy seed and her Seed; it (He) shall bruise thy head, and thou shalt bruise His heel." Jesus said to Nicodemus in John 3:16, "For God so loved the world, that He gave His only begotten Son, that whosoever believeth in Him should not perish, but have everlasting life."

Ezekiel 14:12 prophesied the tree of life characteristics. "And by the river upon the bank thereof, on this side and on that side, shall grow all trees for meat, whose leaf shall not fade, neither shall the fruit thereof be consumed: it shall bring forth new fruit according to his months, because their waters they issued out of the sanctuary: and the fruit thereof shall be for meat, and the leaf thereof for medicine."

The Tree of Life is coming back to be part of the new heaven and new earth. Revelation 22:1-2 says, "And he shewed me a pure river of water of life, clear as crystal, proceeding out of the throne of God and of the Lamb. (2) In the midst of the street of it, and on either side of the river, was there the tree of life, which bare twelve manner of fruits, and yielded her fruit every month: and the leaves of the tree were for the healing of the nations." There are no nations in heaven but back here on earth, so the leaves of the Tree of Life are for the healing of the nations back here on the new heaven and new earth. Revelation 11:15 says, "…The kingdoms of this world are become the kingdoms of our Lord, and of his Christ; and he shall reign for ever and ever." Revelation 5:10 says, "And hast made us unto our God kings and priests: and we shall reign on the earth."

The Greek for the word "tree" denoting the fig tree that Jesus cursed in Mark 11: 13-14 is the Greek word suke, which means a tree with roots. Yet, the Greek for the word "tree" in the Tree of Life in Revelation 22:2 is "xulon," which means a tree that has been cut down and has no roots. The Tree of Life is the Cross of Calvary, and the fruit represents resurrected life, as Aaron's rod that bloomed and had an acorn (Numbers 17:8). Again, the leaves on the Tree of Life are for the healing of the nations that are here in the new heaven and new earth and was symbolized by the green leaves of the evergreen tree in Psalm 1:3, which says, "And he shall be like a tree planted by the rivers of water, that bringeth forth his fruit in his season; his leaf also shall not wither; and whatsoever he doeth shall prosper. "

TURNING TO GOD BY REPENTING BY YOUR SOUL IS A DAILY PRACTICE, AND WHEN YOU DO, YOU WILL EXPERIENCE THE LORD'S FREEDOM

You should practice habitually the repenting of your soul from frequently saying, "Show me the money!" Just turn around and say, "God, show me Your will for today." It is hard to divorce yourself from the avarice love of money because money itself is the reward you think will take care of your problems. The avarice love of money is very insidious and poisonous. Every Believer and person are inundated daily by social media with the philosophies that uses money to make disciples of the fallen world system headed up by the prince of this world (John 14:30).

John 8:44 says, "Ye are of your father the devil, and the lusts of your father ye will do. He was a murderer from the beginning, and abode not in the truth, because there is no truth in him. When he speaketh a lie, he speaketh of his own: for he is a liar, and the father of it." The devil uses lies as a means of deceiving people to obey him or at least adopt the philosophies of the fallen world. Either way, the devil has a hold on you. The devil's lies are not small lies; they are complicated, structured set-ups to totally deceive you when you believe your life will be enhanced by accepting the devil's lies as truth, adopting the world's humanism, or just become self -centered away from God. The devil figures out what motivates you, and he can come and entice you as an angel of light instead of a rebellious fallen angel of darkness (2 Corinthians 11:14).

Satan's malevolent minions in the world are evil principalities, powers, rulers of the darkness of this world, spiritual wickedness in high places, along with demons and fallen angels (Ephesians 6:12; Matthew 25:41). Satan's minions can be sent to lie to you that with money you can be rich and famous, be a leader of this world, and be recognized as a great human being by the world's standards.

Satan sends his minions to steal, kill, and destroy you, primarily through bodily addictions of sins, financial frauds, false promises of riches, set ups with con men, exposure to false witnesses, groundless accusations, defamatory untrue statements published on social media, punishment for not accepting as normal what God's laws state are sins, let others hold you in high esteem and then let you fall in your humiliation, and a host of other evil of what Satan can script in your life, as he is like a soap opera director.

Satan can also tempt even Pastors with money, with illicit sex, and with pride. Yet, the economic sin over wrongful attachment to money, as opposed to sexual sin or sin of pride, normally will not cause the Pastor to have to resign from his office. Some Pastors fall into economic sin because they seek first to be rich and famous instead of seeking first the Kingdom of God and His righteousness (Matthew 6:33). These Pastors fail because they spend the offerings on themselves instead of using the offerings to make disciples of all nations (Matthew 28:19). Yet often the root personality sin of seeking fame and fortune is pride and a failure to exhibit humility before God. An obsessive-compulsive quest and desire to be rich and famous, so you can have stature amongst other religious leaders, fly in your private jet, have an expensive wardrobe, live in a large house, drive an expensive automobile, have income from investment properties, have large savings accounts, own a vacation home in one of the Caribbean Islands, constantly traveling to "minister the gospel" in other churches for a special offering, so this is added money in addition what he receives from his home congregation of tithers and givers. How do you recognize these secret seekers of riches and fame? They hide behind their titles, their licenses, their positions of authority. Not only Pastors, but also professors, lawyers, judges, medical doctors, politicians, and scientists hide their evil and fallen personalities behind titles and positions of authority.

James 4:6-8 speaks how to draw near to God and resist evil and the devil. "But He (Holy Spirit) giveth more grace. Wherefore He saith, 'God resisteth the proud, but giveth grace unto the humble.' (7) Submit yourselves therefore to God. Resist the devil, and he will flee from you. (8) Draw nigh to God, and he will draw nigh to you. Cleanse your hands, ye sinners; and purify your hearts, ye double minded."

In summary, repent means turning around on a new course, and your new course leads you back to the goodness of God, His grace, and agape love in Christ Jesus. In other words, stop trying with your own willpower not to sin. You will sin because you are thinking in your mind what sin you are trying to avoid. The true path of resistance against sin is to let God protect you from sin.

How do you do that? Daily repent and seek first the Kingdom of God and His righteousness. Let this spiritual submission and resolve each morning be your daily practice before you go to work, go to school, go meet a friend, or do any other task during the day. Exercise your will not to focus on not sinning, but concentrate your mind, emotions, and heart on the word of God, pray throughout the day, practice being in the presence of God in Christ Jesus, and submit and be led by the Holy Spirit. When you have fellowship with God in Christ Jesus, you will not want fellowship with the fallen world, and you will not think of sinning. Make this process of seeking God and His only begotten Son, Christ Jesus, His kingdom, and His righteousness daily, being led by the Holy Spirit, and you will not fulfill the lust of the flesh, the lust of the eyes, or the pride of life in your soul. You will serve God and not serve mammon.

If you encounter temptation or evil, immediately reject it out of your mind, emotions, and heart by receiving the presence of the Holy Spirit, Who is always there for you. This takes a little practice but do it. If someone comes to you, and you sense he is trying to convince you to act, is trying to tempt you, or is trying to overpower you, you must practice saying "no," "I don't have time to speak about this," "I will consider what you are saying but I have to leave," or simply say, "I am not interested in your proposal." Never introduce anyone else to that person if you spiritually discern he has evil and sin in his heart.

Jesus said in Matthew 7:17-18, "Even so every good tree bringeth forth good fruit; but a corrupt tree bringeth forth evil fruit. (18) A good tree cannot bring forth evil fruit, neither can a corrupt tree bring forth good fruit." To religious leaders, Jesus said in Matthew 12:34-35, "O generation of vipers, how can ye, being evil, speak good things? For out of the abundance of the heart the mouth speaketh. A good man out of the good treasure of the heart bringeth forth good things: and an evil man out of the evil treasure bringeth forth evil things."

Paul said in Romans 12:9, "Let (agape) love be without dissimulation (subterfuge, suppression, dishonesty, or disguise). Abhor that which is evil (wicked, malevolent, malicious, or immoral); cleave to that which is (God's kind of) good."

Personality Traits of Money

Dr. Nova Dean Pack

Conclusion

CONCLUSION

You may ask of me, "Where did you receive all of this wisdom, insights, knowledge, and understanding that you have written in this book?" Yes, I have a doctorate degree in law, and yes, I have been a lawyer since December 1974 and was well-educated, eating the fruit from the tree of the knowledge of good and evil coming out of law school.

Even though I grew up in church, the fact is I came out of law school as a spiritually ignorant man without God's wisdom, knowledge, and understanding of truth. As a lawyer, I had power and authority as an officer of the court, but I was like Pilate when he spoke to Jesus. John 18:37-38 says, "Pilate therefore said unto Him, 'Art thou a king then?' Jesus answered, 'Thou sayest that I am a king. To this end was I born, and for this cause came I into the world, that I should bear witness unto the truth. Every one that is of the truth heareth My voice.' (38) Pilate saith unto Him, 'What is truth?' And when he had said this, he went out again unto the Jews, and saith unto them, 'I find in Him no fault at all.'"

Three years after I graduated from law school, at age 28, I became severely sick with acute food allergies, trying to work daily with pneumonia and asthma. Although I worked in law during the week, and taught law school at night three days a week, I was bedridden for a season on the weekends trying to recover. My sickness caused me to lose a lot of weight, weighing only about 165 pounds. I was over 6 foot 1 inches and my usual weight was 190 pounds. I looked sick, and I could not get off of steroids that allowed me to breathe. I could not eat very much as it made me nauseated. I went from Allergist to Allergist, and every Allergist said I would be dead by the time I was 44 years old because I could not live without continuous taking of heavy doses of steroids.

I thought, "Well, if I am going to die young, then I better turn around and go back to the God and Savior of my youth, which was Christ Jesus. I knew I was inundated with secular knowledge, and I desperately needed spiritual knowledge. I bought a Bible and started reading it. I first read the book of John, and then I decided to read the whole Bible from Genesis to Revelation. I told friends I was going to church. If they asked what church I was attending, I would say, "The church of the living springs. I lie on my bed, read the Bible, and I watch Christian television." They shook their heads and laughed. I did not care as they did not have a physical death sentence on them like I had. My then wife filed for divorce, partly because she wanted nothing to do with my faith as a Believer, and I think she was tired to be with a husband that was seriously sick. The divorce was private and easy, as we really had nothing to fight over. We both were fair to each other.

As I said, a year later, I received a phone call from Neptune's daughter, and I met Neptune again after five to six years. Later I found an immunologist who cured me of my food allergies, and I felt healthy again, had God back into my life, and had a wonderful relationship with a father figure in Neptune that was a genius and except for Jesus was the best human being that I ever met. Although Neptune did not study the Bible, he did as a young boy. He knew the stories of Jesus and his disciples, and he said he accepted Jesus as Lord and Savior. Based upon his great moral character, I knew that God was in his life. Thus, he became the greatest person I knew in this world to emulate, and he treated me with great kindness, patience, and respect. I truly miss him!

Dr. Nova Dean Pack

GOD'S WISDOM FROM ABOVE

The best thing I can do for you as my reader is to bring forth the wisdom from above in scripture and show you the problems with the wisdom of this fallen world. James 3:15-17 says, " This wisdom descendeth not from above, but is earthly, sensual, devilish. (16) For where envying and strife is, there is confusion and every evil work. (17) But the wisdom that is from above is first pure, then peaceable, gentle, and easy to be intreated, full of mercy and good fruits, without partiality, and without hypocrisy." 1 Corinthians 2:13 says, "Which things also we speak, not in the words which man's wisdom teacheth, but which the Holy Spirit teacheth; comparing spiritual things with spiritual." I sincerely believe the difference between Satan's fallen wisdom and God's eternal wisdom has been proficiently discussed throughout this book which I wrote for your blessing and edification.

All wisdom, knowledge, and understanding for the best kind of life is the truth of scriptures. Isaiah 33:6 says, "And wisdom and knowledge shall be the stability of thy times, and strength of salvation: the fear of the LORD is his treasure." Job 28:28 says, "And unto man He said, 'Behold, the fear of the Lord, that is wisdom; and to depart from evil is understanding.'" Ephesians 1:17-18 says, "That the God of our Lord Jesus Christ, the Father of glory, may give unto you the spirit of wisdom and revelation in the knowledge of Him: (18) The eyes of your understanding being enlightened; that ye may know what is the hope of His calling, and what the riches of the glory of His inheritance in the saints."

The real cure for obsessive-compulsive Personality Traits of Money is to worship and depend upon God and the Lord Jesus Christ (1 Corinthians 8:6), submitting to the leading of the Holy Spirit daily. Changing the direction you are traveling in the world, repenting, and turning around seeking God and the Lord Jesus Christ is the narrow gate to salvation and remission of your sins.

Jesus said in Matthew 7:13-14, "Enter ye in at the strait gate: for wide is the gate, and broad is the way, that leadeth to destruction, and many there be which go in thereat: (14) Because strait is the gate, and narrow is the way, which leadeth unto life, and few there be that find it." You cannot find the narrow gate through religion is what Jesus was saying. The Kingdom of God is not the kingdom of this world nor the kingdom of religion. Do not be confused. Jesus is not only your Provider but also your Provision. Again, Matthew 6:33 says, "But seek first the Kingdom of God and His righteousness, and all these things shall be added to you." You cannot seek first the Kingdom of God if you do not know what the Kingdom of God is.

Seek God when the temptations of this fallen world or the those evil spirits come to confuse you with self-centered and self-exaltation humanism. Psalms 71:1-4 says, "In thee, O LORD, do I put my trust: let me never be put to confusion. (2) Deliver me in thy righteousness, and cause me to escape: incline thine ear unto me, and save me. (3) Be thou my strong habitation, whereunto I may continually resort: thou hast given commandment to save me; for thou art my rock and my fortress. (4) Deliver me, O my God, out of the hand of the wicked, out of the hand of the unrighteous and cruel man."

Romans 14:17-19 says, "For the kingdom of God is not meat and drink; but righteousness, and peace, and joy in the Holy Spirit. (18) For he that in these things serveth Christ is accept-

Personality Traits of Money

able to God, and approved of men. (19) Let us therefore follow after the things which make for peace, and things wherewith one may edify another."

How can the Kingdom of God and His righteousness in my life pay my bills you may ask? Philippians 4:12-13, 19 says, "I know both how to be abased, and I know how to abound: everywhere and in all things, I am instructed both to be full and to be hungry, both to abound and to suffer need. (13) I can do all things through Christ which strengtheneth me. . . (19) But my God shall supply all your need according to His riches in glory by Christ Jesus."

There is an old saying in the midwestern states of America. "I think he is living too high on the hog!" The possible origin of the phrase 'living too high on the hog' comes from 20th century America and refers to the practice of eating expensive choice cuts of meat. In March 1920, an edition of The New York Times stated: "Southern laborers who are eating too high up on the hog (pork chops and ham) and American housewives who "eat too far back on the beef" (porterhouse and round steak) are to blame for the continued high cost of living, the American Institute of Meat Packers announced today." This thought often is used to say about lottery winners, "He has been living pretty high on the hog since he won the lottery."

Understanding the spiritual origin of money and how its use makes people's soul experience an obsessive compulsion to feel safe, to be in control, to be a freedom seeker, to be romantically attractive, to have personal magnetism, or other kinds of Personality Traits of Money, is what I have tried to research and present to you as the reader of a major problem in America and European and other first world countries.

The U.S. has the lowest savings per capita in the first world countries and the highest national debt in the world. Most Americans are ninety days away from bankruptcy, but regardless of how much they earn, at the end of the month they need more to pay their regular bills. I see people in restaurants charging for a single dinner on their credit cards, and that one meal dinner with drinks could have cost them over $150 by the time the tip is paid. If they go out to dinner two times a week as a lifestyle, their maintenance of their lifestyle trying to be like the rich becomes their downfall economically. These same people use their credit cards to buy clothing and things they want on Amazon, where they get deliveries two to three times a week. These people are living a lifestyle on credit because they want to live like the rich and famous.

When my wife and I go out to dinner, I pay cash, not with a credit card because we do not want to go into debtor living practices. If we do not have the cash, we do not go out to dinner but eat at home. Both of us are out of debt, and we enjoy the freedom that being out of debt gives us. We do not seek the almighty dollar, but rather we seek Almighty God in our daily living and devotionals. The law of the spirit of life in Christ Jesus has made us free from the law of sin and death. The spirit of death can be indebtedness, poverty, but mostly is rebellion against God, His Kingdom, and His Truth, personified in Christ Jesus. Truly living or just existing are choices. Money promises life, but really it results in death if you depend on money as your sustenance, your lifestyle, or to enhance your stature.

Moses said in Deuteronomy 30:19-20, "I call heaven and earth to record this day against you, that I have set before you life and death, blessing and cursing: therefore choose life, that both thou and thy seed may live: (20) That thou mayest love the LORD thy God, and that thou mayest obey His voice, and that thou mayest cleave unto Him: for He is thy life, and the length of thy days: that thou mayest dwell in the land which the LORD sware unto thy fathers, to Abraham, to Isaac, and to Jacob, to give them."

Be truthful in your self-examination of your soul, especially your heart where the library of your beliefs is stored. What does money mean to you psychologically, emotionally, and as the foundation of your beliefs? Now that you know the Truth of God's Word, you can be set free from the avarice love of money. If used properly for the building of God's kingdom, money is a good thing to have, so long as there are no ulterior or hidden motives unto gain. If money has attached to it the fulfillment of soulish needs, then you can be treating money as your idol, as it motivates you to seek natural things in your life, business transactions, and relationships instead of seeking first the spiritual Kingdom of God and His righteousness. If money becomes an obsessive-compulsive focus of your goals and attention, then you are robbing yourself of righteousness, peace, and joy in the Holy Spirit, where you have the true sense of contentment in Christ Jesus' abundant zoe life.

In the obsessive-compulsive extreme, money can become an idol, and you can experience in some degree the suffering of the curse of poverty until you make Jesus Christ your true Savior and Lord, not money. The Second Commandment in Exodus 20:4 6 is the prohibition not to make nor worship any carved images, any likeness of anything in heaven or earth. Verse 5 says, "You shall not bow down to them nor serve them. For I, the Lord your God, am a jealous God, visiting the iniquity of the fathers upon the children to the third and fourth generations of those who hate Me."

Why are some family members impoverished generation after generation?   If that is you and your family, consider if someone in your family in history had a major problem or sin with money, and seek the Holy Spirit to see if this wickedness was handed down generationally. Thank God these family iniquities caused by violation of the biblical laws or violation of the law of sowing and reaping that leads to poverty can be lifted off you and your family because Christ Jesus took upon Himself the curse of the law by dying on the Roman cross, so you can have the blessings of Abraham (Galatians 3:13-14). Appropriate the benefits of Jesus' Cross to rid yourself of the work of a curse of generational poverty in your soul and experience the freedom of financial blessings. "Whom the Son sets free is free indeed" (John 8:36).

Having the mind of Christ can lead to prosperity because He will give you His success attitudes, principles, and values. To come out of poverty, you need to have agape love of others, along with humility, obedience, faith, and hope in God through Christ Jesus, which hope will be an "anchor for your soul" (Hebrews 6:19).

Your hope is faith in Christ Jesus and not in money! If you have a problem with money, you must renounce your allegiance as a disciple of mammon. You then must accept God and Jesus Christ as your only Lord and Savior, but especially as your Provider.

Having a giving, compassionate, and loving heart means you want to express that giving, compassion, and heartfelt agape love by feeding the hungry, bringing water to the thirsty, clothing the naked, visiting the sick, and sharing fellowship to those in prison (Matthew 25:34-46). The reason is you know that doing these things to them is also doing these things to the Lord as Believers are the body of Christ. Each Believer must know he is called person-

Personality Traits of Money

ally to bear witness of Christ and to express a giving, compassionate, and loving heart toward those who are suffering. When a Believer who has a giving, compassionate, and loving heart becomes a mature kingdom servant, those who have benefitted his servanthood can glimpse of the deepest source of the immeasurable, intrinsic worth of every human, as every human is made in the image and likeness of God. When you become born again as a new creation in Christ, your soul must submit and invite the Godhead to transform your soul.

The government institutions are important and indispensable; nevertheless, no government institution and its employees can replace the Believer's giving, compassionate, and loving heart in having the developed proclivity of the Believer's own soul by acts of charity when dealing with the sufferings of others. A Believer's acts of charity may be focused on those having physical sufferings, but the Believer must also focus these virtues over the other person's suffering soul that is lost in the quagmire of this fallen world's death camp. There are many kinds of soul sufferings, and lack of money and abject poverty can enhance those feelings of hurt, inadequacies, and the belief you are a second-class citizen. There are no second-class citizens in the Kingdom of God. There is no racial discrimination in the Kingdom of God. There is no disqualifying of a woman or man from ministry (Genesis 1:28; Galatians 3:28). In God's Kingdom all life is precious.

With the knowledge you have obtained, remove the flying demon monkeys in the Wizard of Oz off your money and out of your soul. The Wizard of Oz series of children's books, with its hidden message exposing the Global Bankers' Control of the Money, was written in 1900 by L. Frank Baum.

The popular movie, Wizard of Oz, was filmed in 1939, starring Judy Garland and in truth was all about the Global Bankers in charge of the money. Thus, the 1Timothy 6:10 warning, "For the love of money (avarice) is a root of all kinds of evil, for which some have strayed from the faith in their greediness and pierced themselves through with many sorrows."

Dorothy, the main character in the novel and film, represents the average American patriot, whose character represented the best of what was valued as the American character; she was kind, showed spunk, was level-headed, honest, helped others, was a leader, and was willing to face the unknown to find answers to the issues while trying to get back home. The Munchkins were just everyday little people who knew to tell Dorothy to "Follow the yellow brick road" on her way to the Emerald City. The Emerald City represented the "green back" dollars, and the Emerald City also represented Washington D.C., while the Wizard's Palace represented the White House. The yellow brick road represented gold that is supposed to back the U.S. dollar. The Scarecrow represents farmers. The Tin Man represents a dehumanized and subjugated factory worker, who, through no fault of his own, has had his heart damaged by outside forces. He represents factory workers who were unemployed and are suffering in the economy at that season. The Tin Man was covered in rust when Dorothy and the Scarecrow first encounter him. He had an oil can representing the oil industry, and the Tin Man said, "What will we do if we run out of oil?" The Cowardly Lion represented William Jennings Bryan, who was a hero of the Populist movement at the time and ran as President against those selected candidates of Bankers. Bryan was even referred to as a lion in the press, but he dropped out of the race before election day. Thus, the cowardly Lion. When the Wizard of Oz book was written, the wicked witch of the east and west were Rockefeller and J.P. Morgan. The Wizard behind the curtain in the Emerald City (representing the green U.S. Dollar where the "good life" was and where things were made new) made himself out to be the Great Wizard of Oz but was just a man like everyone else, who manipulated, lied, and lived a pretentious life. Dorothy's shoes were made of silver in the book, but the 1939 film changed them to rubies.

The silver shoes of Dorothy in the book were significant, as she had silver shoes walking on the gold road to Washington D.C. and the White House. Silver and gold are what the Constitution requires to back the U.S. dollar printed by the U.S. Treasury Department, but the Federal Reserve Bankers are not government, but a privately own business; and they can print money without gold or silver backing the dollar. The purpose of gold and silver backing the U.S. Dollar was to restrict the spending of Congress by a limited supply of wealth created by God. When President Nixon suspended the necessity of having gold and silver backing the U.S. Dollar, it caused the national debt to rise like a run-a-way missile headed outer space with the accelerator blasting the missile without control.

Every time a President such as Jackson, Lincoln, or others tried to get the U.S. Treasury to print money instead of the Bankers, the Bankers would print counterfeit "green backs" which were circulated, which inflated the money and made the U.S. Dollar untrustworthy. Then, the Banker Lenders used the counterfeiting of U.S. Dollars as the excuse to demand Gold as payment of debt by the U.S. government instead of the U.S. Dollar. Global world Bankers put people, businesses, and governments in debt to them, so the banker families control people, businesses, and governments. Proverbs 22: 7 is worth repeating, "The rich ruleth over the poor, and the borrower is servant to the lender."

I invite you to repent by going back to near the beginning of this book and take the "Christian Money Beatitudes Test." Just make a copy and take the test. As months and years go by, take the test again, and as you inculcate the teachings in this book, you will see the improvement in your mind, emotions, and heart releasing you more and more from the stronghold of the Personality Traits of Money. When you have completed the test, you will discover areas in which you need improvement and areas where you have received a major of freedom from the knowledge obtained. You will obtain knowledge and wisdom by reading and studying this book with the Scriptures and lifestyle case studies presented of famous historical and present-day people.

May we all find new spiritual liberty as we all are led by the Holy Spirit in our daily commercial and monetary transactions.

Why should you stop serving the god of mammon and start serving the Creator God and the Lord Jesus Christ? Ephesians 4:1 says, "I, therefore, the prisoner of the Lord, beseech you to walk worthy of the calling with which you were called." "Walk worthy of the calling" means God considers you to be desirable to have a relationship with Him in Christ Jesus, as you are His only begotten Son's betroth and eventual bride. God decided you are worthy to be one of His ministers in Christ Jesus as a leader king, priest (Revelation 1:6), lord (1 Timothy 6:15), ambassador (2 Corinthians 5:20), and soldier (2 Timothy 2:3-4). God decided you are worthy to be anointed with the Holy Spirit (2 Corinthians 1:21). God decided you are worthy to receive the spiritual gifts of God the Father (Romans 12:6-8), worthy to receive the spiritual gifts of God the Word (Ephesians 4:11), and worthy to receive the spiritual gifts of God the Holy Spirit (1 Corinthians 12: 8-10).

Personality Traits of Money

My prayer for you is that you do not allow money to have a hold on your soul, especially your heart. Do not allow your heart to be the depository of avarice love of money. You must be freed from the bondage of money. You must serve God and not serve money. Be content with what God has provided you. Resolve that God's provision is enough for you to accomplish your mission and calling. The pathway to freedom is entering the crucifixion of Christ, so you no longer live but Christ Jesus can live His life in you and through you (Galatians 2:20).

As a disciple of Christ, and as the Temple of God, you must learn contentment in every financial condition of life (Philippians 4:11 13). Believe and worship God and Christ Jesus. Romans 8:28 says, "And we know that all things work together for good to them that (agape) love God, to them who are the called according to His purpose."

As you repent and turn back to God, then you will receive health and true prosperity even as your souls prospers (3 John 2).

AMEN!

BIO

Dr. Nova Dean Pack

Dr. Nova Dean Pack's father left the family when he was 3 years old, and at age 10 his mother died at age 32, leaving six children behind. Dr. Pack and his brothers and sisters were raised on his grandparents' farm where there was continuous hard work as chores - taking care of 120 acres, along with feeding many cows, pigs, chickens, duck, geese, and other animals and milking two to three cows morning and night, along with yearly soil preparation, seed planting, cultivating, the harvesting of hay and crops. For solace, on the farm, was a beautiful wooded area where Dr. Pack spent many hours alone praying and seeking God. The farm life was very tough, but the work ethic was engrained in Dr. Pack's foundation of beliefs. Southern Illinois was part of the Bible Belt; so, most everyone went to Church as a lifestyle, although it was mostly a religious experience.

After his mother died, Dr. Pack, at age 11 was born again and had a very intimate relationship with Jesus and the Holy Spirit. He taught Sunday School from the Bible to other students near his age and baptized several people his age and younger in the creeks of Illinois at age 13 and onward.

Dr. Pack moved to California at age 15. He worked his way through college and graduated from Cal State University Long Beach in 1971. He graduated from Pepperdine University School of Law, a fundamental Christian based top rated law school, in 1974. He passed the State Bar exam on the first sitting also in 1974. He immediately started practicing law with other partners, but he left the partnership and started his sole practice of law in 1981.

Dr. Pack personally was ordained by two known prophets in California in 1992; namely Dr. Chuck Flynn and Dr. Richard Maiden. Dr. Pack received ordination papers with the Independent Assemblies of God International (IAOGI), Santa Ana, CA in 1993 and has been the corporate attorney for IAOGI since that year. Dr. Pack was the Senior Pastor of a Church fellowship from 1994 through 1999 in Redlands, CA. Dr. Pack was overseer of two ministries from 1993 through 2020 and ministered monthly at those ministries, along with other churches. In 2004, the Holy Spirit inspired Dr. Pack to use the name "Biblitarian," so Dr. Pack formed the ministry called "Biblitarian Ministries." Dr. Pack in 2022 formed a University called "Biblitarian University."

Dr. Pack broadcasted a radio talk show entitled "Business in Ministry" in San Bernardino, CA., for two years from 1992 through 1994 where he taught business men and women how to make their businesses a place of ministry. In 1994 through 1996, Dr. Pack taught a daily radio teaching that aired in Riverside and San Bernardino Counties, California, where his ongoing sermons in Church became the subjects of radio broadcasts.

During this period, Dr. Pack conducted monthly teachings for 50 straight weeks at several churches, teaching men and women that their businesses were their venue of ministry. Dr. Pack sees his law practice as a place and opportunity for ministry to those in need, where he witnesses to the unsaved, prays for the sick, takes care of those in need, and educates his clients and employees on the Biblical principles of business and economics. Dr. Pack is one of the very few attorneys at law that actually brings the wisdom and principles in the Bible into his law practice for the benefit of his Christian clients and all those seeking his advice.

Dr. Pack is a prolific writer, having written over 30 Christian books on various spiritual topics, some directly for the believer in business. Also, he is an accomplished public minister who teaches under a strong anointing. Dr. Pack has learned how to bring the dynamic of intellectual endeavor under the authority and anointing of the Holy Spirit. He has preached and taught more than a thousand messages over the years.

Dr. Pack's ministry focus is preaching the gospel of the Kingdom (Matthew 24:14) and the message of repentance and remission of sins (Luke 24:47), which Jesus commanded to be the dual priority of preaching and teaching.

Dr. Pack sends his regular teachings to Believers in over 65 different countries. Dr. Pack currently broadcasts his podcasts under the name "Biblitarian Ministries" on the priority of seeking first the Kingdom of God and His righteousness, God's grace extended for repentance and remission of sins, and the receiving of benefits of living in the Kingdom of God. Biblitarian Ministries can be viewed on The Marketplace Network, a Christian media network broadcasting on Amazon Fire TV, Facebook, YouTube and Twitter platforms. Dr. Pack may be contacted at ***packnovapack@aol.com.***

Dr. Nova Dean Pack

Personality Traits of Money

Dr. Nova Dean Pack

www.ingramcontent.com/pod-product-compliance
Lightning Source LLC
Chambersburg PA
CBHW080901030426
42337CB00022B/4538